RESISTANCE AND REBELLION

LESSONS FROM EASTERN EUROPE

Resistance and Rebellion: Lessons from Eastern Europe explains how ordinary people become involved in resistance and rebellion against powerful regimes. The book shows how a sequence of causal forces – social norms, focal points, rational calculation – operates to drive individuals into roles of passive resistance and, at a second stage, into participation in community-based rebellion organization. By linking the operation of these mechanisms to observable social structures, the work generates predictions about which types of community and society are most likely to form and sustain resistance and rebellion.

The empirical material centers around Lithuanian anti-Soviet resistance in both the 1940s and the 1987–1991 period. Using the Lithuanian experience as a base line, comparisons with several other Eastern European countries demonstrate the breadth and depth of the theory.

The book contributes to both the general literature on political violence and protest and the theoretical literature on collective action.

Roger D. Petersen is Research Associate at the Program on International Security Policy at the University of Chicago. Petersen is the coeditor (with John Bowen) of *Critical Comparisons in Politics and Culture* (Cambridge University Press, 1999) and has published in several journals, including *European Journal of Sociology* and *Journal of Politics*. His research is primarily concerned with political violence and comparative methodology.

STUDIES IN RATIONALITY AND SOCIAL CHANGE

Editors: Jon Elster and Michael S. McPherson

Editorial Board:
Fredrik Barth
Amartya Sen
Arthur L. Stinchcombe
Bernard Williams

Titles in the series:

PETER HEDSTRÖM & RICHARD SWEDBERG (EDS.) Social Mechanisms
JON ELSTER Explaining Technical Change
JON ELSTER & AANUND HYLLAND (EDS.) Foundations of Social
  Choice Theory
JON ELSTER (ED.) The Multiple Self
JAMES S. COLEMAN Individual Interests and Collective Action
ARTHUR L. STINCHCOMBE Stratification and Organization
DIEGO GAMBETTA Were They Pushed or Did They Jump?
MICHAEL TAYLOR The Possibility of Cooperation
JON ELSTER & RUNE SLAGSTAD (EDS.) Constitutionalism and
  Democracy
JON ELSTER The Cement of Society
JON ELSTER & JOHN ROEMER (EDS.) Interpersonal Comparisons
  of Well-Being
KAARE STRØM Minority Government and Majority Rule
ADAM PRZEWORSKI Democracy and the Market
GEORGE AINSLIE Picoeconomics
GERALD MARWELL & PAMELA OLIVER The Critical Mass in
  Collective Action

Roger D. Petersen

RESISTANCE AND REBELLION

Lessons from Eastern Europe

CAMBRIDGE
UNIVERSITY PRESS

PUBLISHED BY THE PRESS SYNDICATE OF THE UNIVERSITY OF CAMBRIDGE
The Pitt Building, Trumpington Street, Cambridge, United Kingdom

CAMBRIDGE UNIVERSITY PRESS
The Edinburgh Building, Cambridge CB2 2RU, UK
40 West 20th Street, New York, NY 10011-4211, USA
10 Stamford Road, Oakleigh, VIC 3166, Australia
Ruiz de Alarcón 13, 28014 Madrid, Spain
Dock House, The Waterfront, Cape Town 8001, South Africa

http://www.cambridge.org

First published 2001

Printed in the United States of America

Typeface   Times Roman 10/13 pt.   *System*   QuarkXPress 4.01 [AG]

A catalog record for this book is available from the British Library.

Library of Congress Cataloging in Publication data

Petersen, Roger Dale, 1959–
 Resistance and rebellion : lessons from Eastern Europe / Roger D. Petersen.
  p. cm. – (Studies in rationality and social change)
 ISBN 0-521-77000-9
 1. Lithuania – History – Autonomy and independence movements. 2. Government,
Resistance to – Lithuania – History – 20th century. 3. Europe, Eastern – History – Autonomy
and independence movements. 4. Government, Resistance to – Europe,
Eastern – History – 20th century. I. Title. II. Series

DK505.77 .P48 2001
947.93 – dc21   00-059867

ISBN 0 521 77000 9 hardback

For Daniela

Contents

LIST OF FIGURES AND TABLES   *page* xi
PREFACE   xiii

1   Introduction   1
2   Mechanisms and Process   32
3   Lithuania, 1940–1941   80
4   Rebellion in an Urban Community: The Role of Leadership
    and Centralization   134
5   The German Occupation of Lithuania   153
6   Postwar Lithuania   170
7   More Cases, More Comparisons   205
8   Resistance in the Perestroika Period   236
9   Fanatics and First Actors   272
10 Conclusions   296

BIBLIOGRAPHY   305
INDEX   317

Figures and Tables

Figures

1.1	Map of Svainikai village as drawn by a former resident	*page* 5
1.2	Membership list of Grandis fraternity created by a former member	6
1.3	The spectrum of individual roles during rebellion	9
1.4	Levels of analysis in the study of rebellion and revolution	26
2.1	Examples of hierarchy in an occupied multiethnic state	35
2.2	Sets of possible resistance symbols	39
2.3	Safety considerations during beginning stages of resistance	41
2.4	Status considerations in beginning stages of resistance in two hypothetical societies	42
2.5	Combined utility values of safety and status for two hypothetical societies	43
2.6	Example of a community structure	46
2.7	Normative effects on thresholds	57
2.8	Three hypothetical communities	58
2.9a	An effect of increased density	63
2.9b	The inhibiting effects of high density	64
2.9c	The critical position of a first-acting group	67
2.9d	The effects of centralization	70
2.9e	Centralization and the distribution of thresholds	71
2.9f	The effects of economic fragmentation	74
3.1	A community configuration of the village of Svainikai	121
3.2	The village of interviewee 21	127
4.1	Grandis community structure	136

6.1	Schema of Kasciunai village	178
6.2	Venn diagram of Kasciunai village	182
6.3	Summary of movement during three occupations	204
7.1	The series of ruling regimes in Galicia and Volhynia	211
7.2	An example of occupier strategy	227
8.1	Hypothetical tipping points for various social groups	246
9.1	Cultural schema	293

Tables

3.1	Groups in 1940–1941 Lithuania	110
3.2	Group memberships in Svainikai	112
4.1	Student elections at Kaunas in 1938	139

Preface

This book endeavors to explain how ordinary men and women, in the face of enormous risks, resist and sometimes violently rebel against powerful regimes. Theoretically, the work seeks to identify sequences of mechanisms that combine to produce these phenomena. Empirically, the book devotes the bulk of its pages to four episodes of Lithuanian anti-Soviet resistance (1940–1941, 1944–1950, 1987–1988, and January 1991). The Lithuanian case serves as a base line for comparisons with several other cases of anti-Soviet, anti-Communist, and anti-Nazi resistance.

In an important sense, this book began in the mid-1980s, before I started graduate school. At that time, I was selling housewares to Yugoslavian immigrants in Chicago. In the course of this work, conversation would often turn to the violent events that occurred in Yugoslavia during the Second World War. These conversations led to two insights crucial to this book. First, the memories of survivors of this period were extremely vivid and could be usefully tapped to recreate the social life of the wartime years. Second, it seemed clear that participants in the anti-German resistance and the underlying Chetnik-Partisan conflict did not usually become involved because of ideological or political reasons; rather, they were pulled in through their social networks. There was a connection between participation in resistance and local social norms – a theme pursued throughout this book.

As a graduate student in the Political Science Department at the University of Chicago, I wished to capitalize on my previous experience to write about 1940s Yugoslavia, especially Bosnia. I began seriously planning my research in 1990. Needless to say, events overtook me. For a variety of reasons, research on 1940s Yugoslavia became less feasible. Still wanting to research the local roots of sustained rebellion, I turned to the best available alternative: Lithuania. The Lithuanian center of North American immigration, Chicago's Marquette Park neighborhood, lay only a few miles from the University of Chicago. I moved there during the last years of graduate school to become familiar with the Lithuanian émigré community. I began interviewing émigrés in 1990 and continued throughout 1991. I made two trips to Lithuania to conduct similar interviews. The first trip was not entirely successful. On my second day of Lithuanian fieldwork, January 13, 1991, I was a participant-observer in the Soviet attack that resulted in more than a dozen deaths. These events are the focus of Chapter 9. My second effort, in the summer of 1992, was more successful. The Lithuanian case proved extremely rich. The three successive occupations of the 1940s provided variation along many key dimensions. The events of the perestroika period, as well as January 1991, also provided useful insights into acts of resistance. Although I do not speak Lithuanian, this did not prove a problem with the long-term immigrants in Chicago. In Lithuania, I was able to find someone who was both a professional translator and social scientist to act as guide. The reader will see the results of these interviews and experiences throughout the text.

There is an obvious time lag between the date of these interviews and the publication of this book. The reason for this lag is that the interviews, experiences, and secondary research collected in the beginning years of this book project spawned a second book project. While the present book addresses the puzzle of how the less powerful manage to sustain rebellion against the more powerful, this second project confronts the question of why and when the more powerful commit violence and discrimination against the less powerful. As each project informs the other, I began working on them simultaneously. At the time of this writing, the second manuscript, *Fear, Hatred, Resentment: Delineating Paths to Ethnic Conflict in Eastern Europe,* is nearing completion.

My research (especially this book) is the product of the University of Chicago. I consider myself fortunate to have been a graduate in the Political Science Department. I was even more fortunate to have been able to work with the four individuals who made up my dissertation committee. John Padgett, in his own work as well as his teaching, showed me how to integrate theory with fieldwork. I never left his office without a new way of looking at my work. David Laitin has taught me most of what I know about comparative method. His uncanny ability to cut to the heart of the matter is invaluable. John Mearsheimer, whom I have known since my undergraduate days, has been not only a source of professional insight, but also a constant source of personal support. He has encouraged me to pursue important issues and never shy away from controversial topics. Jon Elster's ideas and scholarship helped form the theoretical foundation of this book. My intellectual debt will be obvious to anyone familiar with his work. Beyond that, his patience, advice, and sometimes blunt criticisms were critical in finally completing this manuscript.

I would like to make several other acknowledgments. The MacArthur Foundation provided funding for the crucial years of this project. I would like to thank the Sidlauskas family for their hospitality, kindness, and strawberry preserves. Arvydas Reneckis was essential during my winter 1991 fieldwork in Vilnius as well as earlier in Chicago. I owe a great debt to Virgiene Valantanavicius, my guide and translator during the summer 1992 fieldwork. These interviews took us into most regions of Lithuania, down narrow dirt roads and through dark forests. Valantanavicius's language skills were only part of his contribution. His social skills and acumen provided entry into Lithuanian communities that I could never have accessed on my own. I owe the greatest debt to the interviewees who made this work possible. Their memories were often painful. I hope this book does them justice.

Julie Stone, John Ginkel, and Gayle Corrigan helped transcribe many of the interview tapes. Tom Kolasa provided computer help.

Finally, and most importantly, I wish to recognize my wife, Daniela Stojanovic, for her unwavering support.

1. Introduction

This book is about ordinary people and the roles they come to play during times of rebellion and resistance against powerful regimes. How is violence against such regimes organized and sustained? How and why do individuals accept enormous risks in the process? On one hand, the subject matter is violence and killing. On the other hand, the subject matter is friendship groups, farming practices, religious and cultural norms – the stuff of the most basic social interactions of everyday life. Whether individuals come to act as rebels or collaborators, killers or victims, heroes or cowards during times of upheaval is largely determined by the nature of their everyday economic, social, and political life, both in the time of the upheaval and the period prior to it. The extraordinary is inextricably linked to the ordinary.

As the reader will discover, this book provides a very detailed theoretical treatment of the process that pushes and pulls individuals into rebellion. Among the most important issues, the work specifies how different social structures tend to change strategic frames and trigger varying sets of causal mechanisms. The book illustrates how variation in community size, homogeneity, and centralization may affect the existence and operation of norms; it examines the role and structural position of "first actors" or entrepreneurs in initiating and sustaining collective action through norms and use of threats; it attempts to identify the conditions when one type of mechanism (rational, normative, irrational) is most likely to prevail over another type of mechanism.

Another aspect of this book is perhaps more important than the development of theory. As much as possible, the work tries to present the story of farmers, students, and workers from their own standpoint. Although much of this work is built on archival and secondary sources, one major part of this project involved interviewing approximately forty elderly Lithuanians in an effort to reconstruct their experiences and the history of their communities during the 1940s. Beyond the theory, I have tried to provide an accurate sense of these individuals' lives and the nature of the decisions they confronted under occupation. If the book accomplishes only this goal, then the effort will have been worthwhile. Before delving into the theory, I wish to provide some examples from these oral histories to illustrate this work's questions, substance, and method.

Lithuania was occupied three times in the 1940s. The Soviets incorporated Lithuania in 1940, the Germans occupied the country during most of the Second World War, and the Soviets again reoccupied the land during the tail months of the war. One of the fundamental questions of the book asks how and why people with less weapons and fewer numbers create and sustain violent rebellion against stronger forces. During the 1940–1941 Soviet occupation, Lithuanians developed a clandestine organization that included roughly 1 percent of the population. In June 1941, in an effort to reestablish independence before the invading Germans could gain control, this underground resistance launched a violent revolt joined by tens of thousands of previously unorganized Lithuanians. How did the organization of this revolt develop? The oral histories suggest that a two-step process occurred, with each step involving a different strategic frame. Early in the initial Soviet occupation, Lithuanians were confronted with a series of opportunities to commit small acts of resistance: accepting illegal underground newspapers, boycotting Soviet elections, attending public religious ceremonies. At this stage, individuals were scanning society at large for signals to help gauge risk and determine how to act. As more and more individuals participated in these small acts of defiance, confidence grew among those desiring more organized, and potentially violent, forms of resistance. Soon, locally based rebellion organizations began springing up across Lithuania. At this stage, thousands of Lithuanians were confronted with another decision – whether to join their friends and neighbors in support of a community-based rebellion organization. Importantly, as the risks increased, the individual's set of closest connections, his community, became the key source of information and influence.

This second stage, the movement toward community-based organization, is an issue of widespread importance. In opposing a regime with superior numbers of weapons and trained soldiers, sustained rebellion depends on significant numbers of individuals occupying roles linking armed, mobile resistance movements to fixed populations. Some clandestine organization that is impervious to the generally superior military power and organization of the occupier or regime must develop and survive. Without this form of organization, rebellion against ruthless regimes (and the cases in this work are the Soviets and the Nazis) is nearly impossible. These actors are important for many reasons: they provide food and information; they serve as a mobilizable reserve for military action; they retaliate against local collaborators and thus serve to deter further collaboration; they are the basis of recruitment for future mobile units.

Several well-known examples can be readily cited to bring out the importance of locally based organizations. The American failure in Vietnam perhaps best illustrates the significance of local organization. The United States won the military battles but could never adequately identify or isolate the locally based support networks despite major efforts to do so. The strategic hamlet program was essentially an effort to weed out local conspirators vital to the perpetuation of Vietcong efforts. The objectives of this program as well as its failure can be seen in *The Pentagon Papers* and other released documents. German occupation forces in the Second World War had a special term for the local organizations, *Hauspartisanen* or "home partisans." As Colonel General Rendulic, commander of a German Panzer army, stated about the situation in Yugoslavia, "the life and tasks of the German troops would have been much easier if the opponent had only closed formations. The home partisans were a much more dangerous enemy because it was from them that all the hostile acts emanated against which the troops could protect themselves only with the greatest difficulty and which caused them the largest losses. They could seldom, if ever, be caught."[1] The Intifada and Northern Ireland are cases in which the rebels operate almost entirely at a local underground level. The Irish Republican Army has at most 500 actual fighters, but there are, "behind the fighters, a network of supporters, farmers, townspeople, and teenagers, who stand ready when called upon to turn their homes into safe houses, to surrender their autos, to hide the fighters, and most of all to hide from the Brits. These are the dickers, the lookouts in every town, out of every window, in the gas station, at the post office, in the cafe."[2]

The oral histories produce detailed insight for examining the process leading to community-level organization. In Chapter 3, the reader will en-

[1] Quoted in Robert Aspray, *War in the Shadows,* vol. 1 (Garden City, N.Y.: Doubleday, 1965), pp. 525–526.
[2] "The Belfast Connection," *Village Voice,* February 8, 1994, p. 30.

counter descriptions of the events of the 1940–1941 Soviet occupation as they unfolded in several rural and urban communities. In some of these communities, local resistance emerged; in others, it did not. For rural communities, elderly Lithuanians were asked to draw maps of their villages, list local prewar membership in political and social associations, and describe the nature of anti-Soviet resistance. In many cases, the level of detailed information that could be gleaned from this process was remarkable. For example, many interviewees can draw an intricate map of their village as it stood on the eve of the Second World War. The respondent's map depicted in Figure 1.1 represents a village described and discussed in Chapter 3, a community that developed resistance during 1940–1941. As can be seen, the respondent could draw each farmstead and designate the number of hectares. He could also list memberships in political parties and social organizations. Finally, he gave a rendition of how resistance was organized in this community. For social scientists and historians attempting to reconstruct social life in the 1940s Baltic area, interviews with elderly survivors are often the only available source of information, especially in terms of rural communities. Not only necessary for research, these oral histories are remarkable for their very richness.

Rural villages are by no means the only communities analyzed in this work. Chapter 4 explores the development of organized resistance among the members of one fraternity and its alumni (the Catholic engineering fraternity at the University of Kaunas). I interviewed seven members of this community (G1–G7), one of whom produced a list (Figure 1.2) containing the name and fate of each member. Again, the question is how, in the face of Soviet harassment and surveillance, did such extensive organization of resistance develop in this community but not others? What characteristics or features of this community worked to facilitate decisions to accept the risks involved with this action?

Chapter 6 also addresses the puzzle of community-based rebellion, this time focusing on the organization of anti-Soviet resistance in the immediate postwar years. When the Soviets returned in the tail months of the war, locally based rebellion organizations again formed. Indeed, Lithuanians controlled much of the countryside (at least at night) until the late 1940s. Consider one particular example. In late December 1944, the Soviets returned to southern Lithuania and the area around the town of Merkine. On Christmas eve, they massacred much of the population of a small village named Klepocai. As the smoke rose from burning Klepocai, hundreds of

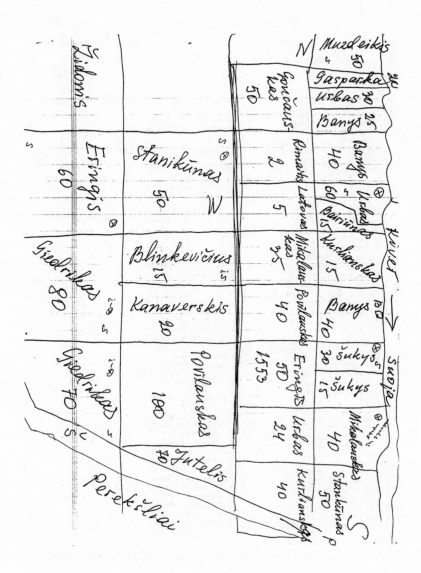

Figure 1.1. Map of Svainikai village as drawn by a former resident

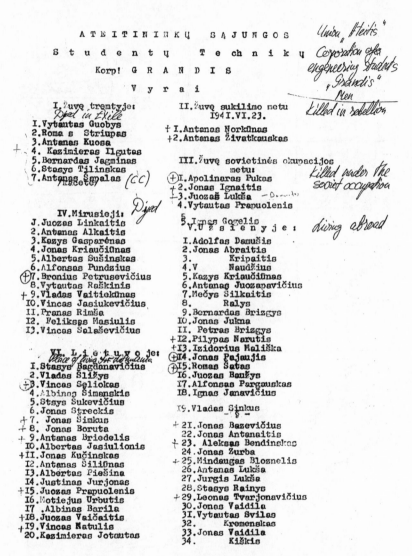

Figure 1.2. Membership list of Grandis fraternity created by a former member

people from neighboring villages, most of them youth fearing conscription into the Red Army, fled into the woods to buy time to consider their options. Within a short period of time, many of these refugees had reincorporated themselves into their communities, and significant numbers of these communities developed into support networks for the refugee-rebels. In fact, some villages created elaborate systems of underground bunkers that were supplied with food and information by the majority of the community. Buoyed by these local systems of support, a partisan resistance to Soviet rule raged in this area of the countryside for several years.

One section of Chapter 6 describes the experience of five individuals from the area around Merkine (M1–M5), a small town in southern Lithuania, during the postwar years. One interviewee became a member of a locally based Soviet collaboration force whose mission was to pacify the countryside. Another tried to stay out of the conflict altogether. A third joined a band of mobile partisan fighters (and was quickly captured and deported to Siberia). Two others were involved in community-based resistance, although the development of resistance in their respective communities differed. As in other interviews, these two respondents produced community maps, lists, and histories.

Again, the interviewees could recall remarkable detail. One of the respondents took out a large piece of cardboard and drew the location of the twelve farmsteads of his community as they were aligned along the Merkys River. He listed the number of hectares and total number of family members. On the right margin, lists of members of various social or political groups can be found. Specific details regarding family history can be found under each farmstead. For example, the Tomas Barysas farmstead comprised forty hectares and sixteen family members. Jonas Barysas was killed as a partisan; Vladas Barysas had formerly been in a Lithuanian military unit and changed his name to conceal that background from the Soviets; Cezaris Barysas became a Soviet informant. This village developed widespread and organized support for the postwar partisans. In these years Lithuanian rebels hid in underground bunkers in several locations indicated on the map by small squares. In the nearby village, no such widespread participation developed, although a few members of the community, including the respondent, served as liaisons for nonlocal partisan groups.

This brief discussion of the multiple cases from the Merkine region illustrates how this type of thorough study can create a field of variation crucial to understanding resistance and rebellion against powerful regimes. First, there is obvious variation among individuals. The five individuals from Merkine played distinctly different roles in the postwar drama: collaborator, neutral, liaison, locally based rebel, and mobile partisan. Further, clear variation occurred at the community level. Some of the communities in the region, like the one just discussed, developed elaborate bunker systems to hide homegrown rebels. These communities maintained their crucial support of partisans until collectivization or significant deportation decimated the village. Other communities were ready to support partisans that passed through and might have a liaison or two but were never organized in even an informal fashion. Yet other communities in the same region remained neutral.

What Is to Be Explained?

With these brief descriptions in mind, the question becomes how to represent the reality of rebellion against powerful regimes. Three methodological points emerge. First, the unit of analysis should not be the "nation" or a "people" because tremendous variation in rebellion activity exists within these large units. This variation can be readily observed at both the community level and the individual level. Second, a great deal of variation exists in the types of roles that individuals come to play during sustained rebellion. As shown in the Merkine example, there are collaborators, neutrals, locally based rebels, mobile fighters, and gradations in between. In much of the rebellion literature, individuals are portrayed as deciding among just two choices, two roles – either to "rebel" or "not rebel" – and then the analyst tries to determine the payoff structures that explain choices to rebel. In particular, this framework is typical of the literature treating rebellion as Olsonian collective action problems solved through "selective incentives." Such treatment obfuscates the actual choices being made during rebellion. Third, the same individuals pass through different roles in the course of rebellion. As indicated in the discussion of the first Soviet occupation, individuals often progressed through a two-stage process, moving first from neutrality to acts of nonviolent resistance and then to participation in community-based rebellion organization.

In sum, at a most fundamental level rebellion involves individuals moving across a set of multiple possible roles. The social scientist must therefore develop conceptions that are able to represent rebellion as a process capable of generating considerable variation. With these points in mind, rebellion behavior in this work will be described with reference to a spectrum of individual roles represented by Figure 1.3. The zero position represents neutrality. The individual does nothing for or against the regime and nothing for or against the resistance. The +1 level represents unarmed

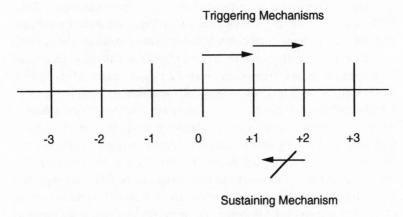

Figure 1.3. The spectrum of individual roles during rebellion

and unorganized opposition to the established regime. Attending a mass rally or writing antiregime graffiti are classic examples of +1 behavior. The +2 position stands for direct support of or participation in a locally based, armed organization. Finally, the +3 node represents mobile and armed organization, meaning membership in a guerrilla unit or rebel army. The left side of the spectrum mirrors the right but represents functional roles in support of the occupier or regime – in other words, collaboration. It is important to understand that these roles are based on observable behavior and not attitudes. For example, an individual either decides to join the local rebellion organization (+2) or remains outside of it.

The advantages of this operationalization are numerous. First and foremost, it captures the reality of the phenomenon to be explained as it allows for multiple roles and differentiates the crucial role played by members of locally based organizations (+2). This spectrum might best apply to populations occupied by a foreign power, but it can be applied to a host of rebellion situations.

Second, the spectrum allows for the treatment of individual and local variation. In addition to identifying individual behavior, the spectrum provides analysis of the way community-based mechanisms influence individuals. As seen in the preceding example, communities tend to develop their own "equilibriums" – that is, their members tend to bunch at particular nodes of the spectrum. Thus, community-level variation may also be discussed in terms of this concept.

This community-level variation holds the key to understanding rebellion. Why would the individuals composing two villages in the same region exhibit different patterns of rebellion behavior? This variation within a single region cannot be easily explained by terrain, history, culture, or the overall balance of power and resources between the regime and the rebels because these elements are roughly the same for all the communities within the area. It is also difficult to explain this variation by reference to attitudinal factors, relative deprivation, or ideology. The argument could be made that charismatic and ideologically driven individuals are the catalysts for rebellion and these individuals are probabalistically distributed across communities. This may, in fact, be part of the story, but I try to show in the following pages that something more interesting and more complex occurs – that relatively small differences in community structure can create different signals for potential rebels that, in turn, produce different rebellion dynamics. By specifying the reasons for variation at this level, the fundamental mechanisms that drive high-risk resistance action can be identified. When remaining at the level of huge aggregates, or relying on relatively vague concepts such as "institutions" or "ideology," the actual causal forces driving individual action are left as too much of a mystery. These individual-level causal forces are the focus of this work and are treated in terms of mechanisms.

Mechanisms

Mechanisms are specific causal patterns that explain individual actions over a wide range of settings. As Jon Elster has summarized, a mechanism is an intermediary between law and description.[3] Thomas Schelling uses the word "template" to emphasize the generalizability of the identified causal pattern.[4] Diego Gambetta has defined mechanism as "hypothetical causal models that make sense of individual behavior."[5] Again, his emphasis is on the

---

[3] As many readers will recognize, the conception of mechanism underlying this work borrows heavily from several works of Jon Elster. See *Alchemies of the Mind: Rationality and the Emotions* (Cambridge: Cambridge University Press, 1999), especially the first chapter, for an overview of Elster's definitions and use of mechanism.

I discuss my own view of mechanisms in greater length in "Structures and Mechanisms in Comparisons," in John Bowen and Roger Petersen, eds., *Critical Comparisons in Politics and Culture* (Cambridge: Cambridge University Press, 1999), pp. 61–77.

[4] Thomas C. Schelling, "Social Mechanisms and Social Dynamics," in Peter Hedström and Richard Swedberg, eds., *Social Mechanisms: An Analytical Approach to Social Theory* (Cambridge: Cambridge University Press, 1998), p. 37.

[5] Diego Gambetta, "Concatenations of Mechanisms," in Peter Hedström and Richard Swed-

specification of causation at an individual level. As described by some, a mechanism approach is a style of theorizing that cannot be given a precise definition, although several examples can be readily given. Gambetta lists several types of established mechanisms identified in the social sciences:[6]

1. Instrumental rationality.
2. Focal points.
3. Biased inferential processes.
4. Cognitive dissonance reduction.
5. Self-validating beliefs, such as distrust.
6. Emotions, such as envy.
7. Passions, such as *amour propre.*
8. Evolved dispositions toward altruism, sex, or children.
9. Special cognitive quirks, such as endowment effect.

I would add to this list a few more examples that are especially salient or relevant to this book's theory and substance:

10. Norms of reciprocity.
11. Threshold-based behavior.
12. Network diffusion.
13. Relative deprivation.

Consider one particular example: "tyranny of sunk costs." An old automobile that is constantly breaking down and being repaired might be retained by the owner despite the likelihood of numerous additional costly repairs due to the tyranny of sunk costs. Although the optimal choice might be to "junk" the car, the owner refuses to rationally calculate probable future costs because he or she cannot bear the thought of previous repair efforts "going down the drain." The same process might be involved in dysfunctional personal relationships or marriages. One or both partners in a relationship may find themselves continuously dissatisfied, in conflict, and on the verge of breaking up. Rather than ending the relationship, they may choose to remain together and ignore the probability that problems will recur because they cannot accept the fact that investments in the relationship have been in vain. The tyranny of sunk costs mechanism is both general in that it can be applied to a wide variety of cases (cars and spouses) and spe-

berg, eds., *Social Mechanisms: An Analytical Approach to Social Theory* (Cambridge: Cambridge University Press, 1998), p. 102.

[6] Ibid., p. 103.

cific and causal in that it explains why an event occurs. This combination of generality and specificity is one of the benefits of a mechanism approach. Another benefit is the wide possible range of behaviors that mechanisms can encompass. Irrational psychological processes such as the "tyranny of sunk costs" or cognitive dissonance reduction are mechanisms, but so are rational adaptation and social norms. Concentration on mechanisms allows the social scientist to deal with realistic actors affected by a complex variety of forces; it forces the social scientist toward *causal* explanations of increasingly finer grain.

The mechanism approach can be clearly contrasted with common alternatives. Variable-based treatments usually aim to estimate causal influence through statistical association. In this method, prediction becomes the primary goal. In opposition, a mechanism approach aims for explanation over prediction. Elster provides an illustration in which prediction can be easily made from a variable (price) but could not be made from any single mechanism:[7]

> To predict that less of a good will be bought when its price goes up, there is no need to form a hypothesis about human behavior. Whatever the springs of individual action – rational, traditional or simply random – we can predict that people will buy less of a good simply because they can afford less of it. Here, there are several mechanisms that are constrained to lead to the same outcome, so that for predictive purposes there is no need to decide among them. Yet for explanatory purposes the mechanism is what matters. It provides understanding whereas prediction at most offers control.[8]

Additionally, while statistical approaches rely on aggregation, the mechanism approach applied here operates at the individual level.

The mechanism approach subsumes rational choice. As several practi-

---

[7] As Elster has elaborated, one of the major reasons for the nonpredictability of mechanisms is that two equally valid but opposing mechanisms (e.g., "absence makes the heart grow fonder" and "out of sight out of mind") may be operating at the same time, but an observer cannot predict which one will determine action in any given situation. Given these difficulties, we may be able to isolate mechanisms, but we can seldom know "the necessary and sufficient conditions under which the various mechanisms are switched on." *Nuts and Bolts for the Social Sciences* (Cambridge: Cambridge University Press, 1989), p. 9. Although Elster clearly does not oppose the search for triggering conditions, he believes the ability to identify them is extremely difficult. As a result, his efforts and priorities lie in development of the logic and plausibility of the mechanisms themselves rather than the conditions that trigger those mechanisms and allow prediction.

[8] Ibid., p. 10.

tioners have pointed out, rational choice is a method based not on the search for laws but rather on the specification of mechanism.[9] As seen in the preceding list, instrumental rationality is only one mechanism among many. Seeking parsimony, rational-choice theorists restrict their analysis to this one mechanism. The method employed here is an explicit rejection of oversimplification of the causes and processes underlying resistance and rebellion. Rational or instrumental behavior is certainly one part of the story, but so are norms and irrational psychological mechanisms.

Restating the Central Question

The central question of this book can be rephrased in terms of the spectrum presented in Figure 1.3: *what mechanisms move individuals from one point on the spectrum to another?* The key movements and their accompanying mechanisms are noted in Figure 1.3. *Triggering mechanisms* work to first push the individual out of neutrality into opposition and, in a second step, into *organized* opposition.[10] The movement to the critical +2 position understandably takes up a significant part of this book. Of course, the organized opposition must stay organized if the rebellion is to continue. There are different mechanisms preventing individuals from leaving organized resistance, which are termed *sustaining mechanisms.* The bulk of this book examines the two sets of triggering mechanisms that move individuals from 0 to +1 and then from +1 to +2. Other movements on the spectrum, for example, the movement from +2 to +3, and the movement into collaboration roles, are only briefly discussed in the chapters that follow.

Sustained rebellion is produced by a sequencing of mechanisms or, in other terms, a process. By insights gained through fieldwork or secondary material, this project hypothesizes which mechanisms apply at which stage of the process. The following chapter outlines in detail these mechanisms and their logic and implications. Here, I simply summarize the key mechanisms in order to address some fundamental methodological issues:

---

[9] One of the most concise statements regarding rational choice as mechanism-based is Jim Johnson, "How Not to Criticize Rational Choice Theory: Pathologies of Common Sense," *Philosophy of the Social Sciences* 26 (1996): 77–91, especially pp. 84–85.

[10] Some clarifying distinctions can be made between riots, rebellions, and revolutions. Riots are unsustained violence; rebellions are sustained violence; revolutions are defined by the amount of social change produced and are not necessarily violent. The focus here is on rebellion and how violence is sustained. I use the term "resistance" to encompass both passive and violent antiregime action.

From 0 to +1 (Triggering Mechanisms, Stage One)
1. Resentment formation.
2. Threshold-based safety calculations with society-wide referents.
3. Status considerations linked to local community.
4. Focal points.

From +1 to +2 (Triggering Mechanisms, Stage Two)
1. Threshold-based safety calculations based on community referents.
2. Community-based norms of reciprocity.

Remaining at +2 (Sustaining Mechanisms)
1. Threats.
2. Irrational psychological mechanisms.
   a. The value of small victories.
   b. The tyranny of sunk costs.
   c. Wishful thinking.

This mechanism-based story aims for generality. None of the specified mechanisms or their hypothesized sequence is unique to any nation, state, or culture. This sequence of mechanisms can, and will, be used as a template to compare the development of resistance and rebellion in a variety of cases.

In essence, the book tells a specified story, something similar to the analytical narratives of Margaret Levi, Barry Weingast, Avner Greif, and others.[11] These practitioners of analytic narrative "seek to explore concrete historical cases," they "wish to examine the choices of individuals who are embedded in specific settings," they "wish to trace the sequences of actions, decisions, and responses that generate events and outcomes."[12] Furthermore, the analytic narrative is a mechanism approach; it does not seek covering laws but rather pursues "a complex middle ground between ideographic and nomothetic reasoning."[13] In a similar vein, I tell narratives of occupations and periods of resistance; however, although the narrative goals are the same, the breadth of the analysis differs. Seeking parsimony and falsifiability, Levi, Weingast, Greif, et al. base their analysis almost entirely on rational choice and mechanisms identified through game theory. In constrast, the range of mechanisms in the preceding sequence is far broader. Although rational choice and game theory play important roles in the analysis of the cases that follow, these devices are too limited to explain crucial actions that create and

---

[11] See Robert Bates et al., *Analytic Narratives* (Princeton: Princeton University Press, 1998).
[12] Ibid., p. 9.   [13] Ibid., p. 12.

sustain resistance and violent rebellion against ruthless regimes. Any realistic treatment of these events must also rely on mechanisms identified in psychology and other social sciences.

This expansion of scope does not mean that parsimony and falsifiability are not valued goals. Given the complexity of the subject, the list of mechanisms is parsimonious. The development of resistance and violent rebellion is explained by reference to only ten mechanisms. Furthermore, these ten mechanisms are sequentially ordered to produce one general process. As Elster states, the mechanism approach is intermediary between laws and description. There is no discussion of laws of rebellion in this work, but neither is there only description of cases. Rather, the goal is to use this relatively short and connected sequence of mechanisms to advance the understanding of important violent events. This specified sequence of mechanisms also provides a measure of falsifiability. If irrational psychological mechanisms are driving individual action in the early stages of resistance, then the hypothesized sequence does not apply. The same could be said concerning threats or other mechanisms.

This sequence also proposes a bold hypothesis regarding the development of sustained rebellion against powerful regimes. Notice that the mechanisms driving individuals to the crucial +2 position are hypothesized to be community-based norms and thresholds. Without the presence of strong communities that provide the conditions to trigger these mechanisms, violent rebellion is unlikely to obtain. As outlined in the next chapter, most of the mechanisms driving individuals from the 0 to the +1 position are not community-based. An implication follows: societies without strong communities may create passive forms of resistance, but they are unlikely to create the locally organized rebellion structures that would be able to spawn sustained violent action against a powerful regime. Clearly, community plays a central role in this work.

Community

Rebellion, or moving to the right on the spectrum, involves the acceptance of risk. Strong regimes threaten harsh penalties against those organized at the +2 level. In the cases that follow, these penalties were generally death or deportation. Strong communities produce mechanisms that are able to drive individuals into these dangerous roles and keep them there despite the possible high costs. Strong communities, as defined directly, promote rebellion by producing accessible information, reducing communication costs, and facilitating recruitment. The specific community-based mechanisms listed earlier – status considerations, norms of reciprocity, and threshold-based action – are related to these general features. Three aspects of community are outlined in this section: general features, specific mechanisms, and community structure.

Basic Definition and General Features of Community

Communities are sets of individuals engaged in regular patterns of interaction. The most common types of community in this work are rural villages, but other types of community such as factory units, neighborhoods, and college fraternities are also addressed. If "community" can be reduced to one measurable aspect, it would be a high level of face-to-face contact, which in turn implies relatively small numbers and stability of social relations between members. Ethnic, religious, and national groups are *not* communities by this definition. A more detailed and useful definition has been outlined by Michael Taylor in *Community, Anarchy, Liberty.*[14] Taylor enumerates five essentials of "community":

A. Direct relations between members (this implies relatively small numbers).

B. Many-sided relations (social and cultural, as well as economic).

C. Reciprocity.

D. Rough equality of material conditions.

E. A common set of beliefs and values.

These elements subsume measures of community used in other fields, namely, density of network ties,[15] community psychologists' "sense of

[14] Michael Taylor, *Community, Anarchy, Liberty* (Cambridge: Cambridge University Press, 1982).

[15] The term "density" generally refers to the overall number of ties within the group. Charles Tilly, *From Mobilization to Revolution* (Reading, Mass.: Addison Wesley, 1978) and Anthony Oberschall, *Social Conflict and Social Movements* (Englewood Cliffs, N.J.: Prentice-Hall, 1973) are two of the most well known works that employ such a conception. Roger Gould, "Collective Action and Network Structure," *American Sociological Review* 58 (1993): 182–196; Pamela E. Oliver, with Gerald Marwell and Ruy Teixeira, "A Theory of Critical Mass I: Interdependence, Group Heterogeneity, and the Production of Collective Action," *American Journal of Sociology* 91 (1985): 522–556; Pamela E. Oliver and Gerald Marwell, "The Paradox of Group Size in Collective Action: A Theory of the Critical Mass II," *American Sociological Review* 53 (1988): 1–8; Gerald Marwell, Pamela E. Oliver, and Ralph Prahl, "Social Networks and Collective Action: A Theory of the Critical Mass III," *American Journal of Sociology* 94 (1988): 502–534. All test or address the relationship between network density and collective action.

community,"[16] and a variety of conceptions defining "solidarity."[17]

This work basically employs Taylor's definition, with the exception of qualifying the role of "equality of material conditions."[18] The *strength or weakness* of the community, a structural distinction that will play a large role in this work, can be related to the presence or absence of these characteristics.

The village in the map depicted in Figure 1.1 and the fraternity listed in Figure 1.2 both clearly qualify as strong communities. The fact that such maps and lists can be created attests to a basic interconnectedness of individuals and the nature of their direct relations. In the substantive chapters, their many-sided relations and notions of reciprocity emerge from the oral histories. Individual farmsteads participated in informal cooperative farming practices, and village members often belonged to the same social clubs or religious societies. As can be seen by the number of hectares written on the map, a rough equality of material conditions obtained. These social groupings could also be characterized as possessing similar cultural backgrounds. Additionally, these communities possessed well-known and longstanding histories. Many of the families in the map in Figure 1.1 had lived in the village since the sixteenth century.

Strong communities facilitate rebellion for such obvious practical reasons as communication and recruitment. When most of the population has become antagonistic to the governing power (the +1 level), the regime will usually attempt to prevent organized efforts to end its rule by instituting a set of measures designed to control the population. As a rule, political parties are banned, the press is shut down, and the right of assembly is denied. The range of policy includes issuance of identification cards, development of a secret police and a network of informants, and the use and threat of high penalties,

---

[16] As an example of work from the field of community psychology, Thomas J. Glynn, "Psychological Sense of Community: Measurement and Application," *Human Relations* 34 (1981): 789–818, found that the best predictors of a "sense of community" were expected length of residency, satisfaction, and number of neighbors one could identify by first name. For an extensive discussion on how to operationalize "sense of community" and how this psychological conception agrees or diverges with the use here, see David McMillan and David Chavis, "Sense of Community: A Definition and Theory," *Journal of Community Psychology* 14 (1986): 6–23; and David Chavis et al., "Sense of Community through Brunswik's Lens: A First Look," *Journal of Community Psychology* 14 (1986): 24–40.

[17] Many scholars from different fields employ the term "solidarity" to help explain how local collective-action dilemmas are solved. Theda Skocpol, *States and Social Revolutions: A Comparative Analysis of France, Russia, and China* (Cambridge: Cambridge University Press, 1979), is one prominent example.

[18] As is shown later, rebellion is facilitated by the existence of social-status groups that are sometimes based on economic inequality.

perhaps death, for involvement in organized opposition. One usual regime goal is to isolate communities and prevent communication between them. Clandestine organization requires numerous and sometimes irregular exchanges of information between members. When travel is monitored, local networks will probably be the safest and most efficient. In line with common sense, Tilly concludes, "the steeper the rise in the cost of communication as a function of distance, the more likely that people will organize their action – if they act at all – around a common territory."[19] Clearly, if the regime is highly effective in isolating communities and preventing communication between them, the locality may be the only basis for organization.

Second, the community allows potential rebels to cope with the high risk involved with recruitment. Individuals are unlikely to recruit, or be recruited by, people they have never met, especially when informants may have permeated the general population.[20] Recruitment may also involve a measure of persuasion, if not outright coercion. Shared community histories produce knowledge of who can be trusted, who can be persuaded (and what the best means of persuasion might be), and who must be isolated (or liquidated). Most individuals are loath to engage in this type of high-risk behavior without some knowledge of the odds of success, survival, and, especially, the odds of betrayal.

This last point leads to a more general issue about communities and the coordination of expectations underlying strategic action. When individuals are confronted with the fateful decision to join (or the idea to found) an organized rebellion organization under conditions of high risk, limited information, and uncertainty about future outcomes, the decision they make is a strategic one. That is, the individual's decision is dependent on the expected choices and actions of others. Only fanatics will engage the forces of a repressive regime without minimal assurances or without significant pressures. Under the conditions of occupation or repression, a community is crucial because, as a set of informal and formal social interactions and institutions, it

---

[19] Charles Tilly, "Do Communities Act?" *Sociological Inquiry* 43 (1974): 209–240.

[20] Even in situations without risk, the tendency to recruit within the memberships of already existing networks and communities is high. See Raymond V. Liedke, "Who Do You Know in the Group? Location of Organizations in Interpersonal Networks," *Social Forces* 70 (1991): 455–474. He finds that "New Organizations should emerge where interpersonal network density is great" (p. 459). Likewise, A. Booth and N. Babchuk, "Personal Influence Networks and Voluntary Association Affiliation," *Sociological Inquiry* 39 (1969): 179–188, have found that new organizations are formed through already existing network ties. The presence of informants and risk certainly works to strengthen this well-established tendency.

can provide both the information and the pressures to assure and/or push individuals to move from +1 to +2.

Consider the following passage from Knight regarding social institutions and strategic decision making:

> Social institutions affect strategic decision making by establishing social expectations, and they do so through two mechanisms: the provision of information and sanctions. Through these mechanisms social actors learn the information necessary to formulate expectations about the actions of those with whom they interact. With these expectations they choose the strategies that they think will maximize their individual benefits. In this way institutions affect strategic choice and, therefore, social outcomes.[21]

The elements of Knight's formulation may need some modification to apply to the subject of rebellion, but they are certainly present. The community is a set of social, familial, economic, and political interactions, indeed, a history of socially shared interactions, which produces information and expectations[22] about how sanctions and rewards will operate during the period of rebellion.

Many students of rebellion and collective action have identified these basic features of strong community.[23] For the analysis here, however, citing these general features is not adequate. Rather, the more specific mechanisms of strong community must be filtered out.

Mechanisms of Strong Community

The mechanisms of resentment formation, focal points, and irrational psychological forces can occur in any society, but four key mechanisms are closely related to the existence of strong community.

---

[21] Jack Knight, *Institutions and Social Conflict* (Cambridge: Cambridge University Press, 1992).

[22] See Dennis Chong, *Collective Action and the Civil Rights Movement* (Chicago: University of Chicago Press, 1991), on the role of expectations.

[23] See Mark Lichbach's section on community (pp. 15–16) in his review of the rebellion literature, "Rethinking Rationality and Rebellion: Theories of Collective Action and Problems of Collective Dissent," *Rationality and Society* 6 (1994): 8–39. Victoria Bonnell shows the importance of community in the specific case of the Russian Revolution in *Roots of Rebellion: Workers' Politics and Organizations in St. Petersburg and Moscow, 1900–1914* (Berkeley: University of California Press, 1983).

Status Rewards.   Status rewards, both positive and negative, are accorded higher weights in communities with high levels of face-to-face contact, that is, in strong communities with high levels of interaction and reciprocity, as well as a commonly held set of values and beliefs. How much you care whether another individual sees you as a hero or a coward depends a great deal on how many times you have contact with that individual. To be coded as a coward in an atomized society is not as meaningful as being so coded in a tight-knit community. It is difficult to be "shamed" by people one does not encounter.

Consider the following two responses to occupation, one an example of weak community and the other strong community, both occurring during the early stages of the Second World War. First, from France, "I had heard de Gaulle's appeal from London and tried to create a small group in Montpellier to do something. We didn't know what. It wasn't easy to find others. Most of them produced some sort of excuse and said, 'we'll be with you when the time comes, but . . .'"[24] Second, compare the response of Montenegrin clansmen. The following is an oath taken by residents of Lijeva Rijeka after just one of their members had been shot in the early stages of occupation: "Each member of this battalion has to be sworn to the people that he would sacrifice his life for their honor and their good, and that he should tenfold avenge any fallen inhabitant of Lijeva Rijeka."[25] Both the French and the Montenegrins may have resented occupation, but the Montenegrins possessed a specific action, an oath, that was enforced by norms of reciprocity and the loss of honor and status if the oath was refused. Within the tight-knit Montenegrin communities, sanctions were automatic and status paramount. Those who came out immediately to speak for action received status rewards for being the first leaders against the enemy. In the French case, individuals could excuse themselves without fear of sanction or loss of honor; there was neither a pursuit of status, the strong desire to be a hero, nor credible sanctions against those refusing to reciprocate the first actions of their fellows. The Lithuanian communities studied here may not have had the level of status reward or sanction as those in Montenegro but neither were they as lacking in status concern as in the French example.

[24] From H. R. Keward, *Resistance in Vichy France* (Oxford: Oxford University Press, 1983), p. 266.
[25] From Milija Lasic-Vasojevic, *Enemies on All Sides: The Fall of Yugoslavia* (Washington, D.C.: North American International, 1976), pp. 45–46.

Furthermore, strong communities produce positive as well as negative status rewards. In communities where a rough equality of material conditions holds (one of Taylor's five criteria in the definition of community), the only way to become a "big man" in the community may be through some sort of courageous action. This seems especially true for young males.[26]

Norms of Reciprocity.   Norms of reciprocity are self-explanatory: if a community member, friend or neighbor, is performing some action promoting a public good, others may feel obligated to participate in that action as well. Alternatively, if one community member is in trouble, then other members should help that member (and, according to the norm, expect help for themselves in the future). There are various norms of reciprocity. In Chapter 2, three specific reciprocity norms are discussed in detail. The broader community effect at issue here is most similar to a generalized "norm of fairness." In practice, it is difficult to treat such norms in terms of strict "tit for tat" behavior.[27] Within the life of a community, a strict sequence of plays would be hard to identify. Among the diverse and complicated interactions of a community, the values of a "play" of defection or cooperation are difficult to compare and perhaps impossible to quantify seriously. Despite these complexities, a sizable amount of valuable literature exists on norms of fair-

---

[26] In a large quantitative analysis, Jack Goldstone found that the presence of economically immobile young males was a major factor in rebellion and revolution. See *Revolution and Rebellion in the Early Modern World* (Berkeley: University of California Press, 1991). There are structural reasons for this finding, as well as status seeking, of course. In the early Gorbachev period, Soviet scholar Jerry Hough believed that one reason why the Soviet Union would avoid nationalist uprisings was that the success of perestroika (which Hough anticipated) would allow an economic outlet for young males that would take them off the streets and refocus their energies.

James Coleman addressed the force of zeal in his work on norms. Zeal relies heavily on status rewards. Coleman held that closed social networks (similar to the use of community here) amplify the rewards of heroic action as the hero actually experiences the admiration or gratitude of those affected by his effort in such a network. "It is for this reason that a performing athlete, musician, or actor may experience far greater motivation than will a book author, who cannot see the reactions of his audience." See James Coleman, "The Realization of Effective Norms," in Randall Collins, ed., *Four Sociological Traditions* (Oxford: Oxford University Press, 1994), pp. 171–189.

The literature on honor often categorizes societies on how honor is gained. A basic dichotomy is based on ascription versus achievement. Status rewards fall into the honor-by-achievement category. Elster lists ancient Greece and seventeenth-centry France as honor-by-achievement societies.

[27] This view differs from the consequentialist norms of many rational-choice theorists such as Robert Axelrod, *The Evolution of Cooperation* (New York: Basic Books, 1984).

ness,[28] as well as a sizable literature on how the norms of fairness can facilitate rebellion.[29] Furthermore, in many of the works that address rebellion at the community level, the discussion of the nature and force of norms plays a prominent role. James Scott[30] and Samuel Popkin[31] have provided well-known examples. This body of work is accessed at various points throughout the book.

For rebellion, the key question is how community norms work to enhance or hinder risk acceptance. During times of resistance and rebellion, will the force of long-term relations of reciprocity in prerebellion economic and social spheres carry over to decisions regarding cooperation in the risk-laden period of resistance? On the issue of carryover of norms, there is some evidence both ways.[32] The evidence in the following chapters clearly supports the conclusion that such normative inertia does operate to affect chances for rebellion.

Threshold-Based Safety Calculations Based on Community Referents. "I will rebel if X percent of the others also rebel." This is the logic of the potential

---

[28] See Robyn M. Dawes, Jeanne McTavish, and Harriet Shaklee, "Behavior, Communication, and Assumptions about Other People's Behavior in a Commons Dilemma Situation," *Journal of Personality and Social Psychology* 35 (1977): 1–11; J. A. Piliavin and H. W. Charng, "Altruism: A Review of Recent Theory and Research," *Annual Review of Sociology* 16 (1990): 27–65; Elster, *Cement of Society,* chap. 5; Steven E. Finkel, E. N. Muller, and Karl-Dieter Opp, "Personal Influence, Collective Rationality, and Mass Political Action," *American Political Science Review* 83 (1989): 885–903.

[29] See Gould, "Collective Action and Network Structure." Bruce Fireman and William Gamson also examine the effects of normative pressure and solidarity for mobilizing resources. See "Utilitarian Logic in the Resource Mobilization Perspective," in M. N. Zald and J. D. McCarthy, eds., *The Dynamics of Social Movements* (Cambridge, Mass.: Winthrop, 1979), pp. 8–44.

[30] James Scott, *The Moral Economy of the Peasant: Rebellion and Subsistence in Southeast Asia* (New Haven: Yale University Press, 1976).

[31] Samuel Popkin, *The Rational Peasant: The Political Economy of Rural Society in Vietnam* (Berkeley: University of California Press, 1979), and "Political Entrepreneurs and Peasant Movements in Vietnam," in Michael Taylor, ed., *Rationality and Revolution* (Cambridge: Cambridge University Press, 1988), pp. 9–62.

[32] Some scholars challenge the idea that norms have inertia. Jack Goldstone, in a summary work on revolution and collective action, holds the opposite view: "In short, research on both historical and contemporary collective action finds that people markedly deviate from one of the assumptions of classical rational choice collective action theory, namely that they make decisions and act as individuals in deciding whether or not to take part in revolutionary actions. Rather, the decision to participate is made by groups of individuals, who were already part of formal or informal groups, and who therefore deliberated and decided to act jointly, as a group. See "Is Revolution Individually Rational? Groups and Individuals in Revolutionary Collective Action," *Rationality and Society* 6 (1994): 142.

rebel in facing the prospect of acting against a powerful regime or occupier. The value of X represents the "tipping point," or the point at which the individual has received enough assurance or pressure to commit to an action.[33] In recent years, many students of resistance, rebellion, and revolution have employed threshold analysis and the closely related assurance game to explain collective actions against repressive regimes.[34] All of these scholars agree that the threshold value represents a "safety in numbers" aspect: the more fellow rebels or protesters, the less chance of being individually sanctioned by the regime.

The key question in terms of a threshold-based mechanism concerns the reference group. That is, X percent of whom? The answer to this question is determined by the type of action that is being contemplated and its inherent risks. If the action is to be a one-shot participation in a demonstration against the regime, the individual may only need assurance that the crowd will be large enough to lower the chances of physical beating by riot police to an acceptably low level. In this case, the reference group may be the total percentage of the population of the city or state attending the demonstration. If the primary risk is being fired from one's job for demonstrating, then the reference group might be the number of employees in the work unit. The authorities could fire a small number of dissidents but could not dismiss a large number of workers without disrupting the operation of the unit.

The movement from 0 to +1 on the spectrum represents unorganized, lower-risk, one-shot actions such as graffiti writing, singing antiregime

---

[33] The assurance game logic was first developed by Amartya Sen, "Isolation, Assurance, and the Social Rate of Discount," *Quarterly Journal of Economics* 81 (1967): 112–124. The work of Thomas Schelling in *Micromotives and Macrobehavior* (New York: Gordon and Breach, 1985) is seminal to any application of the assurance game.

[34] These include Mark Granovetter, "Threshold Models of Collective Behavior," *American Journal of Sociology* 83 (1978): 1420–1443; Chong, *Collective Action;* Goldstone, "Is Revolution Individually Rational?"; Timur Kuran, "Now Out of Never: The Element of Surprise in the East European Revolution of 1989," *World Politics* 44 (1992): 7–48, and *Private Truths, Public Lies: The Social Consequences of Preference Falsification* (Cambridge, Mass.: Harvard University Press, 1995); Rasma Karklins and Roger Petersen, "The Decision Calculus of Protestors and Regimes: Eastern Europe, 1989," *Journal of Politics* 55 (1993): 588–614; Valerie Bunce and Dennis Chong, "The Party's Over: Mass Protest and the End of Communist Rule in Eastern Europe," paper presented at the annual meeting of the American Political Science Association, San Francisco, 1990; Jon Elster, "When Communism Dissolves," *London Review of Books,* January 25, 1990, pp. 3–6; Susanne Lohmann, "Rationality, Revolution, and Revolt: The Dynamics of Informational Cascades," Graduate School of Business Research Paper no. 1213, Stanford University, Stanford, Calif. Anthony Oberschall provides a good summary discussion of the importance of assurance; see "Rational Choice in Collective Protests," *Rationality and Society* 6 (1994): 79–100.

songs on a bus, or showing up at demonstrations (if the regime allows it). These actions are often a test to see how many others are also strongly opposed to the regime, how many others are willing to engage in some form of resistance. The main form of assurance needed is some guarantee of anonymity, some protection from being caught during the act itself. Thus, for the movement from 0 to +1, the reference group is society at large or the larger corporate groups in which the individual is embedded (for instance, students at a university might use the university population as the referent).

In moving from +1 to +2, the reference group changes. At this stage, powerful regimes control much of the outside world but cannot easily penetrate communities; the world becomes smaller, and the battle comes down to the village or workplace. The individual looks for strategic clues for action. When the regime is powerful, the most relevant gauge of "safety in numbers" is the percentage of other community members also involved in underground activity (+2). There is a desire to act, but the potential rebel thinks "I will act if X percent of the community acts, I will have safety in numbers and be protected from informants if X percent of the community is united and organized." In the Lithuanian cases, the Soviets cut off communication between regions and cities but were still not powerful enough to penetrate these communities.

Monitoring and Retaliation: Rational Calculation of Threat.   The ability to threaten and retaliate against informants is a key to the development of any underground organization. If potential recruits have little confidence that the organization can remain secret, they are unlikely to join. Due to their small numbers, stability, and extensive interactions, strong communities allow efficiency in retaliation and monitoring. The rebels know the histories and sympathies of their fellow community members, they know who the probable informants may be, and they know what threats will be most effective to deter their collaboration. Potential collaborators know they are being watched and know they have little ability to avoid retaliation (which, in the cases that follow, often involved their death).[35]

---

[35] Many scholars mention the higher monitoring abilities of smaller groups. Michael Hechter, *Principles of Group Solidarity* (Berkeley: University of California Press, 1987), for example, addresses monitoring issues at length.

Community Structure

Community structure has already been discussed in general terms of strength and weakness. *Weak communities* are characterized by diminished degrees of Taylor's features as outlined earlier – that is, indirect relations between members, one-sided relations, lack of reciprocity, diversity of beliefs and values, and rough material inequality. Within weak communities, individual behavior is less susceptible to the norms, appeals, and threats of other community members. *Strong communities* possess the broad structural features outlined by Taylor, which in turn may produce the mechanisms mentioned earlier.

Central to the argument of this book, not all strong communities are equally able to move individuals toward positions of rebellion on the spectrum. There will be distinct variation among strong communities that is related to the way those strong communities are *specifically* structured. While the strength of a community can be related to the likely presence of these mechanisms, the more specific structure of the community and the strategic interactions those specific structures generate within the community are related to the likely efficiency of these mechanisms in driving individuals along the spectrum, especially to the crucial +2 position.

Communities are composed of various subsets of interactions and institutions. These subsets have different types of reciprocity norms, different conceptions of status and its value, more and less powerful norms of exclusion and ostracism. In these respects, family groups differ from economic groups, which in turn differ from social and religious subsets. The more precise operation of these forces will vary according to the existence of certain subsets, their size, and the nature of overlapping memberships among groups. A knowledge of the distribution of community subsets, *the community structure,* is thus necessary in predicting which communities are likely to form organized rebellion units and which will not.

The Community as the Key Level of Analysis

Due to its importance in generating key mechanisms vital to the creation of sustained rebellion, the community becomes a key level of analysis. Almost every study of political violence can be discussed in terms of the four levels of analysis represented in Figure 1.4. Theoretically, arrows could be drawn going both ways from every box; however, in practice the explicit or implicit assumptions concerning causation and the direction of causation between the four levels generally fall somewhere within the pattern presented here.

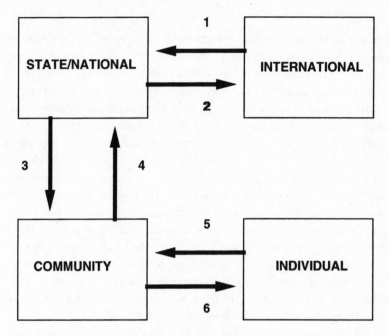

Figure 1.4. Levels of analysis in the study of rebellion and revolution

The following causal sequence underlies the design of the book: community structures produce mechanisms that affect individual behavior driving individuals along the spectrum of roles; these individual actions may in turn change the community structure, most importantly by forming +2 organizations; if enough +2 organizations are formed, then rebellion at the state or national level may be sustained. Thus, an explanation of variation in rebellion behavior at the individual and community levels is also an explanation of aggregate behavior at the state or national level, perhaps the most common and preferred level of analysis for scholars of political violence.

Why is this sequence (6 – 5 – 4) the best way to explain variation in rebellion and resistance against powerful regimes, such as the Germans and the Soviets? As previously mentioned, a powerful regime will be able to cut off or diminish the influence of political parties and nationally based organizations; in effect, links 1, 2, and 3 atrophy. In the post-1945 Soviet cases, they are practically nonexistent. With less powerful regimes, nationally based organizations may survive and their links to the community will need to be examined. Contrary to what many theorists assume, however, the strength of the link between national and community levels may still depend on the type of community structure and how well that structure is able to translate the directives of the national organization into action at the community and individual levels.

Assessing the Theory: The Comparative Method

The comparative method guides the research design. The sequence of mechanisms given here provides a base line for comparison. Cases are then sought that control certain factors and vary others. In a rough sense, the comparisons proceed from most similar to most different design. Chapters 3 through 6 examine the three successive occupations of the 1940s. Chapter 7 investigates resistance and rebellion in four other 1940s East European cases. Chapter 8 expands the analysis across time, studying resistance in the perestroika era. In effect, the goal is to stretch the template of mechanisms to allow for an assessment of its generality and analytical suppleness and usefulness. In concluding this introduction, I will briefly describe each chapter and then explain how the substantive chapters (3 through 8) form controlled comparisons.

Outline

Chapter 2 is theoretical, going step by step through the sequences of mechanisms that form the rebellion process. This template forms the basis for comparison for the next six substantive chapters. Chapter 2 identifies in detail the crucial triggering and sustaining mechanisms addressing in order the movement from 0 to +1 and +1 to +2 (triggering mechanisms) and the prevention of movement from +2 back to +1 (sustaining mechanisms). Building upon the concepts introduced already, the chapter outlines conducive versus nonconducive structures and their inherent dynamics and produces lists of ideal types of community that will and will not provide the mechanisms that push individuals to the +2 node. This chapter includes an explicit discussion of the effects of entrepreneurship, social norms, homogeneity, density, and centralization. The sustaining mechanisms, primarily psychological in character, are outlined much more briefly.

Chapter 3 covers the formation of resistance in Lithuania during the first Soviet occupation of 1940–1941. The chapter aims to vary the type of community. Comparisons among strong and weak communities, as well as comparisons among differently structured strong communities, form the analytical foundation. This chapter also includes a short section on the Soviet occupation of Latvia and Estonia.

Chapter 4 discusses the way in which one urban community, the Catholic fraternity of engineering students at the University of Kaunas, produced clandestine rebels. The chapter focuses on one aspect of conducively structured community – the effect of centralized actors – by tracing the contacts and outlining the connections of two critical rebel organizers.

Chapter 5 covers the German occupation in Lithuania and other Baltic countries. At issue is the general lack of resistance and collaboration.

Paralleling Chapter 3, Chapter 6 explains strong, locally based Lithuanian resistance to Soviet rule, this time in the postwar period.

In an effort to illustrate the robustness of this book's approach, Chapter 7 addresses several other 1940s Eastern European cases: central Ukraine and Belorussia between the Nazis and the Soviets, wartime Montenegro and Albania, postwar Volhynia and Galicia, postwar Belorussia, and postwar Latvia and Estonia.

Chapter 8 addresses perestroika era cases of resistance, including those in Lithuania, Czechoslovakia, and East Germany. These cases are characterized by an absence of strong community.

Chapter 9 breaks from the comparative analysis of Chapters 3 through 8 to address a puzzling question unanswered by threshold models. In using threshold models, a "first-playing" group with a 0 percent threshold must be assumed if action is to be initiated. Whether the size of this first-playing group is 1 or 3 percent might be crucial for starting the tipping process. This chapter explores why one society might have more "first players" than another.

Comparative Analyses

Within-Lithuania Comparisons: Soviet Occupations of 1940–1941, 1945–1952.   The empirical core of the volume consists of three empirical chapters covering anti-Soviet Lithuanian resistance during both the 1940–1941 and 1945–1950 periods (Chapters 3, 4, and 6). The two periods of Soviet occupation of Lithuania are ideal for this study for the following reasons. First, the nature of Soviet control tended to cut off communities, especially rural communities, from outside influences. In both periods, the Soviets had enough power to prevent easy communication between villages but not enough to penetrate into the local community. As a result, these communities can be studied and compared as isolated "microcosms."

Second, due to Lithuania's level of development, a range of types of community structure existed. By the late 1930s, Lithuania was rapidly modernizing but still possessed remnants of premodern social structures. The intermingling of modern and premodern social and economic forms produced weak and strong communities as well as structural variations among strong communities.

Third, while community structure varied, other broader factors were constant across Lithuania. Factors such as culture, relative deprivation, the larger balance between the regime and rebels, terrain, and many others did not vary to a significant degree among villages located in close proximity.

Fourth, as shown by the Merkine example, communities varied in movement along the spectrum; they tended to develop different equilibria in the number of individuals occupying rebellion roles.

As a result of these four factors, it is possible to isolate, at least partially, the effect of community on the dynamics of rebellion.

Comparisons of Lithuania with the Other Baltic States.   Latvia and Estonia witnessed the same three occupations and many of the same general events as Lithuania. Their experience is briefly addressed in Chapters 3 and 7. Regime strategy and strength are almost totally identical across the three Baltic states. What differs is culture, to an extent community structure, and, also to an extent, movement on the spectrum. Lithuania saw more movement into the +2 position than the other two nations. This difference is often attributed to Lithuania's intense Catholic culture, which is thought to produce more fanaticism and martyrdom. The comparisons challenge that thinking.

Comparisons of Lithuania across Time.   During the 1940s, Lithuania was occupied three different times allowing for variation in a set of broader factors. Although "culture" remained constant and no regime allowed nationally based organizations, significant differences in overall regime strategy and strength occurred. In the most basic of terms, regime strategy can be discussed by level of brute force and brutality. During the first occupation, the Soviet strategy could be described in terms of containing a "hearts and mind" element; in the latter period the Soviets generally relied on brute force. By the late 1940s, the Soviets could, and did, deport entire villages and communities to Siberia. The intervening German occupation was relatively mild toward the Lithuanian population.

Comparisons across time create the opportunity to examine the same types of community structures at work in different broader environments. These comparisons will test whether, despite differences in regime abilities and methods, the same structures and same types of mechanisms were effective in producing movement to +2 in both Soviet periods. Additionally, across-time comparisons allow examination of the relationship between regime strategy, change in community structure, and the triggering of mechanisms of rebellion. Clearly, the collectivization and deportations of the late 1940s turned strong and conducively structured communities into weaker and less conducively structured ones, or destroyed the communities entirely.

The inclusion of Lithuania in the analysis of perestroika era cases allows for comparison of 1940s and 1980s anti-Soviet resistance.

Comparisons across State, Nation, and Society. Chapter 7 applies the template of mechanisms to a series of 1940s East European cases that bring important additional factors into the study of rebellion against powerful occupying regimes. While the Lithuanian cases involve only one occupier, wartime Belorussia and central Ukraine involved two roughly equal occupiers, the Nazis and the Soviets, battling over the same piece of territory. How did this battle among ruthless regimes affect movement on the spectrum? In wartime Montenegro, clan-based society still pervaded social life, especially in the rural areas. How did the effects of segmentary society, characterized by very strong communities and overarching "tribal" connections, affect the development of rebellion? Additionally, Chapter 7 examines the significant differences in rebellion behavior among postwar Galicia and Volhynia, two Ukrainian regions with different historical backgrounds. These cases were chosen to stretch the conceptual boundaries of the theory. The comparisons help determine where those boundaries lie and specify what modifications may be necessary.

Comparisons of Resistance within the Perestroika Period. Chapter 8 analyzes the growth of passive resistance in the form of mass rallies that occurred across Eastern Europe in the late 1980s. The effects of communism (and concurrent modernization) on Eastern Europe, and especially the Baltic states, radically transformed the communities located there. Rapid urbanization and collectivization were dual hammers of community destruction. The state intervened to provide the collective goods previously provided by community reciprocity. Increased scale eliminated the direct, many-sided relations characteristic of the previous era. Finally, the assault on and decline of tradition and religion eroded common beliefs and values. The result was societies chararcterized by weak community.

Despite these features, massive, passive resistance (+1) developed. Chapter 8 explores how this resistance developed, why resistance took the form that it did, and why variation occurred among different cases. These questions are examined in an analysis of Lithuania from August 1987 to October 1988 and Czechoslovakia and the German Democratic Republic in the autumn of 1989.

To repeat the central methodological point, each case and each chapter employs the hypothesized sequence of mechanisms as a base line for comparison. The next chapter explains this process in more detail, expands upon its logic, and specifies its implications.

2. Mechanisms and Process

As outlined in the previous chapter, rebellions against strong regimes generally involve multiple stages. Correspondingly, rebellions necessitate multiple mechanisms that serve to drive individuals from one stage to the next as well as mechanisms that sustain action in vital roles. This chapter provides a detailed description of three sets of interconnected mechanisms crucial for initiating and sustaining rebellion:

1. Mechanisms driving movement from neutrality to widespread, but unorganized and unarmed, resistance (0 to +1).
2. Mechanisms driving movement to locally organized and armed rebellion (+1 to +2).
3. Mechanisms sustaining locally organized rebellion (maintaining action at +2).

From Neutrality to Widespread, Unarmed, and Unorganized Resistance

Some of the actions that characterize +1 behavior include writing antiregime graffiti, singing nationalist songs on buses, handing out or accepting antiregime literature, boycotting elections, and participating in "spontaneous" demonstrations. The significance of these actions is that they are public manifestations of antiregime sentiment, and, as each involves the possibility of sanction, they serve as public indicators of the number of risk accepters in the general populace and the amount of risk they will incur.[1] In Chairman

---

[1] As stated in Chapter 1, I am challenging Timur Kuran's argument that the distribution of thresholds is basically unknowable. Individuals are capable of signaling their threshold, at least in terms of its risk component, using symbolic actions.

Mao's terms, +1 actions indicate to potential rebels within the general population, as well as organizers, that there is a "sea" for rebel "fish" to swim in.

Why would any individual accept even a small risk to perform an action that has only an extremely small effect on any outcome? One response might be that the movement from 0 to +1 is not strategic and does not involve calculation. Rather, these types of individual events are borné of frustration and the need for catharsis. In the cases in the subsequent chapters, however, the threat of regime sanctions was so obvious that it would be hard to conceive of an individual who totally ignored them (the interviewees themselves back this up). Given this fact, the present approach borrows from the assurrance game and the threshold mechanism underlying this game. In effect, the threshold mechanism centers the discussion of other 0 to +1 mechanisms.

When a certain percentage of the population is engaged in +1 level anti-regime actions, regime resources are strained and threats become less credible. Individuals find "safety in numbers." Of course, different individuals will hold different ideas about what numbers produce safety. There will be a distribution of thresholds. The intricacies of threshold distributions are discussed in detail later in the chapter, but a couple of commonsense points should be made here. The "first actors" must be willing to accept high risks (possess low thresholds). Also, the lower the thresholds (the more risk accepted by the population), the higher the chances of the entire society moving to a +1 level. This leads up to an obvious question: what mechanisms lower thresholds for participation in low-level resistance? Three mechanisms are especially prominent: resentment formation, focal points, and status rewards.

Resentment Formation

Other things being equal, the more one detests the regime, the more likely one is to accept higher risk in performing +1 actions. If there is going to be a rebellion, there has to be something or someone to rebel against – that is, there must be a perception of an enemy. This point may seem to border on banality, but a great deal of surprising variation in emotion toward different regimes does exist. For the cases in this study, cases of Soviet and Nazi occupation, the question of "an enemy" might seem clear, but in many instances, including some involving the Soviets and the Nazis, the perception of an enemy is a surprisingly complicated matter. For example, the Lithuanian case presents some rapid shifts in perception of enemy. Lithuanians saw

the Germans as predators in the late 1930s but greeted them as liberators in
June 1941; Lithuanians met the first Soviet takeover in the summer of 1940
with some initial ambivalence but then rapidly came to despise the Soviet
regime; Lithuanians had lived relatively peaceably with Jews for centuries,
but many Lithuanians perceived them as traitorous enemies by the end of the
first Soviet occupation. Although the question of the perception, or creation,
of an enemy is beyond the scope of this work, the issue of motivation to act
against occupation cannot be ignored. The mechanism of *resentment formation* attempts to capture the emotional antipathy toward specific occupiers
that appears to vary so much among the cases.

The resentment formation mechanism is based on changes of status hierarchies brought on through occupation.[2] All occupations involve the re-
ordering of political-social hierarchy.[3] At its most fundamental level, hierarchy involves control and force. After occupation, new regimes redraw all
lines of control and force and create a new order in police, military, and political bureaucracy. Hierarchy might be ethnic or political, but for the purposes here, especially for this period of Eastern European history, ethnic
group status is most salient. The occupier obviously places itself at the top
of this hierarchy, while other groups, majority and minorities, are placed
somewhere below. The specific way the hierarchy is reordered after occupation will affect the direction and intensity of resentments that, in turn, provide original motivations for resistance. Consider three different hierarchies
that might follow the occupation of a formerly independent state previously
dominated by the majority people (Figure 2.1).

In hierarchy 1 the occupier agrees to share dominance with the majority
group. The majority, as a distinct and recognizable group, still controls some
administrative and police or military positions and retains a position of dom-

---

[2] Although only a small part of the present study, the formation of resentment and the conditions under which this emotion can lead to violence constitute the core of another book-length
manuscript that I am writing. See Roger Petersen, *Fear, Hatred, Resentment: Delineating Paths
to Ethnic Conflict in Eastern Europe* (Cambridge: Cambridge University Press, forthcoming).

[3] For discussions of ethnic conflict in ranked versus unranked systems, see Donald
Horowitz, *Ethnic Groups in Conflict* (Berkeley: University of California Press, 1985), especially chaps. 3 and 4, which have greatly influenced the present work. Also see T. David Mason, "The Ethnic Dimension of Civil Violence in the Post Cold War Era: Structural Configurations and Rational Choices," paper presented at the annual meeting of the American Political
Science Association, 1994. Many scholars writing on the Soviet Union and Russia have concentrated on the ethnic-status variables. See David Laitin's idea of "Most Favored Lord" in "The
National Uprisings in the Soviet Union," *World Politics* 44 (1991): 139–177. Also, John A. Armstrong, "The Ethnic Scene in the Soviet Union: The View of the Dictatorship," in Erich Goldhagen, ed., *Ethnic Minorities in the Soviet Union* (New York: Praeger, 1968), pp. 3–49.

Hierarchy 1	Hierarchy 2	Hierarchy 3
Occupier/Majority	Occupier	Occupier
Minority 1	Majority	Minority 1
Minority 2	Minority 1	Majority
	Minority 2	Minority 2

Figure 2.1. Examples of hierarchy in an occupied multiethnic state

inance over minorities. In hierarchy 2 the occupier seizes most or all positions of authority, relegating the majority group to a clearly subordinate position, although one still above that of minorities. In hierarchy 3 the occupier not only demotes the majority group but places a formerly subordinate group above it in the hierarchy. As a general principle, individuals of formerly dominated groups resent living in hierarchies that have placed them in newly subordinate positions. After having been on the top of an ethnic hierarchy, most individuals come to see their group's dominant status as part of a natural order. Following this simple logic, they feel more resentment the more they perceive an unjust hierarchy. This sense of injustice is likely to be more acute depending upon several factors: if the policy of the occupier entirely shuts out the majority from positions of authority (the difference between hierarchies 1 and 2); when a majority perceives its position as "below" a formerly subordinate minority or, relatedly, when a traditionally "stronger" group in terms of rule or military prowess finds itself below a "weaker" group (represented in hierarchy 3); and when a group has direct experience of subordination through the actions of an ethnically different police or military. Thus, the majority is most likely to intensely resent the occupier if hierarchy 3 is developed and least with hierarchy 1. In hierarchy 3, minority 1 is likely to become the target of resentment as well. In Lithuania, I argue, the 1940–1941 Soviet occupation was perceived in terms of hierarchy 3, with the Jewish minority seen as occupying an unjust superior position, whereas the German occupation was perceived more in terms of hierarchy 2.

Two points deserve emphasis. First, occupations affect group status and individuals care about group status. For the everyday economic life of most individuals there may be little difference living under the three hierarchies, yet there would be a difference in group status and the subsequent emotion of resentment. This emotion leads to higher acceptance of risk, which can significantly lower threshold points in the decision to commit +1 actions. This factor is cited in not only the Lithuanian case but also the Belorussian and Ukrainian cases as well.

Second, the policy of the occupier in shaping social hierarchies affects resentment and will have an impact on movement from 0 to +1. Although the historical or cultural relationship among occupier and groups may be of some importance – that is, whether there are "ancient hatreds" or "cultural affinities" between the groups – more specific policies might be as crucial, or more crucial, in producing the emotions that drive initial forms of resistance.[4]

Transforming Resentment into Action: The Relevance of Symbols and the Focal-Point Mechanism

Without emotions such as resentment, individuals are unlikely to accept risk at any level, but without minimal assurance of safety even those inclined to accept risk question the point of action. Both factors, motivation and minimal safety, are necessary to move significant numbers from the zero node of the spectrum. Clearly, the recent revolutions in Eastern Europe have emphatically demonstrated that antiregime feeling, or factors such as relative deprivation, are not sufficient to move individuals to action. As various scholars and journalists have noted, citizens of Soviet satellites may have despised their regimes, but most would not act until they saw others perform antiregime acts while avoiding harsh sanctions. Once a certain number of the population demonstrated the possibilities for action and success, the floodgates were opened. For much of the wavering population, the actions of a few served as necessary signals to also act.

Actions are necessary, but the question becomes, Which actions will serve as signals of the willingness to rebel? Not all actions carry the same meaning. Here, focal-point mechanisms become important.[5] How do two separated persons find one another? They use focal points such as clock towers or bridges – clear and unambiguous symbols able to perform coordinating functions. How do those resentful of a powerful regime find each other and

---

[4] Minority 2 is included in the hypothetical hierarchies in support this point: minorities need not be targets if they are not resented. Some minorities, such as Belorussians in Lithuania, never held positions of authority and were not specifically targeted in any occupation.

[5] Thomas C. Schelling, *The Strategy of Conflict* (Cambridge, Mass.: Harvard University Press, 1980).

communicate to one another their desires to resist? They use focal actions that embody symbols that are clear and unambiguously antiregime. As what is antiregime differs by the nature of the regime, this reasoning implies that the ability of any given action to convey the message of resentment and risk acceptance varies according to the nature of the regime. For example, singing or humming a religious hymn is an act of resistance against an atheist-totalitarian regime, and, importantly, others immediately recognize that particular act as resistance and an indication of risk acceptance. Under another type of repressive regime, that same action would not convey the same message. Historical experiences between the regime and the population also provide the possibility for focal action. Showing up in the city square in front of regime headquarters on a certain day may have no meaning under occupier X, but the same action may have great meaning under occupier Y if the date marks the anniversary of some long-ago massacre at the hands of occupier Y's ancestors. Likewise, graffiti slogans written on a wall are more relevant if they have a historical referent.

In this work, the bulk of resistance actions are culturally and historically oriented and involve some risk. It is possible that some symbolic resistance actions can emerge that are not based on culture and are relatively risk-free. In Norway, for example, a common way of showing resistance during the Second World War was to avoid sitting next to a German soldier on public transportation, wearing red caps, or wearing paper clips in jackets. When red caps were forbidden, people showed their motivation to resist by going hatless, even in winter.[6] Importantly, when symbolic action involves little cost, it cannot communicate risk acceptance as effectively. There is a significant difference among low-risk and no-risk actions. Important linkages exist among culture, risk, and communication of risk acceptance.

The movement to +1 action is generally faster when the occupied group and the occupier have a long and repressive history. Although this observation is often attributed to "ancient hatreds" between groups, the more specific point is that this history provides a wealth of symbols, stories, and slogans that imbue many low-risk actions with clear and shared meaning. Eastern Europeans who occupied the region between Germany and Russia had a history of subordination under both powers, as well as ample reason

---

[6] When Norwegians began to avoid sitting next to Germans, the occupying authorities put up posters announcing a fine for standing in the train when seats were available. From Jon Elster, personal communication.

to resent and fear each. However, the wealth and effectiveness of the symbols and slogans toward each differed and the number of actions able to carry meaning of resentment and risk taking varied. Due to historical and cultural factors, Lithuanians had a larger and different set of relevant resistance actions vis-à-vis Russians than Germans.[7]

At issue is the relationship between elite strategy and culture and, relatedly, the malleability of culture. Many political scientists tend to see culture as a "resource" for clever elites, a set of symbols that allows elites to coordinate mass action.[8] In this view, the emphasis is on the role of human agency in using and shaping culture. The treatment of culture in this work differs. Although culture, defined as a set of symbols and symbolic actions with shared meaning, may indeed be a resource for imaginative elites, culture's malleability is lower than many suppose. Furthermore, in the case of rebellion against powerful regimes, culture may be most important in the absence of elites and least important when elites are most free to act.

To understand these points, consider Figure 2.2. Although many actions can serve to signal resentment and risk acceptance, only some will be relevant vis-à-vis any given regime. As just mentioned, because the historical-cultural interactions among Lithuanians and Russians-Soviets and Lithuanians and Germans were different, the set of resistance-relevant symbolic actions also differed. This set differed both quantitatively and qualitatively. Elites cannot simply create coordinative and communicative symbols when they wish; they must choose among existing relevant symbols that have survived the first filter, the historical-cultural filter.

Intelligent and culturally aware elites can choose among the symbols of the middle set of Figure 2.2. Here, with the second filter, is where human agency plays its role. If the regime is relatively weak and cannot stamp out nationally based political organizations or effectively monitor and sanction

---

[7] I do not argue that this factor was most important in explaining the relative lack of resistance versus the Germans. On that issue, the social-political hierarchy created by the Germans was much more favorable to Lithuanians than that of the Soviet regime. Commonly, and not surprisingly, motivation and the wealth of symbolic actions usually operate in tandem. Previous occupiers are not likely to trust populations that they have repressed in the past (and who may have rebelled against them in the past) and are unlikely to implement policies and hierarchies favorable to them. Of course, in resisting a familiar occupier the number of effective symbols and focal actions are likely to be more numerous in comparison to the set relevant to a first-time occupier.

[8] For example, see Jim Johnson, "Symbol and Strategy: On the Cultural Analysis of Politics" (Ph.D. dissertation, University of Chicago, 1991).

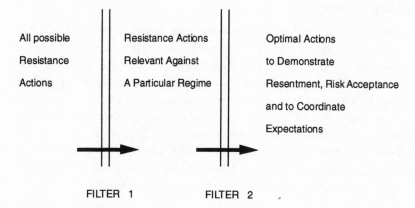

Figure 2.2. Sets of possible resistance symbols

the population, then elites may be able to choose among the set of actions available after the first filter. Elites can encourage, organize, and manipulate the actions and symbols they believe to be most effective in publicizing antiregime feeling and coordinating expectations of further action.

In the situations described in this book, however, elites have often been deported or killed. In these circumstances, culture as elite resource has little relevance. When the regime is very powerful and able to prevent elite choice of action, then the size of the set as it stands after the first filter, the one historically and culturally based, may become crucial. The higher the number of possible relevant actions, the higher the chance that some will occur, *even without leadership,* to perform their signaling functions. If the set is very large, even the most intelligent and powerful occupiers will not be able to anticipate or respond to every action that possesses signaling content. When the regime is weak, on the other hand, the size of the set of relevant actions after the first filter is not as important. Even though the historical-cultural relationship between occupier and occupied may have produced a smaller number of powerful symbolic actions, elites may be able to pick and choose among that smaller set and create much the same effect. In sum, culture and history seem most salient when the regime is powerful and oppostion elites are not. Under a powerful regime, history and culture must play the coordinating and communicating role that elites cannot.

Status Rewards

Community structure is crucial for producing organized rebellion (+2), but it is not unimportant at the earlier stage. Specifically, strong communities are more likely to produce status rewards that help to drive the original actions of resistance. In societies with existing antipathy against an occupier, performing a small act of resistance can enhance one's esteem in the eyes of fellow community members. This mechanism has already been described in a previous discussion of community; recall the comparison between the French and Montenegrin examples. The following section explores the interaction of the status reward and threshold mechanisms and how this interaction affects strategic behavior in the first stage of resistance.

The Strategic Context of Movement from 0 to +1

Variation in movement from 0 to +1 can be explained by resentment formation, the nature of the symbol set, and the presence and power of community-related status gain. All can work to reduce thresholds to levels that can be realistically surpassed. A set of Schelling diagrams shows more precisely how these concepts work together within their strategic context (Figures 2.3–2.5).[9] To simplify, only safety concerns and community-related status reward mechanisms are considered. A significant level of resentment and a sizable symbol set are assumed.

The strategic nature of +1 behavior stems from the fact that both status rewards and the credibility of regime threats are related to the percentage of fellow citizens engaging in +1 behavior. If one is among a very few who are writing nationalistic graffiti and giving speeches to his or her neighbors, the chance of being identified and punished by the occupier is much more likely than if everyone is engaged in such behavior. This reality can be captured by the Schelling diagram in Figure 2.3, which captures the fact that the payoffs for many decisions are based upon how many others are making the same or an opposing decision. The diagram shows a high negative payoff for being one of the first to move to a position of resistance. As more people move to a position of resistance, the occupier's resources become strained and the likelihood of being caught decreases. At very high levels of this type of ac-

---

[9] Schelling diagrams are also used extensively in Chapter 8. The logic of the assurrance game is implicit throughout much of the work. See Thomas Schelling, *Micromotives and Macrobehavior* (New York: Gordon and Breach, 1985).

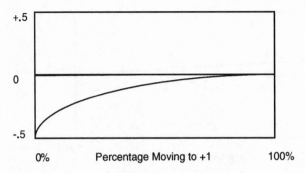

+.5

0

-.5

0%   Percentage Moving to +1   100%

Figure 2.3. Safety considerations during beginning stages of resistance

tivity, the individual chances of being caught drops close to zero. If one remains neutral, the cost is represented by the zero line.[10]

While Figure 2.3 describes the general shape of individual payoffs in
terms of personal safety, it does not say anything about the weight of this
factor in the individual's overall calculus – that is, it cannot say how important the safety factor is in comparison with other factors. Only two issues are
involved: the chance of being caught and the nature of the penalty. The resources and efficiency, as well as the ruthlessness, of the occupying regime
are decisive in both.

The payoffs involved with status rewards, both positive and negative, are
also related to the numbers of people engaged in resistance behavior. In
terms of gaining honor, or becoming a hero, one's payoff for urging resistance and engaging in antioccupier activity is higher at low levels of participation. Heroes, by definition, are not part of a mass of people but individuals who stand above the mass. As more and more people engage in resistance
activity, it simply becomes the expected "thing to do" and no status reward
is attached to such action.[11] Negative status, or ostracism, works the other
way around. When few people are engaged in resistance activity, those not
engaged are not viewed with contempt, but when a majority is cooperating
in a resistance effort, those who remain on the sidelines will receive the con-

[10] In Figure 2.3, I show the costs of resistance decreasing parabolically with increasing numbers of resisters. This may not fit all situations; sometimes the relationship might be better represented as a linear function. In all situations, the costs should decrease with increasing numbers of resisters, at least for the occupations and situations in this work.

[11] In some cases, first actors can be awarded negative status as "hotheads" who follow their
own agenda at the cost of increased risk to the collective.

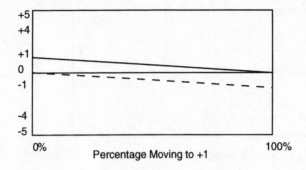

Society A: Low Rewards and Sanctions

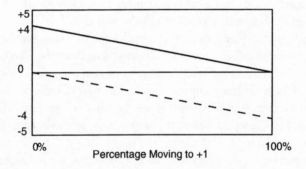

Society B: High Rewards and Sanctions

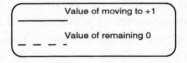

Figure 2.4. Status considerations in beginning stages of resistance in two hypothetical societies

tempt of their fellows. Within Figure 2.4, two Schelling diagrams are drawn to show the different payoffs for 0-level and +1-level behavior in two different societies. Society A represents a society that assigns low-status rewards and low social sanctions for resistance behavior, whereas society B represents one with high rewards and sanctions. There are two individual considerations at this level of activity: costs and risks imposed by the occu-

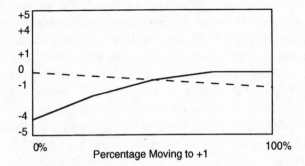

Society A: Low Rewards and Sanctions

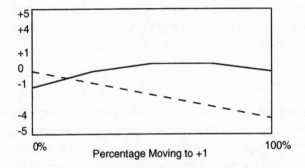

Society B: High Rewards and Sanctions

Figure 2.5. Combined utility values of safety and status for two hypothetical societies

pier, and benefits and costs awarded by fellow members of society (remember, we are leaving out the consideration of resentment and symbols). The weights of these two factors vary from case to case and during each case, but, for illustrative purposes, the arbitrary utility values used in the diagrams in Figure 2.4 are simply added together. This sum represents the two hypothetical societies found in the Schelling diagrams depicted in Figure 2.5.

In society A in Figure 2.5, the optimal play for the average person is to remain neutral until over half of the population has become involved with low-level resistance. Of course, there are individuals who are not driven by "average payoffs," and they will trickle into the +1 level at varying rates. In society B, with more powerful status rewards and penalties, the +1 option becomes optimal at only 15 percent participation. Taking into account even a moderate amount of diversity in personal situations and personality types, and the small difference in utilities even at the 0 percent level, this low percentage could easily be surpassed by less constrained actors, such as youth, students, or idealists. Once the tipping point is passed, a bandwagon effect is predicted by the widening gap in respective payoffs. Figure 2.5 illustrates why a society with weaker status rewards for fighting an occupier may remain at neutrality. First and most obviously, as shown for society A in Figure 2.5, it does not become "rational" to move to +1 until a 55 percent participation level. Additionally, the gap in values at the lowest levels of participation is quite large – four times as large as for society B. Even given diversity in motivations, it is much more difficult to explain the decisions of first actors given such a payoff structure. Finally, the gap in utilities after the tipping point remains small, and thus the sudden bandwagoning effect may be less well pronounced.

Concluding Comments

In explaining variation in movement on the spectrum of roles, the first task is to explain why there is often no movement from neutrality. Three factors have been identified: the presence and depth of resentment, a repertoire of symbolic actions that can communicate resentment and risk acceptance, and status-based rewards and sanctions. Not all occupiers are resented, and not all resented occupiers face resistance. When all three factors are present, rapid movement to +1 can be expected. In the empirical analysis of the following chapters, variation in both movement or lack of movement to +1 and the speed of this movement are explained by these three elements.

Before ending this section, the meaning of the movement from 0 to +1 in the overall picture of rebellion should be reemphasized. The central point concerns risk processing. The individual decision to move from +1, unorganized and nonviolent resistance, to +2 or +3, armed and organized rebellion, involves a huge leap in risk acceptance. Significant numbers of any population are unlikely to accept such risks unless they have confidence that the bulk of the society is behind them and will support their actions in the future. Seeing antiregime graffiti, hearing nationalist songs on a bus, seeing pamphlets distributed, witnessing demonstrations of passive resistance – all of these acts are crucial for defeating resignation, encouraging participation in clandestine organization, and preparing a population for violent rebellion.

Whether a society actually moves to +2 and is able to sustain violent rebellion depends on another set of factors.

The Development of Community-Based Organization

If rebellion is to be sustained against a powerful regime willing to use brutal force, it must have local roots. Whether these roots develop depends a great deal on the types of communities that exist. Certain types of communities are more likely than others to unleash the triggering mechanisms necessary to drive individuals from +1 to +2. This section outlines what types of structures are conducive to the development of community-level resistance organization.

The first task in this effort is the creation of a useful definition and specification of community structure. Consider again the Lithuanian communities mentioned in Chapter 1. These communities were by no means monolithic. Some members belonged to the same social or political organizations, whereas others helped each other in threshing operations. Several individuals belonged to religious groups, while others were seen as drunkards or "uncultured." Community structures are defined by the presence and configuration of these types of groups. In turn, these groups can be represented by Venn diagrams like the one represented in Figure 2.6.

The box in Figure 2.6 represents the entire community while the individual circles represent group memberships. For the cases that follow, examples of A or B groups include cooperative economic groups, families, social-patriotic associations, youth groups, political party membership, and religious groups. In the preceding example, only two relevant groups, A and B, are present. Those in the intersection of A and B, therefore, are members of both groups. There are four subsets, as opposed to groups, in this example community: A, B, AB, and OT. The subset, as opposed to the group, is the primary unit in the analysis that follows. For example, subset AB, with a unique combination of constraint and preference, is treated as distinct from both A and B. Terminologically, *subset* AB is part of both A and B *groups*. Those in the box but not within any circle (OT, outsiders, outcasts) represent a subset of individuals subject to general community influences but not subject to the mechanisms of any subset. Most communities, and recall that the definition of community employed here implies small numbers, have only a few subgroups that will be relevant in influencing decisions to rebel.

Now imagine this particular community coming under the occupation of

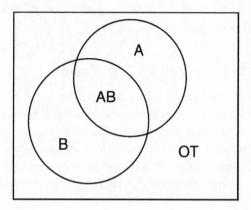

Figure 2.6. Example of a community structure

a despised and resented new regime. Through the observance of +1 actions (accepting leaflets, boycotting elections, attending public religious events), members of this community come to believe that the bulk of society shares their antipathies and attitudes. Once word leaks out that some members of the community are organizing, the second stage of the rebellion process begins. At this stage, powerful regimes control much of the outside world but cannot easily penetrate communities; the world becomes smaller, and the battle comes down to the village or workplace. The individual looks for strategic clues for action. There is a desire to act, but the potential rebel thinks, "I will act if X percent of the community acts, I will have safety in numbers and be protected from informants if X percent of the community is united and organized." When the regime is powerful, the most relevant gauge of "safety in numbers" is the percentage of other community members also involved in underground activity (+2). Given this assumption, *the percentage of total community members engaged in rebellion at a +2 level is treated as the threshold value.*

Within communities, individuals will hold different threshold values. Some individuals, the hotheads or the heroes, may possess very low thresholds – they are ready to act immediately with little assurance needed. Other individuals will be ready to act, but only if significant numbers of fellow community members have already acted. Still others will not participate until most of their friends or neighbors have gotten involved. Communities thus possess distributions of thresholds. With some distributions, the number of low-threshold actors may be sufficient to meet the the safety requirements of medium-threshold actors, with both groups together meeting the requirements of high-threshold actors. This well-known story is excellently portrayed in works by Thomas C. Schelling, Mark Granovetter, and Timur Kuran. In this work, however, the treatment of this story goes beyond these works in two ways.

First, *the distribution of thresholds is linked to observable social structure.* The claim here is that the distribution of thresholds can be gauged from a knowledge of community subsets. This structurally based approach differs greatly from other threshold approaches. In comparison, Granovetter assumed normal distributions and Elster has employed hypothetical distributions of personality types.[12] Kuran's work seems to imply that the distribution of thresholds is basically unknowable.[13] The potential rebel has a history, a set of ties, an ability to estimate probabilities from these ties, a way of reacting to events. While the threshold-based logic of the assurance game guides individual rebellion behavior and is therefore the proper analytical tool for studying these events, without incorporating the social life of the individual prior to the period of rebellion the game loses its predictive power and descriptive validity. The insights of political science and economics must be merged with the methods of anthropology if the benefits of the assurance game are to be fully realized. While a considerable amount of fieldwork is necessary to link community subgroups and thresholds, there is a payoff.

Second, *thresholds are not treated as static* but may be affected by the operation of normative mechanisms emanating from one's community ties. Due to these mechanisms, individuals may change their level of risk acceptance (their thresholds) over the course of the sequence of events underlying rebellion or resistance situations. These two issues are addressed in turn.

Knowing the Distribution of Thresholds

Most communities have a distribution of thresholds that correspond to the type and number of subgroups. In Figure 2.6, there are four subsets: A, B, AB, OT. The thresholds of the individuals within each subset will be closely

---

[12] Jon Elster, *The Cement of Society: A Study of Social Order* (Cambridge: Cambridge University Press, 1990).

[13] Others link thresholds to broader social groups. Chapter 8 treats these larger social groups as the primary basis of threshold reference in the Communist societies of the late 1980s.

related to the preferences, constraints, and mechanisms associated with each group. The relationship of the threshold to the preferences and constraints of the subset is relatively straightforward. For example, if A represents a nationalist organization that requires an oath to fight against any occupying regime (and this is the case in the subsequent empirical material), the members can be assumed to have stronger preferences to move to positions of rebellion, will accept higher levels of risk, and can thus be assigned lower threshold values. If B is an economic group without nationalist overtones and highly constrained in its actions by work requirements, its threshold can be assumed to be relatively high. Members of AB will be subject to the preferences, constraints, and mechanisms of both groups and may be assigned a medium threshold.

Some of the most common and important community subgroupings, at least for mid-twentieth-century Eastern Europe, include the following organizations.

Youth Groups.   Youth organization can generally be linked to low rebellion thresholds for two reasons. First, youth are less constrained than other community members. They do not have to worry about caring for children or heading a family farm or business. Second, youth, especially young males, are on the whole more status conscious than any other demographic group. Rebelling against an occupier or regime seems "adventurous," as well as a way to become a "big man" in a community with few opportunities for economic advancement.[14]

Social-Patriotic Organizations.   Low thresholds can also be found in certain social groups dedicated to defending God and country. Prime examples are religious and patriotic groups, which can be seen in abundance in a couple of the case studies that follow. Religion certainly plays a huge role in resistance and rebellion, but this influence stems as much from religion's localized organizational force as its ability to create and maintain attitudes.[15] An example of a patriotic group that the reader will come across in Chapter 3 is the Lithuanian "Union of Sauliai," an organization founded and sup-

---

[14] See, for example, Edward Banfield, "Rioting Mainly for Fun and Profit," in *The Heavenly City Revisited* (Boston: Little, Brown, 1970), chap. 9.

[15] Stathis Kalyvas emphasizes this local, organizational force while explaining the rise of Christian Democracy in Europe in *The Rise of Christian Democracy in Europe* (Ithaca: Cornell University Press, 1995).

ported by the interwar Lithuanian government to inculcate patriotic values and to serve as a national guard. Similar to corresponding groups in the other Baltic states, all members pledged their life to defend the homeland. Membership in such a group can be taken as an indication of a strong desire to fight against an occupier. Furthermore, this type of group membership, which involved meeting for a couple of hours every few days, involved few constraints.

Economic Organization.   Due to the nature of their constraints and a lack of a clear preference for risk or rebellion, other community subsets must be assigned higher thresholds. Individuals may still move into the +2 position, but only with the assurance provided by high levels of participation. Perhaps the most common and important of these higher-threshold subgroups are those based on economic interactions. Belonging to cooperative work units is definitely a significant constraint on individual commitment to a rebellion movement.[16] After all, there is work to be done and fellow members of work units will have to pick up the slack if an individual devotes a considerable amount of time to rebellion activities instead of work. Membership in an agricultural cooperative constrains each member by requiring that he or she be present at harvesttime to help with the gathering. More than this, occupiers often engage in collective punishment after identifying a rebel's work unit, a ready target. Thus, members of work units will often try to convince an individual considering joining the clandestine organization to remain at a lower level of commitment to reduce the chance of retribution against the entire group. Also, economic groups are not only susceptible to the "stick" of the occupier but to the "carrot" as well. A well-informed occupier might provide benefits to the work unit but withdraw them if a member is identified as a rebel. Such a strategy again tempts the membership of the work unit to constrain its own membership. Less astute occupiers destroy work units and thus destroy their possibilities as constraints.

---

[16] In a community-level study of nationalist violence, David Laitin provides some supporting evidence of these effects in the case of Spain; see "National Revivals and Violence," *European Journal of Sociology* 36 (1995): 3–43. Laitin, citing the work of Robert Clark, writes that Clark "finds that it was the climbing clubs and caudrillas that were the source of ETA recruitment. In his data base of eighty-one ETA militants, not one . . . was from a farming village. The great majority came from small towns where young men commuted to work in small nearby factories. They were workers during the day, but embedded themselves in Basque culture at night. Unlike farmers, they were not members of local economic, but only social groups." This quotation is from Robert Clark, *The Basque Insurgents: ETA, 1952–1980* (Madison: University of Wisconsin Press, 1984), p. 20.

Outsiders.   There may be community subsets that are associated with very high thresholds for participating in local, organized rebellion. These may be sets of individuals that are minimally connected to activities of the community, perhaps newcomers or members of minority ethnic and religious groups. They may hold to generalized conceptions of reciprocity due to living on the same territory or being minimally involved in community social and economic events, but they may not have the same possibilities for status gain or possess the same feeling of a "homeland" that produces a strong preference for rebellion. Their biggest concern may be avoiding total ostracism. As long as many other members of the community are uninvolved, this threat of ostracism cannot be directed at them. If they are the last subset not participating, however, they may feel the need to join to prove that they are still members of the community. As seen in some of the case material, this problem may not arise as the already organized members of the community may find these high-threshold groups as "untrustworthy" and would prefer they not become involved.

Political Parties.   When supracommunity organizations direct community level "cells," the rebellion thresholds of local members of the cell could be either high, medium, or low. The prime example here is the local cell of a political party or organization. It would seem that nationally based political parties would be the logical basis for establishing a resistance movement. Membership might be taken as an indication of a strong preference to act and the day-to-day constraints are less than those of work groups. Political parties may, in fact, become the basis for local rebellion organizations. In practice, however, political parties sometimes have little effect at the community level. Many times, the resources and organization of these parties are decimated by the regime or occupier. The national leadership of a political party is well known and neutralized within a short period, and the more prominent leaders leave the country before the occupier even enters. Most importantly, the communication links between the national and community levels are often to a large degree severed. Without a doubt, the occupier will ban open political meetings. Although battered political parties may try to rebuild an organization, it is difficult to control the activities of members at lower levels.[17] Individuals in communities probably know whether their

<hr/>

[17] Of course, parties that had already been outlawed and battered have some experience in operating under such conditions. The Communist Party is the most common example. In some

party is encouraging or discouraging action against the occupier, but the party may not be able to direct or pressure its members toward an action. If the emerging local rebellion organization is not connected to a party, previous party membership will not be a good indicator to gauge either preference or constraint in the decision to join.

When political groups do retain strength, especially if they are in a position to bargain with the occupier, effects on rebellion thresholds may be negative. If the political party is making a deal with the regime or occupier, it may constrain its membership from joining or cooperating with any nonparty resistance and attempt to dampen a preference for rebellion. In cases when overarching groups can actually control communities, the leadership may find it more politically profitable in the short run to direct its membership to fight other "resisting" politically based groups rather than the regime. The resulting internecine strife often becomes so endemic that the rebellion against the regime becomes a sideshow. While individuals might join local violently oriented organizations, it may have little to do with the stated and original intention of fighting the occupier or regime.

Families and Neighbors. Finally, the most important community subgroups may be family groups and neighbor groups. In terms of constraints and preferences, the effects on rebellion thresholds are again variable. The preference to fight an occupier or hated regime cannot be inferred simply from family or neighbor associations. With these groups, the crucial considerations are normative.

Factors Affecting Threshold Levels

The General Effects of Strong Community

In strong communities, those possessing Taylor's attributes, the thresholds of all subsets, meaning all community members, are reduced through possibilities for higher levels of monitoring or retaliation and coordination of expectations. Thresholds and risk taking are in large part a function of how individuals view nonparticipants. If the action of nonparticipants is not subject to monitoring and expectations of their behavior cannot be clearly formed,

---

ways and some cases, the Communist Party was more like a banned social-religious organization than a political party.

the potential rebel will require a higher threshold (a lower number of non-participants) before undertaking risk-laden action. If nonparticipants are expected to remain neutral or to become participants, then their numbers need not be feared and action can be taken at lower thresholds.

Under conditions of weak community, very high thresholds are required as a hedge against informers and collaborators. Due to the absence of a history of many-sided relations and the potential costs involved, the worst case must be assumed about all nonparticipants. Within even a small minority of nonrebels (those remaining at 0 or +1), there may reside potential informers who, believing that discovery and retaliation is far from certain, will feel free to collaborate. In strong communities, on the other hand, the chances of discovery of informers and retaliation against them are far higher. Knowing that potential informers must fear the threats stemming from the community as much as or more than those of the regime, potential rebels will not fear the nonparticipating population to the same extent. The result is a lowering of thresholds.

Strong communities may also create general beliefs, based on past reciprocity, that the community will develop and maintain solidarity against the occupier. Nonparticipants will then be seen as "likely future participants," and community members will accept a higher number of nonparticipants (a lower threshold) when deciding to rebel. This solution, the coordination of expectations, is an often cited answer to the assurance game puzzle. When the costs are high, however, this coordination of expectations will supply neither the necessary assurance nor the necessary pressure to move a community population to the risk-laden roles of rebellion.

To understand movement to the +2 position, the distinction between strong versus weak community is insufficient. For example, despite both being strong communities, the two similar villages in the Merkine region developed different numbers of organized supporters and partisans. To comprehend these differences, the more nuanced features of community structure must be examined.

Specific Effects of Community Structure: The Role of Norms

The multiple subgroups of a community produce not only a distribution of thresholds but also a distribution of active and latent mechanisms that may work to alter those thresholds. To understand how thresholds are reduced to a point that rebellion can be initiated and sustained, it will be necessary to understand how three basic concepts of this work interconnect – that is, to understand how community structure produces distributions of mechanisms that lower thresholds and create "tipping effects" between low-, medium-, and high-threshold subsets.

The key mechanisms affecting threshold levels are norms of reciprocity. *Norms serve as mechanisms among community members to lower or raise rebellion thresholds.* In effect, community members are faced with a question: how much risk should I accept? The answer comes not only from a rational appraisal of the situation, but also from the norms of one's peer groups. Different norms are activated at different junctures during the dynamic rebellion process. Once some members of a subgroup begin participating at the +2 level, their action pressures fellow members to reciprocate. In reaction, individuals may accept more risk, or in other words, lower their thresholds. When one community subset enters the +2 network, then other community subsets may also experience pressure to reciprocate. This process may continue, as detailed shortly.

The amount that the threshold value is reduced depends on the nature of group norms. In this work, I specify three general types of norms and label them A, B, and C norms.[18]

A Norms.   With A norms, which might be labeled unconditional norms, the action of one or a few individuals triggers a large increase in risk acceptance among other group members. The family unit is the quintessential example: if one family member is in trouble, it is the duty of all other family members to help.[19] Likewise, in times of rebellion, if one family member becomes involved at the +2 level, other members of the family will probably accept far higher risk levels to help that family member even if they had little preference to engage in rebellion at the start of the conflict. In terms of the movement to +2, family members are likely to get "dragged in" to the rebellion organization in order to help their fellow member. In effect, this norm is to

---

[18] By no means am I covering an exhaustive list of norms; rather, I am simply addressing the ones most relevant for the present work. Although my approach is somewhat more specific than that of Jon Elster or Russell Hardin, this section follows both authors on many issues concerning norms. See Jon Elster, *Local Justice: How Institutions Allocate Scarce Goods and Necessary Burdens* (New York: Russell Sage Foundation, 1992), and Russell Hardin, *One for All: The Logic of Group Conflict* (Princeton: Princeton University Press, 1995). These norms form the basis for hypotheses for predicting how individuals will behave when local rebellion units are being formed.

[19] Hardin, in *One for All,* addresses norms of family loyalty in a section entitled "norms beyond interest."

reduce the threshold by nearly 100 percent. Individuals who previously held an 80 percent threshold might reciprocate the action of a fellow family member even if that member is the only person in the community moving to +2. As will be seen in Chapter 6, the long-term resistance against the reestablishment of Soviet rule in Lithuania in the postwar period was in large part the result of families organizing themselves to hide and protect their draft-age sons who had become partisan fighters in an effort to avoid conscription into the Red Army.[20] "A norms" also operate in clan societies where the death of a single member of a clan can move the entire clan to violent action against the aggressor.

B Norms. The logic of B norms, which might be labeled norms of honor, is similar to that of A norms but not as extreme. Within many social-religious-patriotic groups, the first to rebel have disproportionate influence on fellow group members also to rebel.[21] These organizations often have oaths requiring members to defend the organization or the nation, and the action of the very first rebels can trigger the normative power of these oaths and duty. Those not reciprocating will have to wonder whether they are, in fact, cowards.

Here, moral and rational aspects of norms may also come into effect. The first to rebel might label those not rebelling as "cowards" who do not follow through on their oath. If appeals are made to these nonreciprocating mem-

---

[20] Although not addressed in this work, families are also vessels for norms of revenge, or at least the desire for revenge. If a family member has been killed by the regime, the involvement of other family members in clandestine work is more likely as the desire to avenge a fallen relative can outweigh the preference to avoid risk. Lenin comes to mind.

[21] Hardin, in *One for All,* devotes a great deal of time to norms of honor. In line with the view here, Hardin holds that such norms operate largely through the threat of exclusion and "may have force only in relatively small, coherent communities" (p. 115).

Elster, in *Cement of Society,* discusses "codes of honor" in terms of their positive and negative sides: "On the positive side, they tell people to act courageously, to return favours, to honor commitments and to tell the truth, On the negative side, they enjoin people to insult others, to carry out any threats that they might have made and to retaliate if others try to take advantage of them" (p. 116). As Elster notes, an element of both reciprocity and a retribution is involved. Both encourage community members belonging to social-patriotic groups to move to +2 once a conflict starts if some members have started a resistance unit.

Georg Simmel, in *Conflict and the Web of Group Affiliations* (London: Free Press, 1955), describes codes of honor in the following way: "Such a code would imply that every member of the group would feel that his honor was diminished whenever any member suffered an insult or a deprivation of his honor. In this sense the association possesses a collective sense of honor, whose changes are reflected in the sense of honor of each member" (p. 163). Although this description may fit the A norm as well or better, it affirms the idea of the action of the few having a disproportionate effect on the many.

bers, individuals might respond either from some sense of moral duty or simply the wish to avoid retaliation.

The Lithuanian Union of Sauliai, the organization founded and supported by the interwar Lithuanian government to inculcate patriotic values and to serve as a national guard, is an example of a group reasonably assumed to possess B norms. Similar to corresponding groups in the other Baltic states, all members pledged their life to defend the homeland. Although the presence of groups with B norms can be key in initiating and sustaining rebellion, the actual triggering and total impact of these norms depends on the specifics of community structure.

C Norms.   C norms might be labeled norms of conformity.[22] If a minority of the group rebels, there is pressure on remaining nonrebelling members to "not rebel," in effect, to raise thresholds. If a majority of members are rebelling, then there is pressure to lower thresholds and to rebel. The pressure is heaviest against those most clearly nonconformist – the very first "rebels" and the very last "nonrebels." If around half rebel and half do not rebel, there are basically no nonconformists and the effect is nil.

C norms are perhaps most typical of collective economic groups. A worker generally feels that he or she should do his or her "fair share" but seldom feels the need to do any more than that. There is little status reward for baling an extra load of hay, or doing 10 percent more of a quota. In fact, fellow workers may feel that the overworking individual is showing them up. One of the assumptions of this work is that the norms developed in the relationships between community members in prerebellion times will carry over to some extent to the rebellion period. Thus, workers who operated under norms of conformity regarding the distribution of labor also tend to operate under norms of conformity when considering the risks involved in rebellion activity. Members of a work unit may all agree that something should be done against a hated occupier, especially if that occupier has impinged upon the operation and profits of the work unit, but the individual members may ask themselves, "Why should I be the first one to take risks? I will do my fair share if the others do, just as I do when working." As a bottom line, these types of groups may help push individuals into local rebellion units, but only after after a majority of their members have already joined for other reasons.

---

[22] Alternatively, C norms could be termed norms of strict reciprocity or, possibly, norms of fairness.

Summarizing the Relationship between Norms and Risk and an Example.
Once some members of a community subgroup are participating in a local
rebellion organization, their action sets the norms of the group into operation. Nonrebelling members must ask themselves whether they should reciprocate by also participating in the developing +2 group. They must recalculate the level of risk that they are willing to accept in light of the new
circumstances and new pressures. In Figure 2.7, the three norms described
here are assigned a rough mathematical effect on individual risk thresholds.
The vertical axis represents the effect of the norm on the threshold, either its
reduction or increase. At the -1 value, the effect of the norm is to reduce the
threshold to 0. For the sake of symmetry, I have set the limit for threshold
increase at +1, which indicates the possibility of doubling the threshold
value necessary for triggering action.[23] There is nothing firm about the +1
to -1 value of the vertical axis; this value can be changed to represent different weighting effects of norms on threshold values.

To repeat, with A norms the action of one or a few members of the subgroup can reduce the threshold level to 0 percent.

B norms reduce thresholds in a similar though less extreme manner. As
modeled, the B norm effect is to reduce the threshold value by a factor of $1-
(1 - \%$ of subgroup rebelling$)^2$. Thus, under B norms participation of one-
fourth of the subgroup produces a 50 percent drop in wavering members'
threshold values. Substantively, this represents the phenomenon of social
pressure among members of a group holding to norms of honor.

C norms can either reduce or increase thresholds, and their effect is largest
on nonconformers at low and high levels of participation. Mathematically,
the C norm effect is $+/-4(.5 - \%$ of subgroup rebelling$)^2$ (threshold value).[24]
Thus, at 50 percent, C norms have no effect, whereas at a 10 percent participation rate the effect is to *increase* the threshold by 64 percent. Symmetri-
cally, at a 90 percent participation rate the effect is to reduce the threshold
value by 64 percent.

There are only three basic requirements for the structural analysis of rebellion at the community level, and they have just been covered: specifica-

---

[23] This value could be easily changed to incorporate an increase up to a 100 percent threshold: $[f(x) + f(1-X)]$.

[24] I am multiplying by a factor of four to fit the +1 value of the vertical axis. If the percentage of the subgroup rebelling is less than 50 percent, the sign is positive, indicating pressure to
increase thresholds; if more than 50 percent are rebelling, then the sign is negative, representing pressure to lower thresholds.

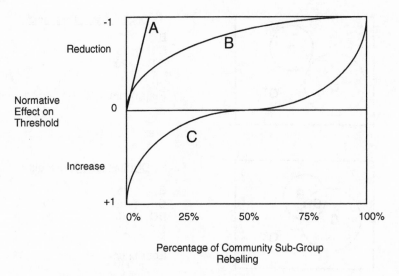

Figure 2.7. Normative effects on thresholds

tion of relevant subgroups; an estimate of the rebellion thresholds of individuals based upon the characteristics of the subgroup (constraint and preference); and function and weight of group norms able to change the threshold value. Each of these can be observed through fieldwork or through a knowledge of community conditions pieced together from anthropological work or diaries.

To see the relative simplicity of this approach, as well as its ability to capture the interaction of community-based mechanisms and generate predictions, consider the following sequence of community structures depicted in Figure 2.8. In each, assume a total of one hundred members and two relevant subgroups (these characteristics roughly fit the rural Lithuanian communities of the 1940s analyzed later). In effect, the only structural property that changes is the amount of overlapping membership between the two relevant subgroups. Assume that community subgroup B is a very low threshold group, perhaps a nationalist organization immediately ready to form a resistance unit. A 0 percent threshold may be assigned. Note that some 0 percent threshold actors must exist in order to begin any "tipping" process.[25] Further, assume that group B holds B-type norms (I continue to label sub-

[25] The subject of 0 percent threshold actors, or "first players," is the topic of Chapter 9.

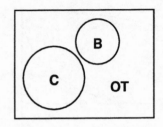

Distribution		Threshold
B	30	0
C	50	50
OT	20	70

Equilibrium = 30

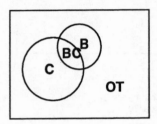

Distribution		Threshold
B	25	0
C	45	50
BC	10	25
OT	20	70

Equilibrium = 35

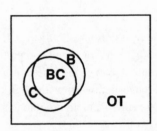

Distribution		Threshold
B	20	0
C	20	50
BC	40	25
OT	20	70

Equilibrium = 100

Figure 2.8. Three hypothetical communities

sets by their norms). Group C, on the other hand, is a relatively high threshold group, perhaps a risk-averse economic group, whose members require a 50 percent threshold level before they join the resistance. For coding clarity, group C holds C-type norms. Members of both groups, found in subset BC, are an amalgam of both group characteristics affected by both B and C norms and an intermediate threshold of 25 percent. Finally, members of the community that belong to no subgroups are represented by OT, are unaffected by any norms, and hold a high threshold of 70 percent. Given the previously developed methodology, what dynamics would we expect to see in these three examples? What equilibria are predicted?

The analysis proceeds sequentially, from lowest-threshold groups to higher-threshold groups. In the upper distribution, individual members of subset B, holding a 0 percent threshold, rebel immediately. Although this action by 30 percent of the community produces a measure of assurance to other community members, it is not enough to surpass the C group's threshold of 50 percent. No normative effects are relevant in this situation as no C group members are confronted by the actions of fellow group members. Thus, only group B rebels producing a 30 percent equilibrium.[26]

In the middle distribution, the dynamic becomes far more interesting. Again, the 0 percent threshold B group immediately starts local organization.[27] The question becomes whether the action of B subset members is sufficient to trigger reciprocation of those holding membership in the intermediate-threshold BC group. Note that members of BC do not act immediately due to the constraints and higher threshold produced by membership in subgroup C. Here, the operation of two sets of competing norms comes into play. First, there is pressure from fellow B members to reduce thresholds, accept risk, and join in rebellion. On the other hand, there is pressure from risk-averse C subset members to conform to the nonparticipation of the C group majority, that is, to increase thresholds and reject the dangerous appeal of B subset members. The percentages of each subgroup are an indication of the power of the norm in changing BC acceptance of risk. Twenty-five of thirty-five B group members (which includes both B and BC subsets) subscribing to norms of honor have already joined the resistance. This produces significant social pressure for reciprocation. However, forty-five of fifty-five C group members are not rebelling, also producing significant pressure but in the opposite direction. Following the functions and weighting procedure above, the effect of the B subset in this particular situation is to reduce BC's threshold by .20 and the effect of C subset pressure is to increase the threshold by .10, producing a net .10 reduction and a new threshold of 15 percent.[28] This 15 percent threshold is surpassed by B's participation, resulting in 35 percent of the community supporting the resistance at a +2 level.

[26] As the reader may have noticed, I am not considering the tipping or "snowballing" effects within groups, only among subsets. There are, of course, such effects, but for the sake of parsimony and for the ability to predict, the within-group effects are less important.

[27] As B norms only work to reduce thresholds, they are not relevant to a 0 percent threshold group.

[28] Of course, the relative weights of norms vary in different societies and must be assigned according to knowledge of the case.

The remaining question is whether the participation of both subset B and BC will be sufficient to drag remaining C and OT members into positions of support. The same C norm applies to members of subset C as subset BC: forty-five of the fifty-five C members are not rebelling. The effect is an increase of .10 in C thresholds or a new 60 percent threshold – which, obviously, is higher than 35 percent. Clearly, the 70 percent threshold of the "outsider" will also not be surpassed, leaving a final equilibrium of 35 percent participation.

In the bottom distribution, the structure produces somewhat different normative effects. Again, B subset members rebel first but this time their normative effect on the BC subset is reduced as the ratio between the two groups falls to 1:2. Still, as modeled previously, the effect of participation of even one-third of a subgroup holding to "norms of honor" will significantly reduce thresholds among the wavering two-thirds of B members located in BC. Furthermore, in this situation the normative effect of C group membership also works to reduce thresholds. As members of the BC subset recalculate the amount of risk they will accept and reexamine social pressures, they will notice that only one-third of all individuals holding C membership (those of the C subset) hold thresholds and dispositions that are clearly against participation.[29] As conformist norms influence individuals against siding with the minority, the effect on the wavering group is toward acceptance of risk and a small reduction of the threshold.

In this situation, as modeled previously, the influence of B norms is to reduce thresholds in BC by .14 and the influence of C norms is reduction by .03. BC's new threshold of .08 is easily surpassed by first-playing B's 20 percent. Total participation now equals 60 percent of the total community. Now it is C's turn to recalculate. As a minority among all C members, the C normative effect on the C subset will reflect the pressure of group members who have chosen participation (or who might still be wavering). For members of BC, the fact that C was a one-third minority created a small incentive to accept risk; for members of C, the knowledge of being a one-third minority creates an incentive to accept risk. In this model, the effects are treated as equivalent: both reduce the threshold by .03. The C subset's new threshold

---

[29] Because we wish to know the normative effect on the wavering group by subsets that are at this point committed to "not rebel," the wavering group is coded as "not not rebelling" and, for the purposes here, is added in with the rebelling group. This assumption is problematic, but it does not affect the conclusions about community structure deduced in the subsequent sections.

is 47 percent, which has been surpassed by the movement of subsets B and BC (60 percent). With a total of 80 percent of the community now supporting local resistance, even the threshold of outsider groups is surpassed and 100 percent of the community will become involved.

At first glance, it is not intuitively clear what equilibria should be expected in the preceding examples. After all, different outcomes result despite the fact that in each case the same types of groups exist in the same numbers. Predictions are possible through a basic knowledge of three characteristics of relevant community subgroups: preferences and constraints concerning rebellion (which serve to set original thresholds), norms, and distribution.

The Structural Characteristics of Community and Their Effect on Rebellion

Several structural features of community influence rebellion. Hypotheses, or at least insights, can be deductively derived regarding five key distinctions of community stucture:

1. Density of ties.
2. The position of first actors or political entrepreneurs within the community.
3. Centralization of ties.
4. Size factors.
5. Homogeneity/heterogeneity.

This section is necessarily abstract and at times quite dense. While those interested in network theory may wish to explore the arguments and methods in detail, not all may wish to read each section. Some may wish to skip to the summary for the time being. In the substantive chapters, I link these theoretical sections to the analysis of actual communities and their rebellion dynamics.

For the sake of clarity, the analysis is centered on the relationship and interaction of B groups (lower thresholds and B norms) and C groups (higher thresholds and C norms).

Solidarity I: Density

Many students of revolution believe village "solidarity" facilitates revolution and rebellion. There is widespread agreement among a variety of social scientists that collective action is more likely with dense and/or homogeneous social networks. The idea is hardly new. Marx believed that the working environment of proletarians, involving constant contact and communication, solved the collective-action dilemma by producing a "habit of cooperation." Some very well known studies have also highlighted the role of social networks or community-level solidarity.[30] Furthermore, the computer simulations of Marwell, Oliver, and colleagues have also concluded that density of social ties within a group increases chances for successful collective action.[31]

Often the term "solidarity" is left undefined. In terms of the Venn diagram structural analysis employed here, two measures might be employed: density and homogeneity. Homogeneity is defined and discussed later in the fifth point. Density concerns the nature of ties within the community. In two of the most relevant network studies, density refers to the number of social ties in a group divided by the total number of possible ties.[32] While in most network analysis the focus is on ties among individuals, here the unit of analysis is the subset that represents a set of ties among individuals sharing similar group membership profiles. With the Venn diagram approach, the essence of density is captured by the amount of overlap among groups (for instance, members of the overlapping group share two ties, thus increasing the total number of ties while the total number of possible ties remains constant across the distributions). In Figure 2.8, for example, the set of distributions proceeds from low density to high density.

Clearly, in the general terms of strong community versus weak community, the present approach supports the findings linking group density and group action. The mechanisms that drive individuals rightward on the spectrum are found in the norms, threats, and monitoring capacities of small interactive communities that are relatively "dense" and homogeneous. In terms of specific structure, though, the findings are more complex. I draw two lessons here.

---

[30] See the general work of Charles Tilly on social networks. Theda Skocpol employs "solidarity" in *States and Social Revolutions: A Comparative Analysis of France, Russia, and China* (Cambridge: Cambridge University Press, 1979).

[31] Gerald Marwell, Pamela Oliver, and Ralph Prahl, "Social Networks and Collective Action: A Theory of Critical Mass III," *American Journal of Sociology* 94 (1988): 502–534.

[32] I am following the definition employed by two works that I refer to later: see ibid.; and Roger Gould, "Collective Action and Network Structure," *American Sociological Review* 58 (1993): 182–196.

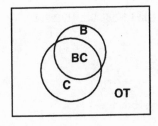

Distribution		Threshold
B	10	0
C	30	50
BC	40	25
OT	20	70

Equilibrium = 10

Figure 2.9a. An effect of increased density

First, outcomes are sometimes sensitive to small shifts in structure and cannot be entirely determined by overall measures of density. Consider the juxtaposition of the bottom distribution of Figure 2.8 with Figure 2.9a. Both communities have the same measure of density (forty members with two ties, forty with one, twenty with zero); the only difference is a shift in the ratio of nonoverlapping subsets B:C from 20:20 to 10:30. Yet, this small structural shift produces a change in the relative power of two norms at a critical juncture in the tipping sequence. In the sequence produced by the structure in Figure 2.8, the effect of B and C norms on reducing BC thresholds effectively tips that subset and creates a cascading effect leading to the 100 percent equilibrium. In Figure 2.9a, on the other hand, the normative effect of the B subset is reduced to the point that subset BC fails to tip and the cascading process fails to develop.

Timur Kuran has shown how small changes in the distribution of thresholds can produce large differences in outcomes. Here, the analysis shows how small changes in structure, which involve not only thresholds but also normative effects of subsets on those thresholds, can produce different equilibria. In some ways, the analysis here takes this ambiguity one step further in that even a similar original distribution of thresholds could produce different outcomes because the normative effects of subsets produce changes in thresholds during the rebellion process. On the other hand, it specifies and identifies what types of small changes commonly produce the "breaks" within the tipping process and ties these "breaks" to community structures. In this regard, this study attempts to provide far more direction in how to understand overall tipping dynamics than the work of Kuran.

Second, although density is far from the sole predictor of equilibria, there are some general tendencies regarding this factor. For instance, some amount of overlap among subsets is ususally necessary to trigger widespread com-

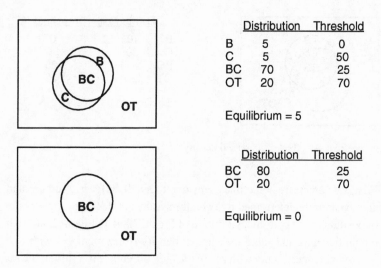

Distribution		Threshold
B	5	0
C	5	50
BC	70	25
OT	20	70

Equilibrium = 5

Distribution		Threshold
BC	80	25
OT	20	70

Equilibrium = 0

Figure 2.9b. The inhibiting effects of high density

munity movement to +2. Consider Figure 2.8 again. Here, the story seems straightforward: with increasing density, more resistance participation is expected because the normative effects of the B group have an opportunity to reduce thresholds (compare the bottom two scenarios to the upper one).

On the other hand, total overlap may produce total inaction. Consider Figure 2.9b. In the lower distribution of Figure 2.9b, there is total overlap of groups, with highest density among nonoutsiders. The equilibrium is 0 percent for an obvious reason: there are no first-playing 0 percent groups to initiate a tipping process. In the upper distribution, the B subset is too small to have much of an effect. Most communities possess both normative forces that push toward risk acceptance and constraints that act against it. Someone needs to be harvesting the crops, building the irrigation ditches, or producing a product. If all members are equally subject to the constraints involved with these activities, however, action may never begin. Very high densities are less likely to produce critical "first actors" subsets.

The overall progression seen in Figures 2.8, 2.9a, and 2.9b suggests that intermediate levels of overlap, not highly dense or sparse ones, may be optimal for reaching high equilibria. The works of Granovetter[33] and Gould

---

[33] In his pathbreaking theoretical 1978 work on thresholds, Granovetter ran an analysis on "acquaintance volume," or the density of friendship ties, on particular distributions of thresh-

have already suggested this relationship. In an approach similar to the one used here, Gould's analytical work on cooperative behavior posited two mechanisms – a calculation of efficacy and a norm of fairness. Strategic individuals participate in a collective action when their individual action has a chance to be meaningful (influence the outcome) and when they are not being played as "suckers" (individuals wish to match the average contribution of those in their network). Gould sums up: "Neither reason accomplishes much by itself: Normative pressure to contribute should have little impact if elicited contributions will be completely wasted, while increasing marginal returns will only reinforce the waiting game in the absence of fairness norms."[34] In his analysis, Gould found that in certain contexts intermediate densities were often superior to higher densities in producing collective action. The reason is a "dilution" effect. This effect incorporates two factors. First, operating with a norm of fairness, the individual is more likely to contribute when the ratio of contributors to noncontributors within his or her network is large. When all are tied to all, however, the action of any original contributor is a very small fraction of the total and the impact of the norm of fairness is very weak. With a lower density of ties, original contributors may have fewer ties but their normative impact on connected individuals will be significantly higher. Within the sparser networks, the effect continues as the individuals connected to the original contributors in turn have a "nondiluted" impact on their own networks.[35] The process, together with the higher sense of efficacy it may produce, can lead to high equilibria.

Although the studies differ in many respects, Gould's "dilution" effect resonates with the present work. In both, individuals are partly driven by the ratio of actors to nonactors among their own set of close ties. In Gould's work, the smaller this ratio, the less the power of the norm of fairness. In the present work, the larger the overlap of B norm subsets with other types of

olds. He found that "the largest effects occur where people know, on the average, about one-quarter of the rest of the group – a moderate level of friendship. The explanation is neither intuitively nor analytically obvious and will require further study" (p. 1430). For this particular question, Granovetter counted each "friend" twice (strangers once) in the overall threshold figure. See Mark Granovetter, "Threshold Models of Collective Behavior," *American Journal of Sociology* 83 (1978): 1420–1443.

[34] Gould, "Collective Action and Network Structure," p. 184.

[35] Gould also posited that the original contributors' impact was greater on immediate connections than on successive nodes. This is another aspect of the dilution effect. Also see Michael Macy, "Learning to Cooperate: Stochastic and Tacit Collusion in Social Exchange," *American Journal of Sociology* 97 (1992): 808–843, for another study that links lower density of ties and cooperative action.

subsets, the more "watered down" the effect of B norms. As modeled here, one of the most powerful forms of normative pressure occurs when a large percentage of a B group (norms of honor) has already committed to action. Remaining wavering members can be persuaded to accept a great deal more risk. However, when the ratio of actors to nonactors within B groups decreases, normative pressure lessens and individual thresholds become substantially higher. As seen in the empirical sections, having such favorable ratios among members of B groups is an important structural factor in triggering community-level rebellion.

In sum, higher densities generally lower ratios of first actors to connected subgroups and thus may produce, given certain other factors, a "dilution effect" on catalyzing norms. On the other hand, low densities may mean that the first-playing group is too unconnected to other groups to have much impact on them. This discussion leads directly into a second issue, the structural position of first actors.

The Position of "First Actors" and Political Entrepreneurs

The existence of "first actors," those holding a 0 percent threshold, is one of the most important factors in triggering community-level rebellion. Without them, no movement can begin. The essential nature of first actors or political entrepreneurs plays a large role in the literature on collective action in general and rebellion in particular. The work of Samuel Popkin is perhaps the best known on this subject. Popkin holds that political entrepreneurs can successfully build local organizations without centrally administered selective incentives by creating a sense of efficacy through small-n organization. In effect, leaders break large tasks into smaller ones in which each individual's contribution becomes meaningful. Additionally, in small-n situations, free riders can be more easily detected and sanctioned. The credibility of leadership is crucial in this argument (as well as the cultural affinity between leaders and followers), as no one will begin to engage in even the first, simple collective actions without having some measure of trust in would-be leaders.

Here, the point is emphasized that not only the presence of leaders but also their structural location in the community is crucial.[36] In fact, in terms of determining final equilibria, structural location may be more important than

---

[36] This is also a major conclusion of Gould's network analysis.

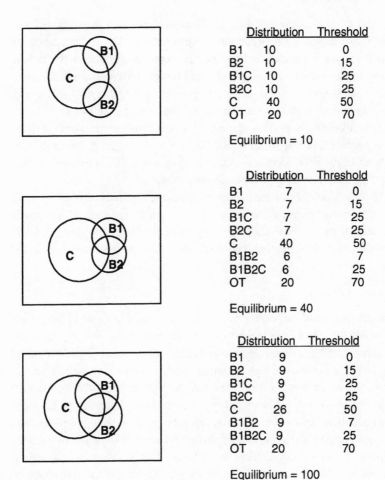

Distribution		Threshold
B1	10	0
B2	10	15
B1C	10	25
B2C	10	25
C	40	50
OT	20	70

Equilibrium = 10

Distribution		Threshold
B1	7	0
B2	7	15
B1C	7	25
B2C	7	25
C	40	50
B1B2	6	7
B1B2C	6	25
OT	20	70

Equilibrium = 40

Distribution		Threshold
B1	9	0
B2	9	15
B1C	9	25
B2C	9	25
C	26	50
B1B2	9	7
B1B2C	9	25
OT	20	70

Equilibrium = 100

Figure 2.9c. The critical position of a first-acting group

even the size of the set of first actors.[37] For instance, in Figure 2.8, the respective ratios of size of first-acting groups to final equilibria are 30:30, 25:35, and 20:100. Clearly, the linkage between groups is critical.

Consider Figure 2.9c. Here we see the same three groups with roughly equal size memberships. One of the B norm groups is "first acting" with a 0

[37] For a very relevant discussion related to the size of first-playing groups, see the treatment of "critical mass" in Pamela Oliver, with Gerald Marwell and Ruy Teixera, "A Theory of the

percent threshold, whereas the other B group holds a 15 percent threshold. The major difference between the two examples is the overlap among the groups. In the upper distribution, the first-acting group, subset B1, fails to tip any other subset, resulting in an equilibrium of 10. In the middle distribution, all B groups' thresholds are surpassed, leading to a final outcome of 40, whereas in the bottom scenario, the equilibrium is 100 percent. In the bottom distribution, the first-playing B1 subset, although smaller than in the upper schema, is able to tip B1B2. Now, the centralized group, B1B2C is subject to multiple normative effects. As modeled, this subset easily tips, sending its effects through all connected subsets.

In sum, depending on the overlap between the B groups and the C groups, the final equilibrium will be either 40 percent or 100 percent. This example shows both the importance of the position of the first-playing group and density factors. It also directly relates to a third structural debate: centralization.

Centralization

For the purposes here, centralization can be defined in terms of a situation in which the qualities or actions of one unit have immediate impact on the actions of multiple connected units. In the network analysis of Marwell et al., Gould, and others, a high degree of centralization occurs when a few individuals within the structure hold a disproportionate number of the total ties. The concept does not smoothly match the Venn diagram type of analysis, but still makes some sense if the unit to be examined is a subset or group. The goal is the same as in network theory: we want to know whether the existence of subsets with multiple direct links – that is, subsets whose actions and norms affect many other subsets – will facilitate or retard movement on the spectrum. For instance, the middle structure in Figure 2.9c can be considered more centralized than that of the upper due to the presence of a subset with three group ties and an additional subset with two group ties. If the threshold of B1B2C is surpassed, all three groups are immediately affected. In the preceding example, the structures with centralized subsets had higher equilibria. Under what conditions should we expect this effect and why?

Although relying on mechanisms and assumptions different than the ones proposed here, other studies suggest that centralization may indeed catalyze cooperative behavior. In their computer simulations, Marwell, Oliver, and Prahl found that collective action is more likely when network ties are centralized. Their logic relates to the structural position of the original actors: centralized organizers can be selective in their recruiting efforts, targeting likely recruits and not wasting time on unlikely recruits. Gould came to the same finding, although for different reasons. He found that centralization could enhance the effect of low density in mitigating dilution effects: "When the volunteer (first actor) is a centrally located actor, high centralization holds that most actors perceive a high average level of contribution because they are tied to relatively few shirkers."[38] Under conditions of high density, however, the impact of centralized first actors still remains diluted by the inevitably high numbers of ties with shirkers throughout the system. Again, centralization helps set up favorable contributor-shirker ratios that trigger norms of fairness (and creates shorter paths between the contributor and other nodes).[39]

In the Venn diagram analysis presented in Figure 2.9d, two effects of centralization can be readily seen. One is quite similar to the effect just described in Gould's work. The upper distribution is simply taken from Figure 2.8. Its dynamic, leading to an equilibrium of 35 percent, has already been described. In the middle diagram, the overall number of members of B, C, and BC remains the same, but the B group now overlaps with four smaller C groups, also producing four smaller BC subsets. In essence, group B has become a centralized group with ties to four other groups (this effect can also be discussed in terms of the fragmentation of C, an issue that is addressed later). In the bottom diagram, the C group is central whereas the B group is fragmented.

Compare the top two diagrams in Figure 2.9d and notice the changing ratio of B:BC, which represents the effect of the first actor upon the medium threshold subset, and the ratio of C:BC, representing the braking effect of the higher threshold group. While the C:BC ratio remains constant, the B:BC ratio is four times greater. The overall effect clearly serves to lower thresholds of the overlapping BC subset.

Of course, this effect works similarly for all centralized groups. In comparing the top and bottom diagrams, the ratio of the C subset, possessing a

[38] Gould, "Collective Action and Network Structure," p. 194.

[39] Gould adds several caveats relating network density and the structural location of the first actor to centralization. Most importantly, perhaps, Gould found that centralization promotes collective action under low density but not under high density. Space does not permit a full discussion here.

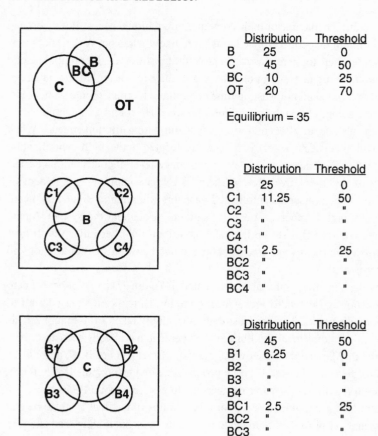

Distribution	Threshold
B	25	0
C	45	50
BC	10	25
OT	20	70

Equilibrium = 35

	Distribution	Threshold
B	25	0
C1	11.25	50
C2	"	"
C3	"	"
C4	"	"
BC1	2.5	25
BC2	"	"
BC3	"	"
BC4	"	"

	Distribution	Threshold
C	45	50
B1	6.25	0
B2	"	"
B3	"	"
B4	"	"
BC1	2.5	25
BC2	"	"
BC3	"	"
BC4	"	"

Figure 2.9d. The effects of centralization

higher threshold and C norm, to the BC threshold increases four times while the effect of the first-acting B group remains constant. A large number of C group members will be pressuring a few wavering members against rebellion. The result will be to increase thresholds of BC members.

A second attribute of centralization concerns its effect on the distribution of thresholds. As modeled previously, the thresholds of overlapping subsets are generally averaged from their constituent groups. Applying this simplifying (and perhaps simplistic) rule to the diagrams in Figure 2.9c, the addition of a centralized subset can produce a distribution of thresholds conducive to a "tipping cascade." In the top diagram, the first-acting group is

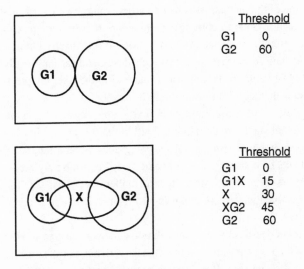

Threshold

G1	0
G2	60

Threshold

G1	0
G1X	15
X	30
XG2	45
G2	60

Figure 2.9e. Centralization and the distribution of thresholds

not nearly large enough to surpass the high threshold of the remaining community members, and there are no interaction effects. In the bottom diagram,
the inclusion of a centralized group with an intermediate threshold creates a
steadily increasing set of thresholds that, along with normative effects, might
easily set a "cascade" in motion. Again, the nature of the centralized group
is critical. The inclusion of a centralized high-threshold group could raise
thresholds and break the entire sequence.

Size Factors

The effect of size has already been addressed in the definition of strong and
weak community. The mechanisms of strong community – normative pressure and automatic social sanction, monitoring and effective threat – rely on
relatively small numbers. Although the local organization of rebellion is not
necessarily a collective-action problem, much of the Olson logic of small
groups and selective incentives applies.[40]

How small is small enough, or too small? Obviously, if the numbers of
members in the bottom schema of Figure 2.9d, for example, were raised by

[40] The literature on the size issue is extensive, but mostly linked to Olson's formulation of
the collective-action problem.

a factor of ten, some of the mechanisms listed earlier would no longer function in the same fashion. Due to complexity, this work does not attempt to quantify the exact effect of size factors and will leave this discussion at a more general level. The complexity of the models developed earlier already exceeds the quality of some of the empirical material in the later chapters. There are two issues that are highly important, however.

First, it seems especially important that first-acting subsets be small enough to overcome obstacles to cooperation within the subset. It is hard to imagine an eighty-member first-actor subset being able to simultaneously coordinate initial acts of conspiracy. A larger first-acting group may create more normative pressure and assurance than a smaller one, but if it is too large, it may not be able to act at all, regardless of its members' characteristics or motivations.

A second size-related issue concerns the relationship between size and the type of norm exhibited by a group. It is hypothesized that A norms are best exemplified by families, whereas B norms can be found among social groups or neighborhood friendship networks. It seems likely, though, that some friendship groups may act more like "families" than do some families and that this may be related to size. Very large family groups, ones with huge age differences between members, may practice a looser form of reciprocity, whereas members of very small friendship groups might behave unconditionally toward one another, in other words, more like a family. This is obviously a slippery issue, but one that can be addressed with the data from actual communities.

Solidarity II: Homogeneity/Heterogeneity

Another possible definition of solidarity might be based on the multiplicity of subgroups. A community with four economic subgroups and three social subgroups can be considered more heterogeneous than a community composed of only one economic and one social subgroup. At this point, in order to lead into important conclusions in the subsequent summary section, let us consider B groups (low threshold, B norms) as social groups (religious, patriotic, etc.) and C groups (higher threshold, C norms) as economic. Given the preceding analysis, under what conditions of economic and social homogeneity/heterogeneity would we expect the largest movement to the +2 node?

Theoretically, the level of homogeneity on outcomes is indeterminate. In order to understand this relationship, consider some of the preceding community structures in terms of a 2X2 matrix representing the different possibilities of economically and socially homogeneous and heterogeneous structures. Figures 2.8, 2.9a, and 2.9b represent socially and economically homogeneous communities, each with only one social and economic subgroup. There are a variety of equilibria within these figures ranging from 0 to 100 percent. Within these diagrams, density is the deciding factor.

Figures 2.9c and 2.9d (bottom) represent economically homogeneous and socially heterogeneous communities. Social group heterogeneity retards movement in Figure 2.9d (bottom) but enhances it in Figure 2.9c. Again, a range of equilibria is produced depending on the location of first actors and centralization, as well as density. Such variation in outcomes can also be seen in the socially homogeneous, economically heterogeneous cases. In communities with heterogeneity in both social and economic subgroups – that is, where countless combinations of groups and overlaps exist – almost any outcome could occur again depending on the position of first actors, the presence of centralization effects, and the level of density.

Whereas the theoretical case may be ambiguous, a more practical analysis (and here I will foreshadow some of the empirical findings) does lead to some tentative hypotheses. In practice, the effects of size and fragmentation favor structures characterized by social group heterogeneity and economic group homogeneity. In theory, Figure 2.9d (middle) would be highly effective as it produces favorable ratios of first players to connected subsets. However, for reasons mentioned earlier, a first-playing group this large may not act as a first-playing group. The level of absolute trust between members necessary to move from a 0 percent level is less likely in a group of twenty or thirty than in a group of five or ten. Second, again in reference to 2.9d (middle), in reality it is unlikely that the fragmented economic groups will be so nicely and evenly distributed. Economic fragmentation will probably leave some groups untouched, while other groups exhibit "overkill."

Consider the example in Figure 2.9f. This example typifies some of the effects of the modernization of agriculture. As individual family farms, or loosely connected neighbor groups, replace previous communal forms of agriculture, many members of the community become more generally unconnected and less subject to community influences. Under these conditions, very high equilibria are difficult to reach. Under conditions of economic homogeneity, on the other hand, the number of rebels found in overlapping subsets of the economic group may reach high enough numbers so that strict reciprocity norms begin either to lose their negative force or to become a

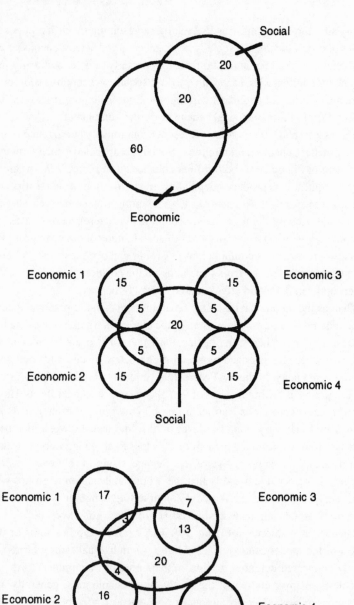

Figure 2.9f. The effects of economic fragmentation

positive force pushing the whole group and most of the community toward rebellion.

Summing Up

The number of community structures that could be represented in Venn diagrams is almost infinite. Although small structural changes can sometimes produce large changes in outcomes, there are some general features and "ideal"/"nonideal" types that can be used for prediction. General features include:

1. Small overall size (strong community).
2. Intermediate density of ties.
3. The presence of social groups, preferably small and heterogeneous.

Community structural factors that may facilitate rebellion under more specific conditions include:

1. Centralization of low- or intermediate-threshold groups.
2. Economic homogeneity.
3. The absence of groups connected to political parties.

These features help establish favorable distributions of thresholds ("cascading" effects) and do not dilute the impact of favorable norms. Both theoretically and empirically, one of the structures most likely to promote movement to +2 consists of multiple, small social groups with substantial links to larger economic groups.

Sustaining Mechanisms: Remaining at the +2 Position

In order to sustain a rebellion, individuals need not only fill the +2 category, but they need to stay there. Once significant numbers of the resistance begin slipping from +2 to +1, the rebellion is in major trouble for several reasons: the number of individuals organized and able to carry out raids against the regime falls; access to food, supplies, and weapons declines or becomes inconsistent; systematic surveillance of the regime's security apparatus, and the general population, ceases. Furthermore, the organic link between the population and the mobile rebels weakens and the pool of recruits to fill the +3 level dries up. Without a reliable source of food and information, rebels may need to resort to coercion against the population, becoming largely indistinguishable from the occupiers. In this section, I identify several mechanisms (rational, normative, and irrational) that operate to sustain +2 numbers. The identification of sustaining mechanisms, while important, does not play nearly as large of a role as the structurally based, threshold-oriented mechanisms outlined in the previous sections of this chapter. The analysis, admittedly, is somewhat of a "laundry list." Still, an explanation of the various sustaining mechanisms is necessary in explaining several important outcomes in the empirical chapters.

Threats

Due to their low numbers, strong communities can easily monitor, socially sanction, and physically threaten members. The development of a +2 organization enhances these monitoring and sanctioning powers. Not only does the organization produce higher capacities, but its members may also possess higher motivations to sanction others. Many individuals within the rebellion organization will have suffered great personal losses and will be driven by revenge or irrational psychological mechanisms. These individuals may strongly pressure those wishing to defect. They have made a sacrifice, so why can't others? The wavering individual might wish to avoid, rationally, possible sanctions that might result from defection.[41]

Irrational Mechanisms

Given the high pressure of belonging to a conspiratorial organization, it is not surprising that several irrational mechanisms affect individual decisions to remain at the +2 level. The irrational "tyranny of sunk costs" was discussed in the introduction. Once an individual has already made an investment or suffered a loss, the human tendency is to continue the same path even when the most cursory cost-benefit analysis would advise against it.

Perhaps less known, "the value of small victories" is another important irrational mechanism.[42] Assume two players are engaged in some sort of game

---

[41] Here, the structure of the +2 organization itself is a factor. Clandestine operations and units, almost by definition, need to be relatively small; their tasks are also usually limited in the numbers of individuals that can be involved. Under these conditions, each individual's contribution is meaningful in that it might make the difference between success and failure in any given task. Along lines of Popkin, unwavering members of +2 have rational motives, as well as emotional ones, to threaten sanctions against those considering a reduction in their level of commitment.

[42] See especially Karl E. Weick, "Small Wins: Redefining the Scale of Social Problems,"

in which there is an objective value in terms of points and a subjective value of winning any given play regardless of the number of points involved. Let us say one player wins a play worth ten points and receives a subjective value of winning for a total of eleven points. The second player wins a game objectively worth one point six times in a row but receives a subjective satisfaction point for each victory for a total of twelve points. Subjectively, the second player is ahead twelve points to eleven and may feel that he is winning, although objectively the first player has won decisively, ten points to six. Of course, in rational-choice theory there is no distinction between subjective and objective values; the second player would be ahead in individual terms. The point here is that the individual subjective satisfaction involved with winning a series of "small victories" prevents a rational evaluation of the overall objective balance between occupier and resistance. In terms of the preceding example, the second player might also state that he was winning the objective game due to the fact that he was winning most of the time. In a situation in which revenge tends to dominate action, the desire to strike back often affects belief formation about the general course of the conflict. The question is phrased, "How can we be losing while we are constantly winning these victories? We must actually be winning."

The phenomenon of small victories is very important because the nature of sustained resistance consists of rebels winning small victories and occupiers periodically marshaling their forces for a large attack. To illustrate this important factor more clearly, some of the material from the Lithuanian case study can be previewed. The height of rebellious activity in Lithuania may have occurred in 1946–1947, when most evidence would have indicated that the Soviets were going to control Lithuania in the long run. The interesting puzzle is why the resistance continued as long as it did in the face of inevitable defeat. Why did so many Lithuanians continue in their +2 roles for so long when they should have been trying to adjust themselves to the new realities by moving down to the +1 or 0 levels? After the Soviets reoccupied Lithuania, they began deporting families who were suspected of being involved at the +2 level. Then they began resettling these farms with Russian families. However, the Soviets started this process without sufficient force to protect the new homesteaders. The Lithuanian resistance, in the form of small raiding parties, conducted nightly attacks against these Russian homesteaders in order to intimidate them from remaining on the land. The Lithuanians were very successful for a relatively long period of time.[43] These raiding groups, formed from local +2 entities, must have been aware of the power of the Soviets, but the fact that they were controlling the countryside and constantly winning small victories caused them to disregard certain evidence and to put their faith in highly uncertain events, which leads us to the final mechanism.

Clearly, when deep-seated desires and reality have little in common, individuals will tend to interpret reality in way that brings the two into line by way of "wishful thinking." For many reasons, rebels wish to continue their commitment to the +2 level even if their action seems futile. When new events come along, they can be used as "evidence" for continuing the struggle. Again, an example from middle-1940s Lithuania can be used for illustration. After the Red Army again swept into Lithuania in 1944–1945, Lithuanian fighters justified continued action on grounds that Western intervention was soon forthcoming and thus action to preserve Lithuania was necessary despite the enormous costs involved. This belief continued for a time even when available evidence failed to support it. Events such as the American explosion of the atomic bomb were seen as evidence that the coming American-Soviet war was at hand. As one underground member relates:

> The belief in the inevitable strong stand of the West against Kremlin designs for world domination had literally hypnotized the LFA command. Even the Lithuanian liaison men from the West, who brought direct and sobering information on the international situation, were unable for some time to shatter that belief. . . . The explosion of the first atom-bomb evoked lively discussions among freedom-fighters throughout Lithuania. The consensus was that the West would confront the Kremlin with an atomic ultimatum and compel the Soviets to free the captive countries. Suddenly a free Lithuania, and the end of a life of want and endless conflict, seemed almost at hand.[44]

These beliefs were not without some foundation, but clearly desires were affecting belief formation and producing an element of irrationality that promoted and justified continued action.

---

[43] In a related point, the social ostracism resulting from defecting from a winning group may be higher than from defecting from a losing group. In a losing group, one could make a better case for defection while defecting from a winning group seems a higher form of betrayal.

[44] K. V. Tauras [pseudonym], *Guerilla Warfare on the Amber Coast* (New York: Voyages Press, 1962), pp. 91–92.

Other Mechanisms

Although the key point on the spectrum is the +2 level, the movement to other positions can also important. The mechanisms involved with a couple of such movements is very briefly outlined here, first the movement from +2 to +3. The movement out of the village-based resistance organization into the mobile organization is generally a matter of rational decision making. Displaced persons, individuals named and targeted by the occupier, idealists, and youth often had nowhere else to go. They are generally unconnected or displaced from their communities. The goals they wish to accomplish are quite different from those of individuals maintaining an organic connection to their home communities. Another group of +3 level participants is simply coerced from the population to join the unit. The Soviet resistance during the Second World War would sometimes enter a town and conscript all healthy males. These conscripts usually played support roles, while the more committed Communists fulfilled the combat roles. The key question is how these units are linked to the communities.

A second movement involves a change from +3 to −3. As mentioned earlier, it is generally suboptimal for the resistance to have all its participants at the +3 level. Because participation in these units brought severe penalties, however, mobile rebels naturally feared the uncertainty and potential vulnerability incurred by leaving the unit. Those who did wish to leave often found that their only real option was to join the occupier's collaborative military organization (−3 on the spectrum). They had to prove their loyalty and were assigned extremely dangerous tasks to perform as evidence of their conviction. Often they were killed anyway.

Concluding Remark

Rebellion is a very complicated matter that cannot be reduced to a few variables. The explanation provided here is more complex than many others but still parsimonious. It will, I hope, provide a coherent means to analyze and generalize the dynamics of rebellion while remaining faithful to the actual dynamics of most sustained violence against powerful regimes. The considerable empirical material that follows should allow the reader to be a competent judge whether this hope has been realized.

3. Lithuania, 1940–1941

Lithuania experienced three successive occupations during the 1940s. The study of each case over the next four chapters generates opportunities for productive comparison by providing differences among individuals and regions, changes over time, and dissimilarities across the three Baltic states. In each chapter, the sequence of mechanisms outlined in the previous chapter is employed as a guide for analysis.

The Lithuanian cases also provide some intriguing puzzles. Perhaps the most puzzling aspect of Lithuanian rebellion behavior is described in minute detail in Chapter 7's review of the second Soviet occupation. In the latter half of the 1940s, a battle between Lithuanian partisans and Soviet NKVD troops devastated the Lithuanian countryside. It was a classic confrontation in many ways. The Soviets controlled the villages in the day, threatening the local population with the wrath of Soviet power if they were caught aiding the partisans. At night, partisans made their own appeals to the local citizens. Despite the mismatch in power, the partisans' hopeless rebellion continued for years largely because many Lithuanian communities developed organizations (+2) that aided the partisans. The costs to these village-based supporters were extremely high: the Soviets "pacified" these uncooperative people by deporting tens of thousands of them to Siberia. Whole villages were removed from the face of the earth; only one in eight Lithuanian deportees would ever return to his or her native land.

This postwar resistance had its roots in the first Soviet occupation of 1940–1941. This case presents a particularly clear illustration of the community dynamics of rebellion. During the first Soviet occupation, underground groups sprung up in localities across the country. The diversity of their names reflected the fact that they had no single political foundation: Committee to Help Lithuania, Punitive Detachment of Lithuanian Fascists, Lithuanian Activist Union, Lithuanian Independence Party, Committee for the Liberation of Lithuania, Saigunas (named after a former prince), Lithuanian Patriots, Committee No. 27, Union of the Patriots of the Fatherland, Exterminators of Parasites, Death Battalion, and on and on. Some of these groups had roots in political parties, but many of them were nonpolitical and local. The formation of these groups appeared to be spontaneous. Many of them were later to be united in the Lithuanian Activist Front (LAF), an organization connected to Lithuanian political officials in Berlin. When Germany launched Operation Barbarossa, the LAF initiated an attack on the Soviet administration of the country. The goal of this rebellion was to take over the government before the Germans arrived and thus force the Germans to recognize the Lithuanians as the true representatives of a sovereign nation.

For the question of rebellion, these political maneuvers are not as interesting or surprising as the social dynamics that had occurred earlier in the year.[1] Perhaps most interestingly, the Lithuanian revolt was primarily formed from local units. In some respects, these local foundations were largely the result of necessity. On July 7, 1940, the Lithuanian Communist Party chief ordered the arrests of all leaders of all nationally based political and social organizations, and on the night of July 11–12 regime officials carried out the order and removed 2,000 Lithuanian elites. In effect, the Lithuanian leadership had been decapitated.[2] On the surface, Lithuania was a country of seemingly average farmers. Yet within a few months they had organized themselves into "Committees to Help Lithuania" and even "Death Battalions" despite the decimation of political and social leaders. The scale of this activity, considering the small size of the nation, was striking. In a country of about 3 million people, the LAF had managed to combine local units and recruit new members into a 35,000 strong clandestine organization. In addition, tens of thousands of other individuals, some organized but not incorporated into the LAF, participated in the June 22 uprising.[3] The re-

---

[1] For a good English-language account of the political maneuvering that went on, as well as an account of the entire June 22 uprising, see Algirdas Martin Budreckis, *The Lithuanian National Revolt of 1941* (South Boston, Mass.: Lithuanian Encyclopedia Press, 1968).

[2] See U.S. Congress, *Report of the Select Committee to Investigate Communist Aggression and the Forced Incorporation of the Baltic States into the USSR,* Third Interim Report, H.R., 83rd Cong., 2nd session, 1954, pp. 344–347.

Stanley Vardys and Judith Sedaitis provide a more precise figure of 36,000. See Stanley Vardys and Judith Sedaitis, *Lithuania: The Rebel Nation* (Boulder, Colo.: Westview Press, 1997), p. 55.

[3] Estimates vary. K. Pelekis, in *Genocide, Lithuania's Threefold Tragedy* (Germany, 1949), puts the figures at 125,000 total, while a Lithuanian general (Rastikis) gives a total figure of 90,000 to 100,000. Many of those who emerged as "partisans" during the actual rebellion were

volt involved considerable personal risk. In the period before the uprising, Soviet secret police made strong efforts to infiltrate Lithuanian society. The revolt itself may have resulted in more Lithuanian casualties in three days of fighting than in the entire 1918–1920 war of independence.[4]

The foundations of Lithuanian anti-Soviet resistance lay in the actions of thousands of individuals who, under considerable risk, organized rebellion in their local communities. This chapter addresses this phenomenon by examining movement from neutrality to widespread, low-level anti-Soviet resistance (the movement from 0 to +1), outlining the salient elements of Lithuanian community structure (the political, social-patriotic, and economic organizations), scrutinizing the structure of one Lithuanian village and its organization of rebellion (the movement from +1 to +2), and comparing communities that did not develop resistance with those that did.

From 0 to +1 in Lithuania under the First Soviet Occupation

The mechanisms that drive individuals from neutrality to unorganized, unarmed resistance are resentment formation, status rewards, focal points, and threshold behavior. The first three mechanisms cannot be properly understood without some historical and cultural background. This background is especially necessary for comprehending focal points. When the occupier is especially strong, a large set of resistance symbols specific to the occupier facilitates communication of resentment and risk acceptance and allows for coordination of expectations – and more likely rapid movement to +1.

by no means partisans in the sense of occupying a +2 position on the spectrum. Many were not involved in fighting the Soviets at all, but simply used the opportunity to wreak havoc and seek revenge on Russians, Soviets, and especially Jews. More comments on this follow in the section on Lithuanian Jews at the end of the chapter.

[4] Budreckis, in *The Lithuanian National Revolt of 1941,* reports that 4,083 Lithuanians died in the revolt while 8,000 were wounded. This means a casualty ratio of about 10 percent. In the 1918–1920 period, only 2,000 Lithuanians were killed. Thomas Chase gives figures of 4,000 dead and 10,000 wounded for the June revolt in *The Story of Lithuania* (New York, 1946). Other Lithuanian scholars believe these figures are exaggerated. Saulius Suziedelis believes that 800 dead might be the upper figure. See Saulius Suziedelis, "Thoughts on Lithuania's Shadows of the Past: A Historical Essay on the Legacy of War" <www.artium.lt/4/journal.html>.

Historical Background

In the course of the union between Poland and Lithuania, lasting from 1386 to 1795, the upper classes of Lithuania became almost entirely Polonized. The Lithuanian language and culture were left to the peasantry, which until the late nineteenth century was essentially devoid of a national consciousness. Even in the period immediately following the Russian incorporation of Lithuania in 1815, there was still little sign of any national awakening among any strata of the population. Only after the Polish-Lithuanian uprising of 1863 (the last time Lithuanians fought under Polish leadership) and the subsequent institution of a Russification policy did a Lithuanian national consciousness emerge.[5] The Russian Empire tried to separate the Lithuanians from the Poles, who were considered the instigators of the 1863 revolt. In order to accomplish this goal, it introduced Russian colonists, harassed the Catholic Church, and abolished the Latin alphabet. The attempt to replace Latin with Cyrillic went beyond an effort to simply reduce the cultural bonds between Poles and Lithuanians. Larger goals involved replacing the local language with Russian, preventing Lithuanians from using their own presses, and establishing Russian censorship in Lithuania.[6]

Much of the small Lithuanian intelligentsia resisted this attack on the local language and culture. Here were the beginnings of a strong perception of ethnic hierarchy and a resulting emotion of resentment. Newly educated and literate, and often newly urban, Lithuanians came to experience the day-to-day feeling of subordination by being told what language, and alphabet, to use, among other humiliations. One special factor in the Lithuanian case was the close relationship between the new intelligentsia and the peasantry; the social origins of the Lithuanian patriotic intelligentsia were almost completely from peasant backgrounds.[7] The established middle classes were too Polonized, and the towns were too Jewish, to be enthusiastic national allies.

[5] For a general history of Lithuania in the nineteenth century, see C. R. Jurgela, *History of the Lithuanian Nation* (New York: Lithuanian Cultural Institute, 1948).

[6] For a discussion of Russian-language policy in the tsarist period, see David Laitin, Roger Petersen, and Jon Slocum, "Language and the State: Russia and the Soviet Union in Comparative Perspective," in Alexander J. Motyl, ed., *Thinking Theoretically about Soviet Nationalities* (New York: Columbia University Press, 1991), pp. 129–168.

[7] Miroslav Hroch, in a fascinating study, concludes that "no section of the bourgeoisie took part in the national movement." Hroch compiled data on 260 active participants in the patriotic movement of the 1880s and 1890s from the editorial staffs of secret newspapers, patriotic stu-

Of 257 leading patriots of this period, only 8 had been born in a town.[8] Given their background, Lithuanian patriots were likely to involve the countryside in their efforts to preserve the Lithuanian culture and language. In practical terms, these patriots created reading circles in the rural areas.[9] With the Russian ban on Lithuanian publications and the Latin alphabet, the operation of these reading circles required a secret organization for smuggling books across the border and distributing them throughout the countryside (the penalty for book smuggling was exile to Siberia).[10] Thus, as early as the 1880s the peasantry was gaining experience in forming clandestine organizations against an "occupier."[11] Furthermore, this early struggle helped develop concepts of status rewards for antioccupation activity and negative status rewards for cooperation. Book smugglers became the first "national heroes." The following passage from a pro-Lithuanian history is typical of the Lithuanian view, both past and present, of these smugglers:

Two heroic types, which became national symbols to future generations, arose during this period. The first was the man, the *knygnesys,* or "book-carrier," who smuggled literature across the heavily guarded border. In doing this, and in spreading Lithuanian literature throughout the land, he was risking his life. He was pursued, persecuted, and not infrequently punished by exile from Lithuania. But he never lost his courage and was ultimately victorious over the huge, oppressive Russian administration.[12]

The image of the courageous Lithuanian fighting the "huge, oppressive Russian," still a vibrant image in 1991 (as described in Chapter 9), became established for the first time. In addition, those who went about reading the

---

dent associations, and lists of the secret book distributors. He draws his conclusions from the locations of patriotic activity and the concentrations of patriots' birthplaces. See Miroslav Hroch, *Social Preconditions of National Revival in Europe: A Comparative Analysis of the Social Composition of Patriotic Groups among the Smaller European Nations* (Cambridge: Cambridge University Press, 1985), pp. 86–97.

[8] Ibid., p. 91.

[9] Hroch finds that there was a very dense network of secret reading circles in the rural areas of Suvalki, for example. Ibid.

[10] The tsarist enforcement of the book-smuggling ban and efforts to break up the book-smuggling circles are described by Alfred E. Senn, "Tsarist Authorities and Lithuanian Book-Smuggling," *Journal of Baltic Studies* 11 (1980): 334–340.

[11] The extent of this activity can be seen in the fact that between 1900 and 1902 alone over 56,000 books were confiscated by the Russian police at the border. See Alfred E. Senn, *The Emergence of Modern Lithuania* (New York: Columbia University Press, 1959) , p. 9.

[12] Jack Stukas, *Awakening Lithuania: A Study on the Rise of Modern Lithuanian Nationalism* (Madison, N.J.: Florham Park Press, 1966), p. 77.

Cyrillic press could be identified as nonparticipants. The Russian book ban allowed the Lithuanians to distinguish individuals along a spectrum of behavior.

The other heroic type was the journal writer. Again, the writing and distribution of these journals required extensive secret organization. The writers and editors came from two sources. The peasant-based patriotic intelligentsia, with appeals directed mainly to the peasantry, formed one wing,[13] while the Catholic Church, also a target of the Russification program, produced a second branch of secret nationalistic journals. Although many of the Lithuanian intelligentsia were not friendly to the church, opposition to the tsarist regime united even the priests and the radicals. Of course, the church also had its largest influence and a system of networks among the peasantry.

It is not so surprising that the Lithuanians developed national consciousness, resentment, and antioccupation symbols in the late nineteenth century. These processes were occurring among other nations in the region. The level of peasant participation and organization was unusual, however. This local and rural basis for resistance provided a strong foundation for the rebellions to come.

Lithuania in the Late 1930s

The resistance of the late nineteenth century helped produce the rebellion mechanisms that were operative in the late 1930s and 1940s.[14] As discussed in the previous chapter, one key mechanism in the movement of individuals from 0 to +1 on the spectrum is the application of positive and negative status rewards. These status rewards are connected to resentment formation and focal points. People must be sufficiently motivated in order to go out of their way to reward or sanction other individuals; this motivation is related to the

[13] In fact, the leading journal, *Ausra,* often attacked the nobility. Hroch, *Social Preconditions,* p. 87. The other main nonclerical journal was *Varpas,* socialist in orientation.

[14] Much important Lithuanian history is passed over for the sake of parsimony. A good source for the important period from 1917 to 1920 is Senn's *Emergence of Modern Lithuania.* For a general discussion of the interwar period in the Baltics as a whole, see the various articles collected in V. Stanley Vardys and Romuald J. Misiunas, eds., *The Baltic States in Peace and War, 1917–1945* (University Park: Pennsylvania State University Press, 1978). Also, Georg von Rauch, *The Baltic States: The Years of Independence, 1917–1940* (New York: St. Martin's, 1995). The most recent treatment of this era is Alfonsas Eidintas, Vytautas Zalys, and Alfred Erich Senn, eds., *Lithuania in European Politics: The Years of the First Republic* (New York: St. Martin's, 1998). Perhaps most importantly, I am passing over the complexities of Polish-Lithuanian relations in the interwar period.

level of antipathy against the occupier. States can sometimes successfully create this emotion, although the task is hard if there are little existing history and animosity to build on. Second, in order to be able to apply the sanction or reward, there must be some way to identify supporters and nonsupporters. Optimally, there will be some sort of "litmus test" that allows identification of neutrals (0) versus resisters (+1). Certain "focal events," such as participation in elections, can be shown to serve as these types of identifying tests.

In Lithuania, the emergence of antioccupation resentments in the late 1930s began not with the Soviet occupation, but with the German occupation of Klaipeda (Memel) in March of 1939.[15] The German action caused an uproar not only through its consequences but also through its blatancy. Adolf Hitler himself came to Klaipeda to head a huge parade (including SA units and local German groups) and festival to celebrate the German takeover.[16] Local Lithuanian residents, fearing the future both in terms of employment and personal safety, fled to the interior cities. The reaction to this national affront and the flood of refugees produced descriptions like the following:

> The surrender of Klaipeda to Germany struck Lithuania with unprecedented effect. Never in its brief political renaissance, whether in the time of the early wars for independence or in the later months of decline, had a blow by an enemy caused the Lithuanian people to demand with such resolute unanimity the realization of national unity and the defense of the nation's liberty.[17]

Political factions of all stripes issued similar calls for united action to prevent the further loss of any Lithuanian territory.[18] On March 23, one day af-

[15] Klaipeda is one of the best seaports on the Baltic coast, and Lithuania's only seaport (about 70 percent of all Lithuanian imports and exports passed through this port). The Germans wanted it not only for commercial and strategic reasons, but also because a large German population had long been established there. The Lithuanians formally acceded to a German ultimatum on the Klaipeda issue on March 22, although a de facto takeover had already been accomplished by that time.

[16] Interview 14. This respondent, a student at the business university in Klaipeda at the time, was present at the parade and saw Hitler and his entourage on March 19. He left Klaipeda for Kaunas as soon as possible, seeing no future for Lithuanians in the area. He was one of 12,000 refugees.

[17] Leonas Sabaliunas, *Lithuania in Crisis: Nationalism to Communism, 1939–1940* (Bloomington: Indiana University Press, 1972), pp. 113–114. Sabaliunas's book is the definitive work on this brief but critical period in Lithuania's history.

[18] Although there was unity among political groups on the necessity to unite the population against foreign aggression, there were some more complicated political maneuverings at this time.

ter the formal concession to the German ultimatum, fourteen military, political, professional, and youth organizations published appeals to the nation asking citizens to carry out their duty to the country.[19] The appeal of the veterans of revolutionary wars was more blunt: "We shall not bear disgrace. Our descendants would curse us if we did not show that we value the Freedom of our Country more than our lives. We must defend ourselves by all means! Not a single foot of our land without a fight."[20] Newspapers imaginatively manipulated the guilt of noncontributors. They constantly published stories about old women who donated their savings to the defense fund, drunkards who gave up drinking so they could contribute the money used on alcohol, or smokers who gave up smoking.[21]

State efforts in propaganda were even more creative. Teachers were to encourage their pupils to sacrifice the money they usually spent for candy and the movies. Furthermore, children were directed to write letters like the following:

> Dear parents! I know that our beloved Country Lithuania is in danger, because there are many enemies that wish to smother its free prosperity. Because you love me more than anything else, it is your ardent desire that I never be a slave. I love the country where I was born, I love the tombs of our ancestors, and I do not want our heroes' eternal rest to be in a subjugated Fatherland.[22]

The state also threatened the wealthier strata of Lithuanian society. A warning went out that the list of donors would be reviewed and action would be taken against those not contributing their fair share.

But did these appeals to honor dead national heroes have any effect? In Lithuania, there seemed to be success. Most importantly, the call to defend the nation increased the membership of several social-patriotic organizations that would later facilitate the growth of resistance throughout the nation. For example, the Union of Sauliai, an organization that combined the duties of the national guard with social activities such as choirs, theatrical clubs, libraries, and orchestras, increased its ranks by 10,000 members.[23] Participation in military training in secondary schools increased dramatically in the

---

[19] Sabaliunas, *Lithuania in Crisis,* p. 116.
[20] Translated from *Lietuvos Aides,* March 28, 1939, p. 5, by Sabaliunas, ibid.
[21] Ibid., p. 132.
[22] From *Karys,* April 13, 1939, p. 479, translated by Sabaliunas, ibid., p. 133.
[23] An extensive discussion of the Union of Sauliai follows shortly.

months following the Klaipeda takeover. Youths aged fifteen to twenty went on lengthy trips to practice tactical maneuvers; they were given rifles and, in some instances, taught to use explosives. Furthermore, the Lithuanian Boy Scouts, Girl Scouts, and their adult leaders greatly expanded their efforts, becoming more militarized in the process.[24] Both organizations began teaching courses on sanitary services necessary for combat support, antichemical and antiaircraft defenses, and medical aid. Of course, their propaganda work and patriotic pressure on their parents also expanded during this time period. On the eve of the Soviet occupation, Lithuanian society had developed somewhat of a "fortress mentality." Despite some political infighting, the population had effectively moved to the +1 position on the spectrum. Although Lithuania remained independent, significant numbers of individuals were contributing to defense funds or participating in social organizations that were gearing the activities of their memberships toward antioccupier military activity.

Lithuanian prewar anti-German mobilization is a good illustration of how elites, both in state and nonstate institutions, chose and created symbols to establish observable acts of resistance. As the state was not occupied, this accomplishment is hardly surprising. In the first Soviet occupation, mobilization would be a great deal more difficult.

The First Soviet Occupation, 1940–1941

At the beginning of the Soviet occupation, very few Lithuanians engaged in resistance activity. In large part, this was due to the gradual nature of the takeover – the Lithuanians did not realize they were being occupied until after the fact. Furthermore, the Soviet arrests of the leadership of almost every social-patriotic group in the nation helped to retard response. Despite these obstacles, within a year of occupation Lithuanian society had again moved to a +1 position and a very significant proportion of individuals had moved into clandestine resistance organizations (+2).

Although the Soviet takeover of Lithuania in the summer of 1940 was remarkably smooth, especially in terms of keeping the local populace pacified, the same cannot be said for the day-to-day occupation policies of the Sovi-

[24] Sabaliunas, *Lithuania in Crisis,* p. 136. The Scouts in Lithuania at that time were a more extensive organization than is commonly found today in Western nations. Membership and activities often continued into adulthood. The relationship to the state was also much different.

ets. The Soviets could move without attracting much attention because most of the public effort, as well as the diplomatic effort, was focused on Germany and the loss of Klaipeda. Of course, the Germans had attacked neighboring Poland on September 1, less than six months after the Klaipeda incident. Before attacking Poland, the Germans had offered the Lithuanians the return of Vilnius in exchange for a simultaneous Lithuanian attack on Poland. Lithuanians were well aware of Germany's aggressive intentions in the region. For all these reasons, Germany, not the USSR, was the focus for many Lithuanians.[25]

Even when the Soviets became the focus of attention, they managed to cleverly deflect animosity. When they pressured Lithuania into signing a mutual-assistance pact on October 10, 1939, they made sure the meaning of the pact would be clouded by making the return of Vilnius part of the deal. The popular celebrations that broke out with the return of the historical capital of Lithuanians overshadowed any consideration that this might be the first step in a total Soviet takeover.[26] Although one clause of the mutual-assistance pact allowed the Soviets to place 20,000 troops on Lithuanian soil, these soldiers were stationed in such a way that the Lithuanian population hardly ever encountered them, at least in the early months of their presence.[27] Additionally, the Lithuanian government was still free to deal with local Communists in any manner they saw fit.

When the Soviets did move, they acted so swiftly and so ruthlessly that

[25] A couple points of interest: in the secret protocols of the Molotov-Ribbentrop Pact of August 23, 1939, Germany was supposed to gain control of Lithuania; it was only in the supplementary provision of September 28 that Lithuania was allocated to the Soviet sphere. The Lublin province of Poland was given to the Germans in terms of compensation (the Germans also gave the Soviets $7.5 million in gold as part of the deal). The Germans apparently lost interest in Lithuania after the Lithuanian government refused to participate in the dismembering of Poland. The Baltic countries had gauged that the best strategy for maintaining control of their own states lay in a policy of neutrality; they hoped that they might form a neutral zone in the balance between Germany and the USSR and believed that siding with one power or the other would disrupt the chances of success of this strategy. Alexander Dallin discusses the Baltic efforts at strategic positioning in "The Baltic States between Nazi Germany and Soviet Russia" in V. Stanley Vardys and Romuald J. Misiunas, eds., *The Baltic States in Peace and War 1917–1945* (University Park: Pennsylvania State University Press, 1978), pp. 97–109. For information on the internal workings of German policy on the Baltic, see Julius P. Slavenas, "General Hans von Seeckt and the Baltic Question," pp. 120–125, also in the Vardys and Misiunas volume.

[26] Vilnius was often described as the "Jerusalem" of Lithuanians. Its importance and meaning can be appreciated by reading Adolfas Sapoka, *Vilnius in the Life of Lithuania* (Toronto: Lithuanian Association of the Vilnius Region, 1962).

[27] Interview 11, among others.

the population was completely stunned and without information.[28] The order of events can be quickly summarized:[29]

May 1940	Lithuania is accused of breaching the mutual-assistance accord.
June 14	Soviets present ultimatum demanding that the current Lithuanian government be replaced by one more favorable to Moscow.
June 15	Lithuanian government accepts the ultimatum; President Smetona flees the country; 300,000 Red Army troops begin crossing the border.
June 15–30	Secret police established under Antanas Snieckus; Communists gain control of regular police; all talk of an "occupation" is banned. Lithuanian Nationalist Party is closed; Communist affiliation is legalized.
July 1	Parliament disbanded.
July 2	Commissar system established in the Lithuanian Army.
July 5	Announcement of new elections to be held on July 14.
July 6	Announcement of new election law. All candidates would have to be nominated at mass meetings at the county level, administered by the Communist Party.
July 7	First wave of arrests. Ex-ministers of government, editors of the press, heads of all social-patriotic organizations are silenced.
July 10	Nominations for elections completed. All candidates are from "The Union of Working People of Lithuania," which includes five groups, one of which is the Communist Party. Even at this time there is no official platform for the incorporation of Lithuanian into the Soviet Union.
July 13	Lithuanian National Guard leadership is liquidated.

---

[28] In addition, the timing of the takeover was planned to coincide with the German attack on France, so that international attention, and especially the attention of the Germans, would be almost totally lacking.

[29] This description of events is addressed in more detail in V. Stanley Vardys, "Aggression Soviet Style, 1939–1940," in Vardys, ed., *Lithuania under the Soviets: Portrait of a Nation, 1940–1965*, pp. 47–58 (New York: Macmillan, 1965). Also see Stasys Daunys, "The Development of Resistance and the National Revolt against the Soviet Regime in Lithuania in 1940–41," *Lituanas* 8 (1962): 11–15.

July 14	Elections (with an estimated 20 percent turnout) extended until ten o'clock in the evening of July 15.
July 16	State of emergency is declared.
July 17	Election commission claims that 95.1 percent of eligible voters turned out to cast 99.19 percent of ballots for "The Union of Working People of Lithuania."
July 20	Lithuanian Boy Scouts and other organizations are banned.
July 21	Elected Diet votes to ask for admission into the Soviet Union.

In the space of five weeks, the independent state of Lithuania ceased to exist, its top 2,000 social and political leaders had been carted away, every press had been silenced, almost every organization disbanded. The whole process had been accomplished with almost no resistance despite the fact that slogans calling Lithuanians to defend the nation to the death had filled the air only a few short months earlier. A state of confusion reigned in the country throughout this period. Several elements of this fog are worth mentioning. First, as mentioned, the public attention had been focused on German action in Klaipeda and Poland. Meanwhile, the Soviets had benevolently returned Vilnius. The overall result was to cloud discussion of Soviet intentions. Second, the Soviets had silenced all talk of an occupation. In the days before the elections, not even Communists mentioned any possibility of annexation. Third, the flight of the unpopular President Smetona on June 15 deflected attention from the Soviets as some people, embittered by years of authoritarian rule, thought that an incoming regime, even one controlled by Moscow, might be better than Smetona's. Fourth, the leaders of organizations were silenced. Fifth, the Soviets had managed to recruit some nationally popular figures into the June 15–July 21 temporary government. For example, Vincas Kreve-Mickevicius, a popular Lithuanian writer, became deputy prime minister (although he had absolutely no idea about Soviet designs on Lithuania).[30] His participation gave pause to both the general public and the intelligentsia. Furthermore, the Soviet takeover of some Lithuanian institutions was not always immediate, thus allowing for hopes that

---

[30] At one point in a conversation between Kreve-Mickevicius and Soviet Foreign Minister Molotov, the latter became so exasperated at the former's naiveté that he rudely spelled out that Lithuania would have to disappear. This enlightening passage from Kreve-Mickevicius's notebook can be found in Vardys, "Aggression Soviet Style, 1939–40," pp. 53–54.

Soviet action might leave some autonomy for the Lithuanians.[31] In the army, for example, political commissars were gradually introduced. The Soviets strategically destroyed the unity and potential for collective resistance action of Lithuanian army units by transferring Lithuanians from region to region while mixing in Red Army soldiers.[32]

By July 1940 the Lithuanians appeared to be a helpless and defeated nation. The calls to defend the nation's honor seemed to be pathetic boasts without foundation. Furthermore, with its government dismantled, its organizations banned, its press muzzled, its army controlled, and its leadership exiled, the possibilities for collective action could have been considered minimal. Yet, less than a year later, over 100,000 Lithuanians would participate in a revolt that would involve violent action against thousands of Soviet soldiers.

Explaining the Rapid Movement to Passive Resistance

Changes in Status Hierarchy and the Formation of Resistance

In the beginning weeks of Soviet occupation, Lithuanian society was effectively in a state of stunned neutrality, position 0 on the spectrum. The nature of the Soviet takeover accounted in large part for this phenomenon. Due to the return of Vilnius, the participation of Kreve-Mickevicius, and the lack of information, the general population did not immediately sense national subordination and a changed social-political hierarchy. For a time, Lithuanians hoped to retain significant levels of autonomy, and they reveled at the chance of being political masters in Vilnius. It seemed as though hierarchy 1 (see Figure 2.1) might be established. These hopes were soon dashed. Not only did Lithuanians come to perceive themselves as subordinate to the Soviet-Russian regime but also to the Jewish minority.[33]

In essence, the first Soviet occupation produced a perceived hierarchy resembling hierarchy 3 (see Figure 2.1). The Soviets-Russians clearly were on

---

[31] In effect, these actions blunted the formation of resentment.

[32] Interview 2. The interviewee was a commissar's assistant and thus had knowledge of Soviet strategies to prevent resistance in the armed forces. One statement was particularly revealing: "The units were all mixed up from one region to another, you couldn't trust anyone. I could only talk to myself and my wife."

[33] I have written about resentment formation against the Jewish population at length elsewhere. See Petersen, *Fear, Hatred, Resentment: Delineating Paths to Ethnic Conflict in Eastern Europe* (Cambridge: Cambridge University Press, forthcoming).

top of the hierarchy. With only a handful of local Communists to rely on, the Soviet presence could not manage to prevent perceptions of "occupier group" for very long. With the Red Army and NKVD at their command, the Soviets obviously could and did use force, visible force, to dominate the population. Soviet deportations, the increasing activity of the NKVD, the introduction of Soviet economic and political practices, the confiscation of land, and the threat of collectivization all hammered the facts of Soviet domination into the hearts and minds of the Lithuanian population.

This experience was exacerbated by the perception of a formerly subordinate group, Jews, rising to a position above Lithuanians. This perception was widespread; in fact, during my own fieldwork I heard several interviewees refer to the 1940–1941 period of Soviet rule as "the Jewish occupation." Although the vast majority of the Jewish population would suffer along with Lithuanians, the visibility of Jews in the Soviet governmental apparatus worked to change totally perceptions of the ethnic hierarchy.

Jews had not held a seat as minister or deputy minister for eighteen years, but during the first Soviet occupation they filled certain sections of the government and party. The minister of industry as well as 70 percent of its highest officials were Jews.[34] Of commissars appointed to nationalize industry, Jews made up a proportion several times that of their numbers in the general population.[35] Although holding only five of the twenty-one seats on the Central Committee, key city and regional party positions were often held by Jews, and not only in Kaunas and Vilnius but also in the smaller cities of Panevezys, Sauliai, Birziai, Utena, and Taurage.[36] Additionally, as was known to the population, some of the top Lithuanian leaders of the Communist Party (Snieckus, Didziulis, Gailiavicius) were married to Jews, a fact that made them not "fully Lithuanian" in the eyes of many in the population. The Jewish presence in the Komsomol was even higher, and the actions of these young Communists were very visible in the day-to-day life of the general Lithuanian population. Komsomol members worked as propagandists for the elections, and Jews probably composed more than half of the Komsomol representatives on the electoral commissions (forty-six of sixty-five in Vil-

[34] Juozas Prunskis, *Lithuania's Jews and the Holocaust* (Chicago: Lithuanian American Council, 1979), p. 13.

[35] Dov Levin, "The Jews and Socio-Economic Sovietization of Lithuania, 1940–1941, Part I," *Soviet Jewish Affairs* 2 (1987): 17–30; see table 1 on p. 19.

[36] Dov Levin, "Jews in the Soviet Lithuanian Establishment, 1940–41," *Soviet Jewish Affairs* 10 (1980): 21–37.

nius).[37] Komsomol youth also were sent into the countryside to organize "socialist competitions." Lithuanian peasants were forced to sit and listen to young Jews, who often spoke poor Lithuanian, on the merits of the Soviet state and how it would transform the countryside. Needless to say, these lectures were less than appreciated.[38]

Lithuanians were outraged more by the Jewish role in the NKVD than by any other aspect of Soviet rule. These important positions were doled out only to the most trusted elements in the prewar Lithuanian Communist Party, and because the tiny prewar party had perhaps been half Jewish, it was natural that Jews would fill the ranks of the security organs. Gladkov, the supreme commander of the NKVD in Lithuania, was a Jew, and the names of his Jewish lieutenants were well known to many in the Lithuanian population: for example, Finkelstein, Dembo, Rozauskas, Singeris, Sermanas, Todes, Komodos, Bloch, Margolinas, Slavin.[39] Jews who performed interrogations in the prisons became hated symbols. Additionally, Jews took a large number of the political positions within the Soviet army in Lithuania.[40] Again, it is not the number of Jews who occupied these positions that is critical. Rather, the fact that any of them occupied these positions of authority at all changed Lithuanian thinking about the nature of the ethnic hierarchy.

Clearly, many Lithuanians believed that they had become subordinate to Jews. At the very least, Lithuanians were no longer dominant in the ethnic hierarchy simply on the basis of being Lithuanian. The depth of resentment and the motivation to act against Soviet rule must, at least in part, be attributed to the perception of the installation of a completely unjust social-political hierarchy.

The First Forms of Resistance

Gradually, individuals began doing small acts of defiance to show their hatred of the occupier. The first forms of passive resistance were exhibited

[37] Ibid., pp. 31–32.

[38] Even within the Komsomol, relations between Jews and Lithuanians were not good. Levin reports the following memo from a Central Committee member visiting Panevezys: "Sitting by a table in the Komsomol club is a Jewish committee member and round him are Jewish comrades speaking Yiddish loudly, while on the other side of the club sits a Lithuanian committee member and round him are Lithuanian members speaking Lithuanian. The Jewish Komosomol members explained the phenomenon by saying that it is impossible to become friends with them (the Lithuanians) there." Ibid., p. 33. Other similar examples are cited.

[39] Ibid., p. 22; Prunskis, *Lithuania's Jews and the Holocaust*, pp. 12–13; Budreckis, *The Lithuanian National Revolt of 1941*, pp. 17–18.

[40] Prunskis, *Lithuania's Jews and the Holocaust*, p. 14.

through splashing graffiti on walls, singing and humming the national anthem, and rewriting prayers and poems in new, sarcastic forms. For example, after the new regime replaced classroom crucifixes with pictures of Lenin and Stalin, students began to recite the following new version of the Lord's prayer:

> In the name of Father Lenin and the son Stalin and their accursed Communism. Father Stalin, who art in the Kremlin, accursed be thy name, thy kingdom perish, thy will not be done in Moscow or Lithuania.... Hail Russia, full of woe, Stalin is with thee. Mocked art thou in Europe and mocked is your uncouth fruit Stalin. Holy Lithuania, our Mother, save us from the Asiatics. We will be grateful now and at the hour of our death.... I believe in stupid Lenin, the all-impotent creator of cruel Bolshevism, and in the devil's son Stalin, who was conceived in Georgia by latrine odors, suffered for his stupidity under Tsar Nicholas, was thrown into prison, almost died, and was not buried. When he alighted from prison, all hell opened up. On November 7, he arose from the dead, ascended into the Kremlin. From thence he came to judge innocent Lithuanians. I believe in the resurrection of Lithuania, communion with cultural countries, the banishment of the red bandits, Bolshevism's debacle, and in joyful life for all.[41]

Another form of passive resistance involved the printing and reading of pamphlets. Soviet intelligence reports indicate that the distribution of these leaflets began almost immediately after the establishment of Soviet rule. They called for the overthrow of communism, the boycott of elections, and the commitment of acts of sabotage.[42] They were often handwritten. The dissemination of these pamphlets was dangerous not only for those passing them out but also for those accepting. Often the leaflets were left in hallways or slipped into the pockets of individuals in movie theaters. As one could never know if a Soviet agent or sympathizer was present, accepting the material was a risk-laden act exhibiting anti-Soviet solidarity.

In the early stage of the occupation, political refugees in Germany founded the Lithuanian Activist Front. The LAF would go on to coordinate and centralize many of the resistance groups that had already formed at local levels. It sent out a plea to the Lithuanian people that echoed the refrains from the Klaipeda crisis: the honor of dead heroes must be defended, the Russian yoke must again be cast off, great sacrifices must again be endured.

---

[41] Budreckis, *The Lithuanian National Revolt of 1941*, pp. 16–17.

[42] Dokladnaia zapiska o raspostaneii kontrrevoliutsionnykh listovok na territorii Litovskoi SSR, 14 April 1941, pp. 1–2.

The LAF, however, combined the usual appeal to Lithuanian antioccupier norms with threats and promises concerning the possible future order. Witness this combination from the LAF appeal issued in the earliest part of the first occupation:

> Those who engage in the struggle without reservations and spare nothing to restore the freedom of Lithuania, who are determined to sacrifice all, even their lives for the freedom of Lithuania, these will also be the master of the new Lithuania. From these fighters will be formed the Government of the new Lithuania, and the social order of the new Lithuania will be based on them. The new Lithuania shall not be one of the lax ones and jellyfish, not one of the lackeys of the party politicians, or led by the plutocrats, but one of the united will of determined men, the best sons of the nation, of those who risked their blood to deliver the new Lithuania. Generation after generation will remember them with honor as the memory of the heroes of the nation.[43]

Even after a few weeks of the new Soviet regime, the slogans of the Klaipeda crisis and traditional anti-Russian attitudes were diffusing throughout Lithuanian society. Individuals were exhibiting their willingness to absorb risks in a multitude of small ways.

Focal Points and Status

Whereas this type of diffuse activity is necessary for creating an atmosphere conducive for resistance, it is insufficient to prepare a society for massive resistance. Consider the following example. Ten individuals are riding on a bus when one of them begins humming the national anthem. Then a second individual joins in. Undoubtedly, these two individuals will reward each other will a certain positive status; they have revealed that they are supporters of at least passive resistance under conditions of risk. But what of the other eight individuals on the bus? The two that were humming will probably not go out of their way to sanction the nonhummers as neutrals or collaborators. The latter will not become identified as neutrals or suffer any sanction for their neutrality.

---

[43] "Lithuanian Activist Front Appeal: All Forward Together to Create a New Lithuania. July–August 1940," in Thomas Remeikis, *Opposition to Soviet Rule in Lithuania* (Chicago: Institute of Lithuanian Studies Press, 1980).

The movement from 0 to +1 on the spectrum requires events that will overcome the murky nature of low-level resistance. There must be "focal events" that facilitate an identification process and the capability not only to confer positive status rewards but also negative status penalties. The first such focal event occurred even before the formal Soviet occupation began with the doctored elections of July 14, 1940. The Soviets went to great lengths to force all citizens to vote in this election. The new election laws passed a few days earlier required mandatory voting, the polls were held open an extra day, and aliens and teenagers were allowed to vote.[44] Clearly, the Communists wanted to create a large turnout to prove to wavering individuals that the regime had overwhelming legitimacy and that resistance was futile. Perhaps more important, all passports were to be stamped upon entering the polling place in an effort to provide the regime a method of identifying noncooperators in the general population.

At the same time, however, the first Lithuanian resisters were using the election to identify and discourage possible collaborators or neutrals. Although even at this late date the general Lithuanian population was unsure of the ultimate Soviet design, there was a general awareness that the elections were fraudulent. Small patriotic groups handed out pamphlets pleading:

> Son of the enslaved Fatherland! Today the hour has struck for you to show that you are a Lithuanian. A real Lithuanian prefers death, rather than raise his hand for Lithuania's traitors. Do not go into the voting hall, because there you will be forced to betray brothers, freedom and faith. . . . Down with Lithuania's traitors. Their fatherland is Moscow.[45]

The election helped reveal positions on the spectrum. Those who willingly voted might be identified as neutrals, if not −1. Those who resisted Soviet threats and did not show up at the polls showed themselves as sympathetic to resistance, as +1 in effect. Only an estimated 20 percent of the population participated. In some settings, such as the University of Kaunas, the elections were met with ridicule and almost total nonparticipation; participants were met with ostracism from fellow students.[46] The election's effect was somewhat blunted by the confusion created by the Soviet's rapid takeover, but it certainly allowed many Lithuanians a rough, early means of gauging

---

[44] Vardys, "Aggression Soviet Style," p. 57.
[45] Circular from July 8, 1940. Cited in Budreckis, *The Lithuanian National Revolt of 1941*, p. 24, n. 2.
[46] Interview 9.

the percentages of cooperation and noncooperation necessary to estimate the costs and benefits of low-level resistance. A given Lithuanian could see the level of nonparticipation in this election (despite announced percentages) and realize that many others were supporting passive resistance.

Other focal events added clarity to the situation. The new Soviet regime required compulsory grain deliveries. For propaganda purposes, the Communists wished to create cavalcades of grain wagons complete with red banners to bring in this grain.[47] Again, those who participated in such parades could be identified while those who ignored Soviet threats and delivered their grain another day (it was impossible to avoid the tax altogether) showed themselves as sympathetic to resistance. When the cavalcades were often composed of only a few grain carts that were jeered by the local populace, as frequently happened, individuals could gauge the level of anti-Soviet sentiment and willingness to resist in their community.[48] Thus events organized by the occupier to convince the population of regime strength and to identify noncompliers can be used by the resistance for the very same purposes.

While the regime attempted to organize focal events, so did Lithuanian patriotic groups, and with much greater success. The Scouts and the Catholic high school youth groups organized the All Souls' Day demonstration of 1940, a watershed for the resistance. All Souls' Day is a tradition held on November 2 of every year to honor the dead. People gather in the cemeteries to sing songs, light candles, and say mass. In 1940 the center of attention for All Souls' Day was at the memorial for those who had died for Lithuania's independence. The event was attended in Kaunas by 20,000 who sang many hymns but one particular hymn over and over: "Mary, Mary, make our slavery lighter, save us from a dreadful enemy."[49] The militia then responded by beating members of the crowd with rifle butts and making arrests. The crowd would dissolve but then suddenly appear at other grave sites to sing as a demonstration of resistance.[50] The event accomplished two purposes.

[47] Budreckis, *The Lithuanian National Revolt of 1941*, p. 17, describes the failure of such a cavalcade in Marijampole.

[48] Both the elections and the grain deliveries, as well as the August 1940 teachers' conference at which an open demonstration of Lithuanian patriotism occurred, are discussed by Juozas Brazaitis in a 1953 testimony before the U.S. Congress. Excerpts can be found in Joseph Pajaujis-Javis, *Soviet Genocide in Lithuania* (New York: Maryland Books, 1980), pp. 62–63.

[49] In popular consciousness, the "dreadful enemy" of this verse was firmly identified with Russia.

[50] Interview 9. The respondent was head of the national Catholic youth group, Ateitis, and thus one of the organizers of the event. Also, see Daunys, "The Development of Resistance," pp. 13–14.

The Scouts and Catholic high school groups that organized it had visited many homes in Kaunas asking people to come; thus, individuals were again forced to reveal their position on the spectrum. Perhaps many people would have liked to have moved back into a position of comfortable neutrality, but events like All Souls' Day did not let them. In addition to identification, the event also served to heighten the status value of resisting.

The Soviet regime revealed itself as so corrupt that the population became anxious to recognize new leaders taking risks in their communities. The national leader of Ateitis – the Catholic youth organization that was engaging not only in passive resistance but had also been trying to develop more organized (+2) resistance – described the effect of All Souls' Day in the following manner:

> From this event we found out one thing. Even in a cemetery we cannot sing. This meant complete occupation. Even innocent things would not be allowed. It was clear that we would have to do things in a stronger manner. Lithuanians began saying we have no life, and they started to hate. And that was the reason that I did not need to organize, for by themselves the people started organizing. News started to come in that there was another group organizing, that there is another leader organizing. And we [those already organized at a +2 level] did not touch them. We said OK. It came from common sense that people needed to start organizing.[51]

After this event, it is safe to claim that most of society had moved from the 0 position on the spectrum to +1. A clear hierarchy formed, one in which the new Soviet authorities, many of them Russian or Jewish, demonstrated a dominant position through the use of force. The high level of resentment and the related intensity of motivation to accept risk became evident.

Threshold Behavior and the Interaction of Mechanisms

"I will resist if X percent of others do": this statement is the essence of the threshold mechanism. In the 1940–1941 Soviet occupation, resentment formation, status rewards, and focal points all served to push average Lithuanians past their "tipping points" into roles of passive resistance. The pre-Soviet Lithuanian government's efforts to mobilize the population against possible German attack provided deepened myths of "heroic Lithuanian re-

[51] Interview 9.

sisters." The latter factor helped make Lithuania a nation with status rewards and sanctions. Figures 2.4 and 2.5 illustrate why high-status societies would be expected to more rapidly move into high levels of passive resistance than low-status societies. Status rewards raise the value of communicating one's antiregime orientation. The required percentage of others, the X percent, is likely to decline in a high-status environment. Given the level of resentment and the high-status payoffs, a relatively low percentage of participation of the population could trigger the action of an average Lithuanian. Most Lithuanians had several indicators to help judge the numbers of those engaged in passive resistance. Graffiti, parodied prayers, and underground leaflets provided signals, as did the boycott of elections and grain cavalcades. This information assured the bulk of the population that the numbers of those already engaged in anti-Soviet action were sufficient to protect them from sure retaliation; these numbers assured Lithuanians that they could act on their emotions of resentment and their desire for status. The result could be seen in the massive participation on All Souls' Day, a focal event indicating that the general "tipping point" had been passed and society was ripe for the development of more-extensive forms of rebellion.

The role of culture within strategic action should be emphasized. Even with motivation and high-status payoffs, the rapid movement from 0 to +1 seen in Lithuania would not have been possible without certain symbolic events specific to the Soviet-Russian-Communist occupation of Lithuania. Consider the revised version of the Lord's Prayer quoted earlier. It is hard to imagine that such a prayer would have been so quickly constructed against a German or a Polish occupier. In fact, regions of Lithuania had been occupied by both Germans (Klaipeda) and Poles (the Vilnius region) without this type of resistance event. The religious nature of the prayer could not have carried the same weight against a Catholic occupier; in fact, it may have seemed blasphemous. Likewise, another occupier would not have gone out of its way to challenge the All Souls' Day observance, and another occupied people may not have gone out of its way to observe it so forcefully. The clash of symbolic sets of the two sides seemed to be on an inevitable collision course. Referring to Figure 2.2, Lithuania's symbol set, pervaded by Catholicism and anti-Russian resentment, seemed bound to produce a set of coordinating symbols even with the decapitation of the Lithuanian elite and the disbanding of open organizational life. Chapter 5 provides a comparison with the German occupation, in which the course of events flowed very differently.

The stage was now set for the crucial movement on the spectrum of resistance. In the course of a year, tens of thousands of Lithuanians would belong to clandestine groups ready to avenge their nation.

From +1 to +2 during the First Soviet Occupation

At the beginning of the Soviet occupation, a small group of émigrés and refugees in Germany named themselves the Lithuanian Activist Front and issued an appeal noted earlier that contained the following passage:

> Let us not waste time but start to create the links of a secret activist chain, groups and units in every Lithuanian village, town, office, factory, in the army and every other place wherever it is possible. Do not expect any particular urgings or directives from above, under the present circumstances, when the leaders of the activists are specially shadowed and watched by the enemy, when they are arrested and imprisoned, the proper directions from above might not arrive. Each one should take independent initiative. Everyone who is determined must find around him some trustworthy friends of the same ideology and should stand at the head of them as their leader and establish contacts with the nuclei of the neighborhood shock organization.[52]

It may seem that Lithuanians heeded this appeal because clandestine resistance organizations did develop locally much in the way the document prescribes. Any causal effect of this appeal is highly dubious, however, not only because few people heard it but because there was really no other way to develop such an organization. Individual Lithuanians were caught in the classic situation of the potential rebel: high uncertainty, high risk. The national leadership had been removed, organizations had been banned, and newspapers and radio stations had been muzzled. Lithuanians did the only thing they could do: they examined the clues emanating from their local environment and acted upon them. Despite similar resentment of the occupier, individuals acted differently depending on the signals they received from their respective communities.

[52] "Lithuanian Activist Front Appeal: All Forward Together to Create a New Lithuania, July–August 1940." Although not directly relevant to the point here, it should be mentioned that this document also contained some fascist and pro-Nazi elements (the two are not the same thing). The document was written in Germany and homage was paid to Hitler's government, some of it simply as appeasement and perhaps some of it as a matter of organizational ideology.

Examining these sets of signals by diagramming the configuration of membership groups within specific communities requires knowledge of groups that permeated Lithuanian society.

Political Groups in Lithuania

The history and nature of political parties during the period of Lithuanian independence can be divided into three eras: 1920–1926, 1926–1938, 1938–1940. After independence was established, the Catholic bloc controlled a majority of seats in the Constituent Assembly, 59 out of 112. This bloc was composed of the Farmers' Union, the Federation of Labor, and, by far the most important, the Christian Democratic Party. The Catholics' policies were progressive compared with those the Nationalists would develop but less radical than the other two major parties – the Populists and the Social Democrats. The Populists, occupying the middle area of the political spectrum and 29 seats in the Assembly, were prevented from cooperation with the Catholics by questions concerning church-state relations. The Social Democrats, holding only 14 of the 112 seats,[53] relied primarily on urban workers and were openly hostile to the Catholic Church.

Catholic dominance held until 1925, when domestic problems became compounded by international Catholic politics. In 1925 the Vatican concluded a concordat with Poland that in effect recognized Poland's claim to Vilnius (Wilno or Vilna) over that of Lithuania. The Vilnius question was paramount in Lithuanian politics, and the Catholic parties could not live down their connection to the Vatican. The result was that a leftist coalition of Social Democrats and Populists took control of the government in May 1926.[54] The new government quickly embarked on a program of concessions to the minority parties (their coalition partners), the lifting of restrictions on civil liberties (which produced an increase in the activities of the Communists), dismissal of Catholics from office, and a reduction in the size of the military. The unrest of this period and the nature of the leftist agenda gave conservative forces an excuse to seize power. On December 17, 1926, military officers seized the government and the authoritarian rule of Antanas Smetona commenced.[55]

---

[53] The remaining 10 seats were held by minority parties: 6 by Jews, 3 by Poles, and 1 by a German. Communists held no seats but were legal at the time.

[54] Populists and Social Democrats garnered 37 of 85 seats while the Catholic parties fell to 30 seats. Minority parties, totaling 13 seats, sided with the leading coalition to form a majority.

[55] For details on the coup, see von Rauch, *The Baltic States,* p. 120. Smetona, not a military

Smetona and his followers had neither the stomach nor the desire to institute German-type fascism.[56] For instance, although they eventually outlawed all political parties except their own (the Lithuanian Nationalist Union), the parties continued to meet "unofficially."[57] Imprisonment, the threatened punishment for party activism, was seldom enforced. The newspaper of the Social Democratic Party was banned, but those of the Christian Democrats and Populists continued to be published in a mildly censored form.[58] The Communists were, of course, outlawed. As for the only legal party, the Nationalists, it never managed to develop widespread membership. It might be said that, on the whole, Lithuanians were not that concerned whether political parties were banned. They had seen them in action for six years and came away thoroughly unimpressed.

The policies of Smetona thus outlawed but did not eliminate political parties from the nation; however, the nature of their membership did substantially change. Without being able to recruit members or hold national rallies, political participation in the countryside, never strong to begin with, was minimalized over the course of the following decade.[59] The semiopen meetings of the parties became more or less debating clubs for intellectuals in urban areas: their views and criticisms were widely known, but their links to locally based memberships greatly atrophied.[60]

Political parties resurfaced after the Klaipeda incident. The German

man himself, had been the first president and a prominent personality who lent legitimacy to the coup. As a university student in St. Petersburg, Smetona had been banished to Vilnius for nationalist activity. There, he joined with other Lithuanian nationalists to form the Tautininkai (Nationalists). The men of this small circle formed a large portion of the first Lithuanian government.

Catholics, who had just lost the majority in the Seimas, at first supported the coup, believing that there would be elections in another couple of years. Soon they came to oppose the regime, withdrawing from the government in early 1927.

[56] See von Rauch, *The Baltic States,* pp. 161–165, for a concise history of the Lithuanian presidential regime. Also see Sabaliunas, *Lithuania in Crisis,* chap. 3, "The Tenets of Modern Lithuanian Nationalism." For an interesting and sympathetic "literary history" of Smetona and his political predicament in this period, see Jurgis Gliauda, *The Agony* (Chicago: Lithuanian National Guard in Exile, 1984).

[57] The Social Democrats were banned in 1929, whereas other parties were not banned until 1935. All of the poitical parties had had little role to play in the period after the coup as the legislature never met.

[58] Interview 7. Respondent was a high-ranking member of the Populist Party.

[59] Interviewee 13, a Catholic priest, notes that there was little activity of Christian Democrats in this period in the rural areas.

[60] The only arena of Lithuanian society open to legal political activity was in the universities. The University of Kaunas was the only major university in Lithuania at the time. The Poles held the university of Vilnius until 1940.

seizure of the port created such a loss of prestige for the Nationalist government that it felt compelled to form a coalition government to deflect the public barrage. Four opposition leaders, from Populist and Catholic parties,
joined the cabinet four days after the surrender of Klaipeda. It was ironic because formally there were no Populists and Christian Democrats – the legal
ban against them was still in effect. With this greater breathing space for oppositional party action, a Patriotic Front composed of all political parties, except the Nationalists, was formed. Its stated goal was to prepare the nation
for defense against external aggression, but its desire to bring down the
Nationalist regime was obvious. In the rallies led by the Patriotic Front immediately following Klaipeda, it was hard to tell who was hated more –
Hitler or Smetona.

Thus, on the eve of the first Soviet occupation, political parties had
reemerged to criticize the Nationalist government and fire up patriotic sentiment against outside threats, but thirteen years of illegality, or semilegal-
ity, had helped reduce political party membership in the countryside, and
thus the majority of the nation, to relatively insignificant numbers and influence. It is important to note that while the pre-Smetona political parties
were weak at local levels at this time, they were also united in their goals
and outlook, both against the Nationalists and the Communists.[61] They did
not play a big role in forming local-level resistance but neither did they per-
meate Lithuanian society with dissension and disagreement. Also, the
Communist Party had been insignificant.[62] Lithuania did not suffer widespread polarization stemming from conflict with the extreme left.

Economic Groups

When considering economic activity in Lithuania in the late 1930s, the focus must be on rural society. Over three-fourths of the population was engaged in agriculture whereas only about 7 percent were occupied in industry.[63] Farm life in Lithuania was characterized by the small and relatively

[61] In the very earliest stages of the Soviet occupation, some Social Democrats may have
shown sympathies to the Communists; however, as shown by the composition of the Provisional
Government formed to take control after the German invasion, Social Democrats were participating in the Lithuanian Activist Front along with the rest of the Lithuanian democratic parties
during the first year of occupation.

[62] There were a total of 190 members of the Communist Party of Lithuania in 1940. See
Sabaliunas, *Lithuania in Crisis,* pp. 47–61, for a discussion of the Communist undergound.

[63] See table 3 in Ancietas Simutis, *The Economic Reconstruction of Lithuania after 1918*

equal size of landholdings and by informal cooperative arrangements between village members. The former attribute resulted from the land reform initiated in the wake of Lithuanian independence. Reconstruction consisted of two elements. First, Polish landowners, who had held 40 percent of Lithuanian farmland in the form of large estates, were stripped of their holdings. Their land was redistributed to create 38,747 new farmsteads and provide about 30,000 smaller farmers additional lots (there were a total of 287,000 farms).[64] Second, holdings were to be limited to smaller numbers of hectares. Originally 80 hectares was the upper limit, although the Nationalist regime moved that figure up to 150 in an effort to gain the support of wealthier farmers. The end result was that by 1930, 90 percent of the land in use consisted of small individual holdings between 5 and 90 hectares.[65]

Although the March 1922 agricultural laws broke up traditional village structures into isolated farmsteads, most small and medium-sized farmers often engaged in informal cooperative forms of agriculture. Before mechanization, tasks required more labor than a single household could provide. This was especially true for threshing grain and treading flax, two prevalent activities of the Lithuanian farmer. Commonly, neighbors would provide unpaid labor in exchange for a feast given by the recipient of the labor. The name of this social institution in Lithuania was *talka,* literally defined as "aid," or sometimes "collective action."[66] Although Lithuanian agriculture became more mechanized and much more individualized in the 1930s, the talka, as well as other forms of informal cooperative work, remained not only a strong informal economic institution, but more importantly, a strong social institution that could be used to code informal friendship networks. Talka groups were informal, and the membership of these cooperative groups shifted. The importance of this institution varied across Lithuanian regions.

(New York: Columbia University Press, 1942), p. 14. Note that these figures are from before the loss of Klaipeda and the return of Vilnius.

    [64] Sabaliunas, *Lithuania in Crisis,* p. 66.

    [65] Lithuanian Central Bureau of Statistics, cited as table 7 in ibid., p. 69. Over 50 percent of the farms were in the 10–50 hectare range, which was clearly above subsistence and clearly below a "big estate."

    [66] There are similarities here to the "bee" common to American agriculture or the *preljo* in Yugoslavia. See Juozas Audenas, "The Cooperative Movement," *Lituanus* 5 (March 1959): 13–17, for information both on talka and the cooperative movement. The cooperative movement was in some ways an outgrowth of the talka but on a more regional or national level. There were over 1,000 cooperatives in Lithuania by the late 1930s. They are not used here for economic "groups" as their size does not allow for face-to-face contact considered necessary for a community "group." Also see Simutis, *The Economic Reconstruction of Lithuania after 1918,* pp. 32–42, for more on all types of cooperatives.

Despite these complexities, these "help groups" are vital for the community mapping that follows.

Economic groups in urban areas consisted of factory units, craftsman associations, and trading associations. Due to their small number and size, urban Lithuanian economic groups are not addressed at great length in this chapter. With Vilnius occupied by the Poles up to 1940, the only large city in Lithuania proper had been Kaunas. Lithuanian industry was underdeveloped even in comparison to the other Baltic countries. Furthermore, union groups could hold little real power under Smetona's Nationalist regime, and the union of Christian Workers was more an adjunct of the Christian Democratic Party than a strong economic group with local roots and organization. Jews were disproportionately involved in trade and business: in the late 1930s, 83 percent of all businesses with gross trade of $15,000 or more were Jewish-owned.[67]

Social Groups

The social groups relevant to the organization of resistance in Lithuania in 1941 can be described in terms of their relationship to the Smetona government.[68]

The Nationalists clearly saw themselves in competition for Lithuania's youth with the Catholic Church, which had strong and extensive youth recruitment practices of its own. In order to meet the political challenge of the church and its Christian Democratic Party, Smetona's Nationalist Party developed "The Union of Young Lithuania" (Young Lithuanians or *jaunalietuvai*) to inculcate their values into youths over eighteen. The 40,000-member group in some ways resembled a leadership cult, as evidenced by the statement of its chief officer, Alfonsas Kaulenas: "The Union of Young Lithuania operates on an authoritarian basis. It knows only one leader – the Union Chief, the Nation's leader, Antanas Smetona. Consequently, all that fails to originate with his thought and the general direction he has decreed is alien and unacceptable to The Union of Young Lithuania."[69] Many youth

---

[67] These figures are derived from the Soviet nationalization of businesses in 1940 cited in Dov Levin, *Fighting Back: Lithuanian Jewry's Armed Resistance to the Nazis, 1941–1945* (New York: Holmes and Meier, 1985), p. 21. There were 1,595 businesses with gross turnovers of over $15,000 at this time. This implies that only about 270 non-Jews owned medium or large businesses in all of Lithuania.

[68] The discussion of social groups in Lithuania has been gleaned mainly from the interviews.

[69] Quoted in Sabaliunas, *Lithuania in Crisis,* p. 36. Also see Gliauda, *The Agony,* p. 82, for an example of the paternalistic relationship between the Young Lithuanians and Smetona.

disdained the Young Lithuanians not only for their dogmatic following of an authoritarian ruler, but because they greatly benefited from patronage in government-controlled jobs.[70] At the university, the Young Lithuanian organization was always quite small, especially in comparison with the Catholic group. At the University of Vytautas the Great in Kaunas in 1938, the largest Lithuanian university, the Catholic organization garnered 466 votes, the Young Lithuanians 177.[71] Clearly, the Young Lithuanians held little status among educated youth despite their privileges in future employment.

The next biggest supporters of the state could be found in the Scouts. The Scouts in Lithuania were more important politically than Scouts in Western countries. Many adult Scout leaders were part of the Lithuanian intelligentsia, and many more adults were involved with the organization in some way. The Scouts also had their own fraternity at the university, garnering 109 votes in the just mentioned election. They could not be compared with the Nationalists in terms of blindly following Smetona, but they were in general a patriotic organization that would support any independent Lithuanian government. Examples of their activity have already been mentioned in the discussion of the Klaipeda takeover.

One of the most important groups in the formation of local resistance was the Union of Sauliai, the name of the national guard.[72] To call this organization the national guard, however, is misleading because it was just as much cultural as military in purpose. Sauliai did prepare localities for defense, but it also had 139 choirs, 126 orchestras, 200 drama clubs, 300 libraries, and a newspaper with a circulation of 30,000.[73] Culturally the organization had some appeal for almost anyone, while politically it was too bland to offend very many. Originally, the organization elected its leaders democratically, but over time Smetona gained the power to pick and dismiss its leadership. At local levels, however, individuals were not conscious of this usurpation; they

[70] Interviewee 13 reports that in rural areas families with members of Young Lithuanians were looked down on as opportunists.

[71] These figures are from the *Lithuanian Encyclopedia*. They are an excellent way of determining organizational membership as students voted almost entirely according to fraternity affiliation. Affiliation was so important that all students wore a "beanie" of the color of their fraternal association. Neutrals, or unaffiliated students, wore white. Of 2,535 students at the university, about 1,600 voted in this particular election.

[72] Von Rauch translates Sauliu Sajunga as "Light Infantry Association." As he describes, "In its original form this association had been composed entirely of Lithuanian veterans. But from 1930 onwards it was expanded by incorporating the older members of the youth organizations, thus creating an armed force comparable to Mussolini's fascist militia, much to the annoyance of the regular army." My own impression is that any comparison of the Union of Sauliai and Mussolini's organization would be vastly overstated.

[73] Sabaliunas, *Lithuania in Crisis*, p. 133.

went about singing, music playing, and military marching with their neighbors and friends the same as always. Religiously, Sauliai often held its meetings and activities after mass, but in some urban units Jews and Lutherans also participated.[74] In many ways, Sauliai could be compared with the Scouts. Both were supportive of the Nationalist regime without being overtly political or tied to any religious group. Their major agenda was building the character of the population, a task that included heavy patriotic inculcation.[75]

While the Nationalist regime had developed blind followers in the Young Lithuanians and had co-opted the Scouts and the Sauliai, they existed in a state of "cold war" with the Catholics and their social groups. Fearful of the former power of the Christian Democratic Party, Smetona's regime had banned the popular Catholic youth group Ateitis (the members of this group are called Ateitininkai). Smetona saw this group as a Catholic recruitment instrument for Christian Democrats;[76] the promotion of Young Lithuanians was in large part an effort to create an alternative organization to wean away the youth. Despite the ban, Ateitis met secretly and probably grew in strength. In Panevezys in the mid-1930's, for example, 300 of the 900 students belonged to the underground Ateitis while only 200 belonged to the government-sponsored Scouts.[77] In the high school in Utena in 1940, the leader of the Scouts estimated that of the 700 to 800 students, only 30 to 40 were Scouts, whereas 80 percent were members of Ateitis.[78] The regime generally did not arrest the students, but arrests did occasionally happen. The Smetona regime drove this youth group "underground" without really hav-

---

[74] Interview JD.

[75] A couple of interesting points about the Union of Sauliai: first, the organization had been involved in some rebellion intrigue in the past and thus had some experience in clandestine operations. After the First World War, French troops occupied Klaipeda. The Union of Sauliai, in contact with the Germans at the time, proceeded to penetrate the Klaipeda territory in civilian clothes and take the territory without much bloodshed. See Julius Slavenas, "General Hans Von Seeckt and the Baltic Question," in V. Stanley Vardys and Romuald Misiunas, eds., *The Baltic States in Peace and War, 1917–1945* (University Park: Pennsylvania State University Press, 1978), pp. 123–125. Second, organizations similar to the Union of Sauliai also existed in Latvia and Estonia, only they were not as developed as a cultural organization.

[76] On the whole, whatever the recruitment procedure, most members of Ateitis were enthusiastic about their membership and duties. Within the interviews, there were a few isolated negative comments about the recruitment practices of Ateitis. One former member of Ateitis described his recruitment in personal conversation. When he was ten, he was invited to the church to a party with plenty of candy, where he was told he was in a group. This group met regularly and then, when its members reached a certain stage, they were told they were now members of Ateitis. Recruitment in terms of methods and selectivity varied from location to location, however, and other respondents said they tried to get into Ateitis but were rejected.

[77] Interview 11 (with a member of Ateitis).   [78] Interview 1.

ing the stomach to take harsh enough action to eliminate it. Thus, a situation developed in which teenagers were becoming acquainted with the basics of clandestine organization, asking themselves who can be trusted and who cannot, learning how to keep secrets. All of these skills would be put to use when the country was occupied by the Soviets. The experience of Adolfis Damusis, an interviewee, is illustrative here.[79] Damusis was imprisoned at the age of sixteen because of his activity in Ateitis. In prison, he met other Catholics and Communists who exchanged information on secret organization and tactics. Damusis later went on to become one of the key organizers of the June 1941 rebellion (discussed at length in the next chapter), and the network of young Ateitininkai members he had met in prison would help form much of the resistance leadership in that revolt. There were other Catholic social organizations, but none so relevant to resistance as the banned Ateitis group.[80]

Multiple memberships in these groups was possible but rare. By all accounts, the Young Lithuanians did not belong to other groups, not even Sauliai. For Ateitis, there was no rule prohibiting dual membership in Sauliai, but in practice it seldom occurred. At the university, all four groups (Young Lithuanians, Scouts, Sauliai, and Ateitis) had their own fraternities with little contact between them.

Employing the methodology outlined in the previous chapter, the following pages develop Venn diagram representations of community structure. Table 3.1 summarizes the most relevant groups by type. Lithuania was a rural country, and resistance groups seemed to sprout up spontaneously in many Lithuanian villages. For both of these reasons the social dynamics of rebellion in the villages is the foremost concern.

Dynamics of Rebellion in a Lithuanian Village

In one Lithuanian village, Svainikai, almost everyone became a supporter of resistance in one way or another. In the late 1940s, the Soviets destroyed this village, sending many of its inhabitants to Siberia. This history has been

[79] Interview 4.

[80] Other Catholic social organizations included a group for farming youth called "Spring-timers" (Pavasarininkai). They could legally meet if they had a permit and a policeman was present. Catholic professional groups replaced Ateitis membership for most Catholic university graduates. "Young Angels" was a group for pre–high school students. It should also be noted that all private Catholic high schools had been closed by Smetona, although the Catholic religion was taught at the public high schools.

Table 3.1. *Groups in 1940–1941 Lithuania*

Political	Economic	Social
Christian Democrats	Talka	Young Lithuanians
Populists	Associational groups	Scouts
Social Democrats	Factory units	Union of Sauliai
Nationalists	Other urban work groups	Ateitis
Communists		

gleaned from two independently conducted interviews in two U.S. cities.[81] The stories of the two interviewees were remarkably consistent.

In an interviewee's map of Svainikai depicted in Figure 1.1, each name represents a family farmstead with the numbers representing the amount of hectares of each farm (e.g., Stanikunas 50). It may seem remarkable that individuals can remember all the names and the size of the holdings of every family in the village they had lived in fifty years ago, but one must keep in mind the nature of Lithuanian rural life. Many of the families of Svainikai had been together in this village for hundreds of years. Farming operations, even in 1940, involved cooperative forms of agriculture. Thus, for almost 400 years the families of Svainikai had been working, feasting, and worshiping together. The amount of hectares owned by a family was the single most important factor in terms of both economics and status and is not easily forgotten.[82]

The fact that these maps can be drawn so easily underscores the fact that Lithuanian rural life involved a heavy amount of face-to-face contact. It was a society dominated by status rewards and social norms. The respondents' memories were also sufficient, with some disagreements of course, to map out economic, social, and political membership groups in the village (Table 3.2).

Economically, the village acted as a unit for threshing grain, which re-

[81] Interviews 5 and 9. Respondent 5 was interviewed three times, while only one interview was conducted with respondent 9.

[82] A couple notes concerning the map of Svainikai. Pereksliai is the neighboring village, found on the opposite side of the highway from the Giedrikas and Jutelis farmsteads. The highway leads to Panevezys, the nearest commercial center and fairly large town. The Suoja River is the eastern border of the village. The farmsteads also had significant hectares in woodland, a fact that later facilitated the survival of resistance fighters.

quired twenty-five to thirty people, but broke down into subgroup talkas for flax operations.[83] The subgroups were clustered by geography and size. Seven adjoining farms on the west side of the village, most of larger than average size, formed one cooperative unit. This unit included Eringis 60, Stanikunas 50N, Blinkevicius 15, Kanaverskis 20, Povilauskas 100, Giedrikas 70, and Giedrikas 80. Many of the generally smaller farms in the eastern half of the village, the two rows near the Suoja River, could be considered a second talka group. There were several familial associations within the village: Giedrikas 80 and Giedrikas 70 were cousins, Eringis 60 and Eringis 50 were distant cousins, Mikolauskas 35 and Mikolauskas 40 were third cousins, Povilauskas 40 and Povilauskas 100 were cousins, the Geidrikas and Mikolauskas families were related, and, finally, Banys 40N and Banys 40S were brothers, with Banys 25 being some distant relation. Although many members of the village were related, location and common size of farms were more important than family relations in terms of economic help groups. Proximity and compatible farm size were often decisive in forming cooperative relationships. Some of the functions of talka groups were time-urgent, such as completing the harvest before a coming storm. Other functions related to the shared use of horses and equipment: a farmer with eighty hectares would not be likely to transport his machinery and horses a considerable distance to form a reciprocal economic tie to a farmer with 10 hectares and little machinery and few, if any, horses.

Social group activity was dominated by the local Catholic church and the local Sauliai unit.[84] Citizens of Svainikai participated in both by singing in choirs and listening to lectures. All residents were Catholic, to one extent or another. The Union of Sauliai was represented in nine to eleven of the thirty-one farmsteads in the village (there was some disagreement between the respondents on two farmsteads). There were no local members of the Young Lithuanians. There were two members of the scouts: Eringis 60 and Mikolauskas 35. Eringis 60 was recalled as a superpatriot and a key organizer of resistance in the village. There was a very active Ateitis group in the nearby

[83] The crops included rye, wheat, oats, and flax, as well as hay for livestock. After the threshing was completed, there would always be a feast and dancing. Also, many fights broke out between younger men at these events. Notably, the size of the farms in Svainikai was considerably larger than the Lithuanian average.

[84] There was also a very active "Young Farmers" organization in Svainkai, but there seemed to be little connection between its membership and the formation of later resistance. After the Soviet occupation, it ceased to meet.

Table 3.2. *Group Memberships in Svainikai*

	No. of Hectares	LAF	Sauliai	Supporter	Scout	Political Affiliation	Comments
Zidomis	?						Moved in from outside area
Eringis	60	X	X		X		5th cousin to Eringis
Giedrikas	80	X	X				Cousin to Giedrikas 70
Giedrikas	70	X	X				Cousin to Giedrikas 80
Stanikunas	50	X	X				
Blinkevicius	15	X	X				
Kanaverskis	20						
Povilauskas	100			X			
Jutelis	70						"Uncultured"
Goncauskas	?			X			
Rimaitis	2						
Latovas	5			X	X		
Mikolauskas	35			X			Shot by either Soviets or partisans
Povilauskas	40			X		Nat.	2nd cousin to Mikolauskas 40

Name	Age			C.D.	Soc.	Notes
Eringis	50			X		Daughter in Ateitis and son active
Urbas	24			X		Daughter in LAF
Kuilanskas	40	X		X		Two daughters are supporters
Muzdeikis	?	X				"Uncultured"
Gasparka	20					Returned from United States
Urbas	30	X		X		Returned from United States, drunkard
Banys	25					
Urbas	60	X				Son in LAF; brother to Banys 40; related to Banys 25
Banys	40			X		
Urbas	60	X				Drunkard and "uncultured"
Bariunas	15					
Kuilanskas	15	X				Brother to Banys 40
Banys	40	X	X			
Sukys	30	X	X			
Sukys	15	X				
Mikolauskas	40			X		Son was very active
Stanikunas	50	X		X		

high school at Panevezis, and two or three students from that school lived in Svainikai.[85] These students would become active in the resistance movements. Overall, however, Ateitis could not play as significant of a role in Svainikai as in other communities that had their own high schools and locally based Ateitis groups.

The role of political parties in Svainikai was similar to the role they played in other rural Lithuanian villages: practically insignificant. Only three citizens were remembered as belonging to a party: Povilauskas 40 was a Nationalist, the southern Banys 40 was a Socialist, and Urbas 24 was a Christian Democrat.[86] None went on to play a prominent role in the development of resistance. In describing politics in Svainikai, one of the interviewees claimed that "in villages in my youth, the political parties were very dull; Smetona's party was not very interesting either. We had a normal life with no political pressures. It was a one-party system, but even that party did not seem too 'political.' Maybe the Populists and Christian Democrats were active in the cities."[87]

Svainikai was home to some special "personalities." Of course, one type of personality was the drunkard. Banys 25, Bariunas 15, and Povilauskas 40 were considered the drunkards of the village. Povilauskas was better tolerated because he would often butcher a cow or sheep and have a big feast for the village. The second type of personality was the "uncultured" man, whose deficiency was treated by Lithuanians almost in terms of a disease. Jutelis 70, Gasparka 20, and Bariunas 15 were hung with this collar. Another personality was the returnee from America. Urbas 30 and Banys 25 had worked in factories and been active in unions in the United States. Apparently, they returned spouting "socialist" ideologies. The result of all this was that they were shunned by the community. Zidomis had recently moved into the community and was not well known. The drunkards, the uncultured, the socialist Americans were all treated in a somewhat different manner than other members of the village.[88] They were not expected to join in community relations to the same extent, they were never trusted at the same level, they were never pressured to join in the resistance movements. In short, social

---

[85] For various reasons, not all students from Svainikai went to the same high school. Some went to high school far away, and their memberships there had little effect when they returned home.

[86] Urbas 24 had been imprisoned for political reasons.   [87] Interview 5.

[88] Perhaps Zidomis could be added to this list. He had come from another region after he had inherited the land through his wife's family. Neither interviewee knew much about him.

sanctions and status rewards were never applied to these "outsiders" in the same way as the core members of the community.

The beginning of the Soviet occupation was marked by the arrival of Soviet tanks along a nearby highway. Respondent 6, who went out to witness this Soviet entrance to the region, described it as a "big tragedy." He and his friends "went to see the machinery (tanks) come in. But few knew that it would be so terrible, so fanatical. For some it was not clear, but for my generation, my friends, it was clear that this was a total occupation. They began arrests, people began disappearing. It was clear." In Svainikai itself, the biggest problem became the total lack of information. Previously, news traveled through national organizations or papers and radio. Soon after their arrival, the new Soviet regime banned the Young Farmers and Sauliai groups (and all other organizations) and controlled all newspapers and radio. In addition to communications from foreign and national sources being cut off, the Soviet land policy hindered the flow of information even at the local level. The Soviet reform limited land ownership to thirty hectares. The confiscated land was turned over to landless rural laborers or very poor farmers. The landowners of Svainikai thus found their village permeated by new residents who may or may not be very sympathetic to the Soviets. No matter what their actual political orientation, these new residents were potential informers, and the long-term residents of the village could not meet or organize openly in their presence. Only the smallest of groups could meet inconspicuously. Thus the all-village threshing groups that had previously been such an important source of interaction and communication could no longer play the same role.

During the first months of occupation, the Soviet secret police did not pose a major problem in Svainikai. There had never been any local Communist in the village, so there were no ready local informants. Most of the resources of the new regime were tied up in the major cities, and the provincial regions saw little if any sophisticated effort by the NKVD at recruitment or infiltration. Still, as everyone had become aware of the deportation of Lithuania's leadership during July, the threat of NKVD action was real and could not be discounted by the local citizenry.

In sum, the residents of Svainikai found themselves in the classic position of the potential rebel. They were filled with loathing for the ruling regime, they were dominated by uncertainty, and they were operating under possibilities of high costs. Under these conditions, the men and women of the village were reduced to working within their smallest interactive environments.

Two distinct segments of the village were the first to act. One was composed primarily of members of the western talka group. It included Eringis 60, Giedrikas 80, Giedrikas 70, Stanikunas 50N, and Blinkevicius 15. This group was marked by a very high level of face-to-face contact, both economically and geographically; in addition, they were all members of the Union of Sauliai. As members of this organization, they had marched, sung, and pledged oaths together. Within this group, the figure of Eringis 60 deserves emphasis. In both accounts, he is seen as a "big organizer."[89] He had more extensive contacts than perhaps any other individual in the village: he was a member of Sauliai, a Scout leader, and a relative to families in other parts of the village. No one else held dual memberships in both the Scouts and Sauliai. This "superpatriot" became one of the leaders of resistance in the village.

An Ateitis group formed the basis for a second early-forming kernel of resistance. It included the son of Mikolauskas 40 and the daughter of Eringis 50 and was led by a demobilized military major living in the area.[90] This Ateitis group would only meet twice during its nine-month existence. Its adult military leader said that a war was coming anyway so it was best to lay back and see what would happen. This attitude was not accepted by the membership, and gymnasium youth began to form their own groups. The Ateitis members in the original organization were joined by the daughter of Urbas 24, the son of Eringis 50, and two daughters of Kuilanskas 40. Again, members of the group had high face-to-face contact: their respective farmsteads were adjacent, and undoubtedly these youth had participated in collective farmwork on innumerable occasions. Outside of the Ateitis members, the friends forming this circle were not members of social-patriotic groups such as Scouts or Sauliai.

Whereas these small segments of the population began their resistance in a spontaneous fashion, the rest of the village was apparently more reticent. Understandably, most residents of Svainikai wanted more information before acting. Only one forum for the exchange of information was available at the time – church services on Sunday mornings.[91] Respondent 5 relates

[89] The "big organizer," or activist (*veikejas*), fit an established type of Lithuanian character or role. The existence of this character type underlines the importance of status in Lithuanian society.

[90] There were about ten members of this group. I failed to get all of their names. Some may have been from neighboring villages.

[91] For a discussion of Soviet policy toward the Catholic Church during the first occupation, see Dennis J. Dunn, "The Catholic Church and the Soviet Government in the Baltic States,

the importance of these meetings: "We met mostly in small groups on Sunday after church. It was a tradition to go on walks after church. Most discussions took place then. It was a good opportunity to meet with university students and Sauliai members; much information was gathered here. From both youth and elders we could get prepared for something." As is evident from this passage, the dissemination of information concerning the local organization of resistance was a delicate matter. Nonetheless, other segments of the population began to join with the original patriots. Specifically, Mudzeikis 50, Urbas 60, Sukys 30, Sukys 15, and Stankunas 50 also came to participate. Significantly, these individuals were the remaining Sauliai members who were located in the eastern talka group. Very possibly, some normative effect among group members was at work here. In the end, every Sauliai member would be involved at the +2 level.

One important point that is unclear from the interview transcripts is the date the local resistance became part of the national resistance organization, the Lithuanian Activist Front. It is relatively clear that every Sauliai member, from both the eastern and the western talka groups, became a member of the LAF. Some of the youth, including the daughter of Urbas 24 and the son of Banys 40, also became sworn members. Interestingly, the farmers who did not belong to Sauliai were not listed as LAF members either. This fact is noteworthy because in both accounts of the village's history a third group of farmers came to play a support role that was functionally equivalent to that exhibited by the LAF members. This group consisted of Povilauskas 100, Goncauskas 50, Mikolauskas 35, Povilauskas 40, Eringis 50, Urbas 24, Kuilanskas 40. All were classified, by one or the other respondent, as "big supporters" willing to provide material goods or information. Although these men possessed an apparent aversion to official membership in organizations, they became part of the informal network of rebellion that permeated most of the village.

Who did not become part of this network? Only nine farmsteads in the village were clearly not active:[92] Zidomis, the outsider; Rimaitis 2 and Latovas 5,[93] the two smallest landowners by far; Banys 25 and Urbas 30; the social-

___

1940–41," in V. Stanley Vardys and Romuald Misiunas, eds., *The Baltic States in Peace and War, 1917–1945* (University Park: Pennsylvania State University Press, 1978), pp. 149–158.

[92] There was conflicting testimony concerning Banys 40N, Banys 40S, Urbas 60, and Jutelis 70. At least one of the informants listed each as possibly active in the resistance.

[93] As a general point of interest, perhaps the biggest discrepancy in the two given histories of Svainikai involved the death of Latovas. Informant 5 claimed he had been shot by the Sovi-

ists from America, Bariunas 15, a drunkard; and Gasparka 20, "uncultured." Only Kanaverskis 20 was a sizable landowner, a "nonoutcast" and a nonjoiner. Only two members of the "outcast" groups, Jutelis ("uncultured") and Povilauskas 40 (drunkard) were mentioned by at least one of the informants as a supporter of the local resistance. The "outcasts" were not part of the community in the same way. Under the high costs involved with occupation, they were not to be trusted. On the other hand, almost every nonoutcast in the village supported the resistance.

No actual fighting occurred in Svainikai, or in Lithuania as a whole for that matter, prior to the June 1941 rebellion. Resistance consisted of preparing and organizing for the long-anticipated German invasion and the opportunities it would provide to wreak revenge on the Soviets. The desire for vengeance was magnified by Soviet deportations occurring on June 14–21, the week prior to the German invasion. About 30,000 people, 1 percent of the total population, were brutally deported.[94] The Soviet action created intense hatred not only by its scale but also by its methods: the NKVD picked up the unsuspecting targets between one and four o'clock in the morning; whole families were deported, husbands were separated from wives and children from parents; the cattle cars used for transportation had no windows or benches. In Svainikai, the teacher of the local school was deported in spite of his socialist leanings. Large landholders from the surrounding villages were also deported. Thousands of Lithuanians fled their homes to avoid being sent to Siberia. Svainikai informant 9 was sleeping outside during this period to avoid arrest.

These deportations set the stage for the violence and chaos that would accompany the German invasion of June 21. In Vilnius, the radio station had been taken by Lithuanian rebels who broadcast the news of the German attack and simultaneous Lithuanian revolt across the country. With only the loosest connection to any central LAF leadership, the Svainikai rebels were on their own. They went in to the volost center to neutralize Soviet soldiers and activists. Along with rebel groups from neighboring villages, they took

ets during the second Soviet occupation, whereas informant 9 said he was accidentally shot by the LAF during the second occupation.

[94] This action was the beginning of what was intended as a deportation of 700,000 counter-revolutionaries, or 30 percent of the nation. Of course, the German invasion prevented its completion. For an English translation of Soviet Order 001223, "Basic Instructions on Deportations," see appendix 4 in Pajaujis-Javis, *Soviet Genocide in Lithuania*, pp. 224–229. In the same volume, see pp. 38–45 for a general discussion of the June 1941 deportations.

over the government offices, and organized a local police, and took Soviet soldiers into detention.

As can be imagined, the rebellion was highly chaotic and very violent. People who had been hiding in the woods for fear of deportation greeted the German attack with immense joy. Informant 9, an activist gymnasium student sleeping in the woods, heard the news on the radio and went with some of his friends to a neighboring town to buy whiskey in order to celebrate. His description of what happened on this journey illustrates a few of the salient aspects of this rebellion:

> The police chief arrested us because he thought we might get shot. So many people were just shooting because they didn't know what the hell to do. He said if I let you go home now somebody will shoot you because you are partisans. . . . but he let us go home and my mother was happy but my father said maybe they will now come to shoot us. Then they arrested my father, but we told the chief maybe we will help him.

In order to understand this passage fully, keep in mind that the police chief has been working under the Soviet regime and does not know at this point who will win out and what his position or punishment might be under the various possible future regimes. He is playing both sides of the fence – on the one hand, he treats the young Lithuanian partisan with leniency; on the other hand, he still goes about arresting the father, a partisan supporter. In either case, Soviet retention of power or successful Lithuanian revolt, he will be able to say he helped the winning side. The last statement, "maybe we will help him," refers to the fact that the son will intercede for the police chief with the local partisans if he in turn will release his father. This passage indicates that during the rebellion itself, as well as in the organization of resistance, the dominant features were uncertainty and high risk.[95] Furthermore, individual actions were calculated from signals emanating from the local environment. The police chief considered his future position in the community, whereas the informant was intermeshed with the activities of family and friends.[96]

---

[95] The Soviets' policy of murdering their enemies during retreat added to this risk. The Lithuanian Research and Studies Center has compiled documents on these actions in *Vengeance on the Run: Documents on Stalinist Atrocities during the First Week of the German-Soviet War, June 1941,* ed. Saulius Suziedelis (Chicago: Lithuanian Studies Center, 1988).

[96] I have also added this passage to illustrate a phenomenon that I have found throughout

Summary of Svainikai Village: Linking Theory and Substance

Most Svainikai families became organized to varying extents to resist Soviet rule. In terms of the spectrum of rebellion roles, the Svainikai community reached a high +2 equilibrium. What drove this outcome?

The general features of strong community helped facilitate movement toward rebellion. By Taylor's criteria – direct and many-sided relations, reciprocity, rough equality of material wealth, common beliefs – the village certainly qualified as a strong community. Obviously, there was a high level of face-to-face contact; some of the families had owned their land for almost 400 years. These characteristics created conditions for efficient communication and recruitment. For example, Sunday walks after church allowed members to circulate information and discuss possibilities for action. As the detailed histories and maps show, this strong community provided members a shared knowledge that could serve as a basis for common expectations and trust. Svainikai's small overall size allowed effective monitoring; the high amount of interpersonal contact produced status rewards as seen in the identification of "big organizers."

This strong community also possessed several specific structural features conducive to movement to +2. In Figure 3.1, Svainikai is divided into its four relevant subgroups (two talka groups, Sauliai members, and active youth and their families); through overlapping memberships, these four subgroups form the six subsets, identified here by the uppermost name in each list in Figure 3.1:

- The Eringis 60 subset comprises Sauliai members of the western talka group. The five members of this subset, along with the youth represented in the upper right cell, were apparently the first to move to +2. All five joined the LAF.
- The Povilauskas 100 subset contains the two members of the western talka who were not members of Sauliai; Povilauskas became a supporter, although not an LAF member.
- The Muzdeikis subset contains the other half of the set of local Sauliai members. The subset makes up about one-third of the eastern talka. Like

my study of the Soviet and German occupations in Eastern Europe: the ability of individuals to combine "partying" with violence. The June 1941 Lithuanian rebellion involved high casualties and drinking and singing. It is doubtful that such a combination of activities is unique to this case or to the region or even the time period.

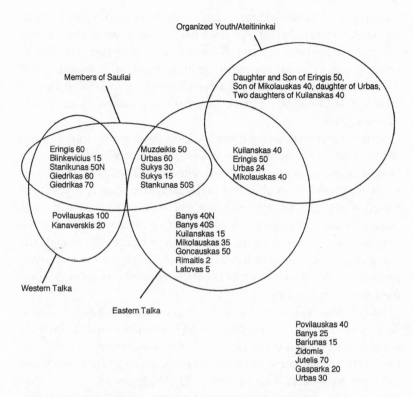

Figure 3.1. A community configuration of the village of Svainikai

their counterparts in the Eringis 60 subset, all would eventually join the LAF.

- The upper right subset represents organized youth, some belonged to Ateitis.
- The Kuilanskas 40 subset comprises farmsteads in the eastern talka with connections to the the organized youth.
- The Banys 40N subset contains members of the eastern talka without ties to either organized youth or Sauliai.
- The list in the bottom right of Figure 3.1 contains community outsiders.

The previous chapter derived four general conditions conducive for rebellion: small overall size, intermediate density, the presence of social groups, and the absence of groups connected to political parties. Each was present in Svainikai.

First, two social-patriotic groups had a presence in the community. Members of these types of groups are more likely to hold low rebellion thresholds and activate norms of honor (B norms). These groups breed the first actors necessary to initiate community-level organization. In Svainikai, both the Union of Sauliai and Ateitis had an important presence. Indeed, both the youth and the Eringis 60 subset were the first to act, and, in each case, so did connected subsets.

Second, the community itself was relatively small and the subsets within this community were correspondingly small (see Chapter 2). The key Eringis 60 subset contains only five farmsteads, while the Muzdeikis 50 subset, making up the remaining set of Sauliai members, also contains only five members. If norms of reciprocity and honor function most effectively in small-group situations with high levels of face-to-face contact, then such norms were likely to affect behavior among members of villages like Svainikai. In this example, the actions of five members of Sauliai from one economic group in the community are likely to have some effect on the five members from another informal group.

This discussion of subset ratios brings up the issue of density of ties. In the previous chapter, it was shown that an intermediate overlap of ties can produce optimal ratios of first actors to higher-threshold actors. If the overlap is high, then the normative effects of the first-acting group can be diluted; if the overlap is low, then the normative effect might never be realized. Consider Svainikai, concentrating on the Muzdeikis subset. These individuals need to weigh the actions of their fellow Sauliai members in Eringis 60, who are organizing, against the reticence of the Banys 40N subset, their fellow talka members. The respective number of farmsteads of these three groups (with the Muzdeikis subset in the middle) is 5:5:7. If norms of honor function as they are modeled in Figure 2.7, then the Muzdeikis subset would be expected to reciprocate its fellow Sauliai members (which it did). When half of a group guided by norms of honor is acting, the other half will strongly feel the need to respond, even if such action means taking on more risk.

Consider, counterfactually, that Svainikai had been differently structured. What if three of the members of Eringis 60 were moved to the Muzdeikis subset? In this case, density of ties, measured in terms of amount of overlapping membership, would increase as the ratio among subsets changes to 2:8:7. The crucial question is whether the two first-acting members of Eringis 60 would now be able to trigger action in the eight members of Muzdeikis. In this case only two of ten members of a group guided by norms of honor are first-acting and the normative pressures may be less compelling. Consider, on the other hand, a situation in which three of the members of Muzdeikis 50 were moved to the Eringis 60 subset. The ratio changes to 8:2:7, meaning a decrease in overlap and density. Whereas the normative effects on the two Muzdeikis members would become very powerful, the ability of these two individuals to influence the seven Banys 40N subset members might very well decline.

These same points can be made concerning the subsets of organized youth and their families represented on the right side of Figure 3.1. Again, the actions of a first-acting subset can sway the decisions of connected individuals. Again, powerful norms, this time family norms (A norms in Figure 2.7), may have come into play. In sum, Svainikai's community structure resembled the cascading structure of low- to high-threshold subsets illustrated by Figure 2.8 (bottom), only with two initial first-acting groups

Finally, note that this local resistance organization formed without the benefit of established political parties. The few individuals who were political did not play significantly more influential roles; in fact, none of the three even became members of the LAF. More likely, the absence of politics meant the absence of infighting and unnecessary debate

In provincial regions, the June rebellion was a haphazard affair. However, a foundation for rebellion against the Soviet occupier was firmly established. In the postwar period, this rebellion would again reach levels that would alter the course of Lithuanian history.[97]

Negative Cases: Communities That Failed to Organize

In 1940–1941 most Lithuanian communities, despite similar overall proportions of members in economic, social, and political groups, did not produce the high equilibrium witnessed in Svainikai. According to one of the central themes of Chapter 2, rebellion is not simply produced by the *existence* of certain groups, but by the *structure* as a whole. This section looks at the communities that failed to organize.

The simplest structures can be examined first. There were types of economic communities with members and former members of Ateitis that did

---

[97] Unfortunately, neither informant knew the history of Svainikai during the second Soviet occupation very well. One had fled in 1944, whereas the other was drafted into the Soviet Army in the same year; the latter never returned to his village. All that is known is that most of the village was deported to Siberia in the late 1940s, perhaps for its support of the partisans.

not engage in resistance activity. By and large, these communities were not organically connected to the unconstrained student and youth groups. Their structure is best represented by Figure 2.9b, with the social group (membership or former membership in Ateitis) being totally within the boundaries of the economic group. In this situation, the appeals of the resistance were ignored as they carried little weight in comparison to the constraints involved with the economic group.

One example was a Catholic-run hospital in Kaunas described by respondent 19. The interviewee, a Catholic priest who was a chief administrator, was primarily involved in fund raising and charitable work and did not directly work with Ateitis or any other Catholic organization, although he was naturally familiar with these groups. The respondent reported a strong motivation to work against the new Communist regime. Not only was the new regime atheistic, but it was constantly harassing the respondent by arresting him on a weekly basis.[98] During the first Soviet occupation, he was approached by members of a Catholic-based underground organization to participate in the resistance. The interviewee did not personally know this man and felt little trust or sense of obligation to him. He refused to participate on grounds that his association might jeopardize the operation of the hospital; he believed that if any staff member were implicated in underground activity, retaliation against the hospital as a whole would follow. The respondent indicated that this belief was held by the staff as a whole, a staff largely composed of former members of the Catholic youth association Ateitis. In effect, the hospital community had no unconstrained first players. The underground appeal was readily dismissed: despite strong personal motivations and a significant group of Ateitininkai on the hospital's staff, the constraints involved were simply too strong.

Respondent 20 tells a similar story, although the constraints may not have been so strong. She was a young former member of Ateitis with an aunt who was an Ateitis adult sponsor. After Vilnius was incorporated into Lithuania, she went to that city to work in a cooperative. College-age members of the resistance came to the store to ask her to hide weapons in the basement. Having just come to Vilnius, she did not personally know this underground recruiter and felt no obligation toward him. Additionally, she believed the other members of the cooperative would not approve. During the German occu-

---

[98] The respondent's brother's family and sister were also deported to Siberia, either in 1940 or 1941; the tape is unclear.

pation, she refused to take underground pamphlets from university students for the same reasons. Again, lack of connection to the unconstrained first actors as well as organizational constraints vetoed participation in underground activity. Despite their organizational memberships, both respondents 19 and 20 never seriously considered such participation.

A more complicated case involves the village of respondent 21.[99] In some ways, this village resembled Svainikai: individual landholdings were similar (above the Lithuanian average in size and roughly equal across village members), and crops were the same – rye, oats, wheat, and flax. Like Svainikai, the village had experienced land and livestock confiscations and was forced to endure compulsory grain deliveries. There was also heavy participation in social-patriotic organizations; in fact, participation was probably higher than that in Svainikai. Despite widespread social-patriotic group membership, respondent 21's village did not witness the development of a villagewide underground organization. There was some apparent movement to +2 but only within some limited sets of ties.

The story of the respondent's own talka is illustrative. His talka could afford to be small – it consisted of only five families – because his family had ten children, seven males, for labor. Flax and threshing involved everyone and was followed by a celebration. Smaller communal jobs were negotiated between families, each agreeing to provide a certain number of laborers. All in all, typical Lithuanian rural relations were present but within a tighter circle of families. The respondent, a Young Lithuanian, was nineteen at the time and had an older brother who belonged to Sauliai. He could remember no one else within the talka who had belonged to a patriotic organization. After the occupation, the interviewee was at a loss for what to do. Smetona had fled and other Young Lithuanian leaders had been arrested. The local Young Lithuanians quickly lapsed into nonexistence. He had no thought of talking with local Ateitininkai as he had not had contact with them before. A brother-in-law was involved in some organization, but respondent 21 related, "There was a lot of work to do on the farm; we just worried about that." In the end, despite the membership of himself and his brother in organizations sworn to defend the country even to death, the economic constraint was given a higher weight. The burden of compulsory grain deliveries, confiscation of livestock, and other Soviet-induced hardships also failed to spur action. They were just two individuals within a larger and somewhat isolated social unit.

---

[99] This respondent did not want to divulge the name of his village.

The village of respondent 21 was much bigger than Svainikai, populated by about 100 families. Three of Lithuania's most prominent social-patriotic organizations were active there. As just mentioned, the respondent belonged to the Nationalist Young Lithuania and claimed that there were approximately thirty-five other members in the village. The Ateitininkai were reported to be slightly larger. The Union of Sauliai also had a considerable presence, including a brother of the interviewee, but the Scouts had little influence.

Relations between these groups were either nonexistent or antagonistic. Fights between Ateitininkai and Young Lithuanians were commonplace. Membership in the latter sometimes produced negative reactions even within families. The respondent told the story of a mother dousing her son with holy water after he had come home wearing the uniform of a Young Lithuanian. Unlike in some other villages, there were few, if any, youth in Sauliai. In smaller villages there was more of a need to combine organizations, but in larger villages generations could separate out into different groups that would all still be sizable enough to maintain viability.

Perhaps the biggest difference between the village of respondent 21 and Svainikai was in their respective economic organizations. In Svainikai, some work involved the entire village and only two talka groups existed. In contrast, there was no all-village communal labor in the larger community of respondent 21. All cooperative work had been broken down into ten to fifteen very intensive talka groups. The respondent could draw and discuss his own talka group, but could not recall the names of neighbors across the lake or grove of trees that separated the respective talkas.

As in most Lithuanian villages of the time, there was little political interest or political group activity. The village of respondent 21 is schematized in Figure 3.2.[100] What explains the apparent low +2 equilibrium in the village?

Theoretically, this village possessed some of the factors favoring rebellion. First, social-patriotic groups were present. Second, outside political groups did not interfere in community relations. Third, taken as a measure of the village as a whole, the density of ties (the amount of overlap) might be described as intermediate.

Other factors operating against movement to +2, however, included, first, its large size, at least in relation to Svainikai. This was not a very strong community. Based on the respondent's lack of knowledge of the village, it seems

---

[100] This is my own interpretive map based on the interviewee's description.

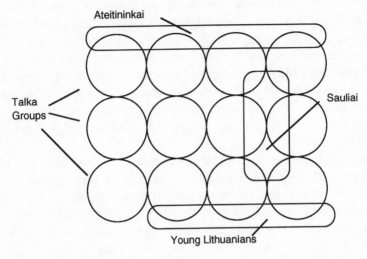

Figure 3.2. The village of interviewee 21

that there was no ability to monitor the village as a whole. Sanctioning and status mechanisms also did not operate across the village. Second, the village was economically fragmented. There were, in effect, many small cooperative economic subsets. Within some of these economic groups, the ratio of first actors or low-threshold players to intermediate-threshold actors may indeed have been favorable, or even exhibited "overkill," and probably led to +2 organization (e.g., in the case of the respondent's brother-in-law). On the other hand, in many other cells, any inclination toward rebellious behavior was outweighed by the work pressures and social exigencies of the immediate local environment and the high number of high-threshold individuals encountered there. The respondent's case, summarized earlier, is a clear example. As illustrated by Figure 2.9f, a fragmented economic structure can produce varying ratios of low- and intermediate-threshold actors that are likely to lead to an intermediate, rather than high, overall community equilibrium.

The structural location of first actors and the strength of the community are the critical features. In Svainikai, there were two single low-threshold subsets, Sauliai and the students, who shared ties with a significant percentage of the rest of the village. In that strong community situation, those first-actors' movements were known and the normative effect of that movement may have reduced thresholds of connected members (and almost all other members were connected). The level of participation of the first actors could then surpass the lowered thresholds. In respondent 21's village, there were first players and, given the abundance of social group members, many low-threshold actors. But their presence did not trigger a dramatic tipping effect. First, within the weaker community, these actions were less known; second, within the specific fragmented structure of the community, the overall normative impact of low-threshold social groups could not be concentrated or optimally distributed.

Additionally, in the larger and more fragmented community structure of respondent 21, there was no mention of centralized actors. A centralized player can choose to use his or her energies with one group first, perhaps one with a low threshold, and then move on to help unite a second group with a higher threshold. In Svainikai, Eringas 60 was in a position to play such a role. With the larger number of social groups in the village of respondent 21, some of which were mutually antagonistic, there were no actors with multiple social group membership to play these efficient linking roles.

The problem of economic fragmentation is, of course, even more prevalent in urban areas than in the village of respondent 21. Respondent 17, an urban dweller who made a living as an organist, was a member of Ateitis in high school and became a member of Sauliai as an adult. When the Soviets occupied his town, he hid his Sauliai uniform in a barn and denied any affiliation with the group. Two problems existed. First, in the case of respondent 17, and also in the rest of Lithuania, the Soviet secret police more easily penetrated the Sauliai organization in urban rather than rural areas. This was because of the relatively higher abundance of informers. The few Communists who did exist in Lithuania lived in the towns. Also, in areas with larger populations it was harder to identify the informers; thus they did not fear retaliation to the same extent. In respondent 17's town, the Soviets quickly arrested the local Sauliai leaders and the organization rapidly withered. In more remote areas, like Svainikai, the organization still exhibited influence. Interview respondent 17 suggests a second issue: unconnected social groups, again generally found in urban areas, experience difficulty in organizing resistance. Immediately after the takeover, respondent 17 could hide his uniform and begin passively riding out the occupation: he was not involved in any communal work organization and he could avoid contact with those who might become active. In fact, he consciously avoided certain people whom he thought might try to get him involved. In villages like Svainikai, avoiding organizers was impossible due to the nature of communal agriculture. Personal pressure was unavoidable as the harvest or flax operations would bring neighbors together. In urban areas, initial blows to social organizations proved devastating as the membership could be "atomized." This was not the case in smaller communities with multiple and diverse ties.

A Brief Comparison with Latvia and Estonia

The similarities between the three Baltic states are manifold: each had undergone a land reform leaving the countryside in a relatively egalitarian state; each had begun with democratic governments that were disposed of and replaced with mild authoritarian regimes (democracy ended in both Latvia and Estonia in 1934); all had paramilitary organizations with the closest resemblance being between Lithuania's Sauliai and Latvia's Aizsargi;[101] each underwent almost identical processes of Sovietization, which incurred similar levels and experiences of hardship; each witnessed massive Soviet deportations a week before the beginning of the German-Soviet war (35,000 in Lithuania, 35,000 in Latvia, and 60,000 in Estonia).

Yet the development of clandestine resistance organization from 1940 to June 1941 in Lithuania was far greater than in the other two cases during the same period. There was some organization in both Estonia and Latvia, but it did not approach the 35,000 LAF members in Lithuania, or the 100,000 total rebels immediately involved in uprising.

In order to make a convincing comparative case in explaining this variation, the same methods used in examining Lithuania would have to be applied to Estonia and Latvia. I do not have such data; however, a few hypotheses based on the theory developed here can be formulated. It seems likely that neither of the two northern states would have had the prevalence of the resistance-capable primary units found in Lithuania. Two factors can be considered. The lesser factor is that Lithuania was somewhat more rural: 17.4 percent of Estonia's labor force and 13.5 percent of Latvia's was indus-

---

[101] In Estonia, the Association of Estonian Freedom Fighters (*Vabadussojalaste Liit*) was a powerful anti-Communist, antiparlimentary movement founded by veterans of the War of Independence. Unlike Sauliai, this organization made active entries into electoral politics – too active for the regime. It was forcibly disbanded in 1934. Interwar Latvia contained many right-wing social-political-military organizations, some more radical, more political, and more anti-regime than Sauliai. For a brief overview of these Latvian groups, see von Rauch, *The Baltic States,* pp. 151–154.

trial, whereas only 6 percent of Lithuania's labor force could be so-classified.[102] As mentioned with the case of respondent 17, rural communities are less prone to penetration and more likely to bring out the pressures involved with social norms. However, the greater factor in explaining variation in resistance organization would seem to be the lack of an Ateitis-type organization in the northern two states. The Catholic organization in Lithuania was an intermediary institution connecting unconstrained actors to larger communities. The Ateitininkai also had experience in operating underground as a result of the Smetona ban. No such group existed in either of the primarily Lutheran northern states.

A Brief Comparison with Lithuanian Jews

Whereas the German attack and the local uprising were reasons for joy and celebration among the Lithuanian population, these events spelled total disaster for Jews. During the first occupation, Lithuanians had come to identify Jews with the Soviet oppressor, and for many Lithuanians the collapse of Soviet rule now meant that the Jews' "time had come." Even before the entry of the Germans, some groups of Lithuanian rebels were engaged in beating, killing, and humiliating Jews.[103] Faced by both a hostile Lithuanian population and the much discussed probability of a German invasion, why were Jewish communities so unprepared to deal with possible contingencies? This is not exactly the same situation and question that has been applied to the Lithuanians, but given the fact that 200,000 Lithuanian Jews would soon be murdered without having any effective means either to flee or to fight back, the issue is historically relevant, if nothing else. The comparison of Jewish

---

[102] Romuald J. Misiunas and Rein Taagerpera, *The Baltic States: Years of Dependence, 1940–1980* (Berkeley: University of California Press, 1983), p. 10.

[103] For personal eyewitness accounts of action against Jews in the aftermath of the German invasion and local uprising, see William W. Mishell, *Kaddish for Kovno: Life and Death in a Lithuanian Ghetto, 1941–1945* (Chicago: Chicago Review Press, 1988), chaps. 2–5; Frieda Frome, *Some Dare to Dream: Frieda Frome's Escape from Lithuania* (Ames: Iowa State University Press, 1988), pp. 22–30; Avraham Tory, *Surviving the Holocaust: The Kovno Ghetto Diary* (Cambridge, Mass.: Harvard University Press, 1990), pp. 3–11; Yitzhak Arad, *The Partisan: From the Valley of Death to Mount Zion* (New York: Holocaust Library, 1979), pp. 28–37. With Lithuania's drive to independence, the controversy surrounding these events has again surfaced. See Benjamin Frankel and Brian D. Kux, "Recalling the Dark Past of Lithuanian Nationalism," *Los Angeles Times,* April 29, 1990, p. M2. A response to that article can be found in "An Open Response to the Editorial Board of the *Los Angeles Times,*" written by the Lithuanian Research and Studies Center in Chicago. Members of the Lithuanian Research Center gave me a copy of this response. I do not know if it was ever published.

and Lithuanian organization may not seem appropriate, but this very comparison was being made by Lithuanian Jews at the time:

> What we could not get over was the fact that while the Germans had not yet entered the city and thousands of straggling Russians were still in town, the Lithuanian partisans apparently were sufficiently armed and organized to pull off that trick. It suddenly dawned on us that all that past year, while we were trying to reshape our lives, the Lithuanians were clandestinely busy arming themselves. They, apparently, even knew the date of the invasion. It suddenly became totally incomprehensible, how we had not noticed anything. Not only were we fooled by the Lithuanians but the entire Russian secret police had missed this organized, heavily-armed military force. This force was now not only in control of the radio station, but most of the country's roads and villages. The rest of the day just did not want to end. The discussion was on edge and every sentence began with the words "we should have. . . ."[104]

In the terminology of this project, Jews had remained at the 0 position on the spectrum during the first occupation. Some leftist youth groups did begin some clandestine organization at the time, but by and large the Jewish communities were "frozen" in comparison to their Lithuanian neighbors.[105]

The most important difference from the Lithuanians was the lack of resentment toward the occupier. Given discrimination in the period of independence, and the present threat from Hitler's Germany, motivation for anti-Soviet action was understandably lacking. Additionally, Lithuanians had developed anti-Russian feeling, symbols, and even underground experience during the period of the tsarist bookban.

In contrast, Jews as a whole did not possess such a clear and unified attitude – neither toward the Lithuanian state nor toward the Soviet occupiers. Their ambivalence created a situation in which a clear "coding" of individuals as "traitors" or "defenders" was simply not an issue: individuals were basically on their own, unconstrained and unmotivated by community sanctions or rewards.

This might not have been the case in the early 1920s. Jews had been among the biggest supporters of Lithuanian independence, believing that

---

[104] Mishell, *Kaddish for Kovno,* p. 14.
[105] See Levin, *Fighting Back,* pp. 24–25, for some comments on the clandestine organizations that did arise at this time.

they could achieve some type of autonomy within the new state.[106] These hopes were thoroughly dashed when the 1926 coup ended democracy in Lithuania. There followed a period of gradual decline in the economic and social circumstances of Lithuanian Jews. This was partly due to a modernizing economy that was squeezing out the small-scale artisans so prevalent in the Jewish community, and partly because of government policies in credit and trade that favored Lithuanians.[107] Furthermore, Jews were discriminated against in higher education: Jewish enrollment at the University of Kaunas had been halved from 1922 to 1934, dropping to 16 percent.[108]

Yet, the situation for Jews in Lithuania was still better than in most other countries of Eastern Europe. There were no pogroms, Jewish education continued to be subsidized by the state, and Smetona himself attended the synagogue on high holidays. Without harassment, Jews remained less assimilated in Lithuania than in any other state in Europe; Zionism flourished there. All in all, the situation was mixed, and Lithuania was described by one historian as "certainly a good country so far as 'Judaism' was concerned, but by the late 1930's it was becoming increasingly evident that it was not a very good country for Jews as individuals."[109]

Then came the Soviets. Again, a situation of ambivalence dominated. On the one hand, all medium and large businesses were nationalized, 83 percent of them owned by Jews.[110] The older generation of established Jewish businessmen really suffered. Jewish religious organizations were also targets of Soviet oppression. On the other hand, Jews entered government positions at an unparalleled rate. Young Jewish leftists enthusiastically took up very visible positions in the new regime.[111] Of course, those knowledgeable about

---

[106] Ezra Mendelsohn, *The Jews of East Central Europe between the Wars* (Bloomington: Indiana University Press, 1983), pp. 217–225, covers the period from 1918 to 1926, considered to be the "Golden Age" for Jews in Lithuania; chap. 5, pp. 213–240, gives a good overview of the whole period.

[107] Another factor is the Smetona regime's policy of reserving government jobs for its Nationalist supporters. Followers of other political and social groups, the Catholics in particular, began entering the business field for the first time as an alternative.

[108] Mendelsohn, *The Jews of East Central Europe between the Wars*, p. 237. Also see Mishell's personal account of Jewish decline in both trade and at the university; *Kaddish for Kouno*, pp. 3–13.

[109] Mendelsohn, *The Jews of East Central Europe between the Wars*, p. 238.

[110] Levin, *Fighting Back*, p. 21.

[111] For a comparative work examining the consequences of Soviet rule on both the Lithuanian and Jewish populations, see Liutas Grinius, "Soviet Consequences to Lithuanian Jews: A Comparison with the Lot of Lithuanians," *Lituanas* 31 (1985): 28–44. Also see Levin, "The Jews in the Soviet Lithuanian Establishment, 1940–41."

the Germans saw the new Soviet regime as the best hope for protection. Under these conditions, there was no clear, overall Jewish prescription for assigning blame or rewarding status to any particular action; individuals were left to make it on their own. Without these broader elements, no coherent focal events, such as All Souls' Day for the Lithuanians, were possible.

Summing Up

This chapter has obviously not been an adequate test of the theory detailed in the preceding chapter. It has, however, illustrated in human terms how mechanisms outlined in the previous chapter operate in sequence to produce organized rebellion. Specifically, this chapter has given life to the abstract conceptions regarding the effects of the density of ties, size factors, and heterogeneity. The analysis has furnished insights in explaining variation among nationalities in the region. The next chapter continues in the same vein but changes the social setting.

4. Rebellion in an Urban Community: The Role of Leadership and Centralization

In the organization of the June 1941 revolt, members of one particular community played a disproportionate role. The students, alumni, and networks of the Grandis fraternity, the Catholic engineering fraternity of the University of Kaunas, were exceptionally influential in creating widespread +2 organization.

A membership roll of the Grandis students was produced by one of the students and can be found in Figure 1.2. This chapter reconstructs the 1940–1941 history of this group through interviews with seven members of the Grandis network and a special focus on the role and action of two leaders. Chapter 2 discussed five important structural properties of a strong community and specified how these properties relate to movement to the +2 position. Chapter 3 discussed three of these characteristics – density of ties, size factors, and heterogeneity – as they operated in various communities during the first Soviet occupation of Lithuania. Here, leadership properties, the role of political entrepreneurs, and the effects of centralization become the primary concern.

The existence of first actors operating at local levels is crucial to rebellion, especially rebellion against strong, invasive regimes. Not only the presence of political entrepreneurs, however, but their specific location in local community structures explain their influence. With this comment in mind, a theoretical review and discussion of leadership precedes and guides the story of Grandis and its development of organized rebellion.

Crucial Characteristics of Leadership

Samuel Popkin, in his work on Vietnam, has written extensively on the importance of political entrepreneurs in catalyzing rebellion.[1] In many ways, Popkin's political entrepreneurs are similar to first-actor, zero-threshold players in the present study. Both act immediately, often out of political, national, or religious conviction; both must be able to convince others to accept risks; both must convince others that the action they consider taking, or the movement they might join, holds some chance of success. As does the present study, Popkin found the basis for rebellion in local community factors – specifically, the presence of local political entrepreneurs. Popkin showed how the local first-acting political entrepreneur, in his cases religious figures or Communists, could solve the collective-action problem for "rational peasants" by breaking up large tasks into smaller actions, each of which required the contribution of the individual to create the collective good. Through this local process, religious or political movements built up a revolutionary surplus that could be used to battle the regime. Although the Olsonian insights of Popkin are relevant for the present study, his points about the credibility of entrepreneurs are more germane in explaining action against the pervasive power of the Nazis and Soviets. Popkin illustrated how local entrepreneurs gained the confidence of residents through their own sacrifice, and how, after leading success in one type of collective action, villagers gained confidence that other collective actions could also be accomplished under these local figures' leadership. Through their reputation, political entrepreneurs provided peasants a sense of efficacy; through their reputation, entrepreneurs could more easily recruit and maintain followers.

Chapter 2 enumerated two important structural features concerning the location of first actors. First-acting groups have low thresholds and often have norms of honor that may lower the risk thresholds of connected actors. When first-actor subsets are centralized, their normative effects may lower thresholds of multiple connected groups (Figure 2.9c); create favorable ratios of zero-threshold to intermediate-threshold actors in order to maximize the power of threshold-lowering norms (Figure 2.9d);[2] and create a cascading set of thresholds more likely to reach high equilibria (Figure 2.9e).

---

[1] See *The Rational Peasant* (Berkeley: University of California Press, 1979) and "Political Entrepreneurs and Peasant Movements in Vietnam," in Michael Taylor, ed., *Rationality and Revolution* (Cambridge: Cambridge University Press, 1988), pp. 9–61.

[2] Recall the favorable B:BC ratios as shown in the middle diagram of Figure 2.9d.

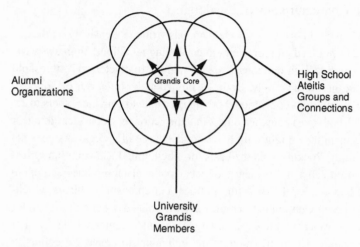

Figure 4.1. Grandis community structure

Each of these effects was present within the structure of the Grandis community, which is represented in Figure 4.1. A set of first actors, highly respected leaders, was positioned in the center of this community. Multiple subsets of Grandis students, residing in Kaunas, looked to these leaders for signals to act. These students, in turn, had connections with the Ateitis Catholic organizations of their home communities as well as connections with alumni groups. This structure produces multiple sets of cascading thresholds in which the first actions of the Grandis core helped trigger the action of Grandis students, who in turn drew in higher-threshold actors.

After a review of the importance and organization of the Catholic youth in Lithuania, especially the Grandis fraternity, these dynamics are illustrated with attention on the influence of two leaders, Adolfis Damusis and Pilipas Narutis.[3]

---

[3] Much of this section, as will become clear, is based on interviews conducted with these two individuals. Mr. Narutis was interviewed three times while Mr. Damusis was interviewed twice. As anyone at all familiar with the history of the 1941 rebellion will immediately recognize both these men in the text, there is little reason for anonymity. Damusis has been interviewed many times about his role in the 1941 revolt, and has written about it as well.

The Ateitininkai, the Grandis Fraternity, and the Broader Catholic Networks

Whereas today fraternities are often envisioned as houses for general frivolity, Lithuanian fraternities were embedded in a political, social, and religious environment that made them important national actors. The authoritarian Smetona regime had officially banned the open functioning of all opposition parties, although they did meet semiopenly. Smetona did allow open political association at the university; in fact, it was the only legal forum for such activity. The university was a battleground, and a recruiting ground, in this national political struggle.

In Catholic Lithuania, the Christian Democrats were a particularly formidable foe of the Smetona forces. Although the two groups were allied from 1920 to 1926, the split between Christian Democrats and Nationalists had widened after the 1926 coup. Given the success of Christian Democracy in other European countries, Smetona had reasons for concern.[4] The Catholic students at the university were well aware of the nation's political struggles and sensed their importance within them.

Grandis was a Catholic engineering fraternity at the University of Vytautas the Great in Kaunas. As Vilnius and its university were held by the Poles throughout most of the interwar period, Vytautas the Great was the only sizable university in all of Lithuania. With a total membership of about seventy-five, Grandis was one of twelve university fraternities connected to the Catholic youth association Ateitis, an organization with roots in the country's high schools. The role of the Grandis fraternity cannot be properly understood without knowing the nature of the larger Ateitis organization. Ateitis stressed an ethos of sacrifice and activism. Members were encouraged to develop an identity as an activist (*veikejas*), and to become part of an elite selected through sacrifice (*elitas*).[5] In short, Ateitis was a classic example of a B group with low thresholds for action and norms of honor.

---

[4] For background on the development of Christian Democratic political parties in Western European states, see Stathis Kalyvas, *The Rise of Christian Democracy* (Ithaca: Cornell University Press, 1996). The relationship between conservatives and Catholics in Lithuania paralleled several Western European countries in many respects. Originally, conservatives saw the alliance with Catholics as a useful one, but came to understand that the organization that formed could not be easily controlled. The Catholics, with strength established at parish and local levels, were more powerful than many originally imagined.

[5] In comparison, the youth group of Smetona stressed personal subordination to the leader.

The relationship between Ateitis and the Christian Democratic Party could be discussed in terms of a family, although a highly argumentative family vexed with issues of control.[6] Both were Catholic and at odds with Smetona and his policies, but distance was maintained between the two organizations.[7] As mentioned earlier, the Smetona regime considered Ateitis to be a breeding ground for future leaders of the Christian Democratic opposition and thus banished it.[8] Ateitis activity was reduced to secret meetings at the church or the home of the priest. Despite the ban, the ranks of the Ateitininkai[9] did not wither but apparently increased. Indeed, conditions were good for recruitment: belonging to a banned organization provided excitement for teenagers, and the Smetona regime did not have the stomach to employ the draconian measures necessary to enforce the ban. Youths were in fact arrested – Adolfis Damusis spent time in a labor camp for his position as an Ateitininkai leader – but, in general, participation involved relatively low risks.

High school Ateitininkai who went on to enter the university continued their activity only in a direct and legal form. The twelve Ateitininkai fraternities, or corporations as they were called, clearly formed the most powerful force in student politics. Student elections give a fair reading of the relative power of each corporation, as the vast majority of students belonged to a fraternity and voted for their own candidates. The election of 1938 fielded the results shown in Table 4.1.[10]

The Ateitininkai maintained some cooperation and contact with anti-Smetona groups before the Soviet takeover. For example, the Ateitininkai, Populists, and the Social Democrats allied several times in the late 1930s to protest the undemocratic nature of the Smetona regime. Although these fraternities met openly, there was a limit on how far they could go in criticiz-

---

[6] The interviews brought out a variety of views on the Ateitis–Christian Democrat relationship.

[7] This debate continues into the present.

[8] Ateitis was naturally very close to the Christian Democrats in terms of ideology; however, there was little official linkage. As far as I can ascertain, most of the Ateitis program was indeed religious and not overly political. Perhaps this was one reason why Smetona was reluctant to enforce a real crackdown.

[9] Ateitininkai is the plural and commonly used name of the members of Ateitis. An English translation is "futurists."

[10] Total enrollment was 2,535. As noted in Chapter 3, all students wore hats indicating their fraternal association. Catholics wore red, neutrals wore white, etc. Respondents claimed it was difficult to get a date if one was not wearing his hat. At any rate, this is an indication of the strength of social boundaries at the university.

Table 4.1. *Student Elections at Kaunas in 1938*

Ateitininkai	446
The Assembly (Social Democratic)	250
Jewish Fraternity	210
Nationalist Fraternity	177
Scouts	109
Liberal (Populist)	102
Officers in Reserve Fraternity	89
Filae Lituniae[a]	68
Neutrals[b]	64
Sauliai Fraternity	35

[a]Filae Lituniae was considered a Nationalist supporter, although during the first occupation it did make contact with the Ateitininkai for the first time ever, an indication that its loyalty to Smetona was not a totally controlling factor, unlike the Nationalist fraternity.

[b]Although they were "neutrals," they still had candidates in student elections.

Source: Lithuanian Encyclopedia.

ing the Smetona regime, because the regime had responded with force at times to break up their rallies.

More importantly, university Ateitininkai, alumni, and members of other Catholic organizations maintained a network. First, university Ateitininkai retained connections with their former high school Ateitis unit. These links allowed the organization to carry information between the center and the provinces, a highly important attribute when normal communications are cut off. For example, immediately after Soviet annexation in 1940, Ateitis groups kept lists of all arrestees and all Soviet activities in their villages. This information was then compiled at the university when Ateitininkai students resumed classes in the fall. In the same way, information about Soviet actions in the cities and the prospects for rebellion were carried from Kaunas to the villages. There were fifty-six local Ateitis organizations active in Lithuania at this time. Although many of these groups were small, some had hundreds of members.[11] Damusis estimated the total number of Ateitininkai in Lithuanian high schools at the time of the revolt to be 12,000.

Ateitininkai played a similar role in communities of Catholic professionals. Each of the twelve Catholic fraternities was linked to alumni through *fil-*

---

[11] Narutis's village in Panevezys is one example.

isters – former members of the fraternity who maintained close contact with students and helped them find employment, among other things. Jobs in Lithuania, especially government jobs, were connected to patronage networks. The Nationalists controlled most of the government jobs and tended to dole them out to graduating members of the Nationalist fraternity. In response, the filister-student bonds in Catholic networks had to become tighter in order to compete.

Perhaps less important were Ateitininkai connections to work groups. One such work group was the Catholic youth farming organization called "Spring." Damusis had been active in trying to bolster this group, which attempted to link students to farming families. During summer vacations, Ateitis university students would work with farming youth and give lectures as well[12] (see Figure 4.1).

The Backgrounds of Two Leaders

Adolfis Damusis and Pilipas Narutis, due to their positions within the Ateitininkai leadership, occupied the core of the Ateitis community. These two men had remarkably similar backgrounds. Perhaps most importantly, they both held the national chairmanship of the Ateitis high school organization. Always held by a university student, Damusis held this position in the late 1920s. As a result, the Smetona regime threw him in prison, where he met other Ateitininkai activists. Damusis was a member of Grandis, as was Narutis, and was a closely connected filister at the time of Soviet occupation. After graduating in 1928, Damusis joined the faculty in the 1933–1934 academic year, teaching technical courses. He maintained connections to the Spring organizations that he had helped to create. Due to his prominence and his track record in underground activity, Damusis became one of the first organizers of the centralized LAF, which in turn was connected to Lithuanian émigrés and diplomats in Germany.

Narutis was the last elected prewar chairman of Ateitis. In that position, he had ties to the Catholic hierarchy, including the bishop. He also maintained contact with the nationwide network of high school Ateitis groups and

---

[12] Although unconnected to Catholic networks, more technically oriented university students were assigned summer employment with a government agency. For instance, Narutis, an engineering student, worked with an electrical crew. While the bonds in these work situations were not as tight as with the Catholic organizations, some resisters like Narutis did have contacts with their assigned summer work groups during the first occupation.

was familiar with the Spring groups of young Catholic farmers. Through membership in the Grandis technical fraternity and association with its fili- sters, he had contacts with Catholic engineers throughout the country. As the head of the most powerful organization on campus, he knew the leaders of the other fraternities. In fact, he had helped coordinate anti-Smetona rallies with the heads of the Social Democrats and Populists. On a more personal level, Narutis was connected to a local work group through his summer job on an electrical crew, and he knew the military officers who provided train- ing at the university. Of course, the personal tie to Damusis cannot be overemphasized.[13]

In addition to the lengthy interviews done with Damusis and Narutis, five other Grandis students or alumni were also interviewed. All were active in organizing anti-Soviet rebellion during the first occupation. The following section traces their activities and contacts during this period in the context of the development of the Lithuanian Activist Front.

Events Shortly after Soviet Annexation

The Soviet takeover occurred during the summer, when the student body was on break. Throughout the countryside, most of the university Ateitininkai were in their home villages or towns, often interacting with local Ateitis and young farmer (Spring) organizations. Within different regions of Lithuania, contact between Ateitis organizations was maintained. These groups' major activity was collecting information; lists of arrests and Soviet actions were compiled and brought back to the university upon the resumption of classes. Narutis, as national head of Ateitis, met with the bishop and other Catholic leaders during this time to determine whether it was too dangerous to main- tain the Catholic networks. They decided that contact should be maintained but become more purely religious in their open activities and meetings so as not to attract the attention of the new regime.

In August the Soviets closed down all organizations at the university. Narutis met with the heads of the Social Democratic and Populist fraterni- ties to resume the ties of cooperation that had been formed during the anti- Smetona rallies. Some university Ateitininkai were in contact with the mil-

---

[13] In addition to belonging to the same fraternity, being heads of Ateitis, and being at the same university as professor and student, Damusis and Narutis had both been born outside Lithuania (Narutis in Georgia and Damusis in Russia) to fathers with technical jobs. At the time of the revolt, both sets of parents were living in Panevezys.

itary men who had formerly been involved with university military training. Finally, some contacts with urban worker groups were maintained in the early stages of the occupation. Damusis, as a member of the faculty and former Ateitis president, was in contact with a group of professors, the adult sponsors of the Ateitis organizations, the filisters of Catholic professional groups, and Narutis.

On October 9, 1940, six leaders, including Damusis, met in Vilnius to centralize the resistance that had already been forming across Lithuania: this was the beginning of the Lithuanian Activist Front in Lithuania. Two headquarters were set up: a Kaunas headquarters in charge of organization of the countryside and a Vilnius headquarters assigned political and military affairs. Of the three leaders of the Kaunas organization (which would go on to lead the June 1941 revolt), two, Adolfis Damusis and Leonas Prapuolenis, were alumni of Grandis. In the opinion of Damusis, this centralization was necessary not to promote resistance activity but to control the local organizations that were springing up across the country. Through his student contacts, Damusis became familiar with the careless practices of many of those already actively resisting. In the end, seventy to eighty of these local units were very loosely united in the LAF.

The Berlin Connection

The Berlin LAF was not formalized until November 17, 1940, under the leadership of Colonel Skirpa. Eventually, the LAF in Lithuania recognized the primacy of the Berlin LAF, which had both access to German information on the timing of the impending attack and the ability to meet openly to develop a political program for a resurrected Lithuania. The relationship of the Berlin LAF to its Nazi hosts is, of course, a highly controversial question. The first contact had been made on July 2, 1940, when Colonel Skirpa, who headed the Lithuanian Legation in Berlin, invited Dr. Bruno Kleist, a Nazi official, for dinner.[14] Kleist intimated that the German-Soviet peace would not hold. Skirpa envisioned the reestablishment of Lithuanian sovereignty and contacted Smetona concerning plans for a united front and a provisional government. In August 1940, a National Committee was formed as a forerunner of a provisional Lithuanian government to be named after the Germans overran Soviet Lithuania.

---

[14] This paragraph is largely based on Algirdas Martin Budreckis, *The Lithuanian National Revolt of 1941* (South Boston, Mass.: Lithuanian Encyclopedia Press, 1968).

Skirpa's staff in Berlin was heavily laden with Voldemarists, followers of the fascist professor, and thus the Berlin LAF's stated ideology and some of its declarations were fascist and racist. Voldemaras was not particularly popular either in Lithuania[15] or among the Lithuanian émigrés in Berlin, but the Nazis had a strong and natural affinity with him. How much the predominance of Voldemarists in Skirpa's staff was a necessary evil that had to be endured to curry favor with the Germans versus how much it represented Lithuanian popular opinion is a debatable question. Shortly after the June revolt, Voldemaras himself attempted an unsuccessful putsch against the short-lived LAF provisional government. This was not surprising given the nature of the provisional government, which had little connection to Lithuanian fascists. The details of this political conflict can be found elsewhere. For present purposes, the relevant question concerns the effects German organization had upon the development of resistance in Lithuania. Clearly, peasants and students knew nothing about events or ideas prominent in Berlin. It is not even clear whether LAF leaders, who in Kaunas were aligned with the Christian Democrats, either received complete information from Berlin or were influenced by it. Local resistance organizations had developed several months previous to the Berlin organization and the connection between the two was always weak.

Cat and Mouse

In the early stages of the occupation, the Soviet secret police were rather inefficient. Narutis relates several illustrative events. Once he was walking in front of his house when he was stopped by a Soviet NKVD officer. The officer had come to "talk" to Narutis but had no idea what he looked like. He actually asked Narutis where Narutis lived. Narutis pointed to his own house and told the officer that Narutis was there now. The officer went on, allowing him to escape. Another time, secret police came to a house where Narutis

---

[15] The affinity for Voldemaras among the general Lithuanian population is a highly complex issue, in part due to the complexity of Voldemaras himself. He was a gifted scholar and, along with Smetona, a primary leader in establishing Lithuanian independence. After the 1926 coup, he became prime minister only to be dismissed by Smetona two years later. Voldemaras then became more and more closely identified with fascism. Supported by the fascist "Iron Wolf" paramilitary organization, Voldemaras attempted to oust Smetona several times, the last attempt in 1934 resulting in a four-year imprisonment. Opinion of Voldemaras varied from time period to time period. Also, many Lithuanians held a high opinion of the man and his love for Lithuania, while disagreeing, or despising, many of his ideas.

was present in order to take in Damusis. Although at the time Narutis was on a general list of individuals to be arrested, the officer in question was not sufficiently informed to recognize Narutis, who again walked right past the Soviet secret police. Also, the NKVD was operating according to rather unsophisticated standard operating procedures, which made it easier for the developing underground to avoid arrest. Apparently, the NKVD worked in two shifts, one from six or seven until midnight and another stretching from midnight until seven in the morning. There was almost no NKVD action from ten in the morning until two or three in the afternoon. Narutis used this as a hard-and-fast rule and operated rather freely during this time period.

With time, however, the NKVD became more effective. Narutis estimates that perhaps one-third of the students at the university were eventually interrogated. Many individuals were forced to sign confessions, which gave the NKVD the legal right to hang or deport them, but they were then freed under the understanding that they would work as informants. Under these conditions, the resistance had to become increasingly clever. As any meeting of three or four people seemed suspicious, the Catholic university students used the meetings of large church choirs to gather and disseminate information and carry out planning sessions. Priests would also hold special youth services as another means allowing a large mass of individuals to congregate. Information from a large number of people could be filtered to leaders inconspicuously. Narutis mentions that women were an exceptionally good source of information as Soviet soldiers and police tended to talk more freely to them than to males. This source of information was again mainly tapped at the church choirs and services.

With increasingly dangerous conditions, Narutis and Damusis reduced their ties, maintaining contact only with the safest and most effective people – that is, the closest and most trusted friends from pre-occupation networks. Damusis dropped ties to general working groups first, in his opinion the most easily penetrated; he also reduced his ties to the military. Ties to Populist professors became purely "tactical" – superficially maintained. Damusis describes how his ties were reduced to long-term acquaintances from the Catholic anti-Smetona networks:

> The most important ties were with people that you trust. I trusted the fifty-six sponsors of the Ateitis groups that I had secret contact with before, and the filisters, and some others. Filisters are professionals who still keep in touch with students and help them. They had proven that they could be

trusted. . . . I trusted completely only Narutis and Prapuolenis, who I knew as a high school acquaintance from Ateitis, and a couple of professors. I met with the professors every month or month and a half, but I met twice a week with Narutis and Prapuolenis.

The evolution of Narutis's ties followed a similar pattern: he reduced connections with workers and the military. Military contact was accomplished through other LAF leaders. Ties with the liberal fraternities were reduced to once every two weeks, and these meetings were again "tactical"; each side just recognized that "the other was still there." The Catholic networks remained the strongest: Narutis met with other Ateitininkai twice a week at the church choir sessions; his technical fraternity was maintaining ties with technical professionals; he was in contact with fifteen high school Ateitis groups; and, of course, he was meeting regularly with Damusis.

In the meantime, the Grandis rank and file was being organized along the lines of the Communist Party underground. Primarily, this involved the formation of "groups of five" (*penketukas*): one member would recruit five others, each of whom would recruit another five. To prevent the secret police from gaining knowledge about the entire network, only cell leaders possessed knowledge of the identity of the immediate superior within the chain. Interviewee G1 was a member of Grandis and a well-known sportsman who had entered the chemistry faculty in 1939. Although he had been expelled from the university after the Soviet annexation, G1 was still in contact with his fraternity mates. At the beginning of the 1940–1941 academic year, a former finance minister who had known G1 through his sports fame recruited him. In turn, G1 drafted four new members to form his own cell. Three of the four recruits were fellow members of Grandis with the fifth being a New Lithuanian.

Throughout most of the period, the organization of rebellion manifested itself at two levels. At a general level, continued gatherings of Grandis members served to produce confidence that a rebellion would occur and the membership would remain solid. At these larger gatherings, G1 received no specific information about clandestine activity, but he did gain several crucial intuitions about the numbers involved and the quality of the leadership. Consider the following exchange:

RP: Did you know the role Damusis was playing at the time?

G1:   Very little. Practically nothing.

RP: But you knew that he was involved in the LAF?

D: Yes, I knew. We were members of one corporation (Grandis). It was at the corporation meeting that there was an exchange of general opinion, but no exchange of secret activity. From that you could conclude that Damusis was involved, it's my comment now, but you couldn't decipher the particular role of Damusis.

RP: I was just curious whether it was well known or not.

G1:   It was a feeling, an intuition. But you had no right to even ask.

RP: What percentage of Grandis was involved in this rebellion?

G1:   One hundred percent.

This "knowledge" of Damusis's participation produced higher levels of assurance of its possible success, as did the intuition that the rest of the Grandis members were involved as well. These intuitions, critical for secret organization, can only be gained by members of strong communities with histories of interactions.

For G1, the only explicit discussion of rebellion took place within the group of five, and even these exchanges were rare and without specific content. G1 described his own group as cultural, political, and ideological. Members of the group knew, in a vague way, that the larger political questions were being dealt with in Germany. They could only concern themselves with keeping their cell intact so that it could be assigned specific tasks at the outbreak of rebellion.

A second Ateitis member, G2, had a long history in the Ateitis movement because his three older sisters were members. He recalled meeting the future LAF leader Leonas Prapuolenis at a secret Ateitis meeting in 1933 when he was fourteen years old. Having met with university Ateitininkai during his high school days, G2 was naturally active in the university Ateitininkai and also joined the Grandis technical fraternity. During the first occupation, the members of his group of five (which was actually a group of six including himself) were all recruited from within the ranks of Grandis. G2 was reluctant to even involve members of other Ateitis fraternities explaining that the members of Grandis needed to keep to themselves for security reasons. One member of G2's cell was working in a sugar plant in Marijampole (two hours from Kaunas by bicycle) as part of his technical training. Information and pamphlets were passed from Kaunas to Marijampole through this connection.

G3 was an Ateitis member from youth and an alumnus of Grandis, having been at the university at the same time as Damusis and Prapuolenis. G3 had maintained tight connections with the Ateitininkai and had suffered politically under the Smetona regime. He had once been confined to his native town and twice been imprisoned for one month at a time for antistate activities. Thus, he had broad experience with oppositional work. Since then, his career opportunities had been blocked. During the first occupation he participated in the LAF underground entirely through Ateitininkai ties, being especially close to Prapuolenis.

Other sections of Ateitininkai alumni and student groups were also drawn into the resistance, although perhaps not to the extent of Grandis. The operation of one professional community is outlined in the story of respondent G4. He had joined Ateitis in 1928 at the age of twelve, continued active membership at the Klaipeda business college, and became a filister who participated in the Ateitininkai patronage networks. During the earlier stages of the occupation, he received information and pamphlets through university Ateitininkai connections. He also heard that Damusis, whom he had known in high school as the head of Ateitis, was a leader of this resistance: "Damusis had been in prison under the Smetona regime. He was later sent to a concentration camp. I knew if he was involved that this was a serious organization." After receiving information through university Ateitininkai, and learning that the leaders of Ateitis were involved, the respondent joined the LAF and went on to recruit ten more members among his acquaintances in Kaunas. Many of them had been fellow members of Ateitis at the Klaipeda business college. He worked solely with fellow Ateitininkai: "Most members of the LAF came from Ateitis. I knew my contacts through Ateitis and could trust them. I would not trust those who came from outside – that would be too dangerous. All ten members that I recruited were Ateitininkai."

Finally, the university Ateitininkai also served to draw in high school groups. G5 was a high school student in Kaunas during the first occupation. Although he was not a member of Ateitis at the time, he would later join Ateitis and Grandis in 1942 when he became a student at the university. He was involved in a clandestine high school group that was connected to the university through a medical student–reserve officer who was almost certainly a member of Ateitis. This group was composed of roughly twenty-five students who met three or four times during the year. They had no official relationship to the LAF. Still, they were ready for action and were easily drawn into the June revolt.

Revolt

The June 1941 rebellion, as well as the larger political context, has been discussed in the previous chapter and elsewhere.[16] Here, the focus is on the activation of ties in the Grandis community network. On June 17, during the five-day period of Soviet deportations, Damusis traveled to Vilnius to meet with Narutis and other surviving members of the LAF to discuss future plans and how to reorganize the LAF after the arrest of many members and several leaders, especially those on the Vilnius staff. At this meeting, Damusis learned that a German attack was imminent. It was decided that Kaunas would serve as the supreme command for the revolt. Because the Kaunas LAF chief, Leonas Prapuolenis, was in strict hiding, the leadership tasks of the revolt were passed on to Narutis, a twenty-year-old student but also a member of the LAF's supreme staff.

Narutis returned to Kaunas and contacted the militia, which was willing to support the LAF and, most importantly, willing to produce access to weapons. Assignments were given out to some groups of five while other groups anxiously awaited orders. On Sunday, June 22, the Germans bombed the Kaunas airport. Narutis and Prapuolenis quickly set up LAF headquarters in a retirement home, while Damusis established another LAF base in the university chemisty building. On June 23, the LAF seized a radio transmitter, and at 9:28 A.M. Prapuolenis publicly announced the restoration of Lithuanian independence using the following words: "The Red executioners, having brutally tortured our land . . . at the moment are fleeing in a disorderly fashion. . . . The hour of liberation for all the Lithuanian lands is approaching. . . . Brother Lithuanians!! To arms. . . . Long live a free independent Lithuania."[17] The revolt was on, and the penketukas went into action guarding or capturing strategic communication and transportation points. Narutis assigned G2's group to reconnaissance at the airport. G3 was assigned to guard a tunnel. G1 had assumed a position of responsibility in the LAF and was himself in charge of directing groups of five to secure certain industrial (the textile plants) and transportation centers. G1 stressed that the revolt itself was rather chaotic and the assignments of the groups of five did not go according to any strict plan but rather were determined as specific needs arose. G4 hid weapons in the basement of his Kaunas store. On the day of the revolt, his group shot fleeing Russians by the Namarus River.

[16] Budreckis, *The Lithuanian National Revolt of 1941,* chap. 5, among others.
[17] *Darbinskas,* June 23, 1961, cited in ibid., p. 68.

While the LAF was largely successful in assigning its organized members to secure strategic points, it also catalyzed the participation of the semiorganized and those who were not previously organized at all. G5, the Kaunas student who was involved with a group within his high school, is a good example of what can be termed "semiorganized." With no official connection to the LAF and only a loose connection to a university reserve officer, G5's high school "conspiracy" group was minimally organized. Yet they were ready to participate immediately on the day of the revolt. With a small group of his fellows, G5 was wandering around town looking for some way to get more involved when they heard that people were gathering at a school where guns were being distributed. At the school, G5's group met an already organized group led by teachers who were former reserve officers. G5 was ordered to stand guard at a shop to prevent looting.

Soon the completely unorganized began to act. The prisons had been taken, and the prisoners, both unorganized and hungry for revenge, took to the streets. In the meantime, captured arsenals became distribution points for weapons. Coming one week after brutal deportations that had split families and removed 30,000 or more Lithuanians from their native land, the mixture of events was explosive. From most Lithuanian estimates, perhaps as many as 70,000 to 90,000 people who had not been in the LAF participated in the revolt in some manner; some took bloody revenge, and the revolt itself in some areas would transform into violence against the Jewish population. In the words of G1: "After that great deportation, very many people were damaged. Most of those who got out of prisons and camps had been beaten and then they got out to find their families deported. They [the LAF leadership] did not anticipate such a spontaneous explosion of violence and action. All those intellectuals were not able to anticipate such cruel things. People were not prepared for such a situation." By the time the Germans entered Kaunas on June 24, Lithuanians were in full control of the city and had established a provisional government. A complex set of politics concerning Lithuania's sovereignty, ultimately doomed to failure, then played itself out.[18]

Linking Substance and Theory

What accounts for the extensive organization of the Grandis fraternity and its alumni? In general terms, the Grandis community was a strong commu-

---

[18] See Chapter 5 on the German occupation.

nity in the general sense. Members interacted frequently and in a variety of ways. They shared common beliefs and history. As in many strong communities, an intuition about other members' behavior and trustworthiness developed that eliminated some of the uncertainty that works to prevent the acceptance of risk. More specifically, Grandis and affiliated Catholic groups stressed reciprocity and norms of honor. Whether these norms actually affect behavior is another matter, one that depends, as this book argues, on structural features.

This strong community was conducively structured. Most conspicuously, a Grandis core group consisting of Narutis, Damusis, Prapuolenis, and a few others occupied a centralized position. They were classic zero-threshold first actors. The reputation of Damusis, and to a lesser extent the twenty-year-old Narutis, provided a sense that something important was happening, something with a fair chance of success. Potential rebels would take more chances, would in effect lower their thresholds, knowing that these individuals were involved. Recall the words of G4: "Damusis had been a prisoner under the Smetona regime. He was later sent to a concentration camp. I knew that if he was involved that this was a serious organization."[19] This core possessed moral authority. When first actors are centrally positioned, they can lower the thresholds of multiple groups with whom they are connected. Knowing, or at least sensing, that Narutis and a set of Grandis leaders were almost certainly involved, the individual Grandis member and his small set of close connections, his roommates or trusted friends, could shirk reciprocation only at a certain personal moral cost.

Second, the structure of Grandis created a cascading set of thresholds. While the core members were certainly classic zero-threshold actors, the other members of Grandis fraternity were just as certainly low-threshold players, needing only the least assurance of other community members' participation in order to choose reciprocation and movement to +2. Notice how quickly and naturally G1 and G2 created cells among fellow Grandis students. Due to their professional or family responsibilities, alumni and connected Catholics may have more naturally held higher thresholds. Yet, when Grandis members, or at least Ateitininkai, approached them during the 1940–1941 occupation, they generally reciprocated and went on to recruit members through their Catholic connections. G3, a Grandis alumnus, had

---

[19] Some former Grandis members would grant me an interview only after learning that Damusis was also participating.

maintained tight connections with Ateitininkai and joined the LAF. After being contacted by university Ateitininkai, G4, an active filister, drafted ten members, all from Ateitis networks developed from his university days.

Conclusions

Narutis and Damusis led a takeover of the radio station that announced the beginning of the revolt. Of the approximately 100,000 individuals that responded to this call, a significant percentage came from community groups with ties to the university Ateitininkai, and the Grandis fraternity in particular. Most interviewees in this project agree that the students were less constrained and more mobile actors who were first movers in various Catholic communities, be they villages, work groups, or professional groups. University Ateitininkai also held ties to intermediate-threshold groups that acted as conduits for information and normative pressure: the high school Ateitininkai in villages, the Spring organization for young farmers, the filisters in professional groups. Two major leaders of the university Ateitininkai, Narutis, the last president before occupation, and Damusis, a past president, were in positions to act as catalysts who could mobilize significant amounts of the population. Because of their multiple number of ties, they could pick and choose the most effective ties, as well as the optimum number of ties, for the given situation.[20] At the start of the occupation when risks were lower, they helped to involve a wide variety of groups. As risks increased, they fell back to smaller and smaller Catholic circles, thus avoiding losses while still keeping relatively large numbers of people involved. In the end, Narutis and Damusis managed to avoid arrest while being crucial in the organization of hundreds of rebels.

Although the Grandis community was not a village community, it was a strong community with a structure conducive to generating rebellion. It illustrates this chapter's contention that the properties of community that

---

[20] Notice that Narutis is credited with eight different types of ties. Both leaders opened or closed ties in ways to optimally maintain the organization. Connections to work groups, with the least history of interaction and common belief, were dropped when pressure increased. Ties to the military, less reliable than those to fellow members of Catholic organizations, were dropped and then renewed immediately before the invasion. In this manner, security was enhanced and weapons became available. Ties to other political organizations were maintained at various levels, but reduced when the pressure increased. The core +2 unit was formed only from the most reliable and committed connections, that is, among selected members of Catholic organizations.

make rebellion against strong regimes possible should be seen not in urban-rural, peasant-worker, but rather along more abstract, generalizable, and, importantly, nonspatial dimensions.

Finally, this analysis produces an important question: what if a few strategically located individuals are removed from the networks of rebellion? Can these types of underground movements be eliminated through "decapitation," or are they driven and sustained by larger social forces and structures? This question again arises in the analysis of rebellion in the postwar years when the majority of politically oriented and previously organized actors had fled, been deported, or been killed.

5. The German Occupation of Lithuania

Lithuanians have a reputation of being among the worst of the German collaborators during the Second World War. Given this reputation, one might expect to see a great deal of movement toward the negative side of the spectrum. There is no doubt that Lithuanians welcomed the invading Germans as liberators in the summer of 1941. As the German occupation continued, however, the bulk of the Lithuanian population maintained neutrality. Contrary to conventional opinion, the number of enthusiastic Nazi collaborators was not high; contrary to some Lithuanian claims, relatively few Lithuanians were involved in active resistance.

This chapter unfolds into three sections: the first establishes movement on the spectrum (or, in this case, its absence) in a short historical review, the second specifies the reasons for the lack of resistance of the Lithuanian population, and the third addresses the lack of collaboration by outlining mechanisms that stymied German efforts to raise an SS division in Lithuania.

Collaboration and Resistance during the German Occupation

As discussed in previous chapters, the leaders of the Lithuanian Activist Front believed that by establishing a provisional government before the Germans arrived they could force, or at least persuade, the Germans to recognize their sovereignty. The leaders of the provisional government, and probably many other Lithuanians as well, were working from a model based on the events and outcomes of World War I.[1] This point cannot be overem-

---

[1] Space does not allow a proper discussion of the impact of the First World War on German-Lithuanian relations. See Vejas Gabriel Liulevicius, *War Land: Culture, National Identity, and German Occupation on the Eastern Front in World War I* (Cambridge: Cambridge University Press, 2000), for an important and detailed analysis.

phasized. Given the nature of Hitler's regime, this strategy really had no chance of repeat success.[2] Although the Lithuanian Provisional Government declared independence on June 23, the Germans refused to recognize its legitimacy.[3] A six-week standoff, punctuated by Lithuanian proposals and German machinations, then began. The Provisional Government attempted to sweeten the pot by offering to raise a national army that would join in the fight against the Soviets. The Germans responded by continuing to ignore officially the Provisional Government and obstruct its communications. In a more desperate effort to gain independence, the Lithuanian Activist Front, still the foundation of the Provisional Government, "declared the acceptance of the nationalist-socialist ideology as the guiding principle of its future policies."[4] Still, the Germans boycotted any participation with the Provisional Government. At one point, the Gestapo facilitated a coup attempt led by the Lithuanian fascist Augustinas Voldemaras on July 23–24. It failed miserably, and the standoff continued.[5]

[2] The following sources describe German plans and internal political maneuvering over Baltic policy: Alexander Dallin, *German Rule in Russia, 1941–1945: A Study of Occupation Policies* (Boulder, Colo.: Westview Press, 1981), especially chap. 10, "Ostland and the Baltic States"; Timothy P. Mulligan, ed., *The Politics of Illusion and Empire: German Occupation Policy in the Soviet Union, 1942–43* (New York: Praeger, 1988), especially chap. 6; Gerald Reitlinger, *The House Built on Sand: The Conflicts of German Policy in Russia, 1939–1945* (Westport, Conn.: Greenwood Press, 1960), especially chap. 4. The strategic logic of German policy is discussed in Alex Alexiev, *Soviet Nationalities in German Wartime Strategy, 1941–1945* (Rand Corporation, Rand Reports, R-2772–NA, August 1982). For a summary of documents, see Timothy P. Mulligan, "The OSS and the Nazi Occupation of the Baltic States, 1941–1945: A Note on Documentation," *Journal of Baltic Studies* 13 (1982): 53–58. In no way does this chapter do justice to the historical and political intricacies of the German occupation of the Baltic. Even Alexander Dallin, in his definitive treatment of German policy in the East, has written, "the internal development of the Baltic States under the Germans is a subject so vast and so distinct from the fate of the 'old Soviet' areas that only the most cursory attention can be paid to it here" (*German Rule in Russia,* p. 182)."

[3] Additionally, the Gestapo was holding the formal prime minister of the Provisional Government, Colonel Skirpa, in Berlin. Skirpa had been negotiating Lithuanian sovereignty with the Germans before the outbreak of the attack on Russia. Juozas Ambrazevicius, a literary historian, became acting prime minister.

[4] Algimantas P. Gureckas, "The National Resistance during the German Occupation of Lithuania," *Lituanas* 8 (1962): 23–28. Gureckas is referring to Memorandums of the Lithuanian Activist Front of July 17, 1941, sent directly to the Fuehrer, and August 5, 1941, sent to the Representative of the German Reich in Lithuania.

[5] For more-detailed accounts, see Zeonas Ivinskis, "Lithuania during the War: Resistance against the Soviet and Nazi Occupants," in V. Stanley Vardys, ed., *Lithuania under the Soviets* (New York: Macmillan, 1965), pp. 68–78, and Algirdas Martin Budreckis, *The Lithuanian National Revolt of 1941* (South Boston, Mass.: Lithuanian Encyclopedia Press, 1968). For an account by an important participant, see Stasys Rastikis, "The Relations of the Provisional Government of Lithuania with the German Authorities" *Lituanas* 8 (1962): 16–22. The Germans brought Rastikis from Berlin to Kaunas in an effort to split the government; however, Rastikis joined the Provisional Government upon his arrival.

Finally, on July 28, the Germans established the Reichskomissariat Ost-land, an administrative unit encompassing the Baltic states and Belorussia. On August 5 the Provisional Government, realizing that sovereignty was un-reachable, composed a written protest against German policy and dissolved itself. The Lithuanian Activist Front, the parent organization of the Provi-sional Government did not last much longer. On September 21 the Germans arrested the head of the LAF, Leonas Prapuolenis, and sent him to Dachau. The following day, the LAF itself was outlawed.

After the June revolt against the Soviets, life for most Lithuanians re-turned to "normal" as individuals went back to their own daily business, farmers returned to their crops and animals, and so on. Of course, Lithua-nian Jews were being herded into ghettos or exterminated during the same period. The political battle between the Provisional Government and the Germans was either unknown (the Germans now controlled channels of mass communications) or of little concern. The general population was op-timistic about the new regime or at least curious about the contours of its policies. Created from a diversity of groups and without a clearly perceived common enemy, the LAF's members and component groups returned to their separate existences. With a decapitated formal structure, the LAF's or-ganizational coherence collapsed.

This very brief summary describes the situation in the fall of 1941. Most individuals were either optimistic about the Germans or would "wait and see." On the spectrum, they occupied the 0 or perhaps −1 position. The ques-tion then becomes whether significant movement toward collaboration and/or resistance occurred after German policies became more pronounced.

Collaboration

The German occupation presented opportunities for both locally based and mobile force collaboration (−2 and −3 on the spectrum). The "Defense Bat-talion" was an armed, mobile collaboration force. Although German au-thorities promised that these units would only be employed within respec-tive homelands, most were sent to the Eastern Front. Some Lithuanian units were assigned tasks of civilian pacification in Yugoslavia and ghetto duty in Poland.[6] At any given time, roughly 8,000 Lithuanians were serving in De-

---

[6] Not surprisingly, I have encountered the most vitriolic anti-Lithuanian statements from Serbs and Jews. From Serbs, the standard statement is that they were "worse than the Nazis." This perception may stem from the types of duties that Lithuanians were involved in more than

fense Battalions (8,388 in August 1941, 8,000 in March 1944).[7] The Waffen SS provided another −3 option. As discussed later, the Germans tried and failed to raise an SS unit in Lithuania. In comparative perspective, the number of Lithuanians participating in mobile, armed collaborationist formations was not large. For instance, in numbers of SS volunteers alone, the Dutch produced 50,000, the Belgians 40,000 (half Flemish, half Walloon), the Danes 6,000, the Norwegians 6,000, and the Finns (despite being unoccupied) 1,000.[8]

The local police force provided an option for local armed service (−2). Lithuanians serving in local police forces performed regular police duties and fought Soviet-sponsored guerrilla units. Because Soviet-based resistance groups did not exist in most of the country, with the notable exception of the area bordering Belorussia, many police never participated in counterinsurgency operations.

The issue of Lithuanian collaboration with the Germans remains controversial even in the year 2000. This controversy, I believe, has more to do with inadequate apologies, the failure to pursue suspected war criminals, and Lithuanian interpretations of the events of June 1941 than with the actual numbers of Lithuanian collaborators. Several recent articles address the legacy of the Second World War in Lithuania.[9]

Resistance

With the lack of a clearly perceived threat and the subsequent organizational disintegration of the LAF, anti-German resistance splintered along prewar political lines.[10] The LAF split into two major groups: the Freedom Fighters

the numbers of collaborating Lithuanians. An alternative view is that this perception stems from the "fanatical" nature of Lithuanians. Chapter 9 addresses the question of the "fanatical" Lithuanian.

[7] Romuald J. Misiunas and Rein Taagerpera, *The Baltic States: Years of Dependence, 1940–1980* (Berkeley: University of California Press, 1983), p. 55.

[8] George H. Stein, *The Waffen SS: Hitler's Elite Guard at War, 1939–1945* (Ithaca: Cornell University Press, 1966), p. 139.

[9] In my opinion, one of the most informed, balanced, and insightful works on Lithuania and the heritage of the Second World War can be found in Saulius Suziedelis, "Thoughts on Lithuania's Shadows of the Past: A Historical Essay on the Legacy of War," and "Thoughts on Lithuania's Shadows of the Past: A Historical Essay on the Legacy of War, Part II" <www.artium.lt/4/journal.html>.

[10] See Ivinskis, "Lithuania during the War," pp. 76–84, and Daniel J. Kazeta, "Lithuanian Resistance to Foreign Occupation, 1940–1952," *Lituanas* 34 (1988): 5–32, especially pp. 11–18, for more complete summaries.

and the Lithuanian Front. Christian Democrats and Ateitininkai dominated the latter, whereas interests less connected to the Roman Catholic Church predominated in the former. In short, the major political division of the pre-war era again came to the fore. The fascist "Voldemaras group," instigators of the failed June coup, first opted for outright collaboration, registering themselves as the "Lithuanian Nationalist Party." After four months, how-ever, the Voldemarists were also forced to go underground after being banned for criticizing German policies. Finally, students at the University of Kaunas formed their own resistance group, the Lithuanian Union Movement.

How should movement on the spectrum be coded? Two questions are most relevant: the nature of the organization and the number of individuals in-volved. Unlike the first Soviet period, the underground organizations were neither composed of local cells nor oriented toward violent resistance.[11] In-stead, resistance groups were politically oriented and their primary activity was the publication of underground newspapers. For the bulk of the popula-tion, any resistance that did occur consisted of accepting and reading these publications, at most a +1 action.[12]

Explaining the Lack of Resistance

Resentment Formation

The lack of movement from the 0 position toward resistance was overdeter-mined. Few of the mechanisms that push individuals from 0 to +1 were pres-ent. First of all, German policies produced far less resentment formation than those of the preceding Soviet regime. Second, focal point mechanisms were absent: the set of focal symbols and symbolic actions available to mobilize individuals against the Germans was far smaller than the set relevant to Rus-sian-Soviet resistance. Third, elites possessed no effective strategy to at-tempt to mobilize resistance to the Germans. In sum, movement could not be expected either from the "bottom up" or the "top down."

The question of motivation is perhaps most fundamental. The lack of re-sentment does not mean that Lithuanians were emotionally neutral or posi-

[11] The Lithuanian Freedom Army was one exception.

[12] Those actually creating and distributing the underground newspapers took on higher risks, including the chance of being sent to a concentration camp. Despite the high risk involved in publishing and distributing underground newspapers, the nonviolent nature of this resistance still represents +1 action.

tive about German rule. Resentment is highest when a hierarchy is strongly perceived, when that hierarchy is perceived as unjust, and when something can be done to change that hierarchy. Under the Germans, the perception of hierarchy was unavoidable, but, in comparison with the nature of the previous Soviet hierarchy, specific aspects of the German occupation made it seem more just. Furthermore, because Lithuanians were working from the World War I sequence of events as a model, which prescribed a "wait and see" strategy, the ability and the need for immediate action was less clearly envisioned.

For Lithuanians, the German occupation possessed many highly unpleasant features. Perhaps most grating was the German colonization policy. By the fall of 1942, 16,300 Germans had taken control of Lithuanian farmland.[13] Furthermore, the German administration did not return property nationalized by the Soviets to their former private owners. Instead, German companies gained control of state farms,[14] textile mills, and other large enterprises. As the war continued, grain requisitions and forced labor conscriptions became more severe. Yet these largely economic hardships did not produce the venom so pervasive during the Soviet occupation. Most regions of Lithuania were not colonized; most small farms, and thus most of the population, remained in the hands of their longtime owners; the restitution of private property was promised (although never carried out);[15] the failure to register for labor assignment was seldom punished. As one former Vilnius resident concluded:

> All those measures caused much inconvenience and hardship, but little real suffering. There was not enough German personnel to supervise the economy, and they had to rely on the Lithuanian administration serving under the authority. The Lithuanian administration tolerated the growth of an extensive black market in food products and, to a lesser extent, in various other goods. The cities were relatively well supplied with food, and the population suffered no starvation. Most of the economic measures created relatively little resentment. They were either ineffective or could be justified by the needs of war. Most irritation and hate was caused by the measures of colonization.[16]

[13] Ivinskis, "Lithuania during the War," p. 75.
[14] Some Dutch companies also were involved; see Gureckas, "The National Resistance during the German Occupation," p. 25.
[15] See Dallin, *German Rule in Russia, 1941–1945,* pp. 192–193.
[16] Gureckas, "The National Resistance during the German Occupation," p. 25.

In effect, although the German policy could be harsh (Timothy Mulligan wrote that "the distinguishing characteristic of German policy in Lithuania remained brute force),[17] the Germans were too overextended to create an offensive presence in the everyday lives of most Lithuanians. As argued in Chapter 2, the perception of hierarchy rests on the visible and everyday experiences of domination and force inextricably linked to the composition of the bureaucracy and the police, the nature of language use, and general issues of sovereignty and control. On each of these issues, the German administration, which possessed neither the resources nor the inclination to attempt a transformation of Lithuanian society, generally rated better than the previous Soviet government.

First, the German need for native administrators dictated that Lithuanians would occupy positions of authority in the bureaucracy and a relatively high position on any perceived hierarchy. The same could be said for police. For the average Lithuanian, contact with local police meant contact with a fellow Lithuanian, and probably a Lithuanian nationalist at that. Minorities, especially and obviously Jews, did not serve in security positions. The importance of this fact was underlined in the preceding chapter. In day-to-day legal matters as well, Lithuanians were most likely dealing with fellow Lithuanians. The pre-Soviet educational system was restored. Unlike the Soviets, the Germans did not generally interfere in the cultural life of the Baltics.

Although the Germans refused to recognize the Lithuanian Provisional Government, they always held out hope that sovereignty, or at least autonomy, was a possibility in the future. As Dallin writes: "the Baltic region was considered an *exception* to the Eastern Mass, and advocating some form of 'recognition' for it was well compatible with Nazism and a fervently anti-Russian approach."[18] Additionally, many Lithuanians believed a repeat of the World War I scenario was possible, if not likely: the war might be settled not through unconditional surrender but through a negotiated settlement that might allow recognition of Lithuanian sovereignty. As in the First World War, this outcome would most likely come to pass if the Germans were to lose while still occupying Lithuania. Many believed that the West – and there was great faith in the United States and Great Britain at the time – would force the Germans out while never allowing the Soviets to reoccupy the Baltics. Thus, German wartime rule was never seen in terms of the finality

---

[17] Mulligan, *The Politics of Illusion and Empire: German Occupation Policy in the Soviet Union, 1942–43*, p. 86.
[18] Dallin, *German Rule in Russia, 1941–1945*, p. 193.

that Russian rule connoted. There were great hopes that sovereignty would be regained, that the Germans would not remain "on top" in Lithuania for long. In contrast, the Russians had been the Lithuanians' imperial "masters" prior to the First World War.

In summary, for the average Lithuanian the perception of dominance of a foreign people was greatly reduced from the 1940–1941 period of Soviet rule. Clearly, the Germans were on top of the political-social hierarchy, but in day-to-day matters Lithuanian citizens were not constantly reminded of their subordinate position. Furthermore, Lithuanians clearly stood above the minority groups on the hierarchy. This was no small matter given the long-standing enmity between Poles and Lithuanians (especially regarding the Vilnius region) and the animosity against Jews created during the first Soviet occupation. Finally, the First World War model informed Lithuanians that the best strategy was to tolerate the problems imposed by the Germans, to wait them out.

Focal-Point Mechanisms

Had there been significant resentment against the Germans, movement from the 0 position on the spectrum might still have been difficult due to the lack of anti-German symbolic actions that could have served to communicate resentment and risk acceptance. A comparison of the wealth of anti-Russian and anti-Soviet symbols with the relative paucity of long-standing anti-German symbolic actions makes this point clear. Perhaps most importantly, the German occupiers tolerated religion. In this fervently Catholic nation, the practice of religion had quite naturally produced anti-Soviet symbolic actions. Recall the importance of All Souls' Day (Chapter 3). As Misiunas and Taagerpera point out, "Although cultural and religious affairs were strictly supervised, the Nazis, unlike the Soviets, did not act on a perceived need to infuse them immediately with a particular ideological aura. The requirements of waging war obviously took precedence over those of eventual Germanization, and so these areas were left largely in the hands of the local authorities."[19]

Furthermore, while Lithuanians had previously lived under both Russian and German rule, the respective historical experiences vastly differed. As mentioned earlier, the tsarist regime had banned the Latin alphabet in an ef-

[19] Misiunas and Taagerpera, *The Baltic States: Years of Dependence, 1940–1980*, p. 52.

fort to stem Polish and Catholic influence. As a result, thousands of Lithuanians became involved in a decades-long underground book-smuggling campaign. Massive numbers of Lithuanians engaged in anti-Russification activities such as home teaching of Lithuanian or support of secret schools. National heroes and legends evolved from this linguistic struggle, Vincas Kudirka perhaps chief among them. A host of religious and educational activities were imbued with anti-Russian overtones.

A smaller number of Lithuanians had lived under Prussian governance, and, of course, the Germans had occupied the country during the First World War. In contrast to the Russian legacy, this experience did not produce the same wealth of everyday resistance actions. There was no language battle; in fact, the Prussian authorities published a considerable number of newspapers in Lithuanian, and Lithuanians served in the German Parliament.[20] One treatment of Lithuanian nationalism describes the differing histories of Lithuania Minor (under Prussia) and Lithuania Major (under Russia) in the following manner:

> Lithuanian patriotism in Lithuania Minor, under German rule, was of a different character from that of Lithuania Proper, oppressed by the Russians. The growth of a national consciousness in Lithuania Major was the result of seditious, revolutionary work. Every patriotic Lithuanian rigorously resisted the Russian authorities and felt superior to them, both morally and culturally.
>
> In Lithuania Minor, at the same time, loyalty and homage to the Kaiser was the rule, and the general Lithuanian ethnic population had quite resigned itself to the German government. This loyalty to Germany by the Lithuanians of Lithuania Minor often surprised and irritated their ethnic brothers in Lithuania Major, but this was understandable. An advanced culture, discipline and material well-being, as well as a systematic and severe denationalization process, subdued the Lithuanians in Lithuania Minor. Any type of insurrection in that area was impossible. To preserve their nationality, Lithuanians faithful to the cause could follow but one path: not conspiracy, but peaceful, cultural work.[21]

Thus, a pattern was set. Resistance against Russians was of a mass and conspiratorial nature. Resistance against the Germans was more passive and

---

[20] Jack J. Stukas, *Awakening Lithuania: A Study on the Rise of Modern Lithuanian Nationalism* (Madison, N.J.: Florham Park Press, 1966) p. 107.

[21] Ibid., p. 112.

public. The experience of World War I only served to strengthen this pattern. Although the Germans had occupied Lithuania during the First World War, they ended up facilitating Lithuanian independence and were one of the first great powers to offer recognition.[22] Lithuanians had felt and remembered the bitter taste of subordination to the Russians and had developed a number of religiously and culturally based responses of a mass character. With the Germans, the mass of Lithuanians, with a smaller set of symbolic actions and less deep-seated resentment, stood by while elites bargained.

Elite Strategy

During the 1940–1941 Soviet occupation, society moved to +1, then local resistance cells formed and were loosely united by the LAF. During the German occupation, this "bottom-up" dynamic did not develop. Whether Lithuanian elites could have initiated a resistance movement from the "top down" is irrelevant because they saw little advantage in fighting the Germans.[23] This viewpoint was reinforced after the outcome at Stalingrad made a Soviet return seem very probable. All Lithuanian political groups hoped for a stalemate between the Germans and Soviets followed by Western intervention. For this scenario to be realized, the Germans had to be strong enough to stall the Soviet return. As Misiunas and Taagerpera write of all three Baltic oppositions, "The organized anti-German oppositions did not encourage armed resistance, which could only help the Soviets. Rather, the aim was one of sabotaging German occupation measures and of keeping alive an organized national political body capable of representing each nation's interest during the post-war settlement. Hope was placed in the Western powers."[24]

For Lithuanian opposition groups, the most appropriate form of resistance was the printing and distribution of newspapers and pamphlets.[25] For most individuals involved, this action was unorganized and nonviolent, in other words, at the +1 level.

[22] Germany recognized Lithuania in 1918. The United States, Great Britain, France, Italy, and Japan waited until 1922 to grant recognition. Of course, German recognition was an attempt to limit Polish and Russian claims and influence.

[23] Based on the preceding theory, they could not have created +2 organizations due to the lack of movement to +1.

[24] Misiunas and Taagerpera, *The Baltic States: Years of Dependence, 1940–1980,* p. 62.

[25] See Ivinskis, "Lithuania during the War," pp. 77–78, for a description of these publications.

While these activities enjoyed some success, their effect in moving individuals from neutrality was limited by the reemergence and lack of unity of pre-1940 political divisions. Again, the widest split was between Catholic-based and secular organizations. The LAF had broken into two groups, each publishing its own views on how to handle the German occupation authorities and what to expect in the future. Other anti-German newsletters were published by the Populist Party, Union of Sauliai, and the Lithuanian Union Movement (students at the University of Kaunas). Furthermore, regional pamphlets and newsletters further diluted the coherency of the message. It was not until late 1943 that the two main groups, the Lithuanian Front (Catholic-oriented) and the Union of Freedom Fighters, joined together to form the Supreme Committee for the Liberation of Lithuania. In the meantime, the general population had become somewhat accustomed to German rule. The mixed messages they were receiving, while providing valuable information on how to avoid labor conscription and mitigate other features of life under German rule, did not produce massive movement on the spectrum. Without a reservoir of resentment and a wealth of symbolic actions, most individuals went on with their lives in a basically neutral fashion.

Collaboration and the Question of SS Recruitment

The definition of the −1 and +1 positions on the spectrum are admittedly rather fuzzy. Many Lithuanians performed actions during the German occupation that would have placed them at various points at both of these nodes. Indeed, this reflected changing Lithuanian thinking on the benevolence of the Germans as well as their estimates of the Germans' chances for success. Given this ambiguity and fluidity, this section concentrates on movement to the −3 position, the most easily identified position of collaboration. As the Soviets approached, the Germans grew desperate for manpower and became more willing to trade political autonomy for cooperation. In August 1942 Himmler approved the creation of an Estonian legion within the Waffen SS. A Latvian legion followed shortly thereafter. The results were fairly encouraging: 15,000 Latvians and 6,500 Estonians enlisted and eventually Estonians and Latvians formed the bulk of three divisions.[26] At first, Himmler refused to recruit Lithuanians due to both racial considerations, because they were "less pure" than their northern neighbors, and political concerns −

---

[26] Stein, *The Waffen SS: Hitler's Elite Guard at War, 1939–1945*, pp. 176–177.

Lithuanians were less reliable.[27] The Germans may have also recalled the June 1941 anti-Soviet revolt as well as the annoying Provisional Government. As the situation grew more desperate, however, the SS and army lobbied to raise tens of thousands of troops from Lithuania for service in the SS.

On March 6, 1943, all men over seventeen were required to register for the Waffen SS legion. Almost no one showed up. As Mulligan sums up, "Out of 3230 candidates summoned to register in six Lithuanian cities, only 177 complied."[28] On March 17, 1943, the Germans gave up their efforts to raise an SS legion in Lithuania, stating that "Lithuanians were declared unworthy of wearing the SS uniform."[29] Of all occupied nations, only Poland and Lithuania had no native SS Legion.

Why was there so little movement toward −3 level collaboration? After all, the Germans used both carrots and sticks to persuade Lithuanians to join. On one hand, the Nazis promised that the legion would only fight in the vicinity of the Lithuanian homeland and would be well armed. On the other hand, it was clear that noncompliance could bring retaliation. Indeed, after their recruiting debacle the Germans deported forty-six Lithuanian leaders to Stutthof concentration camp, closed all institutes of higher education, and initiated manhunts for the missing draftees. Yet despite promises and threats, Lithuanian youth did not report.

The German failure to raise SS units in Lithuania is, on the surface, even more surprising when seen in light of subsequent German efforts to exploit Lithuanian manpower. On February 16, 1944, so many Lithuanians volunteered for a "Territorial Defense Force" that thousands needed to be turned away. One estimate put the number of volunteers at 20,000.[30] There were obvious differences between the two German recruitment drives. The latter appeal was supported by a popular military figure, General Povilas Plechavicius; the units were to be led by Lithuanians (with Plechavicius as commander) and to be employed on Lithuanian soil; perhaps most importantly, the dreaded Soviets were approaching the homeland. Yet the striking difference in mass behavior between the two events, separated by less than a year,

---

[27] According to Dallin, other than SS recruitment the distinctions made between the three Baltic peoples were not large. See *German Rule in Russia, 1941–1945,* pp. 184–185. Mulligan sees the Lithuanian experience as more distinctive.

[28] Mulligan lists further totals for mobilization of non-SS units: "Through the summer of 1943 the mobilization produced a grand total of only 1464 recruits for military and police service," from *The Politics of Illusion and Empire,* p. 87.

[29] Misiunas and Taagerpera, *The Baltic States: Years of Dependence, 1940–1980,* p. 56.

[30] Kazeta, "Lithuanian Resistance to Foreign Occupation, 1940–1952," p. 17.

deserves closer scrutiny. These are clear examples of the "tipping" dynamics of an n-person assurance game. There are two equilibria, one at zero participation and the other at universal support. What were the mechanisms that moved individuals from one equilibrium to the other?

Threshold Mechanisms

The spectrum concept was designed to capture incremental and sequential movements in collaboration or resistance toward one dominant regime. Responses to the SS recruitment drive and the Plechavicius appeal do not neatly fit this concept. Here, the movement is from the 0 (or perhaps the −1 or +1 positions) to a −3 position. Furthermore, these are hardly unambiguous acts of collaboration. Clearly, the primary motivation of the Plechavicius volunteers was not to help the Germans, whose hold over Lithuania was correctly seen as short term, but rather to resist the Soviets upon their imminent return. Despite these ambiguities, the threshold mechanism described in Chapter 2 applies to this movement from neutrality. In short, community-based status reward mechanisms operated to raise or reduce thresholds and the "tipping point" during the respective German recruitment efforts.[31]

During the March recruitment drive, the payoffs of a Schelling diagram "tipping game" can be readily identified. Lithuanian youth faced a binary choice: compliance or noncompliance. As in the hypothetical example in Figures 2.4 and 2.5, status reward mechanisms and the strategic context provide the basis for coding the value of each choice. Avoiding induction involved a measure of risk closely related to the numbers of others also acting to avoid mobilization. If the vast majority of potential inductees boycotted and if support networks were sufficient to help "draft dodgers" safely hide, the risk factor would be vastly reduced, despite German threats. Second, status sanctions and benefits were important concerns. Because mobilization was carried out at a local level,[32] those complying with induction orders could be readily identified by fellow members of the community. The nature of the payoff can be related to the numbers of actors opting for each choice. As the number of "draft dodgers" approaches 100 percent, that is, the num-

---

[31] For more-detailed discussions of the strategic context of military enlistment, see Margaret Levi, "Conscription: The Price of Citizenship," in Robert Bates et al., eds., *Analytic Narratives* (Princeton: Princeton University Press, 1998), and Roger Petersen, "Rationality, Ethnicity, and Military Enlistment," *Social Science Information* 28 (1989): 563–598.

[32] Village elders were responsible for bringing in recruits. See Ivinskis, "Lithuania during the War," p. 79.

ber of compliers is 0 percent, the size of the sanction for compliance (joining the SS) becomes much higher. In strong communities, this effect is generally magnified (refer to Figures 2.4 and 2.5). If the risk involved for noncompliance greatly diminishes while the status sanctions for compliance increases, the gap in values between the two choices at the beginning of the induction effort, that is, at 0 percent compliance, will likely show the optimal choice to be "draft dodging." In fact, the gap might be so large that few would consider signing up even if they were personally so inclined.

The actions and nature of Lithuanian society and its underground organizations helped produce low-risk and high-status sanctions for anyone registering for the SS. Two elements are of special note. First, the underground newspapers, widely distributed through most of the country, unanimously called for a boycott. Given the divergence of political opinion among these organizations, their unanimity on the boycott is notable. These organizations also reduced risk by helping hide unregistered youth.[33] The second factor is more unique: Lithuanian groups raised the negative status of joining the SS by sending retarded and handicapped individuals to the recruiting center.[34] Those who might have seriously wished to join the SS would have found themselves among the mentally and physically deficient. The effect was to ridicule the German effort – and anyone cooperating with it.

Similar to the March 1943 boycott of the SS legion, the February 1944 recruitment of a Territorial Force exhibited a clear "tipping game" dynamic. In the latter instance, in stark contrast, the equilibrium was near universal support rather than near universal rejection. Again, risk and community-level mechanisms can be used to code choices of volunteering or not volunteering. This time, though, resentment can be added to the analysis. The choice in 1943 did not involve joining a Lithuanian-led force fighting against Soviets-Russians at the doorstep of the homeland. In the latter instance, General Plechavicius made his radio appeal for volunteers on Lithuanian Independence Day. The traditional fight against the longtime enemy was again beginning. The value of volunteering also increased through status rewards. All underground publications supported the Plechavicius force.[35] Addition-

---

[33] Mulligan, *The Politics of Illusion and Empire,* p. 87.

[34] Mecislovas Mackevicius, "Lithuanian Resistance to German Mobilization Attempts, 1941–1944," *Lituanas* 32 (1986): 13; Ivinskis, "Lithuania during the War," p. 79.

[35] Mackevicius, "Lithuanian Resistance to German Mobilization Attempts 1941–1944," p. 15; Ivinskis, "Lithuania during the War," p. 83

ally, local groups of friends seemed to join as groups. This phenomenon indicated the power of community-level reciprocity relationships.

Certainly, the decision to volunteer for the Territorial Force involved risk. No one could have been entirely ignorant of the brutality occurring in the war on the eastern front as it rapidly swept toward Lithuania. However, status rewards and resentment served to raise the value of volunteering to a level in which the "tipping point" was very low and easily and quickly surpassed by the least risk-averse youth.

Enlisting in the Territorial Force involved far more risk than could have been realized at the time. In early May 1944, not long after its creation, the German authorities demanded the incorporation of most of the Territorial Force into the auxiliary police of the SS.[36] German officers were to take command, SS uniforms worn, and the "Heil Hitler" salute employed. After ordering his units to disobey, General Plechavicius and his staff were arrested and sent to the Salaspils concentration camp in Latvia. As a warning to the Territorial Force, the Germans randomly picked soldiers out of the Vilnius detachment and shot them as a deterrent to others. Still, most members of the unit fled into the woods, their fate to be discussed in the following chapter. Those surviving but failing to escape, a number estimated at 3,500, were sent to Germany and Norway for ground duty in the Luftwaffe.

Concluding Points

Most Lithuanians went about their own personal business during the German occupation. They may have respected the Germans far more than the Soviets, but their affinity for German rule was much less than commonly believed. Although the German policies were often harsh, they did not breed intolerable levels of resentment. Second, a relative lack of anti-German symbols also worked against the formation of any mass movement to the resistance side of the spectrum. With neither sufficient motivation nor coordinating focal points, resistance to German rule was unlikely. After an initial burst

---

[36] The events briefly described in this paragraph are discussed in more detail in Misiunas and Taagerpera, *The Baltic States: Years of Dependence, 1940–1980,* pp. 56–57; Mackevicius, "Lithuanian Resistance to German Mobilization Attempts, 1941–1944," pp. 16–17; Gureckas, "The National Resistance during the German Occupation of Lithuania," pp. 27–28; Ivinskis, "Lithuania during the War," p. 84; Kazeta, "Lithuanian Resistance to Foreign Occupation, 1940–1952," p. 17.

of enthusiasm, there was little movement toward collaboration either. As just outlined, threshold mechanisms, in combination with status rewards, played a significant role in this outcome.[37]

The causal role of elite politics is difficult to judge, although it too would not have facilitated development of +2 level of resistance. There was no strategic logic in actively and violently resisting the Germans while the USSR remained the bigger threat. Also, the political divisions among Lithuanian factions reemerged under German occupation to fragment the message and signals of resistance.

I end this chapter with the story of M5,[38] which is highly revealing of several aspects of the German occupation of Lithuania. Several Soviet partisans parachuted into the territory around M5's southern Lithuanian village of Merkine (see Chapter 6) and established a camp in the woods. There was no support for them among local residents, but neither was there much desire to fight them. The Soviet partisans, realizing that they had no local support, engaged in no actual fighting and were apparently content to ride out the war in the forest. Soviet partisans and the locals agreed on an arrangement in which each left the other alone except for occassional trade and barter. An obvious logic underlay this neutrality: the Soviet partisans themselves were not a danger unless the German authorities knew about them in which case a fight would ensue that might endanger the community. This lesson was reinforced through experience. Once, Lithuanian police had come into the village while Soviet partisans had been present and had felt obliged to fire upon them. Not wishing to engage in such life-threatening action again, the Lithuanian police, the villagers, and the Soviet partisans developed a system of signals that would allow Soviet partisans to recede to the woods before the arrival of the police. All participants seemed to realize that the war and the final outcome would not be decided at that time and that place and all chose a waiting game. In effect, local residents and even some local police would accept no risk in helping the Germans. They remained neutral. Furthermore, while local residents had felt significant resentment and hatred to-

---

[37] Under the German occupation, the Lithuanian Front published "Judas of Lithuania," which identified individuals who collaborated with the Germans in ways seen contrary to Lithuanian interests. See Ivinskis, "Lithuania during the War," p. 77. Such actions put status considerations into play throughout the occupation.

[38] An interviewee from southern Lithuania; his case is discussed at length in the following chapter.

ward the dominating Soviet regime of 1940–1941, this feeling did not carry over toward the self-isolated, and somewhat pitied, small group of Soviet partisans. This point supports the idea that resentment formation is produced by day-to-day political and social interactions rather than historical and cultural enmities.

6. Postwar Lithuania

The Soviet postwar occupation of Lithuania was far different from the pre-war occupation.[1] First, and perhaps foremost, the Soviets' primary tool in the latter period was out-and-out brutality. There was little of the "hearts and minds" propaganda campaign that accompanied threat and deportation in the earlier period. No doubt four years of savage fighting against the Germans, and the millions of dead produced by it, contributed to the formation and execution of savage pacification policies, especially when these policies were to be applied to a population considered guilty of collaboration.

The Soviet effort in Lithuania, led by General Kruglov, combined the resources of the NKVD, SMERSH (military counterintelligence), and the Ministry of Internal Affairs. The overall strategy included five fundamental

---

[1] In this chapter, I concentrate mainly on the action at the community level while glossing over the policies of the Soviet regime and the politics among partisan factions. Several articles or short sections of books deal with these elements. One concise piece is V. Stanley Vardys, "The Partisan Movement in Postwar Lithuania," *Slavic Review* 22 (1963): 499–522. Also see Thomas Remeikis, *Opposition to Soviet Rule in Lithuania* (Chicago: Institute of Lithuanian Studies Press, 1980), chap. 2; also by Remeikis, "The Armed Struggle against the Sovietization of Lithuania after 1944," *Lituanas* 8 (1962): 29–40. Romuald J. Misiunas and Rein Taagerpera, *The Baltic States: Years of Dependence, 1940–1980* (Berkeley: University of California Press, 1983), pp. 81–91, review the partisan war. More-specific aspects of the postwar struggle are discussed by various authors. On collectivization-deportation, see Kestutis Girnius, "The Collectivization of Lithuanian Agriculture, 1944–1950," *Soviet Studies* 40 (1988): 460–478; John Biggart, "The Collectivization of Agriculture in Soviet Lithuania," *East European Quarterly* 9 (1990): 53–75; Julius Slavenas, "Deportations," *Lituanas* 6 (1960): 47–52. On the growth of the Soviet party apparatus and a general review based on mainly Soviet documents available at the time, see Benedict Vytenis Maciuika, "The Baltic States under Soviet Russia: A Case Study in Sovietization" (Ph.D. dissertation, University of Chicago, 1963), especially chap. 3. Finally, to juxtapose the lives of the hunted with those of the hunters, compare the memoirs of one partisan leader, Juozas Daumantas, *Fighters for Freedom* (New York: Maryland Books, 1975), with the testimony of a former NKVD officer and participant in antipartisan action, Colonel Burlitski, who defected to the West. See U.S. Congress, *Hearings: Communist Aggression Investigation,* Fourth Interim Report of the Select Committee on Communist Aggression, 82nd Cong., 2nd sess., 1952, beginning on p. 1372.

elements: the formation of locally based and recruited militias (−2 on the spectrum), called *istrebiteli;*[2] the periodic combined operation of istrebiteli and NKVD forces in "sweeps" through the forested areas to surround and capture or kill Lithuanian partisans; the infiltration of partisan units with spies; periodic offers of amnesty; and, starting in 1948, collectivization accompanied by deportation, a policy that eliminated much of the partisans' +2 base. The Soviets employed several more specific devices to threaten or demoralize the population. For example, the Soviets punished the families of partisans. In an effort to uncover those related or connected to the rebels, the bodies of killed partisans were displayed in the town square. In addition to providing possible deterrence value, hidden Soviet agents would observe the reactions of passersby trying to gauge who might be the mother or brother of the deceased. Torture was commonplace.

Beyond increased cruelty and violence, the second occupation also differed from the first in other important ways. Of the most politically active and educated section of the Lithuanian population, many had fled with the retreating Germans or had been deported; others were dead. The Soviets had initiated two waves of this decapitation process during the first occupation, one in the summer of 1940 and a second days before Barbarossa. The Germans had forcibly removed many more-important leaders; Damusis and Narutis, for example, were imprisoned in Stutthof concentration camp. Finally, a huge number, tens of thousands in the Baltics as a whole, fled with the Germans to avoid almost certain death or deportation at the hands of the advancing Soviets. Thus, the first occupation eliminated a sizable stratum of the educated and politically conscious, the second began with decimation of this demographic group.

Furthermore, the economic and social organizations that had formed the basic building blocks of Lithuanian social life had withered during the five years of German and Soviet occupation. The Germans viewed social-patriotic organizations like the Union of Sauliai with suspicion. Under Nazi rule, university-based groups suffered, and the educational system as a whole atrophied. The rich texture of social and economic life in interwar Lithuania would never return. The overall situation can be readily summarized: incredibly violent and repressive policies were enacted against a leaderless and socially weakened population.

---

[2] Also referred to as *stribai* or *strebs* by several of the interviewees. The name means "destroyer" and derives from the name of the demolition units implementing the Soviet scorched-earth policy during the 1941 retreat.

Yet Lithuanian rebellion raged; individuals and communities moved to +2 on a significant scale. Estimates place the number of organized rebels at more than 30,000.[3] The Lithuanian underground was able to distribute newspapers, carry out trials of collaborators, and urge the boycott of Soviet elections, in addition to assassinating officials and occasionally attacking a Soviet installation. Official Soviet statistics list the number of dead at 20,000 on each side during this struggle.[4] Non-Soviet estimates put the numbers much higher. By all estimates, the struggle was sizable and bloody. Remarkably, the Lithuanian partisans managed to control much of the countryside until 1948 and the onset of collectivization and mass deportation. Some partisans were able to continue their struggle into the early 1950s.

Common explanations of Lithuanian postwar rebellion refer to Lithuanian obstinacy, level of patriotism or nationalism, or other national-cultural characteristics. Lithuanian sources often credit Lithuanian formal organization. The United Movement for Democratic Resistance, with a separate military arm called the Supreme Committee for the Reconstruction of Lithuania, did unite many partisans. With the creation of Lithuania's Movement of Freedom Fighters in 1949, the formal partisan movement reorganized. The data presented here, though, challenge the national character explanation and downplay the role of formal organization. As in the 1940–1941 occupation, broad factors such as national character cannot explain local and regional differences. As in 1940–1941, organization occurred with bottom-up dynamics. Community structure was again the crucial factor, often unleashing sequences of mechanisms leading to high community equilibria. The formal top-down structures that did exist did not create rebellion organization so much as loosely unite many of the locally based units that had already formed. Centralized organization sometimes hindered rebellion. Indeed, sometimes Soviet infiltrators encouraged the centralization of the underground so that leadership could be decapitated and local units more easily uncovered.[5]

---

[3] V. Stanley Vardys and Judith Sedaitis, *Lithuania: The Rebel Nation* (Boulder, Colo.: Westview Press, 1997), p. 82.

[4] Vardys and Sedaitis point out that this number is roughly equal to the French-Algerian conflict in percentage terms (ibid., p. 84). Of the 20,000 Soviet dead, 13,000 were collaborators, meaning, presumably, that the other 7,000 were Soviet police or military of one variety or another. Misiunas and Taagepera, *The Baltic States: Years of Dependence, 1940–1980,* compare the level of organization of the Lithuanian rebels to that of the Viet Cong in South Vietnam (p. 81).

[5] Vardys and Sedaitis, *Lithuania: The Rebel Nation,* p. 82.

How was this level of rebellion organized and sustained against the powerful and brutal Soviet regime? The mechanisms driving movement on the spectrum of roles are sought again through comparisons within a field of variation. This chapter examines variation within and across regions, surveying twenty individual cases and exploring rebellion dynamics in several communities. The empirical question is whether the same mechanisms are consistently driving behavior throughout a variety of regional and local settings.

Five Cases from the Merkine Region (M1–M5)

During the interwar period, the residents of the small town of Merkine (pop. 2,000 to 3,000) and the surrounding area lived peacefully. Like many other places in Lithuania, Jewish merchants and artisans composed half or more of the population of the town itself while Lithuanian farmers grew hay and barley and raised livestock in the surrounding countryside. For the most part, the two groups lived separately and usually met only at the marketplace. As in other southern Lithuanian towns, many Poles resided in Merkine as well as a few Russian families left from the days of tsarist rule. Until the Soviet annexation, life proceeded in much the same way as it had for decades.

Even after Soviet rule was established in 1940, little changed in the Merkine region. There was some confiscation of land, but most of the farmers of this region were under the limit and thus unaffected. The Communist Party apparently organized some gatherings in the town to encourage enrollment in the party and Komsomol, but these meetings left only the vaguest impression on the interviewees. Although the Union of Sauliai had members living in the region, there is little recollection of the formation of organized resistance on the Lithuanian side.[6] On the whole, it appears that during the first brief period of Soviet rule neither the Soviets nor the Lithuanians had the time, resources, or inclination to challenge or change the inertial life patterns of the region. June 1941 brought severe shocks. Throughout all of Lithuania, the Soviet authorities rounded up and deported the usual cate-

---

[6] There may very well have been units formed similar to those described in Chapter 3, but these respondents did not know about them. As pointed out, the rapid advance of the German invasion, especially in a region like Merkine located so near the Polish border, created a situation in which organized action against the Soviets simply was not necessary. In these rural areas, even members of organized groups might have been acting more or less individually during the tumult, or at least it would have appeared this way to the interviewees. The situation in Kaunas, the focus of major political-military objectives, of course differed.

gories of citizens in the middle of the month. Then, bigger changes occurred only a few days later in the wake of Operation Barbarossa.

First and foremost, the invading Germans, with the help of some Lithuanians,[7] murdered the Jewish inhabitants of the town. One of the interviewees (M5) and his father heard about the shooting of Jews and traveled from their farm to observe the situation. When they arrived in Merkine, he said only eight Jews remained and they were in the process of being transported to the killing site. A second respondent (M4) witnessed a young Jewish woman being shot as she tried to flee.

Although half or more of the population of the town had been massacred, life again returned to a rhythm similar to that of previous decades, especially for the Lithuanian farmers who made up the bulk of the area's population. In the town, Jewish property was confiscated or looted,[8] bricks taken from houses, and potatoes planted in the yards of deserted houses. In the countryside, Germans collected taxes from farmers in the form of produce, but these taxes were not excessive. M5 recalled several positive images of the German tax collectors. Once, the Germans "registered" a pregnant sow to later be taken for taxes. M5's mother then went to town and explained to a German officer that the sow was pregnant and the expected litter was essential to the family farm. The officer drove to the farm, verified the pregnancy of the sow, and had it taken off the tax roll, agreeing upon the importance of the future litter. This story was told to contrast the actions of "uncultured" Soviet agents who were ignorant of basic facts of animal husbandry and whose confiscations in the postwar period left families below the subsistence level.[9]

Not even the introduction of Soviet partisans disturbed the normalcy of life during the German occupation. Soviet partisans were present in the area during German rule,[10] but they made only one insignificant military action.

---

[7] As reported by M2.

[8] Many houses were apparently destroyed by a German bombardment of the town; very little was rebuilt during the war (M5).

[9] M5's point, like many others, was not so much about comparing the cruelty of Russians and Germans as comparing their "culture" and efficiency. Occupiers were going to take produce as taxes, that was obvious, but not to leave a subsistence level would impact upon abilities to produce a future tax base. Such Soviet actions were considered ignorant and deserving of contempt.

[10] These were mobile units largely equipped and supplied from the outside, +3 on the spectrum. According to M5, local residents did sometimes supply them with food; in return these Soviet partisans made no threats toward the local population. According to M2, an agent of the Soviet regime in the postwar period, at least three individuals from the town of Merkine were active in this +3 unit: two Russians and one Tatar.

M5 provides a typical example that was used to end the previous chapter. Members of M5's village and another village feared that if a German soldier was killed, heavy fighting, if not retaliation against the village for suspected Soviet collaboration, would result. To prevent this possibility, a meeting was arranged in the cemetery outside Merkine between the Soviet partisans and the local police. No one, apparently, was interested in fighting, and all agreed on a method to avoid one another. When the police made their rounds into certain villages where they thought Soviet partisans might be present, they were to fire warning shots into the air so that the Soviet partisans could evacuate and avoid confrontation. The armed units of both sides, as well as the rural population, seemed to realize that their own efforts were trivial in influencing the outcome of the war. When the Soviets returned to the area in December 1944, the decades-old rhythms and patterns of life were finally shattered through an unimaginably bloody and drawn-out conflict.

On Christmas Eve 1944, Soviet forces massacred the population and burned the small village of Klepocai. Using information from the samizdat journal *Ausra* and a 1947 partisan report, Kestutis Girnius briefly describes the events in the Merkine region:

> The wave of terror reached its climax on Christmas Eve. The original units were reinforced by a detachment of fifty soldiers who destroyed farms in eight villages. Klepocai and Lizdai bore the brunt of the attack. At least 37 people were killed and 48 farms burned that day. Probably more died, but their bodies could not be recovered from the ashes of their burned homes. The soldiers left shortly thereafter, taking with them more than 120 prisoners. January 13, 1945, the day of the new mobilization, almost no one came to Merkine to report for duty.[11]

This event served to catalyze a deadly rebellion that would last for the rest of the decade and precipitate the killings of hundreds of the area's residents – most as partisans, some as regime collaborators.

The rest of this section outlines the responses of five residents of the Merkine region to the return of the Soviets. The individuals in the first and fifth cases below became involved in local organization of anti-Soviet resistance, one in a village that was almost totally at +2 and the other in a village largely at +1. One respondent (M3) became a mobile fighter (+3), roaming the woods in a small band with machine gun in hand. One (M4) remained

---

[11] See Girnius, "Soviet Terror in Lithuania during the Post-War Years," pp. 36–37.

neutral (0), seeing rough equivalence between the Soviets and Lithuanian partisans. Finally, one (M2) served in the local Soviet antipartisan unit (–2) working to liquidate his cohabitants. In the summer of 1992, all were still living in the Merkine area, the three who engaged in active resistance having previously returned from long stretches in Siberia.

M1 and the Village of Kasciunai (+2)

Upon the burning of Klepocai, M1, being of draft age (born in 1925) and fearing conscription into the Red Army, fled into the woods to consider his options. In the forest, 200 other men, also mostly young and fearing some type of forced service or punishment, had done exactly the same. All remained together for about two weeks, seeking information and wondering what to do next. Some were former members of the Lithuanian military units who faced severe reprisal from the Soviets due to their affiliation with the Germans. No officers were in this original group, however, and it remained a leaderless, unwieldy mass. Two brothers had left the forest to turn themselves over to the Soviets, only to be promptly shot. This action, together with the atrocities at Klepocai and the presence of a major NKVD unit in Merkine, in effect precluded the return option. However, due to its large size, the group could not remain hidden and supplied for any length of time. The group split into smaller units at the end of the first week in January.

Not surprisingly, these fragmented units were based on previous acquaintance. Also not surprisingly, these units generally set up base in their home villages. M1's group comprised up to eleven individuals, nine from Kasciunai, one from a neighboring village, and one German soldier originally from Hamburg who had been separated from his outfit during the retreat from the eastern front. In a short period of time, several villages had formed relatively sophisticated networks of support that were primarily local in nature but loosely linked to a supravillage organization. Two stages were involved: first, families and neighbors worked to hide and support their sons returning from the woods; second, these sons became involved with the resistance efforts of former Lithuanian military officers, and, in effect, brought their local support networks into a wider organization.

The key logistical element explaining the resilience of the Lithuanian postwar rebellion hinged upon the use and construction of bunkers – secret underground chambers used by partisans for hiding from the Soviets and storing supplies. The more mobile partisans built their bunkers deep in the woods or possibly along riverbanks. The village-based partisans generally built their bunkers on the family farmstead. The village of Kasciunai consisted of twelve farmsteads (seventy-one inhabitants) located along the Merkys River. Figure 6.1 shows the geographic position of the farmsteads, and other relevant data, including, most importantly, the location of the bunkers and which families had partisan sons. Participation in the local system can be categorized along three criteria: which farmsteads had bunkers, who had knowledge of the bunkers, and who was supplying the bunkers. Analyzing these three criteria shows how the system was formed and maintained and the specific importance of community-based mechanisms.

Bunkers were located at Jakavonis 1, Packauskas, Barysas 2, and Maksele. Some farmsteads had more than one bunker. The Maksele bunker was actually located in the woods somewhat away from the farmstead. All of these families had at least one partisan son, with the Packauskas family having at least three.[12] No family without a son in hiding built a bunker. For various reasons, not all families of partisans built bunkers. The Jakavonis 3 family felt they could conceal their son without a bunker. The Barysas 1 family had need of a bunker (sixteen family members, one of whom was shot dead for partisan activity) but did not build one because the parents suspected that one of their sons was a traitor who would turn them in. The son of the Rimsha family was arrested before that family could build one.

Obviously, knowledge of the location of the bunkers was extremely sensitive information. For example, not all the family members of the Packauskas farmstead knew where their families' bunkers were or who might be in which one at any given time. M1 explained that the sons of Packauskas did not tell their father all that they knew because they were afraid the NKVD would come and "beat it out of him." For the local system, knowledge and direct supply of the bunkers was largely confined to a small circle of family and friends. Throughout the entire postwar period, the bunkers in Kasciunai served their original purpose as a way of protecting and hiding a family member or long-term local inhabitant. But these bunkers soon acquired other functions during the course of the conflict.

---

[12] During the postwar period, the number of locally based partisans varied according to the number coming of draft age and those killed or arrested. Understandably during this interview, the history of M1's original group of ten became merged with the general history of the village and could not be separated.

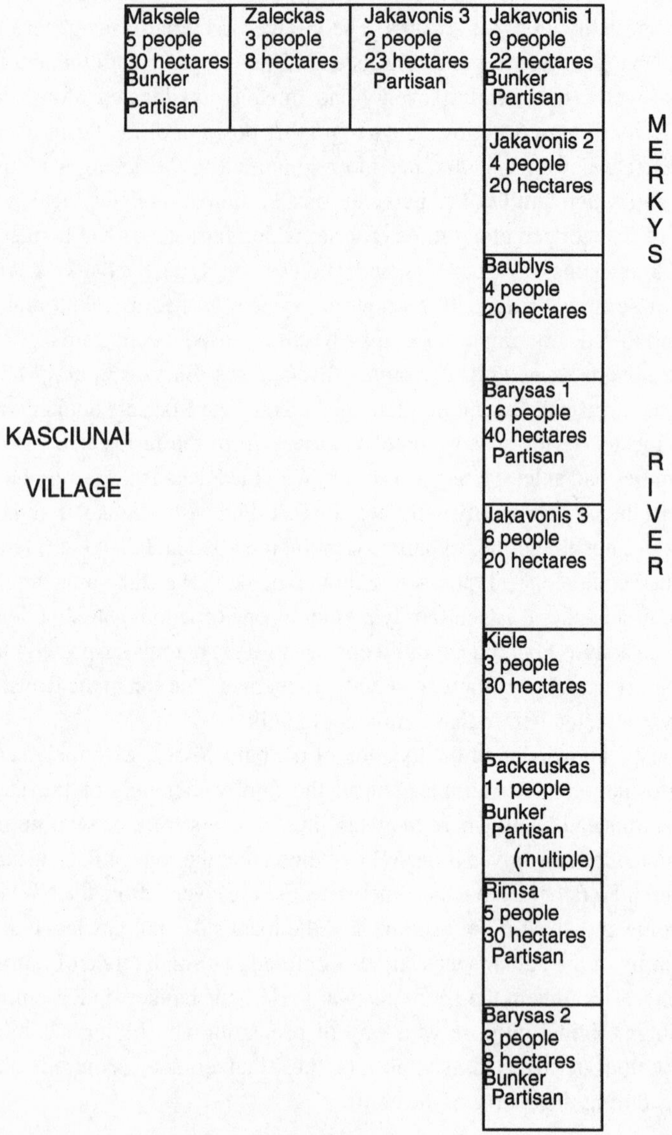

Maksele	Zaleckas	Jakavonis 3	Jakavonis 1
5 people	3 people	2 people	9 people
30 hectares	8 hectares	23 hectares	22 hectares
Bunker		Partisan	Bunker
Partisan			Partisan

Jakavonis 2
4 people
20 hectares

Baublys
4 people
20 hectares

Barysas 1
16 people
40 hectares
Partisan

Jakavonis 3
6 people
20 hectares

Kiele
3 people
30 hectares

Packauskas
11 people
Bunker
Partisan
(multiple)

Rimsa
5 people
30 hectares
Partisan

Barysas 2
3 people
8 hectares
Bunker
Partisan

KASCIUNAI

VILLAGE

M E R K Y S

R I V E R

Figure 6.1. Schema of Kasciunai village

In the spring of 1945, while digging a bunker, M1 met a Lithuanian army colonel named Kazimierietis.[13] In the summer of the same year, he became acquainted with another officer, named Vanagas.[14] They convinced M1 that a war between the Americans and the Soviets would almost certainly occur in the near future and therefore forces should be mobilized to prevent the economic and political consolidation of Soviet rule in Lithuania. Both of these ends required a more formal type of resistance. M1 took an oath of loyalty (very similar to the one for the Lithuanian Army) to this organization in the summer of 1945. Other young men in the village were also drawn in, although to varying degrees.

In practice, the recruitment of an individual also meant a loose incorporation of that individual's local support system into the more formalized supravillage organization (which, for most cases in the present data set, was never that formalized). Thus, in addition to hiding and supplying locals, supporters in the villages were drawn into a variety of other tasks required to sustain the activities of the broader organization. For example, while the mother of the Rimsha family continued to help feed and supply information to the neighboring Packauskas and Barysas 2 bunkers, which had also been drawn into the wider network, she was also active in the communication system of the leadership. Once, when Colonel Kazimierietis needed to go to Alytus, a larger city some distance away, Mrs. Rimsa accompanied him, the two pretending to be a typical rural couple wearing peasant dress in order to escape the scrutiny of any authorities they might meet. A second form of supravillage activity involved "safe houses." When partisans from other localities within the larger network were driven out of their own villages by the NKVD, Kazimierietis and Vanagus would direct them to the Packauskas or Barysas 2 bunkers for safety.[15] Third, due to the general inability of the secluded partisans to communicate with each other, the widened circle of participants allowed a host of messages to be efficiently transmitted. M1 claimed that if some event happened in a certain village nine kilometers away, he would have the information in Kasciunai in two

---

[13] I am unsure of the proper spelling of this name. This spelling was provided by an interviewee.

[14] Adolfas Ramanauskas-Vanagas was the last partisan commander to be captured, managing to hold out until 1956.

[15] The bunker of the Packauskas family is illustrative. The bunker was primarily used by family members, although at least two of the sons spent a lot of time mobile or living in bunkers at neighboring villages. It was not uncommon, however, for partisans from other villages to visit the bunker and stay for short periods, even without an emergency.

hours through a developing network of young girls, usually sisters or daughters of partisans.

After an NKVD assault at a previous base, Colonel Kazimierietis himself came and built a bunker on the Jakavonis 1 farmstead, which became a "headquarters" bunker for the supravillage organization. This bunker existed at an enhanced level of secrecy. Partisans fleeing attack would never be settled at this bunker, only at Packauskas or Barysas 2. Only three families had knowledge of this bunker: Jakavonis 1, Jakavonis 2, and Rimsa. As perhaps the richest family in the village, the Rimsas were seen as the most capable suppliers of basic necessities. The Kazimierietis and Vanagas organization was characterized by three layers of command. An intermediate layer of "adjuncts" transmitted information and orders between the usually secluded leaders and the local village organizations. The transposition of this more "military" system on top of the already developed local systems allowed the military leaders to organize events that could sustain violent anti-Soviet rebellion.

For strategic and logistical reasons, planned attacks on fixed targets were an uncommon form of this violence.[16] Although the Lithuanian partisan war mainly consisted of battles in the forest between insurgents and agents of the Soviet regime, Kazimierietis and Vanagas did manage to organize a sizable attack on collaborationist elements. In the late fall or early winter of 1946, the partisans of M1's village, along with twenty other partisans from nearby villages, met at the house of Jakavonis 1 to review plans for the attack. All, or most, of these thirty were personally acquainted. They would join several other locally based groups connected by the supravillage network. In all, M1 estimates, approximately 150 partisans participated in some way in the attack. M1 himself served as a lookout. During the attack, four partisans were killed along with an unspecified number of istrebiteli.[17] In this operation, the village system played a crucial role by helping disperse the attackers. The 150 participants could quickly separate into small groups and disappear into their bunkers before any Soviet reinforcements could be brought for the chase.

The more common form of partisan violence consisted of ambushes and

---

[16] In general, attacking in force was considered counterproductive because it served to cause attrition among the partisan forces before the ultimate fight – the liberation of the nation in connection with the anticipated Western invasion.

[17] There was disagreement on this issue between M1 and M2. Both agreed that at least one targeted individual had been liquidated.

assassinations against local istrebiteli.[18] As M2 (an istrebitel whose story is given later in this chapter) admits, the partisans around Merkine were quite successful on this score. Of the Merkine istrebiteli unit, twenty-two of thirty members were killed by partisans, usually one or two at a time. The istrebiteli would not go into the woods in groups of less than ten or fifteen for several years after the end of the Second World War.

The partisans' nonviolent activities aimed at the prevention of the region's political and psychological incorporation into the Soviet sphere. For a prominent example, they published and distributed anti-Communist pamphlets discouraging membership in the party and the Komsomol. Vonagas controlled the printing press, which was located in the headquarters bunker at Jakavonis 1. Each small unit was periodically given 200 to 300 "proclamations" to post in small towns or the larger town of Merkine. These activities drew in many members of the local networks. M1's sister transported proclamations to Merkine between pages of a textbook and posted them there. In another effort to prevent Soviet political consolidation, the partisans discouraged participation in elections. In addition to proclamations calling for an election boycott, the partisans fired upon some polling places.[19]

Linking Theory and Substance

The formation of resistance is readily explained by reference to community-based mechanisms and distributions of thresholds previously outlined. A large percentage of the village, ten young men hiding in the woods, held 0 percent thresholds. As they were tied to seven of the twelve families composing the village (see Figure 6.2), a critical mass quickly formed. Even families without "fugitive" sons (certainly, a higher-threshold group) became supporters who provided food for the local system. These supporters were involved to varying extents but were a constant part of local support of violent resistance. Among those more deeply tied to the local system, Jakavonis 2

---

[18] The relations between the regular Soviet army and the istrebitel, as well as between the regular army and the NKVD, were not particularly close. Istrebiteli were considered opportunistic and untrustworthy. The Red Army generally did not want to get involved in the affairs of the istrebiteli, who were only charged with local control. Thus, in the basically localized war between the partisans and the Soviet regime, the partisan-istrebitel struggle was the main day-to-day focus of fighting. Additionally, istrebiteli were considered traitors, and their deaths seemed to bring more satisfaction to partisan camps than the deaths of Red Army soldiers.

[19] Recall efforts at election boycotts in Chapter 3. The efforts of the Ukrainian postwar partisans in promoting the boycott of Soviet elections are discussed in Chapter 7.

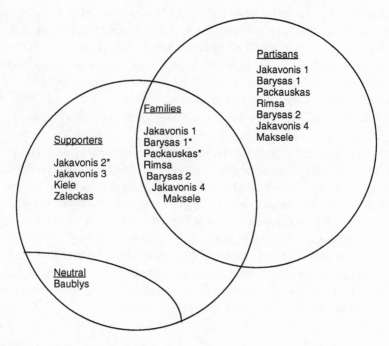

Figure 6.2. Venn diagram of Kasciunai village

was one of the few privy to the headquarters bunker while the Kiele family took in a daughter of a partisan as well as providing food. Jakavonis 3 was not deeply involved but did respond to requests for food (the son of Jakavonis 3 had been a Communist, entering the party in 1940; the Germans killed him in 1941). Zaleckas was described as "supporting." Only one family was not involved at all; its members were of an age to have little connection to draft-age young men and, as M1 commented, "they were not courageous."

Kasciunai was a strong community, with many families tracing their residency back for 400 years; relations were many-sided and involved face-to-face contact; there were a small number of farmsteads; variation in the size of landholdings was not great, and the farms were self-sufficient with no hired labor necessary.[20] The village was also specifically structured in a way

---

[20] Other potentially relevant features included membership in political parties, which had been nearly nonexistent; membership in social groups (although the Union of Sauliai had not fully functioned since the days of independence, now six years in the past, previous member-

to promote rebellion. The bottom diagram of Figure 2.8 represents well the dynamic and outcome seen in Kasciunai. In fact, Kasciunai's structure may be the simplest of conducive structures: a large first-playing group setting off a simple cascade of reciprocation through other community subsets. Favorable ratios among subsets existed at each step of the sequence. Seven first-playing individuals were closely connected through family relationships (A norms) to a larger subset that in turn possessed close connections with the rest of the community. With a very high percentage of the community already active in resistance through family connections, the thresholds of these remaining high-threshold community members were easily surpassed. Clearly, on both normative and rational grounds, support of the community organization was a clear choice.

This local system of support, originated for almost purely local needs, served as the base of operations for the more military-like system that followed. Most of the locally based partisans became involved in this supra-village organization, as did their families.

Sustaining Mechanisms

Although sustaining mechanisms were irrelevant for the brief 1940–1941 occupation and the German occupation (in which +2 rebellion never developed), they were crucial in helping sustain the long, losing battle against the Soviets in the late 1940s. Low monitoring and retaliation costs helped sustain rebellion. M1 recalls an illustrative incident. Jakavonis 3, who was not entirely trusted among partisans because his late son had joined the Communist Party, once came across partisans constructing a bunker. The partisans told him that he could inform on them and maybe they would be arrested, but other partisans would know that he was the informant and enact revenge. Even though this warning may not have been necessary, it shows how threats became a part of the everyday landscape. Local partisans, at least in the early postwar years, could act within their local environs with a certain measure of freedom knowing that possible informants would be deterred by the credibility of these threats.

Slowly, the Soviet regime gained control over the region, and the partisans fell one by one. Supplemented with NKVD troops, Soviet units of sev-

ship, indicated by an asterisk in Figure 6.2, could be taken as evidence of higher motivation to rebel); and family relationships (Jakavonis 1 and Jakavonis 2 were cousins; the relationships with the other Jakavonis families were distant and unknown).

enty to eighty-five troops were able to surround and comb substantial areas. Soviet authorities developed new techniques to find bunkers. Perhaps most importantly, network members were deported or killed. In Kasciunai, almost all members of the Packauskas family were either killed, deported, or jailed. The same result obtained with the Rimsa family, the Maksele family, and some members of Jakavonis 1. Sons of both Barysas families were slain. The strongest links in the local system were eventually removed, and some partisans, sensing futility, went to live in Vilnius where it was easier to "register" as a citizen without being implicated as a partisan. Even Kazimierietis and Vanagas encouraged some partisans to "register" as they felt an organization of such a large size could no longer be hidden and supplied. M1 was captured in December 1946 and deported to eastern Siberia. He returned in the late 1950s.

The 1940–1941 and the Postwar Occupations

From this one example, the dramatic differences between the two periods of anti-Soviet struggle should be obvious. In the latter period, brute force was the order of the day. The mass murder and burning of Klepocai clearly established the parameters of the new struggle for the residents of the Merkine region. For the latter period, a discussion of general 0 to +1 movement on the spectrum is largely irrelevant: risk was thrust on many members of Lithuanian society; there was no need to communicate willingness to accept risk. Rebellion at the +2 level was usually a necessity for survival. A comparison of the two periods can be characterized as one between a high-risk situation and a very high risk situation (more than twenty of the residents of Kasciunai were killed or deported in the postwar period). What difference did this fact have for the mechanisms of rebellion?

First, the importance of status and ostracism seems to decline. In the 1940–1941 period, the members of status-oriented organizations like the Union of Sauliai or the student groups at the university had the luxury to be partly motivated by status; the 200 young men in the woods after the burning of Klepocai did not. As a general hypothesis, increasing chances of death or other severe punishment decrease status seeking.

Second, the groups with the most risk-resistant forms of reciprocity (A norms), namely family groups, became the relevant focus for support and protection. Families may bicker under less pressure, but in general, if one of their member's life is at risk, they pull together. Of course, many family members did end up betraying one another in Lithuania, but, in comparison with other groups, the family became more central to decision making in the latter period.

Third, the importance of monitoring and retaliation increased in the latter period, and strong communities able to accomplish these tasks were more able to carry on rebellion. Unlike in the brief occupation of 1940–1941, sustaining mechanisms were much more relevant to the longer postwar struggle. Here, rational sustaining mechanisms can be highlighted. Threats of retaliation became a very prominent feature of life, especially when the balance started to swing toward the Soviets. And the threats of threatened individuals and groups are indeed credible. Irrational sustaining mechanisms, such as wishful thinking, are discussed later in this chapter.

The question arises of the relative influence of nationalism and ideology. The personal case of M1 is informative. M1 was not politically inclined before the postwar period; he was basically forced to become political through his situation. It was important to make some broader sense out of a life that consisted mainly of hiding in a bunker most of the day; it became necessary to find some hope for a better future. The need for sense and hope required a political ideology, which, given the circumstances, naturally turned out to be nationalistic. It appears rural Lithuanian rebels responded to local events that preceded the development of their ideology.

Similarities between the two Lithuanian-Soviet struggles also exist. In both periods, +2 organizations developed in a bottom-up manner from community-based mechanisms. Furthermore, as seen in the cases compared in the next section, the rebellion dynamics of communities again depended on their general and specific structural qualities. Strong and conducively structured communities appear much more likely to have generated high equilibria at +2 participation.

M2 and the Istrebiteli in Merkine (−2)

As a member of the local Soviet istrebiteli unit, M2, a longtime resident of Merkine, sought to kill or capture M1 and partisans like him. M2 was not forthcoming on all issues, and was certainly lying about others, but most of his information was confirmed by interviews of partisans, and much of it was very blunt. When asked about the primary method of istrebiteli for dealing with the partisans, he simply replied that they hunted, shot, and deported them.[21]

In more detail, the istrebiteli of Merkine were, from an outsider's point of view, active in ordinary and extraordinary tactics in the war against the partisans. They engaged in search-and-destroy operations, especially after reinforcements were brought in. M2 was clear concerning partisan domination in the early postwar period. From his perspective, "half the population of the villages were the liaison men of the partisans and the other ones were suffering from the robberies of partisans." Because approximately two-thirds of his unit were killed by partisans, most ambushed one or two at a time, he would never go into the forest unless he was ordered to do so. M2 spent much of his time guarding a recently established collective farm, which served to establish Soviet control and was a clear target of the partisans. He knew of Vanagas's organization and even seemed to hold some respect for it; other partisans, he said, were no more than "bandits."[22] M2 also admitted that the local Soviet authorities laid out the bodies of dead partisans in an open space on the outskirts of Merkine and then hid to observe whether anyone would try to come and identify the bodies. It was thought that the relatives of partisans could be identified through this operation,[23] which was commonly used throughout Lithuania in the period.[24]

How did M2 become an istrebitel? He was not a Communist; in fact, in reference to the first Soviet occupation, he said only "fools" were joining the party and the Komsomol. He belonged to no organizations and had absolutely no ideology. M2 was, on the whole, a very unconnected individual and really not a member of any community. Although he worked some land

---

[21] Later in the interview, after he had become a little more careful, when asked more specifically about istrebiteli measures, he said he didn't remember which methods were most effective. By the end of the interview, he became rather upset and asked if people would "come for him."

[22] This statement no doubt contains some truth: there were Lithuanian armed groups robbing the population. Vanagas himself, according to M1, saw these groups as highly detrimental to the Lithuanian cause as they would make the general population more quickly accept the stability and order promised by the Soviet regime.

[23] M2 claimed to not be personally involved in this activity. M4 saw the bodies, stripped of their boots, and claimed that relatives could sometimes get the corpses back with a payment to some authorities. He also said that schoolchildren were taken to view the bodies.

[24] As a point of information, M2 was on an operation in the countryside at the time of the partisan attack on Merkine. His unit rushed back to the town but was too late to see any action. M4 observed that nearly all of the young istrebiteli in Merkine were killed because they were too active; most of the older ones, including M2, thirty-seven at the time, were less active and had a higher survival rate.

that his wife inherited, he lived in town. His work life was unconnected to his social life. He was Polish, but married to one of the few Russian inhabitants of the town, which had been mostly Jewish. His ethnic connections were tenuous at best. He was illiterate, which closed off many avenues for personal associations as well.

His own account of joining the istrebiteli is the following. As a farmer with a horse and cart, he had been "mobilized" by the Soviets to transport some bodies (one apparently being the corpse of the wife of a partisan shot by the Soviets).[25] For this action, the partisans threatened to "skin him alive." As M2 saw it, the partisans ruled the countryside (it was 1945) and "were growing like mushrooms." They were highly capable of carrying out their threats and had already robbed his brother. He joined the istrebiteli after receiving a threatening letter from the partisans: after being informed of its contents, he had no choice; it was simply a matter of protection. M2's story is plausible, especially given his ethnic background and his wife's. In the years since his service, the Soviets did not appear to have rewarded him materially for his decision; he seemed to have led a rather bleak and bitter life, consisting of a series of unskilled jobs. This last point would certainly not prove anything about M2's motivations, though, as many individuals did become istrebiteli in hopes of gaining materially or politically and were usually very disappointed. As another interviewee from Merkine (M5) rather eloquently stated:

> The fundamental policy of Soviet rule was to have people annihilate themselves by their own hands and those istrebiteli were used as such a tool until they were no longer needed. Then their fate was not much better than the partisans. Because they were young, istrebiteli were hoping and dreaming that they would be masters, but nothing like that happened. They were illiterate, they were uncultured, and many of them became drunkards. And none of them became officials. When people are uncultured men, they can't reach any higher level. People joked about them. People didn't treat them as human beings; they don't treat them seriously.

The accounts of other interviewees, including those of M4 and M5 discussed later, support the point that many became istrebiteli not from ideological conviction, but to escape very credible threats from partisans. Two points can be made here in reference to community. Many individuals were

[25] Stories concerning mobilized wagons are frequent throughout the interviews.

temporarily conscripted to do jobs for the Soviets, but not many became "coded" as enemies in the way that M2 claimed he had been. Probably, M2's ethnicity, and that of his wife, were critical factors. Supportive actions of Poles or Russians were more likely to be immediately seen as willing collaboration, whereas a Lithuanian performing the same action might be given some benefit of a doubt or chance to explain. Moreover, the fact that M2 was an isolated individual meant that he had no one to intercede for him with the partisans. He also had no community-based barriers to becoming an istrebitel. Because unconnected individuals are less likely to be able to deal with threats, a hypothesis might be formed that more anomic individuals end up in the −2 position on the spectrum. Furthermore, individuals that did see collaboration as a way to move ahead materially or politically would not be faced with community-based deterrents such as ostracism. Some mobile partisans (+3) also had weak community connections, as seen in the case of M3.

M3 and Mobile Partisans (+3)

Certainly, there were different types of "partisans" in the postwar period. At least four categories are somewhat distinct: partisans connected to their local communities and families similar to M1, partisans closely connected to the more formal military structure organized around former Lithuanian military officers, individuals roaming the countryside in smaller mobile military units, and small groups of thieves who may have conveniently borrowed the term "partisan" for their own benefit. In the tail end of the postwar partisan struggle, the third category, for want of supplies in an increasingly hostile environment, may have become indistinct from the fourth category. The second and third categories are considered "+3": mobile and armed. M3 could be classified as a member of the third category. He was the leader of a group of eighteen men who called themselves "Vytautas the Great" after a former Lithuanian king. They had six machine guns and never spent more than a day or two in any location. According to M3 they constantly engaged in skirmishes and battles with their Soviet pursuers.

The history of the unit began before the burning of Klepocai. M3 had not been able to avoid conscription into the Red Army but was able to avoid service by deserting. He managed to make it close to his home village where he hid out in the woods. He was soon joined by many other young men fleeing Soviet consolidation of the territory. As he was older, twenty-seven, and a former corporal in the Lithuanian army, he naturally assumed leadership of the group of eighteen.

The key question is why didn't the individuals in this group try to reintegrate themselves into their former communities, as in the case of M1? For M3's group, the answer is straightforward: the majority of the young men who had coalesced around M3 were from Klepocai; their home base had been utterly destroyed in the Soviet advance. Like many other individuals in the +3 units, the members of Vytautas the Great simply had no place to go. Officers, deserters, those from urban areas, and those whose communities had been destroyed often did not have the same options as M1 (or M5). The military men, like Vanagas, often awaited the next war, which would come with the expected American invasion. Alternatively, the course of events had deposited them far from their home regions, or they were just too "hot," too sought after by the Soviet authorities, and did not want to endanger their families.

Most of the mobile units that were unable to utilize community-based bunker systems were easily caught. M3 lamented his group's logistical difficulties: if members of the group would have stayed anywhere for "more than two or three days, they would have been caught"; if they engaged in fighting, they would have to move a considerable distance away quickly to avoid possible contact with incoming Soviet reinforcements. People were willing to give them food, but their mobility made resupply irregular. M3 remained free for about one year before being shot in the leg and captured. He spent twelve years in Siberia, ten in a labor camp, before returning to Merkine.

M4 and Neutrals (0)

The attitude of M4[26] seemed to be fairly typical for many of the town dwellers: it was best to stay out of the way. Town dwellers who were not deeply embedded in social, political, or economic networks could generally take this option.

M4, born in 1929, became an adult during the era of partisan war but never considered joining either the partisans or the istrebiteli. In his opinion, both were involved in a cycle of violence that was best avoided. M4 saw the bodies of dead partisans laid out at the edge of town; he also knew of officials assassinated by the partisans. He had held a series of low-skilled jobs and

---

[26] M4 was selected off the street in Merkine, the only selection criterion being his apparent draft age, making him eligible for conscription at the time of the partisan conflict.

came into contact with partisans a few times along the way, mostly when working for a cattle farmer. Once, the partisans came to shoot his employer because the employer's brother was an istrebitel. Apparently, the employer convinced the partisans that he should not be held accountable for his brother's action and nothing happened. Yet, the event made an impression on M4.

> *RP:*   Were you more afraid of the istrebiteli or the partisans when they came to the field where you were shepherding?
>
> *M4:*   All of them. But I was not involved and in a way I felt safe because I was not involved.
>
> *RP:*   Was this the general attitude of the people?
>
> *M4:*   A considerable amount of people were acting in the same way. There were fewer people who were active from both sides, and the main body of the people were passive.

M4 had never had much of a family and never knew his father. He had six years of education, no property, belonged to no organizations, and had spent his life wandering from one unskilled job to the next. In short, he had no political, social, or economic ties; he had no connection to any low-threshold actors who might drag him into the conflict. Specific partisan threats might have driven him to a −2 position, as in the case of M2, but these did not occur. He had no strong desires to fight for anything and, being unconnected to any community, he had the option to be left alone.

M5 and the Village of Samuniskiu

On Christmas Eve 1944, M5, as well as other residents of Samuniskiu, saw the smoke rising from Klepocai. As in the village of Kasciunai, the youths of Samuniskiu, including M5's brother, withdrew to the forest to wait for events to play out.

Although actions in the two villages began in a very similar way, their paths quickly diverged. The youths of Samuniskiu were immediately organized by a local schoolteacher who directed the group to return to the village. The residents of the village were instructed to "not tell anything to anybody"; in effect, the youths were to be "hidden" within the normal life of the village. They did not consider the construction of bunkers at this early stage.

Soon, though, the authorities started to register the population officially. The youths of Samuniskiu essentially had three choices: proper registration, meaning conscription into the Red Army; forging fake documents in order to be too young or too old for the draft; going back to the woods (at either a +2 or +3 level). As in Kasciunai, the first option was not at all attractive. Unlike Kasciunai, the second option was a real possibility. For example, M5's brother had been born in 1925, making him a prime candidate for conscription, but with a bribe to the local authority, his birthdate was changed to 1927, too young to be taken by the Soviets at that critical time. As seen in the cases in the next section, such bribes were very common throughout Lithuania at the time. The brother did enter the Soviet army when the 1927 cohort was called up, but at that latter date the war against the Germans had ended and conscription had become less of a "death sentence."

M5 claimed that no one in the village was conscripted into the army in the 1945 period, and no one successfully remained a partisan in the woods or local bunkers either. Two young men had returned to the woods only to be shot in 1945, while the rest had managed to receive forged documents. This is the critical difference between Kasciunai and Samuniskiu: in the former, a sizable zero-threshold group remained in the bunkers and woods driving the action of interconnected members; in the latter, after a short period, no such low-threshold group remained as all of its members had either been killed or had returned with fake documents. Without this set of local first actors, few individuals in Samuniskiu would move to the +2 level, despite the village's many similarities with Kasciunai.[27]

Although its level of involvement differed from Kasciunai, Samuniskiu was quite active in supporting partisans at the unorganized +1 level. M5 himself would be one of the few residents to jump to +2. In the nearby forest, partisans with connections to nearby villages, and some with no local connections at all, had built a set of bunkers, which remained impervious to the Soviets throughout the rest of the decade. In 1948, partisans approached eighteen-year-old M5 while he was plowing in a field near the woods and asked him to describe the situation in his village. Were there Russians there? Could he bring them food? They then asked him to meet them the next day at an appointed time. Thus began M5's career as a partisan liaison man. M5 indicated that he needed little contemplation to make this decision; he was asked and he followed. The decision would eventually lead to nearly seven years in Siberia.

---

[27] Samuniskiu had several Sauliai members and similar family connections. It was larger in size and probably more economically diverse.

In time, M5 came to know of six bunkers. Although located near Samuniskiu, this system was more thoroughly connected to neighboring villages in terms of support networks. Again, Vanagas's organization had incorporated the system, and partisans from outside the locality were regular visitors, including partisans from distant districts attending meetings that may have been national in scope.[28] According to M5, almost everyone who remained in the village was helping occasionally to support the partisans in the forest, although they had no knowledge of the location of the bunkers and their support remained unorganized. The partisans would periodically come at night, and the farmers would give them food and other supplies. M5 could not guarantee that he was the only one who knew of the bunkers, but clearly the actions of other residents gave evidence of his special relationship. If somebody in the village noticed some Soviet movement, they told M5, who in turn relayed the information to an adjutant of Vonagas.

This support is impressive due to the fact that four of the village's residents became istrebiteli with widespread knowledge of the community and its workings. Having fled to Merkine for protection, these istrebiteli no longer lived in Samuniskiu, but they still brought Soviet authorities to the village and helped arrange surveillance and ambushes. M5 told of some interesting family dynamics involved with one istrebitel in particular. Pranas Volunguricius, the brother of Augustus Volunguricius, became an istrebitel from jealousy at his wealthier brother and the urgings of his Communist-sympathizer wife. Eventually, Augustus was deported, his daughter arrested as a partisan liaison in 1950, and his son arrested. The three other istrebiteli were Stasys Baniulis, Karys Baniulis, and Stasys Vitkauskas, all very small landholders who had not belonged to any of the village's formal and informal organizations. M5 said that the istrebiteli knew that the residents were universally supporting the partisans and that the residents knew that the istrebitels knew, so that there was little effort to hide support. The "game" between the population and the istrebiteli went on for several years, with support for the partisans continuing.

Among other reasons for this outcome, the partisans sustained themselves in the area due to their abilities to gain information and, if necessary, to carry out threats. The partisans liquidated the wife of Saturnas Volunguricius due to suspicions that she was an informer. The partisans also killed Juozas

---

[28] These meetings were in 1948 and 1949, and one of M5's duties was to lead partisans from outside the region to the bunkers.

Lapeska, and the story of his killing is highly informative. According to M5, Lapeska was a drunkard and a moonshiner who accidentally set his own house on fire because of his poor home-brewing equipment. Wanting to make up a story for the authorities in Merkine, Lapeska claimed that the partisans had set his house afire. Information had come back to the partisans that during the meeting with the authorities Lapeska had been recruited as an informant. The partisans warned him to "stay at home and never leave it and nothing will happen to you." However, Lapeska did come across the partisans and reported this fact to another local, who he thought was also an informant. Unfortunately for Lapeska, he had given his information to a partisan sympathizer. His death quickly followed. With such solid village support, and with the abilities to carry out threats, regime penetration was very difficult.

The village of Samuniskiu reached a stable equilibrium: the residents almost uniformly were at the +1 position on the spectrum. They unsystematically supported partisans with food and information. Due to the nearly universal involvement, few feared being singled out for reprisal for support of the partisans. With the exception of M5 there was little movement to the +2 position. In order to get involved at the high-risk +2 level, especially during the ruthless Soviet reoccupation, strong normative mechanisms of family and community are necessary. These were not present in Samuniskiu.

Five Cases from Samogitia (S1–S5): The +1 Position

Perhaps most rural villages in Lithuania in the immediate postwar period resembled that of M5 and Samuniskiu: the vast majority supported the partisans but in an unorganized fashion, maybe with one or two well-connected "liaisons" as a bridge. Villages organized at +2, the level of M1 and Kasciunai, are critical for sustaining rebellion, but even in Lithuania these were not the norm. As far as common sense dictates, the +1 position would seem to have been the expected outcome. The role balanced the strong desire to help fellow Lithuanians with the desire to avoid enormous risks. In the postwar era, those who found themselves intermeshed with the partisans at a +2 level were drawn in by strong normative forces involved with family and community. Although the histories may not be as dramatic as in cases of +2 participation, the risks incurred at the +1 level should not be minimized. This role still entailed a dangerous existence between the world of the partisans and that of the istrebiteli and the consolidating Soviet regime. This section deals primarily with this +1 position and the maneuvering that was necessary to persist there.

Five interviews conducted in the Samogitia region located in western Lithuania are employed for comparison. This within-region comparison of the decisions of five individuals juxtaposes the histories of three neutrals (0) with two individuals involved with partisans at a +1 level.

Neutrals

From the viewpoint of a utility maximizer, the neutrality of S1, based on a version of "better red than dead," makes a lot of sense. In a village with local connections to the new Soviet administration, S1 had managed to forge documents and change his age much in the same manner as the brother of M5 had done. His village had produced no partisans (no one had gone to the woods) and had no organized resistance; in fact, it had little resistance at all. In the words of S1: "The village could do nothing against the army. Do you think it would have been better had we resisted and everybody would have been killed?" and "If somebody resists they will come in despite it. . . . if somebody resists they will smash everybody in their way." At another point S1 did admit to seeing some collective benefits in the partisan resistance, stating that Lithuania might not be an independent country today if not for the partisan resistance. However, S1's sense of the collective-action problem presented itself.

> *S1:* In my opinion, if there was no resistance, then Lithuania would be lost.
> *RP:* Do you feel that you should have been a partisan?
> *S1:* Then I would not be alive.

In the thinking of S1, it would be better to infiltrate Lithuanian patriots into the system and manipulate it rather than fight it.

For the other two neutrals in this sample, some of the previous themes emerged. S2, one of the few females interviewed, was from a very poor family and had worked as a servant on larger farms for most of her life. Like M4, she had very little contact with either partisans or istrebiteli, seeing a partisan only one time and experiencing only one visit by an istrebitel. She attributed this lack of contact to her poverty; both sides knew that she would be unable to provide many resources. She and her family, being servants, had not been part of rebellion-prone rural economic or social networks. One day while driving to the forest for firewoood, the returning Soviets happened across her twenty-year-old brother and immediately "drafted" him into the Red Army, where he remained for five years; he had no links to draft evaders. Unconnected and poor, she was uninvolved in the partisan-Soviet struggle.

The third neutral worked in a large meat-packing plant in Taurage from 1939 to the end of the first Soviet occupation and then served approximately the first half of 1942 as a low-level clerk in the German administration before returning to help at the family farm. Unlike most of the other farmers in the sample, whose land could date back 400 years, S3's father had purchased land only in 1939. This property (18 hectares) had not been part of a village but rather part of a large manor (101 hectares). The family did not have long-term economic and social relationships with any neighbors, nor had it belonged to any political organizations. S3's lack of embeddedness was one factor in his neutrality, the other being his association with the German occupation regime. Because he had not held a significant position (he had been a bookkeeper during grain collections), he did not believe the returning Soviet authorities would seek him out for punishment. All the same, S3 wanted to avoid any action that would bring attention to himself. Neutrality was his chosen strategy.

A Balancing Act: +1 Cases

The following two +1 cases again repeat patterns seen earlier. Embeddedness in strong communities prevented neutrality from being an option, yet a lack of direct ties to partisans created a situation in which a higher level of involvement could be avoided. Both individuals supported the partisans on a regular, although unorganized level. S4 was approximately thirty-eight when the Soviets came the second time. He had served as a "warden" for the area on three occassions: for independent Lithuania (1937–1940), for a brief period in the first Soviet occupation, and again for a brief period in the German administration.[29] Additionally, he had belonged to the Sauliai organization.

Like many other individuals in contested areas, S4 played a "double-sided game," meeting regularly with both partisans and regime officials in the post-

---

[29] Being a "warden" involved responsibility for local road repairs and other low-level administrative duties. Under the first Soviet occupation, S4's duty was to help redistribute land; when this job was finished, he was released as warden. His replacement was killed by the Germans, and he was briefly reinstated before being permanently replaced.

war period. Through his contact with the partisans, he believed that eight bunkers existed in the surrounding woods, although he did not know their location. Partisan relatives from another village asked S4 to join their unit, but he declined the offer, citing his family and the high risk of death. S4 indicated that the partisans understood the logic of his decision and did not apply much pressure to change his mind. He remained in contact with partisans, meeting about once a month in the period after 1947, with the last regular contact coming about 1951.

The regime certainly applied pressure to S4, once holding him in jail for fifteen days in 1947. No charges were made and he was released. S4 credits this outcome to vodka payments made by his wife. There was a precedent for this tactic as S4 claimed to have earlier bribed a local official with a half year's supply of liquor. For several years, S4 continued simultaneously to drink with Soviet officials while meeting and supplying partisans at night. He did not consider the situation at all odd.

The final Samogitian case is in the small, eight-family Lutheran village of Osvitis. Like S4, S5 had been a member of Sauliai, a local warden, and was in his thirties when the Soviets returned. He was recruited by partisans, who claimed that America would soon be intervening, but decided not to get involved at that level. Consistent with established patterns, there was no low-threshold group in Osvitis itself. The only partisan, a youth who had served in the German army, had been killed early on. Still, the majority of the village maintained occasional contact with the partisans and supplied them with food and information. S5 had even been inside one of the bunkers.

One particular story illustrates how members of the village often urged the partisans not to engage in acts of violence that might bring regime retribution against the village:

Once, a group of partisans, some seven men or more, decided to spend a day swimming and bathing in the nearby creek. One of the farmsteads in that area had hired workers, and the son of one of those workers was an istrebitel. Suddenly, that son arrived and was face-to-face with those partisans. Those partisans at once put a rope around his neck and were going to hang him, but the master of the farmstead begged them not to kill him. So they made him swear an oath not to betray them and let him go, but he rode straight across the forest to istrebitel headquarters and informed them. The istrebiteli came the next morning; they were afraid to come at night. They were right here in this farmstead. . . . The partisans wanted to resist. They said we will shoot them all with our machine guns. But I told the commander, "don't do that because it would mean a bad life for us."

In effect, individuals at +1, while helping to sustain partisan activity, sometimes acted to protect those at −2. The goal in this balancing act was to remain faithful to partisans without bringing down the reprisals of the Soviet regime.

For S5, the situation became even more complicated when he was elected chairman of the collective farm. In approximately 1948 or 1949, istrebiteli rounded up village inhabitants for meetings to establish collective farms, a primary means for establishing Soviet control in the countryside. Often, the choice was between membership in a collective farm or Siberia. Under these circumstances, the partisans did not hold a grudge against those who were compelled to join, especially in the latter years of the decade when Soviet power was increasing. Nor did they always enact retribution against those elected chairman. In many cases, if there had to be a chairman, the partisans preferred one who was sympathetic to them, as in the case of S5. The position for these chairmen was precarious, to say the least, needing on the one hand to meet Soviet expectations while on the other to avoid offending the sensibilities of the partisans. A classic situation described by S5 was a regional meeting of collective farm chairmen. At these meetings, each chairman was required to give a speech concerning the accomplishments and goals of each collective farm. In the audience, partisan liaison people listened to the speech to make sure it did not cross certain unspecified boundaries. S5 was very scared about his own speech, but it apparently passed partisan standards. Many of the other chairmen who had been too enthusiastic about seizing the property of kulaks or had spoken openly against the partisans were shot the next morning, but no harm came to S5, who believed he had an understanding with the partisans. After less than a year, S5 was replaced as chairman by a party member with an armed istrebitel as a bodyguard. Due to increased surveillance, it became more and more difficult for S5 and other members of Osvitis to continue to support the partisans, although S5 had some contact even in 1955.

In these two cases, as in other +1 cases, the percentage of +1 participation of the general population of the community created assurance against specific reprisals. However, given the lack of first-acting zero-threshold actors, movement to +2 did not occur. Powerful social norms are necessary to reduce the high level of risk involved in +2 resistance, and in these cases the norms were never triggered.

Summary of Other Postwar Data

In addition to the ten cases from the Merkine and Samogitia regions just discussed, ten other interviewees (O1–O10) offered very specific information about their native communities during the postwar period. Five could draw detailed maps. All, or almost all, respondents provided similar accounts of some experiences: the desire of young Lithuanians to avoid Soviet mobilizations, the recruitment of the most uncultured elements of society into the ranks of the istrebiteli, the public display of the bodies of dead partisans, and the ever expanding realm of control of the Soviet regime, the increasingly desperate situation of the partisans, the continued hope of Western intervention and salvation among large sections of the populace.

In terms of movement on the spectrum of roles, the patterns witnessed in the Merkine and Samogitia cases are in evidence. As in the previous postwar cases, three types of outcomes can be observed among rural villages: movement to near universal community involvement at the +2 level, movement of a limited number of community members to +2 with the rest at +1, all members at +1. All rural respondents described their home communities as supportive of the partisans, even if unorganized. The urban respondents, on the other hand, described minimal resistance against the Soviet regime.[30] These outcomes roughly corresponded to similar community-level structural features as seen earlier. First and foremost, these include the percentage of low-threshold first actors within the community and the size of the community. A few brief descriptions exhibit the patterns.

Only one of these cases exhibited movement to a near universal +2 equilibrium. In the village of Lukstai, near the Latvian border, participation in social-patriotic activity had always been high. Nearly half of the seventeen homesteads had participated in the Sauliai organization in the time of independence. The respondent (O1), although only thirteen at the time, recalled how the men of the town, including his father, donned white armbands and immediately seized local control with the start of the German attack in June 1941. Very probably, this village was organized at the +2 level and incorporated into the LAF during the first occupation. During the German occupation, Soviet partisans had made some inroads among neighboring Russian populations and had developed an information base on the activities of the

---

[30] Some of this set of interviewees lived both in their home villages and urban areas during the years 1944–1950.

populace of Lukstai. In Lukstai, unlike villages with no Soviet partisan presence, residents, including the respondent's activist father, had no illusions about escaping the scrutiny and retribution of the incoming Soviet officials. They could either try to flee the country, as in the case of the respondent's father, or take to the woods. Comprising not only youth avoiding the draft but also other activists fearing sure persecution, the first-acting zero-threshold group in Lukstai was larger than in many other villages.

Of the seventeen families, five had partisan members. A community-based support system developed. The respondent served as a "liaison partisan," collecting food from other farmsteads to give to the regularly visiting partisans. He did not know the location of the bunkers; only family members directly visited the bunkers. Although the respondent served as a liaison for his own community-based system, he did not know the liaisons of surrounding villages.[31]

In two cases, limited movement to +2 occurred but did not trigger widespread community organization. In Pagiriai (O2), a village of twenty-three homesteads, a cluster of four neighboring families formed a support network for two sons of one family. This low +2 equilibrium can be related to the paucity of draft-age men. Also, due to its proximity to Kaunas, relations among members of this village were not as numerous and multifaceted in comparison to other Lithuanian villages. Many residents held jobs in Kaunas and were less connected economically and otherwise to the locality. The result may have been a weakened community less able to generate the mechanisms seen elsewhere. In another village, Barteliai (O3), a small network again developed among a set of neighbors, although the community as a whole appears to have remained at +1.[32]

Other interviewees reported partisans periodically visiting farmsteads for food and information, although they did not know of any local, regularized support organization. One respondent (O4) had been drafted into the Red Army but escaped. During 1944–1945, he roamed the Lithuanian countryside as a mobile partisan (+3) drawing food, information, and shelter from

---

[31] As in other cases, this respondent spoke of early groups of 200 men, occasional sweeps of large Soviet security forces, the assassination of the local Soviet official, and hopes for Western intervention. The respondent was arrested in 1949 and served one year in jail and five and a half years in Siberia.

[32] I hesitate to draw any conclusions about this community's partisan activity as the respondent was hiding in a dung heap until September 1945, when he took advantage of the first available amnesty. Still, many events, including the assassination of a Soviet official by one of the resident partisans, could be clearly recounted.

random villages along the way. He describes the experiences following defection from the Red Army in the following manner:

> From this moment we were deserters from the Red Army from the point of view of the Russian officials, but we were now partisans and had strong feelings. I escaped with several of my friends and we made our way back. We went 200 kilometers. Wherever we went people supported us as soon as they found out we were fleeing from the Russian army. They gave us food. Ninety-nine percent of Lithuanians supported us and asked us no questions. They trusted us and we trusted them. Only some people near a big city, an old man indicated the wrong direction toward some Russian soldiers, but we heard them speak Russian and went away. We found out that the man had two sons who were Communists and he was like a traitor. But ninety-nine percent of the people supported us and we started defenses, gathering guns and rifles left by the Germans, exchanged bottles of whiskey (for weapons). We started to pick up such weapons, we started to organize.

These early experiences soon changed, however. Within a short period of time, the big units of partisans could no longer sustain themselves and could be easily hunted by Soviet units. With more and more Soviet agents in the countryside, the trust between partisans and supporters was no longer so automatic. The rare experience of betrayal just described became more common as time went on. O4 continued: "Finally, then our losses became more and more, and the infiltration of the KGB became more and more. Our military method, struggle against the opposition, decreased from 1946. For instance, from our unit there were about thirty young men, my friends, and only five survived." The solution, not surprisingly, was to return to one's native village, as O4 did in September 1945. He was not arrested until 1950. With only unorganized support, mobile +3 fighter groups found it difficult to survive for any length of time. The creation of +2 communities helped solve these logistical problems.

Sustaining Mechanisms

Although sustaining mechanisms have not played a major role in the analysis, their importance in the postwar Lithuanian case is obvious. How was this level of fighting sustained against hopeless odds for so long? In Chapter 1, four sustaining mechanisms were hypothesized and cataloged: threat plus three irrational psychological mechanisms – tyranny of sunk costs, the weight of small victories, and wishful thinking. Threats were addressed in the preceding cases. Here, I wish to concentrate on the pervasiveness of wishful thinking on the part of the Lithuanian rebels.

In almost every interview, the respondent reported the belief that the Western powers would not let Lithuania be absorbed into the Soviet sphere and that a war between the United States and the USSR was imminent. In a general sense, such a belief could hardly be considered irrational. After all, the First World War ended with the West (and Wilson and his Fourteen Points) committed to the independence of small Eastern European peoples. The Second World War began with the West reacting to the invasion of Poland. In the eyes of most of the Lithuanians being hunted, Eastern Europe would again play a central role in a conflict between East and West. The fate of the world would be played out in an irreconcilable battle between the West, and the principles laid out in the Atlantic Charter, and the East, and the godless and barbaric principles of communism. There could be no compromise; a new war was inevitable.

In itself, these predictions simply follow from the world view, the ideology of most Lithuanians, both elite and mass. The Lithuanian political elite during the interwar years was very pro-Western in both experience and attitude; many had been educated in the West and had come to see their native land as an integral part of the Western world. They assumed that their hatred of the Soviets, and perhaps their disrespect for Russians, was shared by their Western compatriots.[33] This attitude was matched, as seen in the interview data, among wide strata of the Lithuanian population. As a result, underground pamphlets were filled with statements predicting salvation from the West. The following two passages are typical:

> The United States has sufficiently understood its mission to be the vanguard of the West, fighting no longer for the liberty of an individual nation, but for all of mankind.[34]

> Only bolshevik agents and weak-willed persons influenced by bolshevik propaganda begin to convince themselves and others that the events, i.e. an armed conflict, will not come soon. Such an opinion, as disseminated, is totally erroneous.[35]

---

[33] Vardys, "The Partisan Movement in Postwar Lithuania," pp. 503–504.

[34] From "Freedom Is Coming from the West," a leaflet from the private archives of Colonel Antanas Sova, reprinted in Remeikis, *Opposition to Soviet Rule in Lithuania,* p. 51.

[35] From the partisan underground publication *Laisves varpas,* no. 123, October 15, 1947, reprinted in Remeikis, *Opposition to Soviet Rule in Lithuania.*

The irrationality of wishful thinking is evidenced not by these general views but rather because so many individuals assigned such weight to scattered bits or pieces of information as reliable predictors of the upcoming war. Churchill's speech at Fulton, Missouri, events in Greece or Turkey, the start of the Korean War – all were revelations that the final battle, the liberating Armageddon, was at hand. For a people enduring Soviet terror, attrition of partisan friends, deportations, and various other tribulations, the tendency to assign hopeful meanings to such events should not be surprising.

The practical effect of these pamphlets and beliefs, however, was to help produce more partisan dead. By 1947 one faction of organized partisans, the United Democratic Resistance Movement, recognized that help was not imminent and that forces should be conserved through less militaristic tactics and strategy. In March 1947 a secret directive stated that "On the current political situation . . . there is no basis to expect a war soon," it went on to confront the irrational tactics of militaristic struggle urged by other partisan groups:

> The question arises: *Who forces us to continue this?* Can it be that they can no longer think coolly and analyze the situation, the provided information? Could it be that a desire to show one's pride, an unwillingness to accept information based on facts and wise tactics, provided by others, is playing a role here? It seems that this is the case. That is why it becomes so sad and frightening because in some places recent days have brought great losses to our struggle and caused pointless suffering. Will this go on much longer?

Despite such directives, it appears that large segments of the population carried hopes of Western rescue well into the late 1940s or even early 1950s. For some, such hopes prevented a rational recalculation of chances that may have led them to accept amnesty offers, or attempts to forge fake documents to reintegrate into society. For others, though, there was no realistic chance at amnesty, or no desire to accept it. There was little choice but to fight on.

Concluding Comments and Comparisons

The postwar rebellion is a central focus of modern Lithuanian history. One Lithuanian literary scholar stated, "Lithuanians remember it in every agonizing detail, and can no more stop talking and writing about it than the Rus-

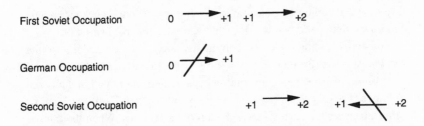

Figure 6.3. Summary of movement during three occupations

sians can stop talking about their great struggle against the Nazis."[36] This rebellion helped to prevent the easy and massive importation of Russian labor in the immediate postwar era, contributing to Lithuania's lower percentage of Russian population today, important demographic and cultural effects that are discussed in Chapters 8 and 9.

Based on an analysis of twenty individual histories, this chapter has discerned general patterns of movement during the postwar years in Lithuania. Comparisons within regions were employed to hold constant broader factors such as geography and implementation of regime policy. Chapters 3 through 6 present opportunities to compare Lithuanian outcomes across the three occupations of the 1940s. The predominant patterns of movement can be summarized in Figure 6.3. Sustaining mechanisms did not come into play in the brief 1940–1941 occupation. The population generally remained neutral in the German occupation, so +1 to +2 triggering mechanisms or sustaining mechanisms are not relevant. Sustaining mechanisms did play an essential role in the second Soviet occupation, however.

Figure 6.3 suggests two direct comparisons, two obvious questions. First, what accounts for the difference in movement from neutrality to +1 among the first Soviet and German occupations? The analysis points to the absence of two key mechanisms, resentment formation and focal points, in the German case. Second, and more directly connected to the present chapter, what accounts for the similarities in outcome in both Soviet occupations? After all, regime strategy differed dramatically in the two periods. The social composition also greatly changed with the killing, deportation, or flight of the educated classes. Yet, the general outcome was the same: manifold commu-

---

[36] Rimvydas Silbajoris, quoted in Anatol Lieven, *The Baltic Revolution: Estonia, Latvia, and Lithuania and the Path to Independence* (New Haven: Yale University Press, 1993), p. 89.

nity-based rebellion organizations developing throughout the country. Moreover, both periods saw significant and puzzling local variation.

Comparison shows similar community structures unleashing similar mechanisms to drive individuals to the +2 role. In postwar Lithuania, draft-age youth fleeing Soviet conscription became first actors within their communities. The normative pressures of the youth on their families (A norms) in turn triggered normative pressures on other families. When the families of these youth were connected to significant other families through previous work and social ties, rebellion movement often reached a high community equilibrium. In cases of few draft-age youth, or cases in which forged documents were readily available, the cascading process never got started. The result was a low number of +2 actors or none at all. In 1940–1941 Lithuania, the first-acting subsets were often fellow members of social-patriotic groups rather than those evading the draft. In both cases, the normative mechanisms associated with these low-threshold groups (family norms in the postwar case and norms of honor in the 1940–1941 case) served to reduce thresholds of connected subsets; in both cases, the specific structure of the community, especially the amount of overlap between low-, intermediate-, and high-threshold groups, was critical in shaping the final community equilibrium. In both cases, similar interactions between structure and mechanism unfolded.

7. More Cases, More Comparisons

How do ordinary people rebel against powerful and brutal regimes? The answer to this question has been sought by envisioning rebellion as a process involving a spectrum of roles. Explaining rebellion entails identifying the mechanisms and sequences of mechanisms that drive individuals across this spectrum. The introductory chapters specified ten mechanisms and how they create movement toward or from roles of resistance and rebellion. These ten mechanisms serve as a template for comparison. Thus far, this template has guided the analysis of rebellion in one nation across three successive occupations. The question becomes whether this approach can provide insight into other cases. The promise of a mechanism-based methodology lies in its generality. The sequences of mechanisms illustrated in the Lithuanian case should be operative in other cases as well. This chapter addresses four puzzles of resistance behavior, all in occupied Eastern Europe during the 1940s. For all four cases, the template of mechanisms suggests answers and testable hypotheses.

The analysis proceeds from cases most similar to Lithuania to cases with major differences in important factors such as regime strategy or nature of society. This gradual stretching of the theoretical framework acts to define and specify its conceptual limits.

Postwar Latvia and Estonia

All three of the Baltic states experienced similar Soviet policies in the postwar period.[1] All three developed anti-Soviet resistance organizations in re-

[1] Benedict Vytenis Maciuika's "The Baltic States under Soviet Russia: A Case Study in Sovietization" (Ph.D dissertation, University of Chicago, 1963) illustrates the similarity of Soviet policy in the three nations. Maciuika, in effect, treats Soviet policy in the three Soviet republics as one case of Sovietization, not three.

sponse. Despite these similarities, all commentators agree that the level of resistance was much more intense in Lithuania than in Latvia and Estonia.[2] Given the similarities, why did Lithuania sustain higher levels of resistance? +2

As described by Laar, postwar resistance in Estonia began much the same way as it did in Lithuania: young men, often soldiers, fragmenting from larger groups to hide in their home districts where they often built systems of bunkers.[3] The support of the local population was the key to survival: the partisans' food was either delivered to a prearranged spot in the forest or fetched by the men themselves. Procuring food for the winter was critical. The "Forest Brothers" got all their supplies, including clothes, tools, everyday necessities, from the farms. They also relied heavily on the information they got from the local people.[4] In Estonia, psychological mechanisms similar to those in Lithuania appear to have helped sustain rebellion. Excerpts from Estonian letters match the wishful thinking occurring farther south: "A new war is more likely now than it was before the war between Russia and Germany. The only things that can prevent it are famine and war-weariness. But the enemy's scales contain enough reasons to outweigh these two factors."[5] Another letter written in retrospect stated: "According to the Atlantic Charter, all nations that were independent before the war were to regain their independence. Our people placed their hopes on America, England, the United Nations, on their 'white ship' of hope, on the departure of the Russians . . . and these stupid hopes sent thousands of Forest Brothers to their deaths . . . not only in Estonia, but tens of thousands more in Latvia and Lithuania. Few of us were able to think clearly, to draw conclusions from what was happening. There really were plenty of clues."[6] Finally, when collectivization drastically and rapidly changed local and regional thresholds, the predicted rapid switches in level of rebellion activity followed the deportations that removed the partisan support base.

A summary of the postwar experience in Latvia and Estonia would closely resemble that seen in the previous chapter on Lithuania: in each, Soviet ter-

---

[2] For example, see Anatol Lieven, *The Baltic Revolution: Estonia, Latvia, Lithuania and the Path to Independence* (New Haven: Yale University Press, 1993), p. 88. Even accounts sympathetic to Estonia, such as that of Mart Laar, *War in the Woods: Estonia's Struggle for Survival, 1944–1956*, trans. Tina Ets (Washington, D.C.: Compass Press, 1992), recognize the more intense level of resistance in Lithuania.

[3] Laar, *War in the Woods*, p. 54.   [4] Ibid., p. 139.

[5] Letter of Estonian partisan Richard Saaliste written in 1945, cited in ibid., p. 110.

[6] Memoirs of Alfred Kaarman, cited in ibid., p. 183.

ror and mobilization efforts sent young men into the woods; in each, the resistance was formed in a decentralized manner; in each, the occupying Soviet regime developed local militias (istrebiteli), occasionally swept the countryside with larger units, offered amnesties, and engaged in massive deportation coinciding with collectivization in 1948–1949;[7] in each, the partisan fighters built bunkers, fought very limited engagements, assassinated collaborators, and attempted to disrupt Soviet elections; in each, the rebel effort was sustained by the belief in the Atlantic Charter and imminent war between the incompatible East and West.

Although the quality of resistance seems fairly similar across the three cases, the quantity differed. There is no precise measure for this comparison, but several rough estimates and gauges can be employed. The numbers of total guerrilla fighters appear to have been disproportionately higher in Lithuania: 100,000 in Lithuania, 40,000 in Latvia, and 30,000 in Estonia.[8] In Lithuania, partisan fighters maintained control of much of the countryside until 1949, whereas the Soviets could operate freely in most of Latvia and Estonia by the end of 1946.[9] The number of Soviet casualties differs in corresponding fashion. The Soviets admit roughly 20,000 casualties in Lithuania while official tallies in Estonia produce a figure of only 891.[10] The number of Baltic casualties also followed similar lines with Soviet estimates of Lithuanian dead put at 20,000 (credible Lithuanian estimates provide a number of 30,000) and Estonian figures at far less.[11]

Common explanations of the quantitative variation in levels of rebellion center on two dissimilarities.[12] First, several sources cite a more disciplined

---

[7] For a comparison of collectivization policies, one can juxtapose the following articles: Kestutis Girnius, "The Collectivization of Lithuanian Agriculture, 1944–1950," *Soviet Studies* 40 (1988): 460–478; John Biggart, "The Collectivization of Agriculture in Soviet Lithuania," *East European Quarterly* 9 (1990): 53–75; Rein Taagepera, "Soviet Collectivization of Estonian Agriculture: The Deportation Phase," *Soviet Studies* 32 (1980): 379–397.

[8] Estimates are from Romuald J. Misiunas and Rein Taagerpera, *The Baltic States: Years of Dependence, 1940–1980* (Berkeley: University of California Press, 1983), p. 84. Other estimates provide lower figures for Estonia. Toivo Raun believes that the number of Estonian "forest brethren" was 5,000 during the 1944–1946 period, but holds that the height of guerrilla strength was in 1946–1948, for which he provides no figures (p. 174). Laar, however, estimates that 30,000 to 40,000 Estonians fought during the prolonged postwar conflict, with half belonging to organized units; *War in the Woods,* p. 155.

[9] Misiunas and Taagepera, *The Baltic States: Years of Dependence, 1940–1980,* p. 90.

[10] On the former figure, see the previous chapter on Lithuanian postwar resistance. The latter figure is from Laar, *War in the Woods,* p. 93.

[11] Laar cites "Soviet sources," putting the number of Estonians "neutralized," killed, or imprisoned at 8,468 through November 1947; ibid., pp. 173–174.

[12] Other differences, of course, exist. In Lithuania, fewer individuals were able and willing

and extensive organization that developed in Lithuania.[13] However, this only begs the question (indeed, the question of most interest to this book) of how this organization managed to form and maintain itself. Lithuanian resistance may have been more strongly developed during the German occupation, but the vast majority of postwar partisans in Lithuania, as seen in the previous chapter, comprised isolated individuals fleeing Soviet mobilization and terror. The Lithuanian resistance organization, never firmly centralized, was built from the bottom up.

A second commonly mentioned explanation focuses on the religious difference among the three states. Misiunas and Taagepera point out that Catholic parishes may have provided a "grass-roots institution" able to provide a "spiritual and national rallying point." They mention that while several Lithuanian clergymen fought with the partisans, only one such comparable case is known for the other Baltic states.[14] The importance of local religious organization was a major part of the explanation of resistance organization in 1940–1941, although for reasons more specific than a moral rallying point. While this general religious factor should not be downplayed, it does not help explain local and regional variation within each state.

The theory developed earlier directs the analyst to look for answers in differences in community structures. An essential difference between Lithuania and its two northern neighbors would appear to lie in the quantity of local support. Both of the specified mechanisms working to drive individuals into the crucial +2 position, norms of reciprocity and threshold mechanisms, operate at the community level. Strong and conducively structured communities are likley to trigger these mechanisms. Thus, a hypothesis can be formed: the quantitative differences among Lithuania, Latvia, and Estonia

to serve in the Communist regime. Lithuania's Communist Party had always been small. Perhaps more importantly, the Soviets had a much smaller pool of Soviet Lithuanians to send in to help establish control and efficiently implement policy. According to the 1939 Soviet census, there were 142,465 Soviet Estonian citizens and 126,900 Latvians, but only 32,342 Lithuanians.

Also, higher levels of participation in the German administration in Latvia and Estonia may have had an effect. Respective figures for participation in the German military are: Latvia 80,000; Estonia 50,000; Lithuania 15,000 (from Maciuika, "The Baltic States under Soviet Russia," p. 64, n. 1). On one hand, these collaborators had the highest incentive to flee the Baltic states to avoid Soviet retribution. On the other hand, they had the greatest incentive to fight if they were unable to make it out of the Soviet sphere. It is hard to establish the direction this factor might work; furthermore, I know of no arguments that are based on it.

[13] Both Laar and Lieven refer to this factor.

[14] Misiunas and Taagepera, *The Baltic States: Years of Dependence, 1940–1980*, p. 82.

were closely related to the number of strong and conducively structured communities found in each case.

Further research would be necessary to test this hypothesis, and not much more can be said at this point. Two demographic characteristics would provide some support, however. First, although all three peoples were primarily rural, Lithuania was significantly more rural than its neighbors. These rural communities would have tended to be strong, at least stronger than the deformed urban communities of the postwar years. Second, the rural population of Lithuania may have been more monolithically Lithuanian. In contrast, there are large Russian populated areas of rural Estonia and Latvia. These Russian or minority areas would have been more likely to remain neutral under Soviet occupation. Thus, the number of ethnically Lithuanian rural communities (those likely to foster +2 organization) would be comparatively greater than the number of similar Latvian or Estonian rural communities.

Variation in Postwar Ukraine: Differences between Galicia and Volhynia

As the Red Army advanced westward in the late stages of the Second World War, it managed to pacify most of Ukraine without great difficulty. One western Ukrainian region effectively defied the reestablishment of Soviet rule, though. In Galicia, a rebel organization developed anti-Soviet resistance for a considerable period after the war. While these rebels maintained sizable mobile forces, their ability to survive the power of the Soviets and the NKVD was clearly based in +2 organization.

It is hardly surprising that Galicia differed from the eastern Ukraine, where very little postwar Soviet resistance ever developed. However, the difference with the neighboring western Volhynia region, where the population rapidly returned to the 0 node, is striking. Galicia and Volhynia[15] shared many similar characteristics: both had been part of interwar Poland and suffered discrimination at the hands of the Poles; in both, Ukrainian nationalists arose to struggle against Polish dominance. Both regions could be characterized as pervaded by strong communities in the sense employed here.

Here is the puzzle: why did two neighboring Ukrainian regions respond

---

[15] I use the term Galicia to refer to eastern Galicia and Volhynia to refer to western Volhynia.

to postwar Soviet regimes in such different ways? Why did one remain neutral (0) while the other develop strong locally based rebellion (+2)?

The theory suggests that the starting point for investigation should be an examination of the four mechanisms operating to drive individuals from 0 to +1. Were these mechanisms present in the Galician case and absent in the Volhynian? The Lithuanian cases present a similar comparative situation. In the first Soviet occupation, Lithuanians moved from 0 to +1 (and on to +2), whereas they remained neutral under the German regime. In that comparison, the difference was explained by the absence of resentment formation and focal points in the German case. I argue that these same two mechanisms were absent in Volhynia but present in Galicia. While both regions may have possessed a strong community able to drive a region from +1 to +2, only Galicia triggered the +1 set of mechanisms. As in the Lithuanian case, historical and cultural background is necessary to understand the presence and absence of resentment and focal point mechanisms.[16]

The Backgrounds of Galicia and Volhynia

Figure 7.1 presents the series of ruling regimes of Galicia and Volhynia during the twentieth century. Each of these periods of foreign rule can be described in turn.

Pre–World War I.   Hapsburg rule, unlike Russian rule, allowed a modicum of national political organization and participation. Under Austrian administration, Ukrainian-political parties, Ukrainian schools, and Ukrainian-language publications existed and helped to create a politically conscious population. Furthermore, in the somewhat free political competition in the Hapsburg realm, the conflict among the Galician Ukrainians and Polish landowners was open and public. In the course of this struggle, Galicians developed symbols and discourse of resistance. Under Russian rule,

---

[16] Throughout the section, I rely on an unpublished work of Alexander Motyl, which, using some interesting and detailed data not developed elsewhere, discusses the different outcomes in Volhynia and Galicia. See Alexander Motyl, "The Organized Ukrainian Resistance Movement and the 1946 Elections to the USSR Supreme Soviet" (unpublished manuscript, 1974). Also by Motyl on a closely related topic: "The Rural Origins of the Communist and Nationalist Movements in Wolyn *Wojewodztwo,* 1921–1939," *Slavic Review* 37 (1978): 412–420. I cannot address all the fascinating background of the development of Ukrainian nationalist organization. Good works exist on this topic, foremost among them being John Armstrong's *Ukrainian Nationalism* (Englewood, N.J.: Ukrainian Academic Press, 1990).

	Pre-WW I	Interwar	1st Soviet	German Occ	2nd Soviet
Galicia	Hapsburg Empire	Poland	USSR	General Govournement	USSR
Volhynia	Russian Empire	Poland	USSR	Reichs-kommisariat Ukraine	USSR

Figure 7.1. The series of ruling regimes in Galicia and Volhynia

Volhynia's Ukrainians experienced far harsher rule; for example, the Ukrainian language was banned until the twentieth century. In contrast to Galicia, Volhynia never developed shared symbols of resistance.

The Interwar Period.   At the end of the First World War, both eastern Galicians and Poles were aware that Austrian rule would soon come to an end. Because both groups were determined to establish national control in eastern Galicia, the struggle was framed in national terms. In October 1918 a Ukrainian National Council was formed from a variety of prominent Galicians, including political and religious leaders. Their goal was to unite all of the western Ukrainians into one single political entity. Other Ukrainians from the region were determined to take even more forceful action: Ukrainian soldiers from the Austrian military took control of Lviv on October 31. Thus began a bitter and violent contestation of the territory between Poles and Ukrainians.[17] For eight months, the West Ukrainian National Republic ruled a region of 3 million Ukrainians and 1 million non-Ukrainians, with an ultimate goal of unification with eastern Ukrainians. During the struggle, the military officers, and most of the 15,000 Ukrainian dead, hailed from Galicia. In the end, the Poles, with their overwhelming numbers, prevailed. However, the Galician Ukrainians had fought a national struggle. As Orest Subtelny concludes, "the Galician Ukrainians, who had clearly demonstrated their ability to govern themselves, failed to achieve statehood for rea-

---

[17] For a more detailed account, see Orest Subtelny, *Ukraine: A History* (Toronto: University of Toronto Press, 1988), pp. 367–372.

sons beyond their control."[18] Nonetheless, the idea of acting as an ethnically based political unit had been firmly established in Galicia, not only in intellectual circles but in the region as a whole.

Under Polish rule, most minority populations experienced institutionalized discrimination, including both Galician and Volhynian Ukrainians. Not surprisingly, given their respective histories, the Galicians began anti-Polish action almost immediately after the new political boundaries had been drawn, whereas the population of Volhynia remained inert. One important form of resistance action was the election boycott, a classic +1 resistance action. In 1921 and 1922, Galician Ukrainians boycotted elections to the Polish Sejm and Senate in large numbers. In contrast, Volhynian Ukrainians participated. As a result, twenty Volhynian Ukrainians were sent to the Sejm and five to the Senate, while Galician Ukrainians were nearly unrepresented until 1928.[19]

The Polish regime countered Ukrainian nationalist activity, which sometimes involved sabotage and arson, with a steady pacification and denationalization campaign. During Polish rule, the number of Ukrainian-language schools declined from 3,662 to 144; Ukrainian teachers, seen as possible organizers, were transferred out of the region to central Poland; and Ukrainian social organizations were limited by official decree.[20]

The First Soviet Occupation.   With this history of repression and subordinate status, the transfer of the area from Polish to Soviet jurisdiction passed with a perhaps predictable outburst of violence. Ukrainians attacked Poles and Polish landlords; the Soviets were seen more as liberators than occupiers.[21] Over the course of the first Soviet occupation, however, disgust with the arrests of citizens, food shortages, and religious persecutions steadily turned the Ukrainian population against the Soviets.

The German Occupation.   As in Lithuania and most of the rest of the western Soviet region, the Germans were greeted as liberators by the bulk of the population. Fearing the potential of Ukrainian nationalism, the Germans administratively separated the western Ukrainian lands. As indicated by

---

[18] Ibid., p. 372.

[19] Motyl, "The Organized Ukrainian Resistance Movement," pp. 12–13.

[20] Ibid., p. 15.

[21] I address this violence in greater detail in *Fear, Hatred, Resentment: Delineating Paths to Ethnic Conflict in Eastern Europe* (Cambridge: Cambridge University Press, forthcoming).

Figure 7.1, Galicia was placed in the General Govournement, whereas Volhynia entered the Reichskommisariat Ukraine. For Ukrainians, the difference between the two areas was significant. In the Reichskommisariat, Erich Koch ruled with incredible severity and the populace suffered enormous deprivations. In the General Govournement, on the other hand, Hans Frank treated the Galician population with some leniency, at least by the standards of the day. In the General Govournement, Ukrainians were not as likely to be subjected to forced labor conscriptions as in the Reichskommisariat. Moreover, Galician Ukrainians served in lower administrative posts and in the police. When the Germans first decided to raise a Ukrainian SS division, they recruited from Galicia. Indicative of the German fear of Ukrainian nationalism and favoritism toward Galicians, this unit was to be named "Galicia" and was to wear the historic emblem of Galicia; reference to Ukrainian nationalism was not allowed. At one point, Himmler issued an order to the officers in charge of training the Galician SS unit forbidding them "for all time to speak of a Ukrainian division or of a Ukrainian nation in connection with the division 'Galicia.'"[22] Whereas Volhynians bore the burdens imposed by the brutal Koch in the Reichskommisariat Ukraine, Galicians lived relatively better in the General Govournement.

Resentment and Focal Points

This historical gloss indicates that Volhynians never had the opportunity to develop a strong perception of ethnic status. Under the Russian Empire and Polish rule, the population remained in a premodern, semiliterate condition, especially in terms of the Ukrainian language. Under the Russian Empire, unlike the Hapsburg, Ukrainians had never been allowed a political voice. Furthermore, in no period had the Volhynians ever experienced any status position other than one on the lower rungs. Under the Russian Empire, Polish rule, and the first Soviet occupation, Volhynians never experienced anything close to equal status. Under the Germans, and Koch's brutal Reichskommisariat Ukraine, the Volhynians were treated as total inferiors. When the Soviets returned in 1944, they were an acceptable alternative to previous regimes.

The Galicians, on the other hand, had developed a political-ethnic con-

---

[22] See V. Dmytryshyn, "The Nazis and the SS Volunteer Division 'Galicia,'" *American Slavic and East European Review* 15 (1956): 7–8. Dmytryshyn is citing "Himmler to All Company Commanders, Field Command Post, July 14, 1943."

sciousness under the Hapsburgs and exhibited nationalist politics, as seen in the election boycotts, under Polish jurisdiction. More importantly, Galicians had some familiarity with higher status than did the Volhynians. This was true in comparing the Hapsburgs and the Russians. Also, the experience under the Germans in World War II differed. For Galicians, the return of the Soviets was surely seen as a step down the ethnic status ladder as well as a blow to chances for higher autonomy or an independent nation.

In his study, Alexander Motyl also cites different historical backgrounds of the two regions but centers his explanation around nationalist ideology and religious heritage:

> The very fact that Volhynia produced so large a number of informers and infiltrators is proof enough that the population, which surely includes these people as well, was not solidly behind the OUN [Organization of Ukrainian Nationalists] and UPA [Ukrainian Insurgent Army]. The basic reason for this fairly widespread postwar lack of support can be found in the pattern of historical development of Volhynia. Unlike Uniate Galicia which served as a kind of incubator for nationalist ideas and activity under Austria and Poland, Greek Orthodox Volhynia remained in the Russian Empire until after the Revolution and was later administratively divided from Galicia. Thus, the nationalists only had a brief twenty-year period to agitate in the province, so that their influence never became as widespread as in Galicia.[23]

Motyl's argument, in tune with political-historical explanation, is elite-led and idea-based: with more exposure to Ukrainian nationalist agitation, Volhynians may have behaved in the postwar period like Galicians. The resentment mechanism also relies on political-historical factors but with a different emphasis. Although elites may be important in creating ethnic consciousness in the mass, the power of ethnic-national consciousness in creating mass resistance derives from the visible elements of governance. Daily experiences of humiliation, status change, and status reversal create the emotion of resentment. Motivation to accept risk is tied to this emotion. The notion of simply being a Ukrainian is less motivating than the experience of being a Ukrainian unjustly ruled by another group. In Galicia, many individuals both thought of themselves as Ukrainians and consciously experienced daily ethnic humiliations. Galician experience, far more than Volhynian experience, produced mass resentment.

---

[23] Motyl, "The Organized Ukrainian Resistance Movement," pp. 35–36.

In addition to more-intense motivation, recent Galician history had produced action with symbolic meanings capable of coordinating expectations under repressive conditions. Galician nationalist resistance against Polish authority included election boycotts and acts of sabotage. As mentioned already, Galicians boycotted the 1921–1922 elections to protest the imposition of Polish rule. In the summer of 1930, Galicians attacked Polish estates, committing over 2,000 acts of sabotage.[24] In response, the Polish government arrested and confined 2,000 Ukrainians to prison and built a concentration camp, Bereza Kartuzka, in 1934 to hold mostly Ukrainian political prisoners. Under the Poles, election boycotts and sabotage developed a meaning: these acts communicated a will to fight a powerful and repressive regime. In the postwar period, these acts would communicate a similar meaning for Galicians.

The Second Soviet Occupation

In Volhynia, the percentage of +1 actors was never high enough to surpass the tipping point and set widespread movement from neutrality into motion. Potential resisters and rebels could never act without the fear of informers; they could never confidently expect support from the general population; they could not expect to successfully build local organization. The words of one report make this fact clear:

> The police terror in Volhynia is so strong that the population is afraid of its own shadow. . . . Under this terror there has developed a mass sekotstvo [informerism]; this is not some kind of lack of political understanding of our struggle, or perhaps moral decay, but it is simply a great fear in the face of the terror. . . . A fear of one's every neighbor. And very frequently, villagers become informers only because they are afraid of being informed upon.[25]

The underlying logic of the assurance game is all about handling fear; surpassing the threshold means that participation rates have reduced fear and risk to a point at which the value of resisting outweighs that of remaining neutral. As the preceding quotation illustrates, this point was never reached in Volhynia. Neighbors could never be sure of each other, let alone of strangers. Given the risks of any type of resistance action in the postwar So-

[24] Subtelny, *Ukraine: A History,* p. 430.
[25] Motyl, "The Organized Ukrainian Resistance Movement," pp. 34–35. Motyl is quoting an anonymous *zvit* written in 1946.

viet Union, the average +1 threshold was naturally high. Without strong motivations to resist, this threshold remains high, probably too high to be surpassed.

In Galicia, despite terroristic regime measures equal to those in Volhynia, the mass of the population clearly had moved to +1 and significant numbers had moved to +2 as well. In fact, rebellion in Galicia covered the entire right side of the spectrum. A mobile armed force (+3) existed in the form of the UPA (Ukrainian Insurgent Army), while the OUN (Organization of Ukrainian Nationalists) worked primarily through operations at the community level (+2). The OUN's underground network operated bunker systems as well as an aboveground membership, mirroring its successful Lithuanian counterparts. Alexander Motyl describes the dynamics of rebellion in Galicia at length:

> Whereas the UPA soldiers were rarely stationed in the areas of their homes, the OUN was so organized that its local cadres were always indigenous to the town or village within which they operated. The necessity for this is obvious, because the OUN worked directly with the population and therefore had to be completely familiar with it and the conditions of its life. . . . Neither the underground OUN nor the UPA could have survived without support from the general population, for it was only the villagers who could provide the underground with food, clothing, occasional shelter and information. Without these essentials, the underground would have been incapable of simple physical survival. . . . The link between the people and the underground OUN and UPA was not direct, for the above-ground OUN acted as intermediary. It was actually these civilian OUN members who were directly responsible for gathering the necessary provisions and information.[26]

These classic rebellion dynamics were predicated on a sympathetic population confident of being able to support rebels without likely retaliation, in other words, a society at +1. When the Soviets returned, they wished to legitimize their rule through mass participation in elections. With the 1921–1922 boycott of elections serving as precedent, Galician rebels again called for a boycott of Soviet postwar elections. Despite clear Soviet falsification of election results, this boycott appears to have been successful.[27]

[26] Ibid., pp. 39, 41.
[27] Motyl's article is concerned mainly with this boycott. See ibid., pp. 20–27, in particular for evidence of the boycott's scope.

Motyl provides supporting data: the Soviet regime assigned a disproportional number of propagandists to the region in anticipation of an election
boycott, and Ukrainian partisan reports indicate purposive boycott and Soviet measures to force a vote. As Motyl concludes, "As the elections of 1922
and 1935 indicate, an election boycott seems not to have been an unusual
course for the Ukrainians of Galicia to have followed. Their high level of national and political awareness, first developed in Austrian times and later for-
tified into a kind of popular unanimity during the twenty years of Polish occupation, had already inured the Galicians to legitimate and political forms
of resistance to an okupant."[28]

The boycott of the 1946 Soviet election is one example of symbolic national resistance in Galicia. Other resistance actions no doubt had historical
referents in the short-lived Ukrainian state and the struggle against Polish
rule. Of course, this boycott provided information at two levels. On the one
hand, the OUN, the nationalist underground, was strong enough to encourage such a boycott successfully; on the other hand, the boycott provided information to both the general population, as well as the rebels, that resistance was possible and that the percentage of fellow citizens active or
supportive was high enough to produce some measure of security (unlike in
Volhynia). The boycott of Soviet elections could not but have buoyed the
confidence of Ukrainian rebels to continue operating at the +2 and +3 levels and produce yet more +2 rebels.

With high levels of resentment and effective symbolic action to provide
communication of common anti-Soviet motivation, the Galician population
moved to +1. In a second step, the strong community structures of Galicia
apparently helped move significant numbers of individuals to the +2 position. Without the necessary fine-grained data, comparisons to the postwar
Lithuanian case cannot be made, but it is likely that many of the same factors were at play: small, rural communities, strong overall communities and
youths fearing conscription, and sustaining mechanisms in the form of beliefs of imminent salvation through a coming war.[29]

---

[28] Ibid., p. 27.

[29] Prewar social organization in the region also resembled that of prewar Lithuania with heterogeneous, locally based social and economic groups flourishing. Of the 4,000 nationally
minded economic cooperatives, 90% were located in eastern Galicia; the village-based youth
organization Sokol and Luh continued from the prewar era and was joined by Plast, the more
urban scouting organization (banned in 1930 as too nationalist). See Subtelny, *Ukraine: A History,* pp. 438–439. Along with the veterans of the post–World War I struggle and the political
prisoners of the era of Polish rule, most communities possessed significant numbers of low-

The Strategies of Competing Occupiers:
Ukraine and Belorussia

During the Second World War, German occupying forces and Soviet partisans bitterly contested areas of Ukraine and Belorussia. In some areas, Ukrainian nationalist guerrillas and Polish forces entered the fray alongside the Germans and Soviets. For the civilians living under these situations of multiple occupation, life was often a bloody hell. In Ukraine alone, an estimated 28,000 villages were destroyed by the war's competing occupiers.[30] The German occupiers often executed more civilians suspected of aiding partisan fighters than actual partisan fighters.[31] In all, roughly one in six

threshold actors and low-threshold organizations characterized by norms of honor (B norms) to produce levels of resistance.

In essential ways, the Belorussian postwar case resembles the Volhynian. Again, the motivation for resistance was lacking. Neither had experienced the relatively open society allowed under Austro-Hungarian rule; both had only known the repressive and Russifying policies of the tsar. While most Volhynians experienced the authoritarian and Polonizing policies of the interwar Polish regime, so did a sizable portion of the Belorussian population. Without this sense, the perception of hierarchy could not develop and, correspondingly, the motivating force of resentment could not develop. In both regions, the Soviets incorporated the area into the USSR under the Molotov-Ribbentrop agreement. In both regions, the Germans stormed the territory during Operation Barbarossa and created brutal wartime living conditions.

Critically, unlike the Galicians, Belorussians and Volhynians had never occupied a top place in any established hierarchy. When the Soviets returned in 1944, it was just another dominant group occupying the region. Soviet establishment of control, not surprisingly, did not produce any level of resentment. In fact, in comparison to the Germans and the Poles, the view of the Soviets, while not overly enthusiastic after the tribulations of the 1930s, was in fact relatively favorable. At least the Soviets had granted them the status of a Soviet Socialist Republic. In short, the Belorussians simply lacked the motivation, especially given Soviet power, to move toward rebellion activity. Not surprisingly, there was practically no movement to +1.

Furthermore, neither population had the organizational or cultural base to clearly distinguish themselves from Russians who carried a similar Orthodox heritage. Neither possessed a history of antiregime action that would produce the symbolic wealth that would facilitate movement toward resistance. As in Volhynia, most individuals in Belorussia simply wanted to rebuild their lives as quietly as possible.

One notable feature of Belorussia should be emphasized. Perhaps in no other area were Soviet partisans so active and well connected to the USSR's support lines. More than 75,000 Soviet partisans were operating in occupied Belorussia. The population could be sure of the Soviet efforts to keep track of the position of local Belorussians during the German occupation; the probability of identification and retribution was high. Jan Zaprudnik, *Belarus: At a Crossroads in History* (Boulder, Colo.: Westview Press, 1993), p. 99.

[30] Bohdan Krawchenko, "Soviet Ukraine under Nazi Occupation, 1941–1944," in Yury Boshyk, ed., *Ukraine during World War II: History and Its Aftermath* (Edmonton: Canadian Institute of Ukrainian Studies, 1986), p. 15.

[31] For example, records show 14,257 civilians and 9,902 partisans executed between August and November 1942. See Taras Hunczak, "The Ukrainian Losses during World War II," in Michael Berenbaum, ed., *A Mosaic of Victims: Non-Jews Persecuted and Murdered by the Nazis* (New York: New York University Press, 1990), p. 119. In this same volume, also see Bohdan

Ukrainians died during the war, 4.5 million of them civilians.[32] The Germans, led by Erich Koch, were brutal. Koch, during his inauguration speech in September 1941, introduced himself to his subordinates by stating, "I am known as a brutal dog. Because of this I was appointed Reichskommissar of the Ukraine. Our task is to suck from the Ukraine all the goods we can get ahold of, without consideration of the feelings or property of the Ukrainians. . . . I am expecting from you the utmost severity towards the population."[33] The Soviets were not much better. After purposely starving much of the eastern and central Ukrainian population a decade earlier,[34] the Soviets initiated three waves of brutal deportations from 1939 to 1941, mostly from the newly acquired western provinces, shipping hundreds of thousands of civilians to Siberia.[35] As seen shortly, in competing for territory with the Germans, the strategies of the Soviet partisan forces were nearly an equal match in raining terror upon the civilian population.[36]

The history of Ukraine (this section refers to east and central Ukraine, not Volhynia or Galicia) and Belorussia during the Second World War is enormously complex and cannot be covered here. Other fine sources exist on this

Vitvitsky, "Slavs and Jews: Consistent and Inconsistent Perspectives on the Holocaust," pp. 101–108, and Aharon Weiss, "The Holocaust and Ukrainian Victims," pp. 109–115, for more information on the plight of the Ukrainian population and, in a subject not covered here, the disaster that befell the Jewish population of the Ukraine.

[32] Hunczak, "The Ukrainian Losses during World War II," p. 124.

[33] Ibid., p. 117.

[34] The western provinces of Ukraine had been part of Poland during the interwar period.

[35] Hunczak, "The Ukrainian Losses during World War II," p. 120. Hunczak also describes the Soviet mass murder of more than 9,000 Ukrainians in Vinnytsia and the numerous Soviet massacres at the beginning of Barbarossa. On the Soviet occupation of 1939–1941, also see Orest Subtelny, "The Soviet Occupation of Western Ukraine, 1939–1941: An Overview," in Yury Boshyk, ed., *Ukraine during World War II: History and Its Aftermath* (Edmonton: Canadian Institute of Ukrainian Studies, 1986), pp. 5–14.

[36] Many acts of brutality and inhumanity that occurred in this region should be remembered. I wish to note one in particular, although its relevance is not central to this chapter. This is the issue of Soviet prisoners of war. The Germans captured 5.7 million Red Army soldiers. Of this number, 3.3 million would perish before the end of the war (57%). Most starved, many died in outbreaks of typhoid and dysentery (an average of 4,600 Soviet POWs were dying per day in camps in the General Gouvernement during epidemics in late October 1941), and many were shot during the marches from the front to the prison camps. Thousands died in the camps of Birkenau and Majdanek in 1941. In Soviet camps, the figures are somewhat better. Of the 3.25 million German prisoners taken by the Soviets, 1.2 million (36%) perished by the end of the war. These figures are taken from Christian Streit, "The Fate of the Soviet Prisoners of War," in Michael Berenbaum, ed., *A Mosaic of Victims: Non-Jews Persecuted and Murdered by the Nazis* (New York: New York University Press, 1990), pp. 142–149. Some Soviet prisoners collaborated with the Germans. On this issue, see Mark R. Elliott, "Soviet Military Collaborators during World War II," in Yury Boshyk, *Ukraine during World War II: History and Its Aftermath,* (Edmonton: Canadian Institute of Ukrainian Studies, 1986), pp. 89–104.

topic.[37] Rather, the present explanatory task is to address the nature of movement on the spectrum of roles. In a region this vast this movement cannot be easily summarized, but two features distinguished much of this region from the Baltic and other cases: in areas in which both the Germans and the Soviets could project force, the population sometimes vacillated between support of the two sides. This vacillation took two forms. At the individual level, a diffusion of roles across the spectrum could be found during the war. At the community level, in certain cases vacillation involved whole villages going from +2 to −2 on the spectrum. It seems that the cruel nature of life created a mentality of "every person for himself" by whatever means possible.

The Project of the Soviet Social System conducted at the Russian Research Center at Harvard University provides much of the source material for this section. This project's investigators, led by Alexander Dallin, interviewed approximately 1,000 former Soviet citizens that had made their way to the West after or during the Second World War. Its summary findings were published in September 1954. I have chosen these documents because they fit with the style of my own interviews. Unfortunately, they provide very little information on the structure of communities in which the respondents had been embedded.

Regions Contested by Both Germans and Soviet Partisans

The bulk of the Ukrainian population greeted the German invasion with optimism, especially peasants who hoped that the hated Soviet system of collective agriculture would be overturned. When initial hopes were not met, the positive attitude became one of watchful neutrality. Finally, inhuman German policies destroyed any remaining Ukrainian goodwill. Between the Soviets and the Germans, the common attitude was a plague on both houses. On the whole, individuals did what they could, and collaborated with whom they could, in order to better their chances of survival. In the summary report of the Project on the Soviet Social System, Sylvia Gilliam and Alexan-

---

[37] See especially Alexander Dallin, *German Rule in Russia, 1941–1945: A Study of Occupation Policies* (Boulder, Colo.: Westview Press, 1981); Armstrong, *Soviet Partisans in World War II* (Madison: University of Wisconsin Press, 1964); John Armstrong, *Ukrainian Nationalism*; Jan T. Gross, *Revolution from Abroad: The Soviet Conquest of Poland's West Ukraine and Western Belorussia* (Princeton: Princeton University Press, 1988); Yuriy Tys-Krokhmaliuk, *UPA Warfare in the Ukraine: Statistical, Tactical, and Organizational Problems of Ukrainian Resistance in World War II* (New York: Society of Veterans of Ukranian Insurgent Army, 1972); and Yury Boshyk, *Ukraine during World War II: History and Its Aftermath* (Edmonton: Canadian Institute of Ukranian Studies, 1986), among others.

der Dallin provide a similar synopsis of the German occupation of the Soviet Union:

> Occupation policies and practices of the Germans varied from one area of the Soviet Union to another. We thus have a fairly good opportunity of evaluating how various strata of Soviet society reacted to different alternatives to the Soviet system. All these experiences are characterized by one common reaction: a strong initial hostility toward the Soviet system developed into an attitude of watchful waiting toward the Germans, to be finally replaced by an overwhelming revulsion caused by German activities which made the Soviet system look not quite so bad in comparison.[38]

Restating these phenomena in terms of the spectrum, regarding the Germans as the negative side and the Soviets as the positive, many communities tended to originally move to −1 (unorganized support of the Germans), then to 0 (neutrality), and finally either to positions scattered across the spectrum or to vacillation between +2 and −2 positions. Although the diversity of experience in this area was enormous, the vacillating movements and scattered positioning are of most interest here.

Most obviously, the diffusion of rebellion roles in the latter half of the Second World War resulted in part from the confusion created by multiple occupation. As a member of the Kaminsky Brigade, a partisan formation operating in Belorussia alongside Soviet partisans and German police noted:

> People didn't know who was raiding them. An old man would not know how to answer if suddenly somebody raided his house. There were cases of people changing their answers every time someone took the village and guessing wrong every time so that he would be beaten and robbed in turn by partisans, Kaminsky, and again partisans and the police.[39]

The confusion, along with the constant brutality by all sides, often made any given strategy unsustainable. Understandably, many of those caught in the

---

[38] Sylvia Gilliam and Alexander Dallin, "Aspects of the German Occupation of the Soviet Union," in *Project on the Soviet Social System* (AF no. 33(038)-12909), Russian Research Center, Harvard University, p. 1. Also see Bohdan Krawchenko, "Soviet Ukraine under Nazi Occupation, 1941–1944," in Yuri Boshyk, ed., *Ukraine during World War II: History and Its Aftermath* (Edmonton: Canadian Institute of Ukrainian Studies, 1986), pp. 15–38.

[39] *Project on the Soviet Social System*, file 358. Interviewee 32 told a similar story: "The peasants had a hard time telling what groups they were dealing with; usually they could tell by listening to the group's songs at night. Many people kept changing sides from one group to another several times."

middle without decent information were resigned to tactical cooperation with both of the two undesirable sides of the spectrum. The following passage is fairly typical:

> None of us had any concrete ideas about how the future would develop. Besides, we were poorly oriented about the course of events in general. I just floated with the stream of things, not knowing what the future would bring. . . . In a narrow circle one kept asking "what next?" The only concrete way out of the situation was to join the partisans. But, let us say it frankly, one did not want the Soviets to win either. The only activists you had under the occupation were the Communists, the out-and-out pro-Nazis, the Ukrainian Nationalists, and the criminals.[40]

Other informants did not even recognize that the Soviet partisans and German-recruited police could be seen as activists, but rather saw them as collections of similar individuals who ended up on opposite sides simply through idiosyncratic circumstances: "I'm not aware of any special personal animosities between partisans and police. After all, they were the same sort of people on both sides. Conditions forced people to side with one side or the other."[41] The nature of their violent and vague circumstances led many to the conclusion of yet another interviewee who stated, "There seemed to be a general feeling on the basis of one's own experience that under certain conditions one must be able to collaborate with anybody."[42] Indeed, the major factor was often simply who seemed to be winning at any given time. Many individuals who originally sided with the Germans eventually went over to the Soviet partisans as the tide of war turned, a conversion without conviction or passion.[43]

Often individuals were forcibly recruited by one side or the other while at other times individuals or families fled to the woods on their own. Some-

---

[40] Ibid., file 322 B6. Another typical quote: "People made no value judgements of 'collaboration.' People did not turn in Communists to the Germans, not even the most zealous ones. Deserters were given asylum from both the Reds and the Germans. People had no general ideas of what the future would bring; they just hoped for a change, any change for the better" (ibid., 32 AD B6).

[41] Ibid., file 219, passage J. The same interviewee noted that "A number of people kept changing sides from partisans to police or vice versa."

[42] Interview 144, B6, passage 6.

[43] I am leaving out the whole issue of Vlasov and the German efforts to raise an anti-Soviet force from Soviet prisoners of war. On this subject, good material has been written. See Sven Steenberg, *Vlasov* (New York: Knopf, 1970). Also, Armstong's *Soviet Partisans in World War II* addresses Soviet countermeasures to the Vlasov movement on pp. 241–249.

times communities remained largely intact under the leadership of a *starosta* (a village elder). When this happened, the position of the starosta, having to appease two or more ruthless entities, often became nearly impossible. Peasant communities required imaginative balancing solutions to survive. Again, the strategies of the community reflected the exigencies of survival, which, in turn, often entailed switching sides of the spectrum (or trying to occupy both sides simultaneously) to meet current conditions. The following quote reveals one apparently common local solution to the problem of survival under multiple occupation:

> When the partisans began being annoying, our village decided to rotate the starostaship. For ten or fifteen days at a time, the pro-German starosta would hold the job, then for ten or fifteen days it would be the turn of the pro-partisan starosta. Actually, neither of them were pro-German or pro-partisan. They just happened to get along with them. The Germans knew this alternating arrangement, but there was nothing they could do about it. The peasants thought it up as the only way they could protect themselves.[44]

In other localities where the local German and partisan forces were more brutal (and this brutality certainly did vary according to local administration and personalities), peasants developed risk-sharing arrangements: "In some areas where both partisans and Germans operated, sometimes peasants established a system whereby each of a number of local residents were starosta for two weeks at a time as to minimize personal risk."[45] Given the fact that 28,000 villages were destroyed, apparently no mixed strategy or insurance plan could guarantee that a community would not be destroyed.

Weak Community

Confusion and barbarity were two primary reasons for the vacillation on the spectrum seen in the latter stages of occupation, but there are three more-specific reasons why movement in one direction or the other could not be sustained in the regions occupied by both Germans and Soviets. The first two

[44] From the *Project on the Soviet Social System*. The passage here is from file 46 AD B6, passage 3. Other passages indicate similar strategies. For example, file 142 AD B6 indicates that the length of tenure of starosty could be even more brief than noted earlier: "Our village for a while was in German hands in daytime and in partisan hands at night. From then on nobody wanted to be starosta. So it was decided to alternate the position. In a number of villages somebody else became starosta every week. Later the job was rotated almost daily."

[45] Ibid., file 219, passage 9–K.

are relatively straightforward and follow from two of the basic tenets of this study.

The communities of most of Ukraine (again, excluding Volhynia and Galicia) and Belorussia were relatively weak. The autonomous subgroupings and organizational elements seen in the Lithuanian study had been destroyed through two decades of Soviet rule. Religious groups and organization had withered; non-Soviet social groups were banned; informal sets of middle-class peasants had been labeled kulaks and deported to Siberia; in some regions, millions had died of starvation. Furthermore, with the situation in the countryside ever more hopeless, millions of the most able had immigrated to Soviet cities during the 1920s and 1930s, again weakening the previous village communities.[46] The new community was based on hated state collectives – often of large size and always ultimately directed by outside policy.

Under these conditions, movement toward any side of the spectrum is hard to sustain for several reasons, both rational and normative. First, larger and weaker communities do not possess strong reciprocity norms. Second, weak communities are not able to effectively monitor and threaten their members. In strong communities, members get pulled into a +2 position through family and social group norms. They remain there through reciprocity norms and threats. None of these mechanisms was effective in the weak communities of World War II Ukraine and Belorussia.

Ethnic Hierarchy and the Lack of Resentment

Had a strong perception of ethnic hierarchy existed in central and eastern Ukraine and Belorussia, and had the Germans chosen to exploit it, there might have been rapid movement on the spectrum toward collaboration. As it was, widespread movement toward the −1 position occurred during the period immediately after invasion and then was reversed. The simple fact of the matter was that neither the Germans nor the Soviets were willing to allow policies that raised the status position of national groups above a certain level. In comparative terms, the Soviets did a better job on this score by creating a Ukrainian Soviet Socialist Republic and developing Ukrainian-language outlets.[47] German occupiers only offered national groups any sig-

---

[46] See George Liber, "Urban Growth and Ethnic Change in the Ukrainian SSR, 1923–1933," *Soviet Studies* 41 (1989): 574–591.

[47] Although arrests and starvation mitigated the power of these factors.

nificant recognition in the desperate days before Soviet reconquest.[48] In effect, the ethnic-national factor was taken out of the equation through German and Soviet policies that were similar in practice. Given the German, and Soviet, failure to exploit the national issue, there was little motivation to counter material and safety benefits produced through vacillating movement on the spectrum.

Scholars have discussed at length the failure of the Germans to take advantage of national grievances.[49] The German bureaucratic staffing policies indicate the extent of the Nazi's distrust of Ukrainian self-rule. The Germans decided to mobilize 200,000 Reich Germans rather than allow willing Ukrainians to fill administrative positions.[50] The Ukrainians, far down the scale on the Nazi racial hierarchy, were judged most fit for slave labor; indeed, perhaps as many as 2.2 million Ukrainians were sent to Germany, where they were clearly treated as second-class citizens.[51] These numbers cannot describe the day-to-day corrosive effects of Nazi racism. Summing up the interview data, Gilliam and Dallin state that "almost every inhabitant sooner or later, personally or second-hand, encountered instances of what he perceived as duress, humiliation, or colonialism."[52]

Furthermore, the very perception of ethnic hierarchy in most of the Ukraine (the exception of Galicia is discussed earlier) and Belorussia was weak. Unlike the Baltic states, these nations had never firmly established a nation-state in which they experienced a sense of dominance. There had been no sense of status reversal. In many ways these peoples had not reached a point in modernization where the national idea had become fully formed. Finally, much of the most nationally conscious sections of the elite had been killed, deported, or otherwise eliminated during Stalin's harsh nationality policy of the late 1930s.

---

[48] Here, the issue of SS divisions is relevant. For discussion of the creation of the Galicia division, see Dmytryshyn, "The Nazis and the SS Volunteer Division 'Galicia.'"

[49] In *German Rule in Russia*, Dallin discusses the battle between different Nazi factions over nationality policy in great detail. A shorter summary is found in Alex Alexiev, *Soviet Nationalities in German Wartime Stategy, 1941–1945* (Rand Corporation, Rand Reports, R-2772–NA, August 1982).

[50] Alexiev, *Soviet Nationalities in German Wartime Stategy, 1941–1945*, p. 12.

[51] Hunczak, "The Ukrainian Losses during World War II," p. 120.

[52] Dallin and Gilliam, *Project on the Soviet Social System*, summary report, p. 12. Not surprisingly, Dallin and Gilliam found little evidence for the importance of ethnicity in the German occupation of much of the Soviet Union.

Soviet and German Pacification Strategies

Although ethnic status considerations and weak community did not prevent vacillation on the spectrum, it was the interaction of occupier strategies that produced the positive incentives to move back and forth. During the occupation, contested areas witnessed an escalation of brutality that created tremendous variation in rebellion behavior and effectively scattered the population across the spectrum. In this section, a relatively simple method is created to analyze the effects of interacting strategies.

In any occupation, the new regime has basic choices in trying to influence the nature of roles of the newly occupied population. For instance, should it spend scarce resources on chasing mobile partisans (+3) or use these same resources to police the suppliers and sources of refuge and communication found in networks of organized villages (+2)? Should it try to force the neutral members of the population (0) to move into collaboration roles? Should it use resources to build up local collaboration organizations (–2)[53] rather than simply policing or destroying the bases of resistance (+2)?

In the words of one often used phrase, occupier strategies can be examined in terms of sticks and carrots. The sticks include physical repression, deportation, forced military and labor conscription, higher taxes; the carrots include political, economic, and religious autonomy, provision of foodstuffs, tax relief, work relief. Such policies involve costs to the occupier, which can only absorb a finite amount of cost.[54] While one element of occupier strategy is the mix of sticks and carrots to be played, a second is the choice of recipient: against whom should the sticks be used? To whom should the carrot be offered?

Both of these elements (stick-carrot, target-recipient) can be analyzed with the use of the spectrum concept of rebellion roles. Assume that the occupier has resources worth 100 units of value that can be divided up into smaller packages of carrots (represented by positive values) and sticks (rep-

---

[53] Here, for example, the essence of the strategic hamlet program the United States employed in Vietnam comes to mind.

[54] Of course, some of these costs are hard to compare. The costs and benefits of destroying villages versus the cost of granting them self-government are hardly comparable with the cost-benefit analysis of investing in one stock versus another. The analysis of threat is especially difficult to model in any coherent fashion. The effectiveness of threats often depends on the imagination of those making the threat. Despite a paucity of resources, some exceptionally cruel operators in the Ukraine could effectively threaten a locality by use of particularly barbaric devices such as mutilation of local leaders, letting them live but cutting out their eyes, etc. Despite the problems of weak analogy, the "economic" analysis of occupier policies can yield important insights.

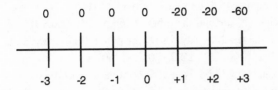

Figure 7.2. An example of occupier strategy

resented by negative values). Various occupier strategies can be represented by aligning the stick-carrot value with the spectrum position for which it is targeted. For example, the occupier may wish to use all resources to either hunt down partisans or close off their supply bases. This *partisan hunt* strategy might then be illustrated as shown in Figure 7.2. More simply, this strategy could be designated (0,0,0,0,-20,-20,-60).

Other logical occupier strategies and logics included the gradient strategy (0,0,0,-10,-20,-30,-40), in which the occupier arranges a series of sticks and threats to encourage individuals at each level of resistance or neutrality to move leftward toward collaboration. In the strategic hamlet strategy (+20,+60, +20, 0,0,0,0), the occupier spends all resources providing incentives to the population to resist the rebels themselves. The -2 node is seen as most critical. A version of this strategy might be *hamlet destruction* (0,0,0,0,-20,-60,-20), where a disproportionate amount of resources are used to destroy or threaten bases of rebellion support.

With the mixed stick and carrot strategy (+20,+20,+10,0,-10,-20,-20), the occupier both tries to woo collaborators and discourage rebellion through an even and symmetrical diffusion of sticks and carrots. Of course, there could be several variations of this strategy, such as (+10,+40,0,0,0,-40,-10). In the neutral scattering strategy (0,0,-30,-40,-30,0,0), the occupier wishes to move the population off of neutrality in order to be able to identify supporters and rebels along the logic of "if you are not for us, you are against us." This step might be the first part of a two-stage strategy. Neutral scattering creates visible targets, which are then sought in partisan hunt or hamlet destruction strategies. Of course, many other strategies are conceivable and have been employed by various occupiers. Also, the chosen strategy might not become the actual strategy due to misinformation or lack of ability to identify the individuals at each node.

In cases of multiple occupation, the strategic interplay of the competing occupiers helps shape movement on the spectrum. To consider a simple example, assume two occupiers with an equal number of resources. Regard one occupier as the negative side and the other as the positive side. If both sides play partisan hunt, the resulting payoffs for the population at each node of the spectrum would be (−60,−20,−20,0,−20,−20,−60). Given this structure of payoffs, individuals could be expected to move toward the highest payoff, in this case, neutrality with a value of 0. Given the pressure on both sides of the spectrum, the population flees to neutrality to avoid sanctions and threats.

A somewhat more complicated situation is produced by a combination of gradient and strategic hamlet strategies. Here the outcome is (0,0,0,−10,0,+30,−20), and movement into the +2 category would be expected. If the game has multiple and sequential rounds, the gradient strategy could be expected to be adjusted by one player in order to counteract the benefits accruing at the +2 position.

This last point brings out the problems and ambiguities of this type of analysis. How free are occupiers to choose their stategies? Do they have the information and capabilities to adjust their strategies? How much does ideology constrain the original choice and subsequent choices of occupiers? These issues are beyond the scope of this section. I only use this form of analysis to help explain the outcome witnessed in central and eastern Ukraine and Belorussia: vacillating movement on the spectrum, a scattered distribution of rebellion roles, a very high level of atrocity and barbarity.

Germans and Soviets in World War II Ukraine and Belorussia

As mentioned already, individual movement on the spectrum was not strongly constrained by community-based mechanisms or ethnically based motivations of resentment. Basically, it was every man (and woman) for himself. Thus, occupier strategy was a decisive factor in explaining movement on the spectrum. The Germans, constrained by their ideology and racism, were less free to choose optimal plays than the individuals whom they sought to rule. Recall Koch's statement: "I am a known as a brutal dog. . . . I expect the utmost severity toward the population." Given this orientation, it was highly unlikely that the Nazis were going to play strategic hamlet, or any other carrot-oriented policy for that matter. Rather, they were going to use threats and punishment almost exclusively. Although German policies varied from area to area, the general strategy was to apply pressure across the board but most severely to the localities supporting partisans and the partisans themselves. In a rough fashion, they had chosen the gradient strategy $(0,0,0,-10,-20,-30,-40)$.

The Soviets did not have comparable resources to compete with the Germans on their own terms. Because they possessed fewer resources than the Germans in much of the region, the Soviet partisans adopted tactics aimed to change the German strategy. As the Germans promised to retaliate against any village where German soldiers were found dead, the Soviets placed killed Germans near neutral villages to trigger punishment against that village. In effect, the Soviets wanted the Germans to help carry out a neutral scattering strategy and drive the population toward the ends of the spectrum. They hoped that the Nazi strategy of retaliation would create enough anti-German animosity to drive the bulk of scattered neutrals toward the Soviet end.

The Soviet partisan strategy can be seen in the comments of those affected by it:

> Germans also practiced taking reprisals for each German killed and killing many in the local population in retaliation. This brutality was exploited by the partisans. The partisans would make an ambush far from the village and kill one German and leave without accepting any battle. The only mission was to kill Germans and not to accept battle. Then a German attachment would appear and either burn down the nearest village or shoot part of the inhabitants, especially the men, without any trial or investigation. Whole groups of people felt threatened by the Germans whether they had done anything or not, which naturally meant fertile soil for the partisans.[55]

The neutral scattering effects are seen yet more clearly in other passages from the Project on the Soviet Social System:

> It was well known that when the partisans came into a village and killed Germans in that village, there would be trouble for the villagers. So therefore partisans forced villagers either to join the partisans or join the Germans, leaving no middle ground. . . . Very often when the partisans would kill two Germans they would kill them right in the village when it would

---

[55] *Project on the Soviet Social System,* File 143, AD B7, passage D15. Also see file 193, HD B7, passage 19. This strategy was also employed by Tito in the partisan-civil war occurring in Yugoslavia during the Second World War. Mihailovich, leader of the nationalist partisan force was unwilling to provoke German retaliation against the civilian population, while Tito saw the potential for creating anti-German hatred.

have been just as easy to do it outside of the village thereby to spare villagers. The partisans did not care if a whole village was destroyed.[56]

Of course, conditions varied across such a large region. Sometimes the Germans could control a large area, as did the Soviet partisans.[57] In the contested areas, the German "neutral scattering" effect appears to have been common. For many of those located at the −1 or 0, collaboration with the Germans at the −2 or −3 level would have seemed a likely choice. Indeed, many individuals fleeing destroyed or threatened villages found themselves working for the Germans in local police (−2) or in some other capacity. As an informant stated, "Now our village was under pressure and it was only a matter of time before it would be destroyed by the partisans or by the Germans. The villagers had two choices. Some fled to the German cities. . . . Those who went to the cities practically always had to join the German police."[58] Similarly, those determined to avoid German collaboration, and this number increased after the outcome of Stalingrad became known, found their best option among only bad options at the +2 position. Furthermore, those village communities that remained intact, as seen earlier, sought their salvation in a strategy of moving back and forth between the −2 and +2 positions.

Although much of the population of Ukraine and Belorussia would have preferred to have remained neutral, the combination of German and Soviet policies clearly tended to drive individuals from the −1, 0, and +1 positions. Given the local and theaterwide changes in balance of power between the Germans and Soviets, the scattered and fluctuating set of rebellion roles was hardly surprising. Strong community or ethnic status considerations might have stopped this oscillation, but these factors were not present or weak. The occupation of these territories was one of the most brutal witnessed in this century. The major reason for this barbarity was the racist and severe nature of German policy. However, the Soviet's strategy also had little regard for human life and apparently used the Germans' barbarism as a vital part of their own strategy. In combination, the German and Soviet strategies naturally created an outcome of carnage and death.

---

[56] Ibid., file 41, B7, passage 13B.

[57] For the areas held by Soviet partisans and nationalist partisans, see Armstrong, *Ukrainian Nationalism*. Also see Martin Gilbert, *Atlas of Russian History* (Great Britain: Dorsett Press, 1972), p. 127.

[58] File 41, B7, passage 13.

Rebellion in Segmentary Societies: Montenegro during Wartime

During the Second World War, Montenegro witnessed vacillation between the +2 and −2 positions. This movement differed from that witnessed in the Ukrainian-Belorussian case. In Montenegro, it was not the individual or the community that switched from one position to the other, but rather whole sets of communities connected by clan and tribal relations. Two questions stand out here. How did communities develop universal +2 equilibria? What explains the ability for sets of communities to move between −2 to +2? Some historical background is required to answer these questions.

Montenegro and the northern highland region of Albania functioned as segmentary societies well into the nineteenth century and still retained many of the features of such a society at the beginning of the Second World War.[59] Perhaps best described by Evans-Pritchard in his study of the Nuer, segmentary societies have political structures that order basic social units.[60] Individual households combine into clans (unilineal descent groups with one surname and generally found in the same village), which in turn combine into tribes that ultimately form an intertribal government. Concerning rebellion, the most important aspect of segmentary societies is their rapid system of mobilization and ability to create unity. Two clans within a given tribe may be engaged in a bitter and deadly feud, but an attack upon their common tribe immediately brings them together as allies.

In traditional Montenegro, as in other segmentary societies, the clan was the basic unit of warfare. Consider the description of Montenegrin mobilization that took place in 1853:

> Every village (clan) formed a company, varying in number, according to its population. . . . Such an organization seems to promote emulation and maintain concord, because all the soldiers of a company are for the most part related amongst themselves; whilst the companies and divisions emulate each other by their deeds. The warriors of the village, having formed a circle, propose the candidates for the command; these candidates address their hearers by turns; the seniors having the preference, their com-

59 An earlier draft of this work included a section on wartime Albania.

60 E. E. Evans-Pritchard, *The Nuer: A Description of the Modes of Livelihood and Political Institutions of a Nilotic People* (Oxford: Clarendon Press, 1940). Also Marshall Sahlins, "The Segmentary Lineage: An Instrument of Predatory Expansion," *American Anthropologist* 63 (1961): 322–345.

rades relating their exploits, enumerating the battles where they fought and exhibiting the wounds they consider the most deserving, they swear to obey him and to lay down their heads where his should fall.[61]

In response to outside threats, the clan went as a whole to the +2 position on the spectrum and fought as one coherent unit. This was true for feuds, when the clan fought as a unit against another clan, and for warfare, when the clan joined other clans of the same tribe to confront a larger threat. All able-bodied men participated and all pledged total devotion to a leader chosen largely in terms of his heroic status.

With the onset of the modern state, the characteristics of the segmentary society slowly eroded.[62] In 1878, the Congress of Berlin recognized Montenegro as an independent state. Under Prince Nikola, the tribal chieftains were reduced to agents of the state in their home territories. A bureaucratic and administrative apparatus replaced the functions of tribal councils.

This process of state building and modernization had some effects at the clan level also, but the essential structures of clan self-defense and organization remained the same even at the beginning of World War II, especially in the highland areas.[63] The organization of self-defense of the clans of the Vasojevic tribes during the beginning of the Italian occupation and concurrent Communist-Nationalist civil war is a good illustration.[64] After the Communist murder of only one member of the Orivic clan, that clan and its closest neighbors set the traditional mobilization methods into motion. As

---

[61] Count W. S. Krasinski, *Montenegro and the Slavonians of Turkey* (London: Chapman and Hall, 1853), quoted in Christopher Boehm, *Montenegrin Social Organization and Values: A Political Ethnography of a Refuge Area Tribal Adaptation* (New York: AMS Press, 1983).

[62] Ivo Banac, *The National Question in Yugoslavia: Origins, History, Politics* (Ithaca: Cornell University Press, 1984), pp. 275–276.

[63] An autobiographical account of social conditions in Montenegro in the 1920s can be read in Milovan Djilas, *Land without Justice* (New York: Harcourt, Brace, Jovanovich, 1958). His descriptions of the norms of revenge and honor that permeated Montenegrin society are particularly striking. He writes: "The word 'blood' meant something different in the language I learned in childhood from what it means today, especially the blood of one's clan and tribe. It meant the life we lived, a life that flowed together from generations of forbears who still lived in the tales handed down. Their blood coursed in all the members of the clan, and in us, too. Now someone had spilled that eternal blood, and it had to be avenged if we wish to escape the curse of all those in whom the blood once flowed, if we wish to keep from drowning in shame before the other clans. Such a yearning has no limits in space, no end in time" (p. 106).

[64] The Vasojevic clan lived in Nahija in a region of mixed populations: Serbs of the Hasani tribes, Montenegrins, and Moslem Albanians. The distinction between Serbs and Montenegrins is somewhat artificial and always very slippery. The Vasojevic are actually Serbs who expanded into the region during the sixteenth and eighteenth centuries. They were instrumental in efforts to unify the Montenegrin and Serbian states.

described in a memoir of one of the participants, "We decided that the men of each village should be organized in a military manner. The traditional military organization would be utilized. For example, it was accepted that the Boricic, Dujovici and Mujovici belonged to the third company; Milosevici, Vesovici and Djudici to the first company . . . and so forth.[65] The more distant clans in the Lijeva Rijeka region of the Vasojevic tribe were recruited with the help of a proclamation that stated the purposes of the organization:

1. To protect against all the honor, life and property of any inhabitant of Lijeva Rijeka.
2. If there is any evidence that anyone does anything contrary to the honor, dignity, and the traditions of the people of Lijeva Rijeka and our tribe, Vasojevic, he will be tried exclusively by an appointed popular court but not by any irresponsible group of men.
3. In this organization are included all capable able-bodied men of Lijeva Rijeka from 18–70 years old.
4. This organization has no party organization. . . .
7. Each member of this battalion has to be sworn to the people that he should sacrifice his life for their honor and their good, and that he should tenfold avenge any fallen inhabitant of Lijeva Rijeka.
8. At the head of the battalion is the headquarters of the battalion, that is, the commander and his adjutant.[66]

This proclamation was read before other assembled clans. In theory, every member of the clan could discuss and vote whether the clan should join in the mutual-defense organization. In practice, the vote was often immediate and always unanimous. Formally, the process involved equal individuals voluntarily swearing an oath of honor; in actuality, the overwhelming force of clan and tribe social norms predetermined the matter. In the end, the death of one member of the Orivic clan precipitated the birth of a resistance battalion of 469 locally based fighters, the same number as in the Lijeva Rijeka battalion that was raised in 1912 to fight for liberation from the Turks.[67] The whole process took only five days.

The theory and the template of mechanisms suggests that two mechanisms are crucial in developing +2 organization: reciprocity norms and community-based thresholds. The reciprocity norms among members of these Mon-

[65] Milija M. Lasic-Vasojevic, *Enemies on All Sides: The Fall of Yugoslavia* (Washington, D.C.: North American International, 1976), p. 45.
[66] Ibid., pp. 45–46.   [67] Ibid., p. 49.

tenegrin communities need little commentary. Thresholds were passed in one shot. Here were communities ideally suited for locally based armed rebellion; here was a society able to rapidly mobilize a large number of villages to fight against occupation.

Although the first question regarding rapid movement to +2 has been answered, the second question regarding shifts between +2 and −2 nodes still needs to be addressed. On this issue, the centralized nature of supravillage relations comes into play. Both the intertribal leadership and the individual clan heads had the ability to bargain with outside forces or to cease fighting. Thus, they could effectively remove significant numbers of fighters from any rebellion in an instant, or move them into collaboration. As a counterexample, recall the Lithuanian village of Svainikai. In that community no single individual wielded that much influence. Certain individuals occupying centralized nodes within that structure may have served as catalysts in distributing information and recruiting members in different subsets, but it was not clear that their personal defection would cause other already organized community members to also defect. A diversity of subsets within a community may act as a brake upon rapid disintegration: one subset may defect, but the unit as a whole may remain viable.

In Montenegro during World War II, tribal heads made deals with the occupier. The southern tribes, never having been strongly enthused with the inclusion of Montenegro into the Yugoslavian state, collaborated in the beginning with the Italians. When it became clear that the Italians intended to make Montenegro a puppet state, these tribes did go into action; however, by that time the Communist partisans had made significant inroads. Defections of clans were also common. Djilas describes this problem during the Austrian occupation of World War I:

> We Montenegrins did not hold a grudge against the enemy alone, but against one another as well. Indeed, our enemy – the Austrians and their minions – were called to intervene and to help in these quarrels. Two notable clans entered into a blood feud. No one really knew what it was all about. While one side did their shooting as guerrillas, the other side joined the Austrians. The Austrian shadow hovered over all these crimes. But the root was in ourselves, in Montenegro.[68]

[68] Djilas, *Land without Justice*, p. 77.

By World War II the situation had not changed that much. The memoirs mentioned earlier speak of early clan defections to the Communists and rapid disintegration of the aforementioned self-defense system when the chances for victory dimmed. At one point, the memoirist writes of clans that "wait to see which side will be the stronger, and then take sides." His claim that this phenomenon is new, is hardly likely.[69] Segmentary societies are efficient at raising warriors quickly, but they are focused at the local level. In a drawn-out conflict against an unbeatable foe, the incentives for a local leader to save his own clan from severe punishment and to save his own local power by cutting a deal are simply too strong. The clan's survival will be placed above tribal unity (this was especially true in the decaying segmentary societies of the Balkans in the 1930s).

Conclusions

The worth of any social-science methodology might be best seen in its ability to bring fresh insight to perplexing social variation. This chapter has shown the suppleness of the present approach, especially the use of mechanisms and the spectrum of roles, in explaining variation in resistance and rebellion. This chapter has analyzed four types of puzzling variation: the differences among the Baltic states in the postwar period, the differences between western Ukrainian regions in the immediate postwar period, the vacillating movement in central-eastern Ukraine and Belorussia during World War II, and the rapid mobilization and supravillage shifts in wartime Montenegro. This variation could not be easily explained by national culture (witness the differences among Ukrainians in the postwar period) nor could it always be explained by the policies of the occupier (witness the differences among the northern Baltic states and Lithuania in the postwar period). Here, the explanatory goal has been the identification of fine-grained causal forces and the linkage of these mechanisms to larger observable forces (the number of conducively structured communities, status hierarchies).

---

[69] One of the major findings of Boehm's study of nineteenth-century Montenegro is that the Montenegrins survived against the Turks for so many centuries not only because they were fierce warriors, but "because they knew how to evaluate political problems, and because they knew exactly when to submit to the Ottomans without permanently losing their local autonomy." From *Montenegrin Social Organization and Values,* preface, p. 3.

8. Resistance in the Perestroika Period

This chapter continues both the substantive and theoretical agendas of the book. Substantively, sections of this chapter and the next complete the history of Lithuanian anti-Soviet resistance (the events in Vilnius, Lithuania, in January 1991 are the subject matter of the following chapter). Theoretically, this chapter continues the process of applying the template of resistance mechanisms across new and expanded contexts. Here, the same template of mechanisms used previously is employed to investigate resistance in the perestroika period. Does this approach yield insights in a more modern time? Let us consider first what is to be explained.

Open anti-Soviet resistance resurfaced in the late perestroika period. It was not a violent rebellion involving community-based cells but rather took the form of mass rallies. This resistance was nonviolent, and loosely organized; individual participation meant moving from 0 to +1 on the spectrum. The essence of this participation was the same as in the 1940s: individuals accepting risk in resistance action against an opponent holding superior force.[1] This chapter covers only a small part of the Eastern European "uprisings" of the late 1980s; the selection of cases rotates on the existence of clear risk in terms of personal safety and possible threats to jobs and careers.[2]

---

[1] Participation in these rallies did indeed involve calculations of significant risk. In retrospect, it seems that Gorbachev "let Eastern Europe go," but when protests began in Czechoslovakia and East Germany in October 1989, neither the dissidents nor regimes expected that they would produce fundamental political change in a few short weeks and the repressive powers of the government still were a foremost consideration. As in the People's Republic of China, these governments had the abilities to attack demonstrators physically and to punish them afterward by denying jobs, promotions, and other goods, and they were in command of these abilities as late as the summer of 1989. As discussed later, Honecker ordered a crackdown in East Germany on October 9, 1989, only to be stopped at the last moment by his security chief. The option of imposing martial law, witnessed in 1981 in Poland, was also available.

[2] Much of this chapter grows out of an article I cowrote with Rasma Karklins, "Decision Calculus of Protestors and Regimes: Eastern Europe 1989," *Journal of Politics* 55 (1993):

These conditions obtained in the USSR in 1987–1988 when the limits of glasnost were still untested and were present in Czechoslovakia, the German Democratic Republic, and Rumania in the fall of 1989. They were absent in Poland and Hungary during the same time. This chapter compares Czechoslovakia in November 1989, the GDR in October of 1989, and Lithuania between August 1987 and October 1988.

Despite the fact that massive rallies occurred in all these cases, there was a great deal of variation in the way that the process unfolded. First, there were differences in the timing and speed of the general protest process among different countries. This fact is captured in the famous slogan, "Poland ten years, Hungary ten months, East Germany ten weeks, and Czechoslovakia ten days." Second, populational subsets – students, workers, party members – moved from 0 to +1 at different junctures.

The antiregime rallies of the perestroika period were nonviolent and largely unorganized. On the spectrum, the puzzle involves movement from the 0 to +1 positions. Four mechanisms were identified as crucial for this movement: resentment formation, focal points, community-based status rewards, and societally based thresholds. Although the causal logic of these mechanisms is general, broader structural changes affect their operation in various ways.

The Effects of Modernization and Communist Rule

Since the 1940s, decades of modernization and Communist rule transformed Eastern European society. Perhaps the biggest change involved the weakening of community. This theme has been discussed by countless scholars including Weber, Simmel, and Durkheim. Writing more than 100 years ago, Ferdinand Toennies added new terms to our lexicon with his discussion of the continuous weakening of *Gemeinschaft* ties, those of the village, guild, and family, and the development of *Gesellschaft* relations, characterized as associational and impersonal.[3] More recently, Robert Nisbet has summed up:

> In earlier times, and even today in diminishing localities, there was an intimate relation between the local, kinship, and religious groups within

---

588–614. The sections on Czechoslovakia, East Germany, and deassurance borrow heavily from this article. I am indebted to Karklins for many of the points in these sections. The work on Lithuania is mine alone.

[3] See Ferdinand Toennies, *Gemeinschaft und Gesellschaft* (Leipzig: Fue's Verlag, 1887).

which individuals consciously lived and the major economic, charitable, and protective functions which are indispensable to human existence. . . . For the overwhelming majority of people, until quite recently the structure of economic and political life rested upon, and even presupposed, the existence of the small social and local groups within which the cravings for psychological security and identification could be satisfied.[4]

As the state and the economic large-scale corporation replace the functions of smaller communities, so the argument goes, those communities decline in salience.

This broad debate about community and modernity is important, but it goes beyond the scope of this chapter. Here, as noted in Chapter 1, community is defined according to Taylor's criteria: direct relations between members, many-sided relations, reciprocity, rough equality of material conditions, common sets of beliefs and values. In these terms, the number and variety of communities in Eastern Europe declined in the period from the 1940s to the 1980s. Beyond the general contours of modernization and the growth of the state, the type of modernization and state growth occurring under Soviet-style communism diminished the strength of community.

Consider Lithuania as an example. As seen in the detailed 1940–1941 case study, Lithuania was a nation of strong communities. Villages maintained cooperative work ties and dense social ties; in some cases, families had resided on the same land for several hundred years. Various Catholic communities maintained ties over time and distance. Taylor's definitional characteristics – many-sided, direct, reciprocal, and iterated relationships – pervaded these communities. In contrast, fifty years of Soviet rule had destroyed these communities by the late 1980s. Collectivization and deportations obliterated the pre–World War II rural societies.[5] To a great extent, new social relationships were no longer the result of iterated voluntary agreements made between independent individuals. Rather, the state structured new social relationships that were less likely to be direct and many-sided, and arguably less able to generate the reciprocity norms oi previous voluntary arrangements. Naturally, the Soviets banned social organizations such as the

---

[4] Robert Nisbet, *Community and Power* (London: Oxford University Press, 1962), p. 53. The first half of Nisbet's book aptly frames some of these larger community issues. Relevantly, this work includes an entire chapter entitled "History as the Decline of Community."

[5] The process of rural change in Lithuania is documented in Augustine Idzelis, *Rural Change in Soviet Lithuania 1945–1980: Problems and Trends* (Chicago: Lithuanian Research and Studies Center, 1990).

Union of Sauliai and worked to diminish the influence of the Catholic Church. The number of face-to-face functional relationships in nonwork organizations declined in rural Lithuanian society.[6] The Soviets also speeded the process of urbanization, entailing destructive effects on community. Most high-rise apartment dwellers in Vilnius, for instance, cannot name many of their neighbors, let alone draw a detailed map as shown earlier.[7] Formally, tenant organizations were created, but they never gained legitimacy and were not voluntary.[8] As in rural society, social and religious organizations that formed the cement of many communities were banned or went into decline in cities as well. The situation was not much different for much of the Eastern bloc, with Poland as a possible exception. The special situation in the GDR is discussed subsequently.

While strong communities disappeared or declined, Soviet-style modernization created new social forces, two of particular relevance to mass rallies. While community-level groups disappeared, modern Communist society created new divisions in the form of broader corporate groups. Four such broader groups might be identified in "mass" society: dissidents, students, workers, and party supporters.[9] Similar entities can be found in the regime: low-level officials, security forces, and party elite. Despite efforts by the regime to control information, however, urbanization and modernization brought new capabilities for diffusion of information.

Mechanisms

These changes – the weakening of community, the corresponding development of corporate groups, new possibilities for communication – affected the way that the four 0 to +1 mechanisms operated as well as the likelihood

---

[6] For a general study of the process of Sovietization in the Baltic States, see Benedict Vytenis Maciuka, "The Baltic States under Soviet Russia: A Case Study in Sovietization" (Ph.D. dissertation, University of Chicago, 1963).

[7] I base this statement upon conversations with residents in Vilnius during January 1991.

[8] As an illustration of the lack of community in Soviet cities, a student who had served in the Peace Corps in Latvia once told me that the roofs of Latvian apartment buildings are covered with antennae. His explanation is that residents do not trust or know one another well enough to get together to solve the collective-action problem of installing one common antenna capable of servicing the entire building.

[9] Other observers have used these groupings in their analysis of Eastern European society. For example, William Echikson, in *Lighting the Night: Revolution in Eastern Europe* (New York: William Morrow, 1990), divides his section on "people" into chapters on intellectuals, students, workers, and the nomenklatura.

of their being triggered. The similarities and differences in comparison to the earlier periods can be discussed in turn.

In previous chapters, resentment formation was linked to the perception of an unjust ethnic-national hierarchy. In 1980s Eastern Europe, hierarchies were perhaps as much political as ethnic. Ultimately, Soviets-Russians were in control, but they ruled through local administrators and the party personnel of the majority nationality. The largest minorities of the prewar period, Jews and Germans, had been murdered or deported and borders had been shifted, leaving homogeneous populations. The Soviets were the invisible masters at the top of the hierarchy, but the perceived hierarchy also included a local party elite followed by the rest of the population. The sense of unjust hierarchy, and hierarchy dominated by ethnically different outsiders, still endured, however. During demonstrations in Lithuania in the late 1980s, for example, people chanted "occupier" at Soviet military parades; the rightfully sovereign people were not rulers in their own house. In turn, resentment formation remained as a relevant motivational mechanism with the same effect: the acceptance of risk and the reduction of thresholds.

Although their role differed from the 1940s cases, focal-point mechanisms continued to act as crucial devices for translating resentment into action. In the 1940s cases, the size of the cultural symbol set was used to explain the rapid and nearly universal movement from 0 to +1 against the Soviets. Prayers, songs, histories, and stories were all important parts of the opening stages of resistance. In contrast, the slow or nonexistent movement versus the German occupation was tied to the relatively small size and general nature of the anti-German symbol set.

The Communist regimes of the 1980s did not threaten death and deportation in the same way as Nazis and earlier Soviet regimes. Due to comparatively lower risk and better informational channels, the need to communicate in symbolic "code" was no longer as necessary. Still, focal-point mechanisms played a crucial role in the 1980s. Unlike the earlier period, demonstrations became possible. In this situation, people needed to know where and when to assemble and focal points provided this information. The surprisingly limited role of dissident leadership in organizing the rallies intensified this need. Long-standing dissidents took on a leadership role only in the last phase of protest when someone was needed to negotiate with the authorities. Instead of being elite-led, or even elite-facilitated, the rallies had a life and an organization of their own during the phase of highest risk. As shown in Figure 2.2, symbolic mechanisms are envisioned as working through two filters: the first is historical-cultural; the second is manipulated by elites for their own purposes. A major point connected with this illustration suggested that movement to +1 may be possible under a highly repressive regime and *without the leadership of elites* if the symbol set is rich enough. The peculiarly Communist heritage and tradition, filled with commemorations, provided a rich set of focal mechanisms that enabled mass resistance events even without leadership of elites. Ironically, people were conditioned for anti-Communist mass events from the orchestrated parades and assemblies so prevalent in Communist rule. In turn, these rallies provided clear knowledge of the numbers underlying the threshold-based assurance games described later.

Whereas resentment formation and focal points played important roles in the 1980s, community-based status rewards did not. Eastern Europe of the late 1980s was not composed of strong communities. Consequently, status seeking did not play a huge role in pushing individuals from the 0 to +1 position. Societies with less face-to-face contact generally do not dole out harsh sanctions for being a "coward." Why should one neighbor incur the costs of sanctioning another when they hardly ever see each other or interact? Likewise, the value of being a "hero" in the eyes of a virtual stranger is less than in the eyes of intimate and long-standing family and communal associations. Although hero status remains important for potential leaders operating on a larger political arena, within weak communities, status cannot be so easily translated into local influence as in the strong communities of the past. Eastern Europeans did not condemn one another for failing to take risks against the regime. In fact, in the early stages when risk was highest, those pushing for resistance might have been seen as rabble-rousers or dreamers who would only bring suffering to others. The status gain or loss was not at all clear.

The absence of strong community and status rewards heightens the puzzle of the the 1980s anti-Communist resistance. Figure 2.4 compares strong and weak community societies in the movement from 0 to +1. The decision to engage in +1 resistance involves risk but risk that can be mitigated through "safety in numbers" and counterbalanced by incentives created through status. Society A in Figure 2.5 shows a weak community society with a tipping point of around 50 percent, whereas society B in Figure 2.5 represents a strong community society in which status-based and normative mechanisms operate to lower tipping points to around 15 percent. Here is the real puzzle: Eastern Europe witnessed rapid and massive movement toward the +1 position in the absence of strong community mechanisms. In the early stages of the demonstrations, movement surpassed a relatively high tipping point, the situation characterized by Society A.

In summary, in the Soviet-dominated 1980s Eastern Europe, community-based status mechanisms were absent but resentment-forming mechanisms and focal-point mechanisms were present.[10] At this point, the basic questions remain unanswered. How did these societies move to +1 so rapidly? What accounts for variation in the process? The presence of these mechanisms does not solve the puzzle of such rapid "snowballing" resistance. Nor do these mechanisms, which were present to roughly the same degree in all the cases considered in this chapter, help explain differences in timing and participation of social groups. In order to understand these differences, it is necessary to comprehend the operation of threshold mechanisms in 1980s Eastern Europe.

Thresholds

"I will act if X percent of the others act." This is the logic of thresholds, with the value of X representing the "tipping point," the point at which the individual has received enough assurance or pressure to commit to an action. A most fundamental question concerns "X percent of whom?" – that is, the question of the reference group. The second major issue concerns the mechanisms that operate to raise or lower thresholds. A final issue deals with the way in which thresholds can be structured to produce cascading effects.

In the previous analysis of strong community societies, thresholds were tied to subsets of the community. In the weak community context of Eastern Europe in the late 1980s, these community subsets either no longer existed or had lost their relevance. By no means does this fact mean that individuals ceased searching for signals of assurance in terms of "safety in numbers." The clues would just have to come from a different source, one relevant to the nature of risk inherent in the type of resistance action under considera-

---

[10] One should be cautioned, however, about the depth of open resentment in 1989. For instance, most analysts of Czechoslovakia have written that the failure of the 1968 Prague Spring and the consumerist policies that followed produced a profound political apathy and acceptance of the status quo. Many Lithuanians, especially younger ones with little accurate knowledge of history, were rather apathetic and resigned to a Soviet future. In the early stages of the demonstration process described here, the level of antioccupier fervor could in no way be compared with that seen in the post-Klaipeda days of 1939–1940 or that of the first Soviet occupation in general.

tion. In the late 1980s, resistance involved participation in protest rallies set within a series of protest rallies. For this series of rallies, I argue, there were two distinct threats to the individual and three relevant thresholds for dealing with these threats.

First, and most straightforward, all individuals who attend a rally must deal with the threat of physical beating or arrest at the demonstration site. Obviously, the chances of being beaten or identified in a crowd of 100,000 are less than in a crowd of 1,000. Here, risks are reduced by the overall size of the crowd. The relevant threshold is the percentage of the overall population attending the protest.

Second, individuals must fear sanctions in the local environment – for instance, at the university or workplace. Again, these risks could be significantly reduced through "safety in numbers." For example, a worker employed at a certain factory might skip work to join a demonstration of 10,000 students. He might be protected by the size of the crowd from suffering a beating, but if he is the only worker from that plant participating, then the management of the factory can single him out for job sanctions. The situation would be different if a significant number of workers at the same plant participated in the protest, because the same type of sanctions against this larger group would damage the operation of the entire factory. The same logic holds true for university students and others. Therefore, a second threshold can be linked to percentage participation within broader, associational social groups such as workers and students.

Third, when resistance occurs in the form of a series of public protests, the possibility of prediction exists. Individuals think strategically and base decisions not simply on the percentage of protesters at one point in time but also on what percentages might hold at future times. A given demonstration is rarely seen as a single self-contained event but rather as part of a series of events with updated information. Each potential protester wishes to know the chances of achieving protection at the protest site as well as in the group environment. Furthermore, all potential protesters will wish to know the probability of regime collapse. They prefer to participate in activity that might possibly bring about meaningful change and are looking for clues and assurances that other social groups may join the protests to further weaken the regime.

The question is *how* protesters make predictions. Here, the nature of modern Eastern European society, in terms of its corporate groups, helps provide answers. As is outlined in the model in the next section, the percentages of participation within one social group can serve as a referent in decision making for members of other groups. For example, risk-averse workers may use less-risk-averse students as a referent: if students as a group protest without suppression by regime forces, the probabilities that workers will escape repression can be upwardly reevaluated. When certain groups achieve protection, individuals within other groups recalculate probabilities.

In sum, three thresholds, linked to three observable percentages, become relevant to the potential protestor: the percentage within the overall population linked to physical safety at the rally site, the percentage within one's broad social group linked to safety of job or career, and the percentage in a referent group used for prediction purposes. These three thresholds form the basis for the model presented here.

Protest as a Combination of Multiple-Assurance Games: A Model

In Eastern Europe in the late 1980s, resentment worked to lower thresholds. Focal-point mechanisms helped thresholds become public knowledge, but, in conditions of weak community and high risk, the thresholds remained high. Yet, in each case, a series of rallies added new segments of the population to the resistance until the regime collapsed. If thresholds were in fact so high, how were they surpassed with such rapidity and seeming ease? Also, what accounts for variation in order of social group participation?

The game theoretic device most appropriate to analyze protest in Eastern Europe is again the n-person assurance game, or tipping game, that was used in describing the movement from 0 to +1 on the spectrum in Chapter 2. However, in a society of weak communities where corporate groupings become the source of the most relevant signals, some revisions of the game must be made. First, the simple form of the assurance game, with only one threshold, provides little basis to discuss the needs for prediction sought by potential protesters acting within a series of protests. The revised game must take into account all three of the thresholds described earlier: (1) the overall threshold for protection against beating and arrest at the demonstration site, (2) the percentage within the social group for protection against career and job threats, and (3) and the percentage within a reference group that might serve to predict the turnout at future rallies. Second, the revised model must take into account the interactive effects among these three thresholds.

In order to understand possible variation in this process, an "intuitive" tipping order can be laid out as a base line. This order is closely linked to the overall tipping game illustrated on the right side of Figure 8.1. Taking into consideration risk aversion and susceptibility to regime threat, dissidents would be expected to hold the lowest thresholds and be the first actors in any tipping process. Dissenters have usually already been sanctioned with prison, loss of job, or at least the loss of upward mobility. For this small segment of society, regime threats do not hold the same deterrent power as they might have with the rest of the population. Correspondingly, this group can be assigned a low overall threshold. Because "students" usually have more to lose – they may jeopardize their future careers by participating – their thresholds are somewhat higher. "Worker" thresholds are higher yet because they can be fired from their jobs and they are more likely to have a family than other groups. "Party supporters," many of them officials, bureaucrats, or professionals, do not begin demonstrating until they believe that they have to deal with a new order. This belief justifies the assignment of a relatively higher threshold than workers. Of course, a great deal of variation exists within each group but each group can be thought of as having a "mean" value with a range of deviation in the statistical sense. (Only the subgroups composing the "mass" are considered in this section; the actions of regime subgroups will be addressed later in the chapter.)

Given this order, the next step is specifying the interrelationships between protection and prediction within the process. Figure 8.1 illustrates both the overall tipping game and the intragroup tipping points and serves for reference.

As the dissenter group has no group preceding it in the tipping order, it tends to make predictions based upon other criteria. In the Czechoslovakian and East German cases, protests in neighboring states formed a referent.[11] The dissidents were the group most clearly attuned to the significance of the accelerating success of the reforms in Poland and Hungary and the creeping repudiation of the Brezhnev Doctrine. In this sense, exogenous influences set off the endogenous process. If dissidents reach an internal tipping point and are able to continue protesting without brutal regime repression, their action sends a signal to students. The most courageous, or least risk-averse, students will begin protests that possibly pass the internal student tipping point. Meanwhile, the participation of both groups is raising the overall tip-

---

[11] In Lithuania, the events in Poland were closely watched.

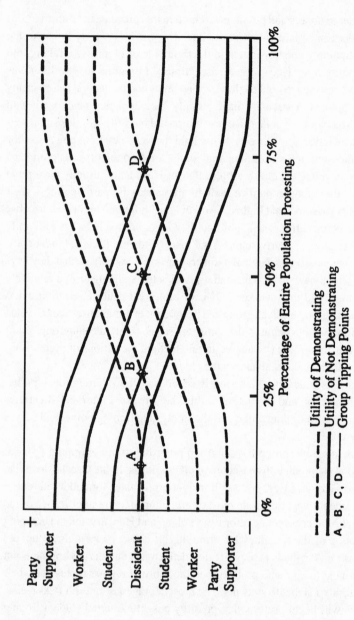

Figure 8.1. Hypothetical tipping points for various social groups

ping point to significant figures. In turn, once students have passed their group tipping point, workers can be pretty certain that students will continue to attend protests in at least the same numbers. The regime's failure to deter or stop the students produces the perception that it will do likewise in the case of workers. Individual workers and factory units will be acting upon their recalculation of regime strength and probabilities of regime collapse. Their action will push percentage cooperation in the overall assurance game closer to the relevant tipping point, eventually surpassing it. This process is especially critical for the next group in the tipping order, the party supporters. After the workers, the supposed backbone of the Communist Party, have reached their tipping point and are protesting without fear of repression, the party supporters must recalculate relevant probabilities. Thus, the protest process can take on a life of its own by linking the achievement of protection by one group with the recalculations of other groups.

Although this model adequately describes at least the Czechoslovakian case, its major contribution is its service as a heuristic device for analyzing the development of a chain reaction of protest. It shows that heterogeneity of actors is the key in the solution of the assurance game and in the depiction of the "snowballing" process. Heterogeneity within each group must be taken into account as well. Individual propensities to protest vary due to differences in age, education, sex, family responsibilities, and personal psychological makeup. Some individuals within each group need more assurance than their fellows: some might act when all three strategic clues are satisfied, others after one is satisfied. Thus, bolder students may be joining at the same time as more timid members of the dissenter group and younger workers may be joining at the same time as the more constrained students.

Consider the following example of how a cascading effect can result from the original action of a very small percentage of the population. Assume there are four social groups in a society: a group of dissenters and idealists contains 5 percent of the population, a group of students and young people contains 10 percent, workers contain 55 percent, and a group of party members and regime supporters contains 30 percent.

Each group looks to three strategic cues on whether to support a protest movement: an overall tipping point, a group tipping point, and a reference group tipping point. Assume the following overall tipping points: dissenters 1 percent, students 7 percent, workers 30 percent, and party supporters 60 percent. Furthermore, assume that each group has a 50 percent internal tipping point.

Now each individual will key in on his or her respective overall tipping point, internal tipping point, and reference group tipping point. Without having sufficient knowledge to weight these three factors, we assume they are of equal value in the individual's decision calculus. Within groups, however, individual circumstances vary considerably due to differences in age, family responsibilities, and personal psychological makeup. Thus, some individuals need more assurance from the set of strategic cues than others. To represent this fact, assume that one-third of each group demonstrates with the assurance of one of the strategic cues, one-third needs two positive assurances, and one-third needs all three strategic signals in order to trigger an action. For convenience, let us call these three groups bold, average, and timid.[12] Thus, we actually have nine different groups, each with different thresholds.

Only one further assumption is needed. We must account for an original spark to set the process in motion, so assume that outside events act as a cue for the dissenter group.

This series of events follows:

1. Outside events act as a reference cue that sets off the bold one-third of the dissenter group. Total protesting = 1.7 percent.
2. The preceding figure sets off overall tipping point of dissenter group with the two strategic cues precipitating action by the average dissenters. Total protesting = 3.4 percent.
3. Internal tipping point of dissenters is reached, thus setting off the timid dissenters acting upon the satisfaction of all three strategic cues; also, the bold student group is set off by the fact that the students' reference group, the dissenters, has reached its tipping point. Total protesting = 8.3 percent.
4. Student overall tipping point is reached, triggering participation of average students. Total protesting = 11.6 percent.
5. Requirements of timid students are met as well as those of bold workers. Here is the real breakthrough in the protest movement. Total protesting = 33.2 percent.
6. Average workers set off by overall tipping point and reference group tipping point. Total protesting = 51.5 percent.

---

[12] The bold might also be called idealistic or noncalculating, and the timid might also be called bandwagoners or opportunists. There are various reasons why a member of each group might act on different conditions of the cues being met; the important point here is to capture the fact of individuals within groups having different thresholds for joining a protest.

7. Timid workers and courageous party-oriented members join. Total protesting = 79.8 percent.

This abstract version of a protest process roughly corresponds to the dynamics of the Czechoslovakian case.

Czechoslovakia, Fall 1989

Between January and October 1989, an increasing number of dissidents engaged in some form of protest.[13] In January, hundreds of dissenters participated in week-long demonstrations to mark the twenty-year anniversary of Jan Palach's self-immolation in protest of the forcible suppression of the Prague Spring.[14] In response, the police beat and arrested several activists (and bystanders as well). Vaclav Havel received a nine-month sentence. At first, this repression appeared to have accomplished its prophylactic purposes. Neither dissidents nor other groups responded with further protest. (Indeed, Havel himself was later to urge potential protesters against open demonstrations in August.) However, within the dissenter community, the regime repression failed entirely to stop antiregime actions: Havel's show trial and the accompanying media campaign gave all dissenters an issue to rally around. New independent dissenter groups formed at increasing rates, and 40,000 people signed a petition protesting against persecution of dissidents.[15]

Developments in neighboring Communist states also contributed to the activization of the dissidents and must be cited as a key reason for the failure of previously effective forms of repression.[16] The renewed legalization of Solidarity and its meteoric rise to power in the summer of 1989, as well as the emphasis on reform in Hungary, the Soviet Union, and (by October) East Germany, could not have helped but bolster the beliefs of Czechoslovakian dissidents that continued activity could bring lasting change.[17]

[13] For a brief overview of leading dissidents, see Gale Stokes, *The Walls Came Tumbling Down: The Collapse of Communism in Eastern Europe* (New York: Oxford University Press, 1993), pp. 149–153.

[14] For a more detailed description of these events, see Bernard Wheaton and Zdenek Kavan, *The Velvet Revolution: Czechoslovakia, 1988–1991* (Boulder, Colo.: Westview Press, 1992), pp. 26–29. This book provides perhaps the most extensive information on this case.

[15] Ibid., p. 28.

[16] As the focus of this work is on the decisions of individual protesters, I am passing over critical developments and ideology of the Soviet Union. Concerning the influence of the Soviet Union, see Jacques Levesque, *The Enigma of 1989: The USSR and the Liberation of Eastern Europe* (Berkeley: University of California Press, 1997).

[17] Wheaton and Kavan, *The Velvet Revolution*, pp. 31–36.

October 28 marked a new stage of protest in Prague. For the first time, thousands of students joined committed dissidents in an unauthorized rally commemorating the seventy-first anniversary of Czechoslovak independence. This demonstration made clear that prophylactic repression had failed to stop open protest in spite of the intensive efforts by the regime. Before the demonstration, the official press published numerous warnings and many dissenters were arrested under false pretenses, detained, or ordered out of Prague. Clearly, some people were scared off, but between 10,000 and 20,000 others joined in the biggest demonstrations since 1969. Once the demonstration was under way, the police arrested 355 and used some force,[18] yet this open form of repression was limited in relation to the next stage.

When students planned a demonstration for November 17 to mark the fiftieth anniversary of the killing of a student demonstrator by German occupation forces in 1939, the Czechoslovak regime first tried to co-opt the demonstration by authorizing it. When roughly 50,000 students turned the event into a prodemocracy rally, however, police riot troops engaged in unprecedented violence. In the words of Timothy Garton Ash:

> They were met by riot police, with white helmets, shield and truncheons, and by special anti-terrorist squads, in red berets. Large groups were cut off and surrounded, both along Narodni and in the square. They went on chanting "freedom" and singing the Czech version of "We Shall Overcome." Those in the front line tried to hand flowers to the police. They placed lighted candles on the ground and raised their arms, chanting, "We have bare hands." But the police, and especially the red-berets, beat men, women and children with their truncheons.[19]

---

[18] "Milos Jakes, the Communist Party leader, ordered out heavily armed police officers, who bashed dozens of heads with their truncheons, to put down the October 28 demonstration." This is the description by R. W. Apple, *New York Times,* November 13, 1989, quoted in Bernard Gwertzman and Michael T. Kaufman, *The Collapse of Communism* (New York: New York Times Press, 1990), pp. 200–201. Furthermore, Wheaton and Kavan, *The Velvet Revolution,* state that ninety-seven civilians connected to the state security apparatus were at work discovering the identities of students in order to impose sanctions. This fact indicates both that risks were significant and that many demonstrators were not the usual dissenters but students who needed to be identified.

[19] Timothy Garton Ash, *The Magic Lantern: The Revolution of '89 Witnessed in Warsaw, Budapest, and Prague* (New York: Vintage Books, 1993), p. 80. Also see Tony Judt, "Metamorphosis: The Democratic Revolution in Czechoslovakia," in Ivo Banac, ed., *Eastern Europe in Revolution* (Ithaca: Cornell University Press, 1992), pp. 98–99. Wheaton and Kavan give a nearly identical rendition: "Brutal treatment was meted out indiscriminately; as depositions later showed, the police did not hesitate to attack the elderly, professional people, and even parents with children. Indeed, the youngest casualty was thirteen and the oldest eighty-three" (*The Velvet Revolution,* p. 46).

The entire process then entered a new plane. The brutality at this event became the focus for the demonstrations that immediately followed and the general strike called for November 27.

At this point the fear of massive physical repression as well as career sanctions played as prominent a role as ever and the outcome remained in doubt. Wheaton and Kavan sum up the students' decision calculus:

> The state of student opinion was by and large still unknown, even though the demonstration was the talk of student and artistic circles. For many, the nagging worry induced by the knowledge that the state was able to apply sanctions at almost any time in their school or professional careers was, in conditions of relative isolation, wound up into outright fear by the thought that next time they could be shot at.[20]

These fears were overcome by the signaling and snowballing processes involved in a series of mass demonstrations from November 18 to 20. On November 18, the day after the crackdown, 2,000 individuals returned to the scene of the violence to lay flowers in commemoration.[21] On November 19, an estimated 20,000 individuals, mostly students, demonstrated against the regime action. On the morning of November 20, even the Communist youth organization at the university, the Socialist Union of Youth, was cooperating with student resistance.[22] Later the same day, the rally in the Wenceslas Square totaled 200,000, and for the first time it appeared that some workers and nonstudent and nondissident groups became active (there are only 136,000 students in Prague). The levels reached half a million by November 25.

These numbers and conditions match the story theoretically outlined in the preceding section. The first 2,000 on November 18 (perhaps dissidents or student activists) signalled to the rest of the students that the regime effort at deterrence was not going to be entirely effective. The 20,000 of November 19 (mostly students) signaled to the rest of the students and the pop-

---

20 Wheaton and Kavan, *The Velvet Revolution*, p. 51.

21 The numbers for participation for November 18–21 are gleaned from Radio Free Europe Research Reports, especially the weekly *Background Reports* and *Weekly Record of Events* 1989 and the weekly *Report on Eastern Europe* 1990. Other sources agree on the general cascading nature of participation but provide somewhat conflicting specifics. For example, Wheaton and Kavan, *The Velvet Revolution*, talk of student participation on the morning of November 18 as a "section of youth," do not mention November 19, and give a figure of 150,000 for November 20. The *New York Times* gives a figure of 200,000 for November 20 that is based on the official radio figure. The precision of all these estimates is questionable, but the general cascading phenomenon is not.

22 Wheaton and Kavan, *The Velvet Revolution*, pp. 59–60.

ulation at large that the regime had no will to continue the violence and that the Soviets would not be intervening. The 200,000 of November 20 showed that the tipping point had been reached within the student group and that some workers were beginning to become active for the first time in twenty years. The possibility of a societal tipping point being reached, one that would force a change of the regime, became a real possibility, thus activating even hesitant members of the population.

At this point, however, it still was far from clear that the regime was going to collapse in the near future. The party was not yet falling apart internally; the students and dissidents were unified, but their action did not necessarily mean that the regime was in its death throes. The crucial issue from November 20 until November 27, the day of the general strike, concerned the decisions of the workers. Attention by all groups focused on this critical reference group, which had always been given preferential treatment by the Communist regime.[23] In the words of Jiru Masek, a student at the University of Prague and a strike organizer, "We won't win if the workers are not on our side. To the leaders of our country, we students are nothing. But workers are the power here. To persuade them is critical to our cause."[24] In order to win support, "missionary" students went to the factories with their appeal for support.

The workers also saw themselves as the critical group. As one worker at the CKD semiconductor factory bluntly stated, "If the factories close down, the government will fall." The outcome was in doubt, and deliberations occurred at most factories. As another worker pointed out about discussions at her plant, "This was not spontaneous support. We talked about what would happen if the strike didn't work, what kind of repression there might be. But we decided we can't support a government that beats its students. Next time it will be us, and then who will strike?"[25]

---

[23] All commentators agree on the pivotal nature of worker support and the uncertainty that surrounded the workers' response. Judt writes that "It is worth noting that until November 27, students and intellectuals were nervous (and in some cases pessimistic) as to the degree of support they would get from the industrial working class. What chance did a revolution led by actors, writers, and students focused upon Prague (and to some extent Bratislava and Brno) have in a country where 60 percent of the working population were still blue collar working class and where the latter had been carefully cosseted and sustained in reasonable living conditions by the party, the better to isolate intellectual and political oppostion? In short, the intellectuals had tended to believe the regime's own propaganda." ("Metamorphosis," p. 101). Also, see Echikson, *Lighting the Night,* pp. 112–113; Wheaton and Kavan, *The Velvet Revolution,* p. 61; and J. F. Brown, *Surge to Freedom: The End of Communist Rule in Eastern Europe* (Durham: Duke University Press, 1991), p. 173, for nearly identical statements.

[24] Gwertzman and Kaufman, *The Collapse of Communism,* p. 240.   [25] Ibid., p. 242.

In terms of a counterattack, the regime began to offer minor concessions to pacify the protesters and defuse the demonstration process before it could become consolidated at an unmanageable point. Older, hard-line ministers were replaced, and promises to punish and rein in the security forces were given. Instead of exhibiting strength and the possibilities of compromise, though, regime concessions were seen as a sign of the weakness and fragility of the regime – a sign that continued pressure would bring the regime down. The general strike of November 27 demonstrated the failure of the regime strategy: millions of people participated; at least 900 factories and businesses were closed, with only hospitals, nursing homes, and a few other enterprises continuing to function. In different ways, roughly 75 percent of the population participated in the protest.[26]

Indeed, workers had clearly followed students. The party, having to face up to this fact, employed desperate strategies in the form of major concessions. By this time, however, many party members realized that the probabilities of the regime remaining in power, especially without support of workers, were not very good. The party itself began to unravel and disintegrate. The end of the regime became inevitable, and even hard-liners and true believers were forced to evaluate their future under a new order.

"De-Assurrance" among Regime Groups

The preceding dynamic provides an explanation of how tens of thousands of individuals decide to demonstrate despite possible sanctions. Surely, though, a large part of the story of the Czechoslovakian collapse has been left out. Repressive regimes do not fall simply because citizen protests illustrate the regime's lack of legitimacy, but also because regime subgroups became "de-assured" through many of the same signals that were providing assurance for the "mass." Some of the first defections came from officials in the media and the judicial system.[27] They were followed by some lower-level security organs. The police, reevaluating their position after the growth of protest numbers and the opening of information channels, began fearing the "mass" more than the regime. The events of November 17 made the police a focus of protest, one whose indiscretions could be publicized daily by a new Civic Forum newssheet. Soon after the rallies reached massive propor-

---

26 Wheaton and Kavan, *The Velvet Revolution*, p. 95.

27 After some of the early protests, 380 journalists met to discuss open dialogue in the press and 142 Prague judges signed a petition asking for a dialogue on reform. See ibid., p. 62.

tions, militia units connected to factories began to vote themselves out of existence. Wheaton and Kavan summed up their decision calculus and the increasingly desperate position of the party elite:

> The younger members, though given certain minor career and financial advantages, evidently decided it was not worth becoming involved in the party's struggle for power as a previous generation of militiamen had done in the late 1940s, though under very different historical circumstances.
>
> The failure to mobilize the People's Militia shifted the attention of the Central Committee to the army as a possible means of preserving the party's power.[28]

By this point, not even the army could be trusted to carry out the party elite's orders. The military option was apparently narrowly defeated in the Central Committee, and Jakes, with no remaining options, soon resigned.

Explaining Variation: Some Theory and Another Example

As with the "mass," the process within the "regime" appears to follow the intuition that those with the highest stake in the regime are the last to defect. In the Czechoslovakian case just seen, the party regime seemed to unravel from the bottom up, but this was not always the case in the rest of the region. Sometimes the party elite preceded sections of the "mass." In order to provide such an explanantion, the actual process of change and connection between the "mass" and the "regime" needs better explication. This section contains some speculation about the signals and assurance games that affect regime calculations and includes an analysis of Lithuania, a case in which some party elites "defected" early.

As Mancur Olson has recently pointed out, authoritarian regimes and dictatorships are inherently fragile as they rest upon the perceptions of their guards, officials, and administrators.[29] If these perceptions suddenly change, the officials will cease to carry out their orders: "If the cadre observe a moment of vacillation, an incident of impotence, a division of leadership, or even a collapse of analogous regimes, all the power of an imposing regime can vanish into the night air." Crucially, perceptions of regime officials may be changing most dramatically during the demonstration process itself. Al-

---

[28] Ibid., p. 71.

[29] Mancur Olson, "The Logic of Collective Action in Soviet-Type Societies," *Journal of Soviet Nationalities* 1 (1990): 8–27.

though there are few available data, the same dynamic behind the actions of individuals who compose the "mass" can be applied to the decision process for the individuals who compose the regime: both have needs for protection and prediction that are related to various assurance games played out versus the society as a whole, within one's own social group, and within referent groups.

As with the "mass," it is important to recognize the heterogeneity of the regime. At least four groups make up the repressive apparatus of the regime: civil regime officials (including managers and the media), regular police and the army, security police, and the regime elite. Their choice of actions is not so clearly binary as with the mass, but it is possible to speak about options of "repress" versus "don't repress" for each of these groups. For the media, the choice may be rephrased as "censor" or "don't censor," for soldiers, perhaps "shoot" or "don't shoot." Individuals within these groups operate under different sets of constraints and will consider defecting from their support of the regime at different junctures of the protest process. The timing of defection may be related to signals emanating from various assurance games.

The logic of the internal group assurance game is similar to the one for protesters. Journalists and officials wishing to defect will feel protected from possible sanctions if a significant percentage of their own group is about to defect or has already done so. A majority of journalists or factory managers cannot be fired without resultant high costs. If an individual soldier plays "don't shoot" while the vast majority of fellow soldiers play "shoot," the regime will survive and the individual will face court-martial or even more severe sanctions.

The case of soldiers emphasizes the need for prediction by the individuals serving the regime. Soldiers must try to predict the solution to their internal game. At the same time, security police are doing likewise, although their position is different from that of the regular army and the police. They might not be able to avoid sanctions under a new regime even by playing "don't shoot." Regime administrators too are trying to predict whether the regime will survive. Once doubts are established, they have little motivation to support regime repression, especially harsh repression, because the latter might close the door to governmental employment in the future. The more visible elements of the regime – journalists, for instance – will be striving to predict the chances for regime change at the earliest possible moment because future job prospects will be brightest for those who appear as leaders rather than those who are simply joining the "bandwagon."

The basis for these predictions or changes in perception probably lie in the same cues for action used by the demonstrators. When the society as a whole has reached the tipping point and is demonstrating day after day without individual fear of physical sanctions, regime officials upgrade the probabilities of regime collapse. When the social groups that have joined the protest process include not only students but workers, soldiers recalculate the chances of other soldiers firing on the crowd. In turn, the regime elite needs to recalculate its ability to rely on the soldiers under these new conditions.

Thus, there are two processes occurring simultaneously. On the one hand, social groups of the mass are becoming assured of protection versus sanction and upgrading the possibilities of regime change. Simultaneously, groups within the regime are using signals from the "mass" to become "de-assured" of the regime's ability to survive. Within the mass, the distribution of thresholds, and thus the "tipping order," was hypothesized as dissidents, students, workers, and party members. In the regime, a corresponding order might have officials "tip" first, followed by army and police, security police, and finally the regime elite itself.

These "tipping orders" may follow commonsense logic, but they certainly do not describe all cases. There are not enough data at this time to effectively consider all the factors that might produce variation in the tipping order, but there does seem to be one major characteristic that can help explain a considerable part of it: *the abilities of the regime elite in self-rehabilitation.* Like the dissidents, the regime elite is most sensitive to international events. A combination of international events and some initial movement toward tipping points in domestic society may cause the regime elite to believe the best strategy is to lead, rather than follow, the demonstrations. If the elite chooses this strategy, then the order in the "mass" will also be different. Party supporters will be attuned most closely to the words and actions of the regime elite and may tip before workers and students. The Lithuanian case presented in the next section illustrates this pattern.

Clearly, not all elites can perform self-rehabilitation. Certainly, Czechoslovakian leader Jakes could not have done so. Jakes had supported the invasion of August 1968, led the hunt for reformers in the period thereafter (helping to expel 450,000 party members), and was rumored to be closely connected to the KGB.[30] A regime elite that is tied to security police may

[30] See Brown, *Surge to Freedom*, p. 165.

prove unredeemable. The more regime elites are tied to security forces before the beginning of mass resistance, the more the intraelite assurance games in the military and security forces will determine their fate. Honecker, Ceausescu, and the Soviet leadership after the 1991 coup attempt are good examples and are discussed briefly in this chapter's conclusions. In contrast, regime elites who are unconnected to the security apparatus and can make a plausible argument that their participation in the regime was a matter of necessity are better able to accomplish self-rehabilitation. In Lithuania, for example, many local leaders could claim that they had always had Lithuania's interests at heart even while serving in the regime, that they had compromised only because it was absolutely necessary. The Czechoslovakian hard-line leadership could not plausibly make such claims and was bound to hold out until the end of the tipping order. The outline of Lithuania clarifies these differences.

Lithuania: August 1987–August 1988

On August 23, 1987, a few hundred demonstrators gathered in Vingis Park in Vilnius to publicize and condemn the Molotov-Ribbentrop Nonaggression Pact that had been signed on that day forty-eight years earlier. Undoubtedly, thousands more sympathized but were too fearful to come close. Some drove by the tiny rally to see what was going on, but they spent more time trying to spot KGB agents writing down license plate numbers than actually observing the rally.[31] Attendance at such an event was expected to bring immediate sanctions at the job or university. Exactly one year later at another demonstration marking the same focal event, an estimated 200,000 Lithuanians filled the same park. The Communist Party would soon be out of power. While the result was similar to the one in Czechoslovakia, the process was not.

As in Czechoslovakia, Lithuania witnessed a series of rallies with different social groups participating at different times. As in Czechoslovakia, dissidents were the first to begin protesting. Lithuania's dissident community included some radical elements. Due to the length of the rebellion in the late 1940s, many partisans had been arrested and deported to Siberia, lost relatives somewhere along the way, and never had a chance to start a career. Some of these former prisoners, having little to lose, found themselves in the

---

[31] Personal conversation with an eyewitness.

clandestine Lithuanian Freedom League (Lietuvos Laisves Lyga), which had perhaps been operating since the late 1970s.[32] A second set of dissidents were connected to the samizdat *Chronicle of the Catholic Church in Lithuania,* maybe the longest running and most prolific underground paper of the Soviet era. A less radical set of potential early protesters originated in early environmental demonstrations. Found across all the Baltic states, these environmental groups at least had some experience in organizing politically acceptable rallies against nuclear power or phosphate mining.[33]

Lithuanian dissidents were undoubtedly taking encouragement from events in Moscow as well as Latvia and Estonia, Baltic neighbors who at this point were moving more quickly toward reform. In November 1987, the Lithuanian Artists' Union disposed of its entire leadership. On February 16, 1988, sizable unofficial demonstrations commemorating the 1918 date of Lithuanian independence showed that the dissidents had reached an internal tipping point and were demonstrating without fear. Smaller dissident groups were organizing during this period. The rallies of May 22, called by the Lithuanian Freedom League, provided further evidence of the decline of effectiveness of government threats. Knowing that these dissidents could not be stopped from bringing their numbers out in the street, the regime sponsored a demonstration itself for the same day in order to overshadow the league.

At this point, some members of the Lithuanian regime took a different course than the one chosen in 1989 Czechoslovakia. They chose to join with non-Communist intellectuals. On June 3, members of the Lithuanian intelligentsia, including some key younger members of the regime, formed "The Lithuanian Movement for Perestroika," better known as Sajudis. Of the thirty-six founders of the Initiative Group, seventeen were members of the Communist Party.[34] Some of the group were KGB informers; none had been present at the August 1987 rally.[35] Clearly, some members of the party were

---

[32]   The Lithuanian Freedom League became public on July 3, 1988. For a more general discussion of Lithuanian dissent, see Kestutis Girnius, "Lithuanian Dissent: Proud Past, Uncertain Future," *Radio Free Europe Research,* October 5, 1988. Also see V. Stanley Vardys, "Lithuanian National Politics," *Problems of Communism* 38 (1989): 58.

[33]   Environmental protests occurred in Riga in November 1986 and in Tallinn in the spring of 1987. Lithuanian protests focused on the Ignalina plant in eastern Lithuania. As most nuclear power plants required labor emigration from the Russian Republic, the motivations for protesting carried ethnic-political overtones. See John Hiden and Patrick Salmon, *The Baltic Nations and Europe: Estonia, Latvia, and Lithuania in the Twentieth Century* (London: Longman, 1994), p. 149, for a commentary on how early protests may have affected regime calculations.

[34]   Anatol Lieven, *The Baltic Revolution: Estonia, Latvia, and Lithuania and the Path to Independence* (New Haven: Yale University Press, 1993), p. 226.

[35]   Ibid., pp. 224–225.

anxious to take control (or had been directed to take control) of the direction of the perestroika reforms in Lithuania, especially in light of the upcoming Nineteenth Party Congress, an expected watershed for reform. Demonstrations and public meetings were at the core of Sajudis's political strategy.[36] These events were needed not only to show the viability of Sajudis in relation to the established local Lithuanian powers, but to prevent the radical Freedom League from gaining too much influence and creating what Sajudis members saw as counterproductive provocations. At this point, Moscow was Sajudis's ally, not the rabble-rousing and unrealistic league.

A June 14 rally called by the Freedom League attracted 6,000 people. Sajudis responded with its own rallies on June 21 and June 24, the latter being a send-off for delegates to the Nineteenth Party Congress in Moscow, which drew an estimated 20,000 people.[37] The rally was "politically correct" in asking for a return to "true" Soviet rule based on Leninist principles of sovereignty. Crucially, a Central Committee secretary, Algirdas Brazauskas, spoke in favor of Sajudis initiatives at this gathering. He announced that the cabinet of ministers would ask Moscow to stop construction of the controversial nuclear power plant at Ignalina. Vilnius party leader Kestutis Zaleckas also spoke on June 24. Even though the Lithuanian Communist Party still refused to recognize or bargain with Sajudis, important leaders of the party began to defect, or at least hedge their bets.

These signals did not go unnoticed. Upon their return from Moscow, the delegates of the Nineteenth Party Congress were met by another Sajudis-sponsored rally, this time with 100,000 attendees. Pollsters and sociologists surveyed the crowd. Although this was not an antiregime rally, their findings were still somewhat startling. Over 70 percent of the respondents to their questionnaire were "specialists and administrators." These positions usually require some party background. Only 10 percent were workers and 13 percent students.[38] The social composition of these rallies was radically different from that seen in 1989 in Czechoslovakia. It seems that the party supporters in the mass were most ready to pick up on the signals produced by the early defections of key party leaders.

[36] For more details on the day-to-day operations of Sajudis, see Kestutis Girnius, "Three Months of Change in Lithuania," *Radio Free Europe Research,* August 31, 1988, pp. 1–5.

[37] V. Stanley Vardys puts the number at 50,000 in "Sajudis: National Revolution in Lithuania," in Arneds Trapans, ed., *Toward Independence: The Baltic Popular Movements* (Boulder, Colo.: Westview Press), p. 13.

[38] "Lithuanian's Views on Independence," Service for State Delegation for Interstate Negotiations with U.S.S.R., Supreme Council of the Republic of Lithuania, Vilnius, November 1990.

The nature of the rally meant that risk would no longer be a factor in this type of protest (until the stakes became higher again in 1990–1991). The Lithuanian Republic's security forces were not going to consider violence against this type of crowd. Furthermore, Communist leaders who could rehabilitate themselves now had every incentive to do so. First and foremost among such leaders was Algirdas Brazauskas. Brazauskas had a reputation as a potential innovator, had a grasp on economic problems and realities, and was rumored to have been the last member of his school class to have joined the Komsomol.[39] He was undoubtedly aware of his own reputation and the political possibilities it might hold, especially the possibilities produced by placing himself between the party and Sajudis, a strategy of "hedging bets." There is a small window for self-rehabilitation during such a reform process: the act cannot come so early that the regime is still able to eliminate party dissenters, but it cannot come so late that one is accused of simply "bandwagoning." Brazauskas found this moment at the July 9 rally greeting the return of the party delegation. This time he made concessions to nationalists that he was not legally entitled to make: the party and government would be legalizing the display of the traditional tricolor flag and seeking legislation making Lithuanian the official state language of the Lithuanian Republic.

He had rehabilitated himself. Not only was he not held accountable for the past "sins" of the Lithuanian Communist Party, but he would soon become the most popular leader in all of the country. Less than a year after the aforementioned speeches, and even after serious confrontations with Sajudis in November 1988, Brazauskas received an 84 percent favorable rating, significantly higher than Landsbergis and overwhelmingly higher than the party's 22 percent rating.[40] Brazauskas was only able to accomplish this feat because he was unconnected to police actions and other highly distasteful functions of the regime. His counterparts Songaila and Mitkin, the two top party secretaries, could not separate themselves so easily from past policies. Because these two individuals were so thoroughly disliked, they could be

[39] Alfred E. Senn, "Toward Lithuanian Independence: Algirdas Brazauskas and the CPL," *Problems of Communism* 39 (1990): 21. Also, see Hedrick Smith, *The New Russians* (New York: Random House, 1991), chap. 16, "Lithuania: Breaking the Taboo of Secession," for an extended comparison of Brazauskas and Landsbergis. Also see Lieven, *The Baltic Revolution*, pp. 232–233, for another direct comparison of the two leaders.

[40] Kestutis Girnius, "The Party and Popular Movements," in Arveds Trapans, ed., *Toward Independence: The Baltic Popular Movements* (Boulder, Colo.: Westview Press, 1991), p. 62. Figures are taken from the Lithuanian newspaper *Komjaunimo Tiesa*, June 16, 1989. For more on Brazauskas, see Saulius Girnius, "A New Party Secretary: Algirdas Brazauskas," *Radio Free Europe Research*, October 28, 1988, pp. 19–22.

successfully blamed for almost everything. Many party officials would soon come to follow Brazauskas's lead.

Sensing that the party was losing ground to Sajudis, Alexander Yakovlev came from Moscow on August 11–14 to try to salvage the party. Apparently believing that the local Communist Party could remain a viable entity if it adopted a more popular program, Yakovlev pushed Lithuanian Communists toward a truce with Sajudis. Second secretary Mitkin responded by telling the heads of local party units to cease harassing individuals sympathetic to Sajudis. Furthermore, leaders of Sajudis could announce their events on television.

In effect, there was now no credible sanction against participating in the next demonstration. The size of the crowds extinguished fear of even the slightest possibility of physical beating, while the new party policies removed the "stick" in the localized environment. The August 23 rally to condemn the Molotov-Ribbentrop Pact resulted, with 150,000 to 250,000 in attendance from all walks of life, including students and workers. The tipping point for the society as a whole had been reached on this day, as Senn describes:

> After the meeting in Vingis Park, the public behavior of the Lithuanians changed radically. No one had been sure what would happen that evening in August; after the fact, few seemed to remember how nervous they had been before the meeting. The public now spoke more freely of its concerns; it raised new demands.[41]

It was the beginning of the end for the Soviet Lithuanian Communist Party. Sajudis support groups immediately formed in offices and factories across the republic; a Sajudis newspaper spread information across the nation.

The local party made one last-ditch effort on September 28, employing violence against an unauthorized Freedom League demonstration. The action had little serious effect and only served to unite the opposition. The next day, members of Sajudis and the Freedom League stood on the same platform for the first time and called for the resignations of Songaila and Mitkin, the "unsavable" first and second party secretaries. By now the mass party and the regime elite had reached internal tipping points. Various local party units appealed for the removal of Songaila and Mitkin. In a few short weeks, the two top Lithuanian Communists were gone, replaced by Brazauskas. In

[41] Alfred E. Senn, *Lithuania Awakening* (Berkeley: University of California Press, 1990), p. 136.

its traditional form, the Communist Party ceased to be a significant oppositional force. In the first elections, held in March 1989, it would win only four
of forty contested races.[42]

As in Czechoslovakia, the Communist Party's fall followed in part from
a series of demonstrations. "Tipping" occurred more slowly and with a different order of social groups, but similar protection and prediction dynamics were nevertheless present. Communist leaders such as Brazauskas and
Prunskiene could more easily separate themselves from the regime than the
majority of the leadership in Czechoslovakia. Unlike actions in the Eastern
European satellite states, the early actions of some Lithuanian Communist
leaders produced movement within the party's mass and elite membership
groups. While the internal dynamics of the cases varied, the overall result
turned out to be the same: the "mass" reached a tipping point that demonstrated the illegitimacy of the Communist Party and brought its downfall. Of
course, in Lithuania only half the battle was fought. The Lithuanian party
had disintegrated, but the struggle with Moscow loomed ahead, the subject
of the following chapter.

The German Democratic Republic

In terms of cascading numbers, the German Democratic Republic witnessed
a series of rallies much like those in other Eastern European states: 5,000
to 8,000 on September 25, 15,000 to 20,000 on October 2, 70,000 on
October 9, 150,000 on October 16, 200,000 on October 23, and 500,000
on November 6.

These numbers,[43] and the resulting collapse of East Germany, are all the
more remarkable when the ruthless nature of the Honecker regime is taken
into consideration. The repressive capabilities of the East German state far
surpassed those in neighboring Communist regimes (with the exception of

[42] Election results are discussed in Saulius Girnius, "Sajudis Candidates Sweep Elections,"
Radio Free Europe Research, April 21, 1989, pp. 19–22.

[43] Again, in absolute terms, these numbers should be taken with a great deal of caution. In
his analysis of these events, Karl-Dieter Opp estimates that the demonstrations were probably
a great deal larger than published figures. Estimating three persons per square meter in the Karl-
Marx-Platz, not an unlikely estimate given photographs of a very crowded square, the figure
would be 124,500. See Karl-Dieter Opp, "Repression and Revolutionary Action: East Germany
in 1989," *Rationality and Society* 6 (1994): 107–108. Also see the discussion of numbers of protesters in Karl-Dieter Opp, Peter Voss, and Christiane Gern, *Origins of a Spontaneous Revolution: East Germany, 1989* (Ann Arbor: University of Michigan Press, 1995), particularly pp.
20–24.

Rumania). A network of 120,000 full-time agents and 100,000 informants penetrated a society of 16 million, numbers reflecting both the capabilities and will of the regime in controlling opposition.[44] Given the power of the secret police and the general nature of the regime, individual thresholds were high and, correspondingly, the need for signals to produce assurance was intense.

This section will concentrate on the critical period running from September 25, the beginning of a series of large rallies, until October 9, the date when a reported 70,000 East Germans marched in Leipzig in open defiance of regime threats. In the view of most commentators and participants, October 9 was a turning point, a day in which demonstrators lost their fear and put into motion the rapid demise of the East German Communist Party.[45]

So far, this chapter has identified a "bottom-up" tipping phenomenon (as seen in Czechoslovakia) and a "top-down" process (as seen in Lithuania). The movement to +1 resistance in East Germany was neither. Rather, outside events and the odorous nature of the Honecker regime rapidly moved the East German society toward massive +1 level resistance. Although the process looked similar in terms of numbers, there were major differences with other Eastern European nations' experience. The basis for these differences lay in the East German state's many unique features, especially its relationship with the other half of the German nation living next door in the Federal Republic. Still, although many of the elements of the model did not come into play, many did. Most importantly, the fundamental view of the potential protester that underlies this entire book – a strategic actor searching for signals in terms of thresholds – still applies. Specifically, dissidents were aware of their group level of participation, most potential protesters were aware of the overall societal numbers, and members of the regime were "deassured" through percentages of participation.

This section describes the buildup of protest in the GDR with explicit comparisons to the Czechoslovakian and Lithuanian cases. The analysis relies heavily on Dirk Philipsen's *We Were the People: Voices from East Germany's Revolutionary Autumn of 1989*. Philipsen conducted 106 interviews

---

[44] Dirk Philipsen, *We Were the People: Voices of East Germany's Revolutionary Autumn of 1989* (Durham: Duke University Press, 1993), p. 10.

[45] The October 9 demonstration is considered a turning point by Ash, *The Magic Lantern*, p. 67; Opp, "Repression and Revolutionary Action," p. 102; Stokes, *The Walls Came Tumbling Down*, p. 140; and Charles S. Maier, *Dissolution: The Crisis of Communism and the End of East Germany* (Princeton: Princeton University Press, 1997), p. 142, among others.

lasting from forty-five minutes to four hours. Consistent with the methodology of this chapter, he divides his subjects into "the Party," "the workers," and "opposition intellectuals." The interviews he reproduces therefore serve to illustrate the decision calculus of individuals across the social groupings of the preceding model.[46]

Most obviously, few individuals in the East German regime had the range of options available to Brazauskas in Lithuania. That is, most of the political elite of the Honecker regime had little hope of self-rehabilitation. The connection and existence of this leadership to previous Soviet leaderships was evident, and the distance between the regime and its citizens was enormous. Any hope of closing this distance had been lost with the rigged May elections. Picking up on Gorbachev's glasnost and perestroika campaigns, some reform-minded workers, environmentalists, and dissidents believed that the party could be induced to respond to criticism by casting no-votes in the elections of May 7, 1989 and election-observing groups had been formed to monitor the vote. Three quotations from the Philipsen book – one from a pastor, one from a worker, and one from a party member – help set the scene. First, Pastor Klaus Kaden describes the devastating impact of election fraud on the legitimacy of the Communist Party:

> Many things happened after the elections, which revealed beyond a doubt that the party had been cheating – it was clear election fraud. They "improved" the results by up to 20 percent. People knew. We had a lot of "no-votes" in Leipzig. There was a lot of grumbling going on. People had become very aware of what was going on. There was simply no longer any legitimacy for this party, for this parliament, or for this local leadership.[47]

Crucially, the effect of this election fraud was felt not only in dissident and religious circles, but among longtime party supporters as well. One of those hopeful of reform was Maria C., a decades-long active union member. She recalls her disillusionment and the beginning of resistance:

---

[46] Opp et al., *Origins of a Spontaneous Revolution,* provide a more complete account of the East German events based on survey research. Anyone interested in the East German case should consult this volume.

[47] Philipsen, *We Were the People,* p. 154. Also, see Naimark's remarks on the effect of the May 1989 election fraud. Norman Naimark, "'Ich will hier raus': Emigration and the Collapse of the German Democratic Republic," in Ivo Banac, ed., *Eastern Europe in Revolution,* (Ithaca: Cornell University Press, 1992), p. 82.

Marcia C.:   It really started after the elections of May 1989. I remember that the day after the elections I accompanied our enterprise director, our factory union chairman, and the party secretary on a tour through the factory during which they congratulated certain colleagues who had been elected. The official results were not yet known. I just remember that colleague W., or rather then comrade W., asked "do you already know the results?" Both the enterprise director and the party secretary replied, "Well, we've been to about three polling stations, and in each case the outcome was about 10–15 percent no-votes." I was flabbergasted by this response, and so was comrade W. But when we went home the same evening and read the newspapers, the official result was still 98 percent.

Phillipsen: Did any of your colleagues participate in the organized attempt by the opposition to send out election observers to all polling stations?

Marcia C.:   Yes, of course. And later they tried to tell us that the absentee ballots had all been in the party's favor, and this is how the high approval rate could be explained. Of course, we did not believe a word – in fact, we were outraged – and that's when open resistance began.[48]

Doris C., an engineer and party member, developed a similar view of the importance of election fraud in delegitimizing the party. Her comments further show how disparate dissident forces later came together:

And, you know, the election in May was decisive for a lot of people, because we simply said to ourselves that most governments in the world that receive 10–15 percent no-votes would kiss their own feet. After all, what government receives 80–85 percent support? But that they had to even lie about these 10–15 percent – we were really upset about that. So more and more people went to the church, not because they liked the church, but because they were seeking protection in the church. Women my age all the sudden ran to church on every 7th of the month, lighting candles and all, simply because we no longer knew what to do with our bottled up anger. . . . this election fraud just pushed things beyond the breaking point. After that, a lot of people just thought: "It doesn't matter anymore. Let them come, let them accuse me of crimes, let them arrest me, I just can't take it anymore. I will no longer say 'yes' to all this."[49]

48 Philipsen, *We Were the People,* p. 116.   49 Ibid., p. 125.

This quotation reveals the operation of two mechanisms that helped to counteract and lower the high thresholds created by the GDR's repressive apparatus. First, motivation to accept risk was evident: "Let them come. . . . Let them arrest me." Second, focal mechanisms connected with the Lutheran Church benefited the opposition. In its relationship and negotiations with West Germany, the East German regime had left the church considerable freedoms. Even those not sympathetic to the church or religion knew that the churches and their regular Monday prayers could serve to cover antiregime messages.[50] Therefore, communication problems were considerably minimized, at least at the local level.

These original church-based meetings were crucial in organizing rallies as dissidents faced an uphill battle in the GDR. The emigration or compulsory expulsion of antiregime actors to the FRG had served to weaken the size and abilities of the set of dissidents. In effect, the "exit" of some oppositionists had reduced the "voice" of those left behind. The repressive GDR regime apparently used this tool to an extent more than any other Eastern European state.[51]

Clearly, dissidents saw the need to reach an internal tipping point to hinder easy state repression. Harald Wagner, founder of Democratic Awakening, states the logic of uniting the dissident groups that were forming in the summer of 1989:

> You have to realize that opposition activists were oppressed in the most severe kinds of ways. It was not at all farfetched when people began talking about internment camps. We found whole Stasi lists of oppostion activists to be arrested and interned in times of crisis. Even the execution of oppositionists was, according to the documents we later found, seriously considered.

---

[50] Monday prayers had, for example, been held at Nikolai Church in Leipzig since 1982 with only perhaps a dozen people attending. In February 1988 activists were invited to take part in peace prayers and attendance began rising into the hundreds. These Monday prayers became the focal point for the subsequent politically powerful demonstrations. For an extended treatment of the role of the church in East Germany, see Niels Nielsen, *Revolutions in Eastern Europe: The Religious Roots* (Maryknoll, N.Y.: Orbis Books, 1991), chap. 2, "Germany: Springtime in Autumn."

[51] In their analysis of the GDR's political strategy, Manfred Tietzel and Marion Weber reconsider the nature of "exit and voice": "When critics leave the organization, they may weaken the potential for effective voice for those left behind. Thus the act of exit is not a perfectly private good, but may impose negative externalities on others in a similar situation" (p. 62). From "The Economics of the Iron Curtain and Berlin Wall," *Rationality and Society* 6 (1994): 58–78.

So this is precisely why it would have been important to get together all 300 or so people who were seriously committed to such an initiative, and not only the thirty that came together for the founding meeting of New Forum.[52]

Events began to proceed so rapidly, however, that the lack of unity within the dissident group mattered little. During August and September, tens of thousands of East German tourists were fleeing through the newly opened channels in Hungary, or through the West German embassy in Prague.[53] On September 12, New Forum, one of the first nationwide opposition groups, was founded. Sebastian Pflugbeil, a nationally prominent physicist and op-positionist, provides a litany of factors that helped create the widespread opinion that "something had to happen":

There were a lot of catalysts for people to come to this conclusion: we had no reform-minded party politician like Gorbachev in the GDR; there was this whole election fraud in May of 1989; there were the political changes in Hungary that led to the opening of its border with Austria; there was a clear decline in economic performance; there was an obvious inability to act or respond to all these problems within the government. The leader-ship was, among other things, just too old; it was way past the time in which the leadership should have been replaced; then there was the spec-tacle of Politburo member (and later general secretary) Egon Krenz con-gratulating the Chinese for the Tiananmen Square repression; and then, of course, the huge wave of people fleeing the country through Hungary and Czechoslovakia. All these combined factors resulted in people saying "enough is enough." Somehow things started to happen; no one knew ex-actly how. And the population understood that there was a real chance to move things. People understood that very quickly after it began.[54]

Because the social differentiation between workers, students, and officials was not sharp, East German society was not structured to provide clear sig-nals across groups.[55] Whether the reference group signals so evident in the

---

52 Philipsen, *We Were the People*, p. 230.
53 For a review of the context of these events, see Maier, *Dissolution*, pp. 120–131.
54 Philipsen, *We Were the People*, p. 304.
55 See Philipsen's conversation with Ludwig Mellhorn (ibid., p. 89) on this issue. Maier de-scribes the role of university students and professors as "ambiguous" due to the pervasive power of the Communist Party: "Those that could not make their peace with the authorities never en-tered academic institutions" (*Dissolution*, p. 121). In comparison with the Czechoslovakian case, the boundary between the university and the regime was not as clear.

Czechoslovakian case would have played out during the events in the GDR is not clear. The question, however, is moot in the present case because the combination of problems and signals enumerated by Pflugbeil, most originating outside the system, were both very powerful and widely available across different social groups. Once the dissidents and a more random set of other disaffected individuals reached a certain threshold, the rallies would turn into a flood, rather than a cascade.

This does not mean that certain thresholds did not play critical roles in providing assurance leading to the series of rallies. The September 25 demonstration in Leipzig after Monday prayers numbered 8,000, the largest since 1953. Would-be emigrants were perhaps the core of this rally, called to recognize New Forum. The following Monday, the crowd grew to 20,000 and almost certainly involved wider circles. On October 7 and 8, antiregime rallies involving tens of thousands occurred not only in Leipzig but in East Berlin, Dresden, Plauen, Jena, and Potsdam as well. They were met with brutality, setting the stage for October 9.[56]

At this time, the regime declared that it would suppress any demonstration "with all due force." Clearly, the protests of the preceding week provided the assurance that this possibility would be avoided. Philipsen's conversation with Werner Bramke, party member and chairman of the history department at Karl Marx University and first-time protester on October 9, provides insight into the calculations of participation:

> *Philipsen:* Is it correct that the party, the police, and the Stasi tried to convey a very clear message prior to 9 October that anybody who participated in the 9 October demonstration would be considered an enemy of the state and should thus expect the most severe repercussions imaginable?
>
> *Bramke:* This is exactly how I understood it.
>
> *Philipsen:* How do you explain the fact that you yourself and thousands of others dared to go anyway?
>
> *Bramke:* Well, I think that many people did not perceive it that way. The demonstration on 2 October had already been a mass demonstration – there were different estimates, but I think 25,000 is realistic. Since the police had not intervened, there was hope that it could be repeated.

---

[56] Ash describes police action in the following terms: "Young men were dragged along the cobbled streets by their hair. Women and children were thrown into prison. Innocent bystanders were beaten" (*The Magic Lantern*, p. 67).

The movement had also generated a sort of "automatism"; it could not be stopped any longer.[57]

Seventy thousand marched with no violence. These numbers apparently convinced members of the regime that the opposition could no longer be stopped. The police had received orders to shoot but did not consider obeying them. A few even began to speak with demonstrators making sure that their intention to disobey orders was known.[58] Within the top ranks of the party elite, the same conclusion had been reached. Again, the numbers seemed to change the decisions of the elite; it did not receive enlightenment in the space of a few days.[59] Take, for example, two comments by Erich Mielke, the security chief under Honecker. On October 7 and 8, when the demonstrations were relatively small, Mielke is reported to have said, "Give those pigs a sound beating."[60] On October 9, when the demonstrations had grown much larger, Honecker called for violence but was approached by Mielke who said, "Erich, we can't beat up hundreds of thousands of people."[61]

Conclusions

In the late 1980s, Eastern European witnessed unorganized, nonviolent resistance against authoritarian regimes. Significant variation occurred in these 0 to +1 movements. In Czechoslovakia, the movement proceeded from "bottom up," whereas in Lithuania the process appears to have been more closely connected to elite signals. In East Germany, the population seems to have moved over more in "one-shot" fashion. If the set of cases were to be expanded, yet more variation might be witnessed. Surely, Poland and Hungary, not to mention Rumania[62] and Albania, had their own paths to the dissolution of communism.

---

[57] Philipsen, *We Were the People,* pp. 265–266.   [58] Ibid., p. 201.

[59] Maier discusses the thinking of the elite on pp. 150–162; Opp summarizes the "blunt weapons of the Stasi" in Opp et al., *Origins of a Spontaneous Revolution,* chap. 9.

[60] Naimark, "Ich will hier raus," p. 90.

[61] Gwertzman and Kaufman, *Collapse of Communism,* p. 219.

[62] The Rumanian resistance appears too spontaneous, for instance, to fit the model presented here. However, even here the assurance games played between various social groups within and between the regime and the mass can be seen as critical. The immediate context of Ceausescu's downfall was the massacre at Timisoara and the huge public rally held in Bucharest four days later in Bucharest. Within the crowd on December 21, students were the first to begin chanting anti-Ceaucescu slogans. After a moment of shock, the rest of the crowd started to join in. The army then sided against the Securitate, and the end was sealed. The violent and short revolt in Rumania was determined in large part by the fact that in extremely repressive states the costs

In this chapter, the same set of mechanisms used to analyze earlier resistance has been applied to help explain variation in resistance in the perestroika era. Resentment of foreign domination provided widespread motivation for rapid action. As in earlier cases, focal mechanisms coordinated the actions of tens of thousands of individuals. In Czechoslovakia, previous official gatherings made Wenceslas Square the obvious place for antiregime rallies. Anniversaries of both Communist and anti-Communist martyrs supplied coordination of timing. In Lithuania, history provided August 23, the anniversary of the Molotov-Ribbentrop accord, as a focal date for key protests. In the GDR, the Monday prayer services in Leipzig effectively created a focal point for protest.

The analysis, though, has centered on the threshold mechanism. The causal logic of this mechanism remains the same across all time periods. The potential resister thinks, "I will be sufficiently protected and I will act if X percent of others also act." In all cases, the percentage of the overall society serves as a reference point in regards to personal safety. Although the advance of modern Communist society did not fundamentally change the operation of the threshold mechanism, it did produce new wrinkles in the movement from 0 to +1. First, with the decline of strong community, threshold-reducing status rewards were diminished. Second, the corporate nature of society and the division between mass and regime created new possibilities for prediction. In the Czechoslovak case, workers could look to students for signals. In Lithuania, individuals in the mass could look to the actions of regime leaders for clues. In the GDR, on the other hand, the more repressive nature of the regime, led by the pervasive Stasi, molded a more homogeneous society lacking the differentiation necessary for such intergroup signaling.

are so high that there was little room for any party to find safe ground: the regime's men know that they will be heavily punished for past crimes if they lose, and the opposition knows they will suffer extremely harsh penalties should they lose; thus there is little bargaining ground and no opportunity for self-rehabilitation. The result is that neither side has much to lose by fighting as violently as possible (Jon Elster, "When Communism Dissolves," *London Review of Books,* January 25, 1990, pp. 3–6).

In addition, due to the preceding cases of successful protest in Eastern Europe, the demonstration effect was stronger in Rumania. Yet despite these exceptional features, reference groups were used in calculations of how to act and a heterogeneity of actors was seen in the demonstration. Students and youths were the first to act; the mass of citizenry hardly would have burst into violent revolution without their original action. Furthermore, the army and the mass served as clues for each other: the army may not have acted if the mass had not surpassed its tipping point, and it is likely that many protesters would have calculated a different course of action had the army not solved its own assurance game by fighting against the Securitate. In such a concise revolt, and the 1991 events in Moscow might also be included here, the signals between mass and army may be the most decisive.

The model developed in this chapter builds on the core assumptions of the book. The movement from neutrality to passive resistance is explained by a process specifying the interplay among a small set of mechanisms. In terms of specific cases in modern societies, the analysis highlights two important variables: the ability of elites for self-rehabilitation (the Lithuanian case); and the strength of linkage between dissidents, students, and workers (the Czechoslovakian case). Societal movement to passive resistance can be facilitated by signals from elites able to rehabilitate themselves. On the other hand, movement from 0 to +1 can be retarded if numbers of protestors in groups early in the tipping order are insufficient to help trigger action by more risk-averse groups. Indeed, the analysis here helps form the hypothesis that the Chinese series of demonstrations failed to bring down the regime due to a break in the tipping process between students and workers.[63] On the whole, the model here emphasizes the need to examine the heterogeneity of modern society and the operation of threshold mechanisms within and among groups.

Finally, this chapter has continued the story of Lithuanian anti-Soviet resistance. While pursuing the theoretical puzzle of first action, the next chapter completes this story with a description of events in January 1991.

[63] Karklins and Petersen, "Decision Calculus of Protestors and Regimes," pp. 609–611.

9. Fanatics and First Actors

For any given threshold analysis, there must be a set of "first players" who begin the interactive "tipping" process. If the underlying logic of multiple-person assurance games is correct, these first players have an impact totally disproportional to their numbers. For example, in the preceding chapter covering 1989 Eastern Europe, the model represented by Figure 8.1 assumed a very small percentage of "first actors" in a dissident group, and then went on to explain how their action could trigger a strategic interactive process resulting in hundreds of thousands of participants. In cases fitting this model, the entire snowballing process leading to the downfall of regimes may never be catalyzed without these first actors. In many types of mass activities, only a very few individuals are needed to show that "the emperor has no clothes." A small number of hecklers at Ceausescu's last rally revealed that resistance against his tyrannical regime was possible and helped lead to the end of his rule.

In essence, first players hold 0 percent thresholds. They act in the absence of visible signals and actions that help to estimate risk.[1] Their existence poses a fundamental challenge to some of the basic tenets of this work. From its opening sentence, this book has concerned itself primarily with "ordinary people" and how they become involved in resistance and rebellion. While incorporating norms and emotions, the analysis has placed strategic calculation and sensitivity to risk at the center of the explanations. The spectrum concept is based on a logic of risk. Individuals usually begin resistance with low-risk actions such as writing graffiti or abstaining from elections. The movement toward riskier forms of resistance generally occurs after signifi-

---

[1] For analytical reasons, this chapter concentrates (but not exclusively) on "first action" as the clearest example of risk-insensitive behavior. The decisions of players acting in the later stages of interactive resistance processes may also be driven by risk-insensitive factors. These decisions take place within the context of interactions between other groups and regimes, and the nature of risk-insensitive factors is therefore often difficult to isolate.

cant numbers of the population also are engaging in similar low-risk actions. The less-risk-averse players are given a "signal" by the more-risk-averse players that their actions are supported and will continue to be supported by the bulk of the population. This story assumes a distribution of risk thresholds, but also assumes that the players are risk sensitive and use strategic signals to gauge risk. Likewise, the interlocking thresholds described in the preceding chapter posited actors attuned to signals emanating from the process itself. Students, workers, party members, regime actors all used each others' actions as clues for measuring risk.[2]

Given the pervasive consciousness of risk, how do individuals come to hold 0 percent thresholds? Two questions drive the rest of this chapter. First, what mechanisms might produce 0 percent thresholds? Second, if these mechanisms can be identified, can they be used to explain regional or cross-cultural variation in the number of first players? (Can we specify conditions under which nation A or culture X will consistently produce more 0 percent threshold actors than nation B or culture Y?)

While the first issue is rather straightforward, the second is truly thorny. The question of variation involves at least three troublesome dimensions. The question of variation in the number of first actors is never great. In most situations, the vast majority of individuals will remain inactive until certain signals provide assurance of safety. However, in certain situations the difference between 0.2 percent and 2 percent may be decisive in catalyzing movement. Framing these figures another way, the analyst might be explaining the difference between a society with 99.8 percent non–first actors and another with 98 percent non–first actors. Second, unlike other actions, variation in first action cannot be linked to observable changes in others' behavior because there have not yet been any changes in this behavior. Finally, first players appear to perfom risk-insensitive actions only at certain times. Why does the same individual engage in risky protest activity under conditions A but not under conditions B? Under the same set of conditions, why might more individuals of nation X engage in risky protest action than in nation Y?

The chapter addresses these qusetions. First, I provide several examples of first-playing and *fanatical* behavior from an event I personally witnessed

---

[2] The dissidents were "first actors," that is, those with a 0 percent threshold operating without signals of assurance from other actors. In the Eastern European context, statements by Gorbachev and demonstration effects did produce some confidence that risk had been reduced. However, there are other important situations, which I describe in detail shortly, in which first players act without the benefit of exogenous signals.

during fieldwork in Lithuania. I define fanatical behavior as *embracing* risk. First-acting behavior and fanatical action need not overlap; one can certainly have a 0 percent threshold but still dread the incumbent risks. Often, though, the first actors seem to thrive on the risks and thus are fanatics as well. At their core, the two behaviors both involve risk acceptance and can be coherently studied as part of the same family of action.

Second, these examples serve as concrete illustrations for the analysis of the second section, a review of relevant mechanisms. Two criteria are applied in evaluating these mechanisms: their overall plausibility, especially in terms of the Lithuanian examples, and their ability to explain variation in first action in more general terms.

Third, I identify a new mechanism, which I call "the small risk of martyrdom." This mechanism may be especially prevalent in some cultures and might explain first action in a number of cases.

Vilnius, January 1991

In January 1991 I became a participant in the events precipitated by the Soviet assault on communication facilities in Vilnius. There, I observed individuals engaging in resistance activity that involved at least a small chance of death. What seems most remarkable in certain cases of "first action" is that a chance of death may be involved. It would seem relatively uncontroversial to assume that human beings are death-averse. Yet, people do risk their lives in some situations even when they know (or should know) that their own individual contribution is insignificant in affecting the outcome.

I present four examples of behavior gleaned from my personal observations and field notes, all of which involved considerable risk as well as a paucity of strategic signals.

1. Early on the morning of January 13, 1991, I witnessed the Soviet assault on the radio-television building in Vilnius.[3] An anonymous "Lithuanian Salvation Committee" along with Soviet paratroopers, claimed to be taking control of the government. Supporters of Lithuanian independence

---

[3] The Soviet action took place at two locations, the television tower, where all of the deaths occurred, and the radio-television building located a few miles away, where the action was certainly violent but not lethal. Altogether, the casualties totaled fifteen or so dead, a few hundred injured. I was at the radio-television building at the time of the initial assaults. A detailed written account of these events can be found in Alfred E. Senn, "The Crisis in Lithuania, January 1991: A Visitor's Account," *Association of Baltic States Newsletter* 15 (1991): 1–12. Many of the numbers and estimates are gleaned from this source.

had anticipated the attack on communication centers and stood around the buildings. While the tanks and armored personnel carriers performed their work, the crowd chanted out "Lithuania." At the radio-television building, the shock waves from explosions blew out the windows of neighboring apartment buildings, raining glass upon the crowd below. When the main action was over, my Lithuanian friend turned to me and, referring to the Parliament building perhaps a mile or two distant, said, "They will attack the Parliament building next, we must go to the Parliament building." I tried to explain that our individual contributions were insignificant in the whole scheme of things, but this argument fell on deaf ears. At the time, it seemed quite probable that the Soviets would forcibly crush Lithuanian resistance, no doubt killing a few more people along the way. And my friend wanted to be part of this event.

Anatol Lieven provides an extensive account of the January events that concurs with my own notes.[4] He quotes a student waiting at the Parliament at length:

> We all thought that they would come next to the parliament. I was afraid, and so were others, but in general the mood was more angry. That was so even when people came from the TV tower and told us what had happened; some of my friends came, and their faces had quite changed, stony. It took months for some of them to get over it. Landsbergis broadcast over the loudspeakers, asking us to move to the side, so as not to be caught in the crossfire when the parliament was attacked. He said something like, "we need live witnesses, not more victims"; but we didn't move. . . . All sorts of rumours ran through the crowd, and it would surge in one direction or another – that was dangerous, because the square was completely packed. There was a fear of spies. I saw people catch one man – they were screaming that he was a provocateur, and they were going to throw him in the river, but they let him go. . . . A Catholic priest, Grigas, was going through the crowd, leading prayers and talking to people, and I remember admiring him because he was so calm, but also being irritated, feeling that he was using the occasion to make his own religious propaganda.[5]

These impressions matched my own. When we arrived at the square in front of the Parliament, uncertainty, fear, and some silent anger seemed to per-

---

[4] Anatol Lieven, *The Baltic Revolution: Estonia, Latvia, Lithuania and the Path to Independence* (New Haven: Yale University Press, 1993), pp. 244–255.

[5] Ibid., p. 251.

meate the crowd. Everyone knew that casualties had already been suffered; almost everyone believed that more would be killed or wounded at the Parliament. Similar to the experience of the student just quoted, I was told that Soviet agents might infiltrate the crowd to gain access to the Parliament prior to the impending attack. I also recall hearing that the Soviets might land helicopters on the roof.[6] Yet, despite these fears and rumors, the square remained packed.

Three observations relevant to the discussion below should be added. First, I don't think anybody took Landsbergis's suggestion to leave as a serious suggestion; rather, it was part of a "script." Second, the scene was one of enormous confusion without hardly a trace of leadership. In fact, while Lithuanians acted courageously, their leaders, with the notable exception of Landsbergis, panicked. The newly appointed prime minister, Dr. Albertas Simenas, disappeared on the bloody night, turning up in a nursing facility, and the foreign minister, Algirdas Saudargas, remained abroad. A retired Lithuanian émigré colonel from the United States Army found himself in a leadership capacity advising the defense of the Parliament.[7] Third, throughout the confrontation, a Catholic presence, seen in the form of the roving priest mentioned by the student was common.

2. Two nights after the assault on the television and radio facilities, I accompanied my friend into the Parliament building, still considered to be the target of a possible assault.[8] I noticed that a few hundred Lithuanian patriots had barricaded themselves in the first floor, turning the Parliament into a military barracks. Their weapons were primitive: many had only shotguns and hunting rifles; most had gas masks that might prevent them from being smoked out. I knew that they had sworn to defend the Parliament building in a dramatic ceremony that involved President Landsbergis and a priest. Everything seemed to indicate that they would indeed defend the building, as their oath stated, "to the last drop of blood." In addition to the regular Soviet garrison located in Vilnius, a plane full of Soviet paratroopers had arrived a few days earlier. A hundred tanks had rumbled through the city a few nights before the crackdown; surely the Soviets had the capability to crush the Lithuanian volunteers. They had no military purpose; their purpose was to die.

---

[6] In fact, the Lithuanian Guards inside the building unscrewed the support beams to the roof in order to thwart such an attack. Ibid., p. 250.

[7] Ibid.

[8] The reader may wonder about my own motivations for this action. Simply, I would have been ashamed to be studying resistance and rebellion and forgo such opportunities out of fear.

Lieven again provides a relevant quote from an interview with a Lithuanian parliamentary guard: "The intention is not to win, because we all know that is impossible; the intention is to die, but by doing so to make sure that Moscow can't tell any lies as they did in 1940. To make sure the whole world knows that Lithuania was prepared to fight for her freedom."[9] The defender was referring to the fact that Lithuania had become absorbed into the Soviet Union without violence in 1940; he wanted to make sure that the event would remain an aberration in Lithuanian history.[10]

3. On the night preceding the assault, the area around the Parliament building had been turned into a festival. Fearing a Soviet move, residents of smaller towns and villages had come in on buses to stand around the Parliament. They had brought banners proclaiming the name of their hometown and had set up a vigil. In one section of the square, folk dancers held the ground while a hundred yards away a younger group of Lithuanians danced to American and English rock music. As far as I could discern, a mixture of old and young, rural and urban, modern and traditional had either set up vigil or returned to the Parliament when the Soviet troops took over the nearby communication facilities. An hour after the attack several hundred Lithuanians of mixed backgrounds had situated themselves in front of the Parliament.

4. While inside the Parliament building, the lights temporarily went off and one frightened person speculated that perhaps the Soviets had somehow cut the power and an attack was imminent. When the lights came back on, I tried to convince my friend to leave as soon as possible but he insisted that we stay longer. He told me how comfortable he felt in this building, more comfortable than he had in days. He was conscious of a specific feeling that he called the "we" in opposition to the "I." He said that he had always struggled against the "we" that takes hold of Lithuanians while chanting at Mass or cheering in the crowd. But on this occasion he admitted being exhilarated by the feeling of the "we" that he was sensing inside the Parliament building.

The essence of the Vilnius events can be briefly summarized: the overwhelmingly powerful Soviets came in and killed and wounded a small percentage of Lithuanian demonstrators. In response, some Lithuanians, acting as first players, rushed to the next possible site of violence. Some Lithuanians, a very small number, ensconced themselves inside a building that was

[9] Lieven, *The Baltic Revolution,* p. 253.
[10] I heard reference to "not repeating the mistake of 1940" several times during these days.

a possible target of further violence. Furthermore, at least a few individuals appeared to *enjoy* their roles, thereby earning the classification of "fanatic."

Mechanisms

What mechanisms can explain these types of first-action and fanatical behavior? I address rational mechanisms, personality-based mechanisms, and participation-based mechanisms in turn.[11]

Rational Calculation

There are several rational mechanisms that might explain why an individual would choose to be a first player. Political entrepreneurs might wish to advertise their courage, vision, and leadership through such daring.[12] Sensing the impending collapse of the current regime, entrepreneurs may believe that the chances of securing a leadership position in the future can be enhanced

---

[11]   Due to space limitations, I discuss two mechanisms, efficacy and norms, in this footnote rather than in the text. By efficacy, I am referring to the belief that one's individual contribution is meaningful in affecting the outcome. In the context of the 1991 Vilnius demonstrations, such a belief would be clearly irrational. There is evidence for the plausibility of such a mechanism; see Steven Finkel, E. N. Muller, and Karl-Dieter Opp, "Personal Influence, Collective Rationality, and Mass Political Action," *American Political Science Review* 83 (1989): 885–903. This form of irrationality can be treated, I believe, in terms of a personality type with the attendant problems discussed here. Furthermore, it was not my impression that most of the crowd in Vilnius actually believed their action might create a difference in outcome. This is especially true for example 4.

As outlined previously, norms have a strategic context. If other people do not act upon a norm, it loses its force. In the case of first players, explanations relying on norms are plausible only if the actions of others are anticipated; otherwise others' nonaction would free the individual from participation. Another treatment of norms, however, is found in the work of Russell Hardin, *One for All: The Logic of Group Conlict* (Princeton: Princeton University Press, 1995), and Paul Stern, "Why Do Individuals Sacrifice for Their Nations?" *Political Psychology* 16 (1995): 217–236. Both emphasize the abilities of leaders to respond to communal norms. Stern posits that leaders are most effective when they "manipulate those forces so as to socially construct the nation as an object of primordial attachment" (p. 229). If the proper symbols are used, the moral norms of the family can be extended to elicit action on behalf of the nation. Hardin believes leadership appeals to norms are most effective when they overlap with self-interest. In these cases, first players may simply be the ones who are most attuned to the symbols or have the greatest self-interest. Both link the nature of the leaders' appeals to action. Stern's account generates testable hypotheses concerning the nature of leadership rhetoric. Neither, however, seems applicable to cases like 1991 Vilnius in which first action (example 1) took place without leadership in the midst of considerable chaos.

[12]   See Morris Silver, "Political Revolution and Repression: An Economic Approach," *Public Choice* 17 (1974): 63–71, and Gordon Tullock, "The Paradox of Revolution," *Public Choice* 11 (1971): 89–99, for a more extended discussion of these types of incentive.

by enduring risks in the present. In Lithuania, Landsbergis's stock certainly rose while holed up in the Parliament building. The problem is that few potential leaders took advantage of this opportunity. As mentioned previously, some stayed abroad or ended up in nursing homes. Only around 40 percent of parliamentary deputies chose to remain in the building during the crucial period.[13] If risk taking was an optimal strategy for leadership status gains, few took advantage of it. It would seem that such a mechanism would need to be supplemented with reference to personality.

Furthermore, most of the first-playing or fanatical individuals stood to secure few political or career gains through their action. Many were elderly people past the age for any career enhancement; many were youth not yet embarking on careers. This point leads to other possible rational mechanisms that emphasize the cost rather than the benefit side of the equation. As pointed out in the preceding chapter, structural explanations for first action show that individuals in certain social categories, youth or dissidents for example, have less to lose than others and are therefore less risk-averse. Members of other social categories may have something to gain by participation in risk-laden action. In his study of revolution, Jack Goldstone has found that revolutionary behavior is linked to the proportion of youth in the population.[14] Youth are less constrained by family and career and are much more likely to hold lower thresholds for action. The same logic holds for dissidents who may have been stripped of jobs and families. Following the logic of a structural explanation, we would expect to see a skewed distribution in the participation levels of various social groups. The difference in participation in first action between nations might simply be correlated with the differences in the respective sizes of these social groups.

Hypotheses linking rational mechanism to social category are unconvincing, or at least incomplete, for several reasons. First, when the risk of death is involved, even a small one, the question of ignoring risk becomes less amenable to common, structural explanations. There is little evidence that individuals of one social group value their lives less than those of another. If any group of people should be death-averse, it is the group with the most life ahead. By this logic, we would expect to see a preponderance of old people as first players in high-risk situations with students holding back. Structural arguments emphasize varying cost-benefit ratios tied to social groups, but in

[13] Lieven, *The Baltic Revolution,* p. 253.

[14] Jack A. Goldstone, *Revolution and Rebellion in the Early Modern World* (Berkeley: University of California Press, 1991).

relation to events like those in Vilnius, they do not provide a convincing explanation of the benefits of first action that must exist in order to overcome the obvious costs. Second, in a point discussed later, structure-linked explanations do little to explain the form of action that first players take, and the form itself can sometimes be politically crucial.

Most importantly, there are specific instances when the set of first actors is drawn across social groups. From my own perspective, this was the case in Vilnius the night of the killing. Whereas my friend and the volunteers inside the building were young males, the crowd that stood in vigil around the building in the early hours of the morning was of mixed backgrounds (see example 3). In some cases, the actual demographics of first players may match structurally based predictions. For instance, dissidents (and/or students) appear to have been the first players in the demonstrations in some Eastern European states during 1989. But this is not true of all cases. These observations lead back to the crucial issue. If risk-insensitive first players do not always come from the same social groups, then how do we explain variation in the numbers and composition of first players?

Personality-Based Mechanisms

First actors might also be seen as a personality type subject to specific psychological mechanisms. They might be acting according to a sense of duty in the broadly Kantian sense, asking themselves "But what if *no one* showed up at the Parliament?" Or, they may simply be thrill seekers gaining some psychic benefit from participation.[15] Indeed, Muller and Opp have found that participation in antinuclear demonstrations went up when danger of arrest was present.[16] No doubt some of the first players in the Vilnius events were Kantians or thrill seekers. In the absence of the ability to measure the exact motivations of first actors (indeed, they can't precisely describe their motivation themselves), these types of explanations might seem as plausible as any. However, there is again a major problem concerning variation. It is difficult to explain why one society would have more of a particular type of personality than another or why within the same society different events might produce varying levels of first action.

[15] Tullock, "The Paradox of Revolution"; Silver, "Political Revolution and Repression"; and Edward Banfield, *The Unheavenly City Revisited* (Boston: Little, Brown, 1970).

[16] Edward Muller and Karl-Dieter Opp, "Rational Choice and Rebellious Collective Action," *American Political Science Review* 80 (1986): 472–487.

This problem is highlighted in Kristen Monroe's study of "John Donne's People," a survey of twenty-eight altruists, thirteen of whom were involved in efforts to rescue Jews in Europe during the Second World War.[17] Monroe failed to find any sociocultural predictor for the actions of altruists. Instead, rescuers were motivated by a common perception of being strongly connected to others by a shared humanity. The action was triggered by an emotion or belief of organic connection. Quite relevant here, she failed to find any structural or national factor that could explain why individuals helped save Jews or engaged in other types of altruistic behavior. Although she was dealing with a non-risk-averse, nonstrategic personality type, she provides us with no way to link this personality type to any explanation connected to an observable independent variable.

Monroe provides two useful insights for the present discussion. First, the study highlights the paucity of the risk-insensitive, nonstrategic personality type. For instance, the names of all the known rescuers of Jews in Europe can be written on a few walls as a memorial. Sadly for humanity, the numbers of "John Donne's people" are numerically small. The percentage of first actors in Vilnius, while small, seems far greater than the number that could be explained by the presence of altruistic personality types.

Second, Monroe's study brings us, ironically, to another type of "personality" that needs to be considered: the nationalist fanatic. Monroe found a set of actors driven by the idea of being part of a collective group of human beings. For her respondents, that collective group was all of humanity. For much of the twentieth-century world, however, the limit of that collective group is usually not all of humanity but the nation. One of the rescuers in Monroe's study explained his actions by stating that "We (all human beings) are as much together as the cells in our body are together." Parallels with the organic, nation-centered imagery of fascist thought come to mind. This brings up the question of whether a deeply felt nationalism (of being "one" with the rest of the nation) can be the trigger of first action. As with Monroe's rescuers, a deeply held feeling of communal unity may override strategic considerations and the calculation of risk.

This type of explanation is often used in reference to Lithuanians. One often hears that Lithuanians are a very nationalistic people, perhaps with a strong fascist strain in their culture and history. Therefore, it is not surprising that such

---

[17] Kristen Monroe, "John Donne's People: Explaining Differences between Rational Actors and Altruists through Cognitive Frameworks," *Journal of Politics* 53 (1991): 395–433.

nationalistic culture would breed a higher number of first players. At first glance, this line of reasoning seems amenable to standard methods of political science. In terms of cost-benefit analysis, participation in nationalist activity surely provides a benefit for the nationalist, one strong enough to outweigh considerable risk. Proxy variables could be created in order to deal with national variation. An index of government propaganda effort or national suffering could be formed to assign country "means" in the force and effects of nationalism. First action could be explained in terms of a normal distribution around an overall mean: those lying two standard deviations from the overall mean being the fanatics that make up the first-actor group. Nations with higher means would, of course, produce higher numbers of first players, whereas nations with means lower than the overall mean would produce fewer first actors.

This argument has some merit. Nationalism is obviously an important force and was certainly present in Vilnius on the night of January 13. Also, understanding participation as a benefit is helpful in understanding first action. The solution to the collective-action problem in this case, and perhaps others, may lie in the psychic benefit of participation. Of course, this is not a new theory. As Russell Hardin has written, "It is the desire to be there, to take part in history, to have oneself develop through participation in significant, even world-shaping historical events and movements."[18] When nationalism and participation are treated in such a general way, however, they can no longer account for specific actions. Crucially, the argument does little to explain first action because first action is simply one form of nationalist action. For example, a deeply nationalistic individual (two standard deviations from the mean) might just as easily hold to the logic "those who run away, live to fight another day" as to the logic or nonlogic of first action. The fanatic might just as easily go home and build bombs in his or her garage than be the first one to show up at a rally. In some nationalistic countries, people might think it is stupid and a waste of resources to stand in front of buildings or try to defend them with outmatched and pathetic weapons. Some of the supporters of Petain and French accommodation with the Germans in World War II were no doubt very nationalistic and patriotic Frenchmen who believed that this route was the best for their country under those particular circumstances (of course, some were scoundrels).

A comparison of the Baltic nations supports this point. In the beginning

---

[18] Russell Hardin, *Collective Action* (Baltimore: Johns Hopkins University Press, 1982), p. 109.

stages of perestroika, the Estonians and Latvians, despite generally being considered less nationalistic than the Lithuanians, were the most active of the region's peoples in pushing for republic autonomy. Only later did the Lithuanians begin taking the most radical actions. Does this mean that the Estonians and Latvians were somehow less nationalistic than the Lithuanians? This type of question is not helpful.

Explanations relying on personality and nationalism do no better in addressing variation in levels and types of risk-insensitive behavior than structural ones. Variation in action must be linked to differences in some antecedent factor. The next set of mechanisms attempts to link variation to the nature of the resistance event itself.

Participation-Based Mechanisms

Participation in and of itself can produce rewards. Facing danger for a cause generally brings some measure of respect, an obvious example being veterans of popular wars. Status rewards are one of the key mechanisms driving +1 behavior. The theory here treats status rewards as compensating or offsetting the dangers of protest. Status rewards and resentment formation operate to reduce thresholds but they do not work to create actors who willingly embrace risk. Status seeking is not a convincing or complete explanation of first action, at least not for participation in rallies. First, given the actual progression of demonstrations, status benefits would seldom outweigh risks. Consider the likely possibilities. If the first actors are not joined by others, they will be identifiable as first actors and probably receive a great deal of status reward; however, the regime will also be able to identify everyone present, driving potential cost to extremely high levels. Alternatively, if the first actors are joined by thousands, or tens of thousands, the status rewards will drop precipitously (with the possible exception of identifiable leaders). Others may know if an individual was a participant or a nonparticipant, but they may not know whether this individual showed up first or last in the growing crowd. The status reward for doing what tens of thousands of others did cannot be large enough to overcome the original risks of first action. Second, status seeking would seem to be linked to structural arguments, with the attendant problems mentioned ealier. Male youth and political entrepreneurs are generally assumed to desire status more than other groups, but this would not explain the number of older people standing in front of the Parliament in Vilnius, or other events. Finally, and very importantly, in different cultures and nations, different actions bring different status rewards. An explanation of first action would need to address this relationship between culture and status reward.

Although seeking the respect of others through risk-laden participation would seem to play a role for first actors, others argue that one's *self-respect* may be just as important. The argument holds that expressive motivations, in the form of roles, may drive the behavior of a small number of individuals. When the event itself creates such roles, individuals might accept high levels of risk, 0 percent thresholds perhaps, to receive expressive, internally driven rewards. The next section develops one particular mechanism, "the small risk of martyrdom," which follows the logic of expressive motivation and matches my intuitions and experience in Vilnius.

Participation in a Paradigmatic Event: "The Small Risk of Martyrdom" or "Pseudomartyrdom"

Here I follow Stanley Benn's view that expressive motivations may drive human behavior.[19] Benn proposes that individuals act in different roles and that each role has its own preference ranking: an actor can rationally and consistently prefer *a* to *b* under role A, while preferring *b* over *a* under role B.[20] The individual switches "from one socially-defined role to another as different social situations confront him."[21] The obvious problem with this formulation, as Benn recognizes, is that "different social situations" needs better definition if we are to know when an individual might switch from one role to another. In addressing this particular issue, Benn notes:

> Political activity may be a form of moral self-expression, not for achieving any objective beyond itself (for the cause might be lost), nor yet for the satisfaction of knowing that one had let everyone else know that one was on the side of the right, but because one could not seriously claim, even to oneself, to be on that side without expressing the attitude by the action most appropriate to it in the paradigm situation.[22]

Benn expands upon the meaning and importance of action conforming to a paradigm situation:

---

[19] Stanley Benn, "The Problematic Rationality of Political Participation," in Peter Laslett and James Fishkin, eds., *Philosophy, Politics, and Society (Fifth Series)* (New Haven: Yale University Press, 1979).
[20] Ibid., pp. 301–302.   [21] Ibid., p. 302.   [22] Ibid., p. 310.

The smaller the possibility that the relevant states will be significantly altered by the individual's decision, the more strictly the expressive act must conform to some socially understood pattern for expressing that attitude. . . . It is rather that only by using such standard modes can the protester claim, even to himself, to have made his protest, to have expressed his attitude, and so to have been true to himself.[23]

Socially understood patterns are connected to the rituals and symbols of a society. For example, in many democratic societies elections possess strong symbolic significance. The apparent irrationality of voting is overcome as the individual switches to a role where the expressive motivation to show support for democracy in a paradigm situation overcomes the costs involved in going to the polls. Of course, not all individuals in democratic societies have similar role rankings, and not all will turn out to vote. For some, voting may have little symbolic significance at all and the opportunity to play the role of voter has very little meaning or value.

Benn's explanation is based on the nature of the event and provides a culturally oriented lens to address the question of variation in risk-insensitive nationalist participation (fanaticism).[24] Normally, an actor occupies roles that are risk-averse, but if an event produces opportunities to play a paradigmatic role, then the individual may, to use Benn's langauge, "switch over" to this socially understood role in order to express some core attitude. A certain percentage of the given society, a small percentage no doubt, will value this role highly enough to become first actors. The more the event produces opportunities to play a paradigmatic role, the more individuals will feel compelled to be "true to themselves" despite the risks. Thus, it is the specific match-up of events and paradigmatic roles that produces first action and other risk-insensitive actions, not personality types, general levels of nationalism, or a simple lack of structural constraints (although all of these may have some place in the overall explanation).

This approach addresses risk in at least two nonexclusionary ways. First, the value of playing this role produces enjoyment as a benefit. Again, it is doubtful that this benefit would overcome chances of death. Second, and more important, *the paradigmatic role may redefine the meaning of risk and in certain cases turn risk from a cost into a benefit*. In this event, one plays

---

[23] Ibid., pp. 310–311.

[24] There is one very major difference between my treatment and that of Benn: I am trying to show the importance of identifying roles independently of the actions they bring about. Benn does not emphasize this point at all. I return to this issue later.

the role not only despite the risk, but because the role itself informs one that enduring risk within the context of the particular event is a good in its own right. I return to the events of Vilnius to explain and illustrate this crucial but difficult point.

Returning to Lithuania

During the past sixty years, the Lithuanians have not always been fanatical anti-Soviets. In 1940, they acquiesced to Soviet takeover without any mass response or a single shot being fired. In the early period of perestroika, the Latvians and Estonians were more active in pushing for autonomy. However, the Lithuanians seem to have very high and enthusiastic levels of participation when the event calls for standing in front of tanks, at least in 1991.[25] This variation in behavior, I believe, is related to a Lithuanian identity of national martyrdom, which in turn is the basis for paradigmatic roles able to drive self-expressive behavior of a significant number of individuals.

Clearly, as the most Catholic nation in the former Soviet Union, a religious martyr imagery existed in the current of Lithuanian cultural self-perception.[26] Undoubtedly, this religious influence plays a part; of course, other nations are Catholic and possess similar stories and images of martyrs and saints present in their own cultural foundations.[27] There is a stronger and more specific historical side to Lithuania's martyr imagery that is more enlightening but involves a richer study of relevant identities. There is no "we"

[25] A few cursory examples emphasize this point. A few months after the Vilnius events, the Russian Parliament would be under siege by Communist hard-liners, but it is safe to say that the number of first actors standing vigil outside the Russian White House was far less impressive than the number in Lithuania. In the United States, the Kent State shootings had a noticeable impact on the number of students attending rallies, although only four were killed. In Lithuania, immediately after a significant number of demonstrators were killed and wounded, the lure of participation in a resistance event appeared to produce a relatively sizable number of individuals who eschewed risk and became first actors in a new demonstration that would eventually involve tens of thousands by the next morning.

[26] For some, the term "martyr" may bring up connotations of valuing salvific defeat over victory itself; it may conjure up an element of passivity. Most Lithuanians value historic victors, such as Vytautas the Great, more than national martyrs. When the event creates high probabilities of being on a "losing" side, however, then self-sacrificing participation does carry with it elements and possibilities of martyrdom. This does not mean the individual, in more favorable circumstances, would not prefer the victor's role and would not prefer to be more active than passive.

[27] For a general discussion of the relationship between Catholicism and nationalism in the late Soviet era, see Kestutis Girnius, "Catholicism and Nationalism in Lithuania," in Pedro Ramet, ed., *Religion and Nationalism in Soviet and East European Politics* (Durham: Duke University Press, 1989), pp. 109–137.

without an "other." For the Lithuanians, there seem to be two relevant "others": the Soviets-Russians and the West.[28] Clearly, the identity of the Lithuanians to the former is one of oppressed to the oppressor. The relationship to the West is complicated by its ambivalence, and to understand it one must go back to the partisan war of the late 1940s. This guerrilla war, which maintained its intensity far longer than in Latvia and Estonia, resulted in the deaths of tens of thousands of Lithuanians. During the same period, the Soviets deported hundreds of thousands of Lithuanians to Siberia as part of the collectivization campaign, some of whom were deported as a pacification measure in quelling the resistance in the countryside. During the carnage, the Lithuanian partisan movements felt compelled to develop a justification for their losses and develop reasons to continue to struggle in what appeared to be a futile and losing cause. The following excerpts are from the Instructional Bulletin of the United Democratic Resistance Movement of Lithuania, dated March 16, 1947.

We are fighting because we want to show the world that there are ideals that inspire and enable a dwarf to become a giant, that give so much power and strength that the powerful tyrant no longer knows how to suppress it, if he is still ashamed of publicly hanging everyone. . . . We are fighting because we think and believe that one day the hour will come, and the world's patience will run out, and it will tear off the mask of the rapacious tyrant, it will rally all its forces and it will help free the enslaved millions, the martyrs, the exiles. . . . our struggle is a continuation of that struggle with the minions of evil that was begun by the handful of fishermen of Genesareth inspired by His ideas, the banner of which has been borne by the martyrs of the Coliseum and all times into these days of ours.[29]

---

[28] Shmuel Noah Eisenstadt and Bernhard Giesen hold that collective identities and the cultural codes by which they are formed are, in general, trichotomous: "Between inside and outsides lies the boundary, between left and right is the center, between past and future is the present, and between God and the world is the human subject. Even on the most elementary level, codes exhibit a *trichotomic structure* inserting a mediating and separating realm 'in between.' *This mediation and separating realm is the phenomenal focus of identity:* the center, the present, the subject. . . . Constructing a world means starting at this given and immediate identity and extending the construction of this center to further and distinct realms, from the present to the past and the future, from the subject to God and the world." "The Construction of Collective Identity," *European Journal of Sociology* 36 (1995): 72–102. I interpret Lithuanian collective identity as founded on such a trichotomy, but I am not sure this is due to a universal principle as much as its precarious geographic position between East and West.

[29] This document, and others, can be found in Thomas Remeikis, *Opposition to Soviet Rule in Lithuania* (Chicago: Institute of Lithuanian Studies Press, 1980).

In essence, Lithuanians cannot win by themselves, but their sacrifice will help show to the world the true nature of the Soviet opponent. One day, the West will shed its hypocrisy and come to the aid of the enslaved. Lithuanian martyrdom and courage will be instrumental in these events; thus, the "dwarf becomes a giant."

This image was not confined to the partisans themselves but was perpetuated in fictional accounts long after the resistance had been entirely broken. Émigré plays, such as *Five Posts in a Marketplace* written in 1958 by Algirdas Landsbergis, positively portrayed suicidal partisan missions in the last stages of rebellion.[30] In the play, the following dialogue between a Lithuanian woman and a partisan illustrates the meaning of the hopeless struggle in the mind of the partisan:

> *Aldona:*   You know, as I do, that armed resistance lives by hope. But there is no more hope.
>
> *Antanas:*   To panic is a feminine privilege!
>
> *Aldona:* Have you been listening to the foreign radios? Nothing! Nothing!
>
> *Antanas:*   The silence must be only temporary. They'll have to understand. Aren't we fighting for the freedom of the entire world?

In the play, Aldona gives a seemingly more clear-headed appraisal of the situation: the time for open resistance is over, and Lithuanians must preserve themselves through other means. Although the playwright presents different sides of the argument, in the end the suicidal actions of the partisan are seen more as heroic than foolish. In the last scene, the authorities have publicly placed the corpse of the partisan on an anthill so that his rotting and ant-eaten body will serve as an example for the town. A young girl who loved the partisan rushes down to "marry" her dead beloved. Her parents, who had made peace with the Soviets, try to stop her, as such an act will identify her to the authorities as a subversive. The following exchange takes place:

> *Mother:*   It's death! Death ends everything!
>
> *Grazina:*   Nothing ever ends!
>
> *Father:*   Go after her!
>
> *Mother:*   Stop her! She is running to her death!
>
> *Commentator:*   Too late. She's on her way to the altar.

[30] Algirgas Landsberbis, *Five Posts in a Marketplace,* in Alfreds Stranmanis, ed., *Confrontations with Tyranny* (Prospect Heights, Ill.: Waveland Press, 1977).

With the music of a wedding song being played, the young girl kneels by the bullet-pierced body of her "betrothed." The last line reads, "How beautiful is my beloved, like a deer frozen in an eternal leap."

Even inside Soviet Lithuania itself, themes of martyrdom remained common in the postwar period. In *The Red Forest*, Romualdas Granauskas, in an apparent attempt to summarize Lithuanian history, develops an imagery of thousands of crucified women stretching back endless generations in a blood-red forest. In the end, a little girl asks, "Mama, when I grow up, will they nail me to a cross, too?" Other stories of the period, written in code to avoid censorship, show that the meaning of the partisan war was still a live issue for some.[31]

The martyr role continued to be physically played out decades after the end of the partisan war. On May 14, 1972, nineteen-year-old Romas Kalanta burned himself alive in Kaunas in front of the theater in which a jury-rigged assembly had proclaimed the incorporation of Lithuania into the Soviet Union in 1940.[32] It was rumored that a group of youths, some students and some workers, had drawn lots for the planned suicide.[33] When the Soviet authorities secretly buried Kalanta's body to prevent publicity, riots broke out in Kaunas requiring the efforts of internal security troops. The prevention of Kalanta's funeral became the cause of one of the great riots of the Brezhnev era.

This material also provides a context for the events immediately after the January Vilnius killings. The dead of January 1991 were honored with wakes held in the state sports stadium. Tens of thousands stood in freezing temperatures to file past the corpses; tens of thousands attended the funeral. The path from the church to the cemetery, winding its way past the Soviet garrison, was lined with mourners standing respectfully for hours in freezing weather. Lit candles and makeshift shrines were everywhere. Everyone seemed to have a designated role – a group of schoolchildren holding candles stood for hours in two neat rows, old women were planting their lit can-

---

[31] Granauskas's story, as well as other pertinent stories from the Soviet period, can be found in Violeta Kelertas, ed., *Come into My Time: Lithuania in Prose Fiction, 1970–1990* (Urbana: University of Illinois Press, 1992). The quoted passage is from Romualdas Granauskas, *The Red Forest*, in ibid., p. 46.

[32] Descriptions of the event appeared May 22, 1972, in the *New York Times, Washington Post, London Times,* and many other major newspapers.

[33] Thomas Remeikis, *Opposition to Soviet Rule in Lithuania* (Chicago: Institute of Lithuanian Studies Press, 1980), pp. 118–119.

dles in the gutter. All were careful not to disturb the aura that permeated this communing with the dead.[34]

Lithuanians love their dead. Especially the dead killed at the hands of the Soviets. This form of martyrdom conjures up a rich and obvious meaning that has historically and culturally manifested itself in both action and art. To utilize Benn's term, for the Lithuanians, the martyr role is paradigmatic.

The Operation of a "Pseudomartyrdom" Mechanism

A "pseudomartyrdom" mechanism consists of at least three elements. First, martyrdom must have socially understood symbolic significance. The case for such significance in Lithuania was just presented. Second, events must produce martyr *roles* and the opportunity to play them. The events of January 1991 created opportunities for individuals to play paradigmatic roles. The identities of all the actors had fallen into place. Lithuania called for the West to help, if not diplomatically recognize, the new freely elected and self-declared independent state. The West's response was, of course, clearly seen as inadequate. Again, the West was perceived as sacrificing the Lithuanian nation out of self-interest. As events played out during the early hours of January 13, the scene was set for Lithuania to play out its martyr role at the Parliament building. The West would be shamed, the Soviets would oppress, some Lithuanians would die. Clearly, the dead in Vilnius were martyrs who suffered at the hands of the traditional Soviet enemy. However, it was not only the fifteen individuals who died, but the Lithuanian nation as well; the "we" had suffered at the hands of the "other." The individuals who had been in the crowd, *through their participation,* had become a part of the "we."[35]

At the peak moment of uncertainty and risk, Landsbergis had told the crowd, "we need live witnesses, not more victims." No one was swayed by this statement; in fact, the words allowed the milling crowd to make a decision to stay as potential martyrs. Martyrs must volunteer for their role; they come to it through choice, not coercion. Landsbergis knew that his fellow

---

[34] Personal impressions.

[35] Eric Hobsbawm makes a related point about the vicarious identification of sports fans with national struggles: "The imagined community of millions seems more real as a team of eleven named people. The individual, even the one who only cheers, becomes a symbol of his nation himself." From *Nations and Nationalism since 1780: Programme, Myth, Reality* (Cambridge: Cambridge University Press, 1990), p. 143. Of course, George Orwell had made this point earlier.

Lithuanians would not leave. His statement simply allowed the unfolding script to be more clear and dramatic.

My friend's rapture in the Parliament building (example 4), as well as the presence of the Lithuanian volunteers (example 2), makes some sense in light of this discussion. The Parliament was a symbol of Lithuanian resistance, a target of Soviet aggression, an object of Western betrayal (as well as media attention) – and he was in the bowels of the building. The nation was playing its historical role and the nature of individual participation allowed one to both be absorbed into the nation and become a symbol of the nation by playing a parallel role. The benefits of this role were not confined to any single age group or gender; members of all demographic categories could play this role simply by being present (example 3).

The third element integral to a pseudomartyr mechanism regards the level of risk. The event must not involve overwhelming risks. Recall the self-immolation of Romas Kalanta. Kalanta became a hero and one of the most famous individuals in modern Lithuanian history. But he did, of course, burn to death. Very few people actually wish to become a martyr. This is evident from the fact that it is very easy to martyr oneself: all you need is a can of gasoline and a match. Many Lithuanians revere the role that Kalanta played, and many would certainly like to enjoy a small modicum of the honor that he received, but they would also like to be around to enjoy it. Logically, one cannot have it both ways, but I would suggest that one can come close. By enduring a risk of getting killed, the willingness to die for a nation or ideal is exhibited. In the ideal situation, the risk is high enough to demonstrate this willingness, but low enough so that the chances of death are "tolerable." In Vilnius, even those rushing to stand in front of the building were certainly not suicidal. The chance of death was not high; Soviet troops were not indiscriminately machine-gunning crowds. This is not to discount the risk, which was still considerable, but rather to view the risk in its overall context.

In sum, the elements of a "pseudomartyrdom" mechanism were in place; the event created a paradigmatic role that transformed risk into a benefit. Most important for the purposes here, this mechanism provides a plausible explanation for the creation of first actors. As the events of January 13 unfolded, those heading toward the Parliament (as well as those previously present at the Parliament and choosing to remain) became first actors in the mass action against subsequent Soviet threats. My friend took little thought of others' actions when he said, "They will attack the Parliament next, we must go to the Parliament" (example 1). Rather, historical events were unfolding and he had a role to play. His threshold was 0 percent. For some individuals, very few no doubt, risk may be overcome by the expressive nature of the role itself.

Two Concluding Points

Relationship to Various Social Science Approaches

It is possible to see paradigmatic roles in microeconomic or rational-choice terms. There are, indeed, few contradictions with such an approach. Taken in its entirety, however, these mechanisms are more fully explained in anthropological terms. A full outline of role-based mechanisms might follow the diagram in Figure 9.1. The centerpiece of this mechanism is the "cultural schema," that is, the ordering of symbols and myths that events may create. In effect, the schema is a socially familiar plot line that creates roles, some of which may convert risk into a benefit that drives first action. In Vilnius in 1991, political myths of heroic martyrs, and of Lithuania as a symbolic martyr oppressed by the East and forsaken by the West, lay in the Lithuanian symbol set. The January events ordered the myths and produced a familiar plot line with a recognizable pseudomartyr role. A small percentage of Lithuanians, the fanatics and first players, then acted out this role.

The concept of a cultural schema is aptly explicated by Sherry Ortner:

> In effect, the cultural schema has been moved by an actor from an external to an internal position, from an abstract model of deeds done by ancient heroes and ritual participants to a personal program for understanding what is happening to one right now, and for acting upon it. . . . there is a distance between actors' selves and their cultural models, in the sense that not all of a culture's repertoire of symbolic frames make sense to all actors at all times.[36]

One controversy among the social sciences concerns the "distance between the actors' selves and their cultural models." Those using a "thin rational view" posit an actor whose more immediate and personal economic or po-

---

[36] Sherry B. Ortner, "Patterns of History: Cultural Schemas in the Foundings of Sherpa Religious Institutions," in Emiko Ohnuki-Tierney, ed., *Culture through Time: Anthropological Approaches* (Stanford: Stanford University Press, 1990), p. 89. Also, see Lowell Ditmer, "Political Culture and Political Symbolism: Toward a Theoretical Synthesis," *World Politics* 29 (1977): 552–583, for a review of the use of political culture and symbols primarily in the field of political science.

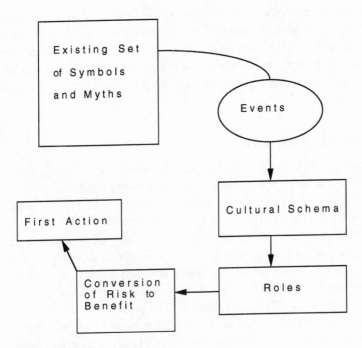

Figure 9.1. Cultural schema

litical goals dominate the murkier cultural frame pushing its significance to the background. Along this line of thinking, culture is more likely to be viewed as a resource rather than unconscious constraint. Following Figure 9.1, culture might help produce a set of roles, but the individual is relatively free to choose among them. Other scholars, more likely to practice sociology or anthropology, see the cultural frame as heavily constraining, or even programming, the individual's choices. Roles are not chosen, but rather accepted. Ortner takes an intermediate position where "actors may internalize a schema under certain conditions and thus may be constrained by its forms, but under other conditions may reestablish a distance between themselves and the schema."[37]

In helping to explain rebellion and resistance, or at least its most risk-accepting participants, a qualified version of this intermediate position seems appropriate; *some* actors may internalize a schema with a plot and roles that

[37] Ortner, "Patterns of History," p. 84.

under *specific* conditions may produce expressive motivations to perform a first-playing or fanatical action. When events produce a more clearly paradigmatic situation, the number of actions triggered through this mechanism will be higher, but the numbers of individuals involved will never be large if the costs and risk are significant. This point brings up another, and final, issue.

A Theory of Fanatical Action?

This analysis leads to the issue of explaining variation in first action across cultures and nations. Is it possible to develop a theory that would allow us to predict when more first players will be present? Currently, some theories hypothesize a relationship between the type of rhetoric used by leaders and the number of actors willing to incur high risk.[38] The preceding argument is much more complex and incorporates several variables. First, each nation or culture possesses a unique set of salient political myths and symbols. Second, the events that shape this symbol set, such as those in Vilnius, are themselves complex and difficult to categorize. This process produces roles that leaders cannot blatantly manufacture; the forces behind such role creation must remain latent or they will lose their force. Furthermore, as just emphasized, variation among cases is minimal. In all cases, the number of those voluntarily performing risky action is quite small. Even under the most paradigmatic conditions, "the small risk of martyrdom" mechanism will drive the actions of only a small percentage of the population.

With so much complexity in culture and the nature of the event, combined with so little variation, a coherent theory of first action or fanatical behavior is currently, and may always be, beyond the reach of social "science." On this issue, we will be left with explanations heavily relying on interpretation and intuition. This does not mean, however, that social scientists, especially political scientists, should abandon efforts to bring some order to these issues. Events like those in Vilnius in January 1991 are too important to be ignored. Many commentators believed these events were a precursor for the failed Moscow coup the following summer. As Lieven has written:

> They [Soviet hard-liners] clearly thought an assault would not meet serious popular resistance. The dead outside the television tower cured them

---

[38] Paul Stern, for example, in "Why Do Individuals Sacrifice for Their Nations?" *Political Psychology* 16 (1995): 217–236.

of this illusion. To have stormed the parliament would have meant dozens or even hundreds more dead, and it seems that for this the Soviet leadership lacked the courage, or possibly in some cases even the ruthlessness, in the face of a storm of protest that was building both in Russia and in the West. . . . the humiliating failure of nerve in January may well have undermined the resolve of officers to support the counter-revolution in August. If so, the dead of 13 January deserve recognition not only from Balts but from tens of millions of people across the former Soviet Union. . . . Despite the sleazier aspects of Lithuanian politics at the time, the episode has provided Latvians and Lithuanians with their own modern martyrs, a feeling that they have fought and suffered for their independence. The solidarity and courage of the peaceful, unarmed crowds outside the parliaments in Riga and Vilnius, convinced that they were about to be attacked, but standing their ground, is indeed one of the most moving political images of modern times, not only for Balts, but for Europe.[39]

[39] Lieven, *The Baltic Revolution,* p. 254.

10. Conclusions

This book has been about ordinary people and the roles they come to play during times of resistance and rebellion against powerful regimes. In pursuing this aim, the work has intertwined two agendas, one theoretical and methodological and the other substantive. In this conclusion, I discuss both in turn.

A mechanism-based approach was developed to answer the question of how ordinary people rebel and resist against powerful regimes. Mechanisms are specific causal patterns that explain individual actions over a wide range of settings; they are intermediary between laws and description. Ten mechanisms were identified: four that triggered movement from neutrality to passive, unorganized resistance, two crucial in producing movement into armed community-based resistance organizations, and four that help to sustain these organizations. When possible, the mechanisms were linked to observable social structures.

These ten mechanisms are seen as forming a process that originates, catalyzes, and sustains rebellion against strong regimes. This template of mechanisms was formed from an understanding of Lithuanian resistance, especially the events in the first Soviet occupation of 1940–1941, and knowledge of the theoretical literature on political violence. Because the mechanisms forming this process, and the process itself, should hold generalizable properties, the essential question asked throughout the case material is whether this template of mechanisms could apply across space and time. Could it help to explain puzzling variation? For example, could it help explain why one community develops an extensive rebellion organization while a neighboring community does not? Could it help explain why some, but few, urban communities develop organized, armed rebellion? Could it help explicate why the same nation rebels against one occupier but remains passive with another?

This template of mechanisms was systematically and progressively applied to a series of cases. Each case expanded the context. An investigation of variation among Lithuanian communities in the first Soviet occupation was followed by an analysis of the German and postwar Soviet occupations of Lithuania. While keeping the time frame and occupiers the same, a new set of cases expanded the geographic scope of analysis by examining outcomes in postwar Latvia and Estonia, postwar Vohynia and Galicia, wartime Ukraine and Belorussia, and wartime Montenegro. A further comparison changed the time frame, contrasting the passive resistance of modern Communist societies of the 1980s to the earlier period.

The systematic application of hypothesized mechanisms across these various cases produced a series of lessons about the nature of resistance. I address each of the six main mechanisms (leaving aside the sustaining mechanisms) and discuss whether they were in fact operative across settings.

Resentment Formation

An essential question regards variation in motivation to resist an occupier. Because the focus of this work has been on ordinary people, the most relevant motivational mechanisms are those affecting the action of the broadest strata of the population, not elite actors. Resentment is an emotion that forms from the day-to-day experience of humiliating subordination and affects the entire population. Resentment is reinforced by everyday policies that heighten the perception that one's group is located in an unjust position on a status hierarchy. These policies can intensify resentment and encourage individuals to accept risk and act against the occupier. Differences in perception of ethnic status hierarchy and intensity of resentment are crucial in explaining two substantive puzzles: the contrast between Lithuanian reactions to Soviet and German occupation, and the difference in reaction to postwar Soviet rule in Galicia and Volhynia.

Although there are certainly numerous mechanisms that are able to shape motivations to resist an occupier or regime, resentment formation has been common to Eastern Europe and especially crucial to the creation of resistance. The First World War and the collapse of empires brought forth a plethora of new nation-states based on the conception that the majority nation should rule the state. Throughout the region, language use, educational policies, bureaucratic staffing, and other government policies served to cement a commonsense idea that the eponymous nationality should be first among all ethnic groups in the state. Within the ethnically heterogeneous states of the region, slogans such as "Poland for Poles" became standard fare. Foreign occupations established new ethnic-political hierarchies. New regimes shaped perceptions of status hierarchy through the relative placement of majority and minority individuals in visible positions of authority. Individuals would in effect ask if their group was "still on top" or whether formerly subordinate groups were now "above them." The answer to this question consistently produced an emotional reaction that, in turn, affected movement toward resistance.

The prominence of resentment as an emotional mechanism points to new avenues for research. Social scientists have seldom explored the interaction of emotions and politics in any depth. Few people doubt that hatred, fear, resentment, and other emotions are essential parts of the human experience, and their relationship to ethnic conflict and violence would seem apparent. As Donald Horowitz has written, "A bloody phenomenon cannot be explained by a bloodless theory."[1] However, emotions are difficult to operationalize or to quantify. Emotions are not the stuff of survey research; few would readily admit to being influenced by hatred or resentment. Perhaps not surprisingly, the number of articles on relative deprivation (employing available income and education data for proxy variables) and political violence dwarf the number of articles on emotion and political violence. While the field of emotions and politics is wide open, those who wish to pursue the issue will need to take an interdisciplinary approach, merging political science with the insights of psychology.

The study of the relationship among ethnic status hierarchy, resentment formation, and rebellion begs for comparative research. In Eastern Europe, the collapse of empire, the nature of subsequent nation and state building, and the shocks brought on by occupation created the resentments that drove not only antiregime rebellion but pogroms against minorities.[2] Is this same story being played out again in postcolonial Africa and India? What role has resentment formation played among the Serbs, Croats, Muslims, and Kosovars during the collapse of Yugoslavia and the subsequent ethnic wars?

---

[1] Donald Horowitz, *Ethnic Groups in Conflict* (Berkeley: University of California Press, 1985), p. 140. Horowitz's work stresses the ideas of hierarchy and is an essential starting point for the study of resentment, emotion, and ethnopolitical conflict.

[2] I have written an offshoot of this work focusing on four emotional mechanisms. See Roger Petersen, *Fear, Hatred, Resentment: Delineating Paths to Ethnic Conflict in Eastern Europe* (Cambridge: Cambridge University Press, forthcoming). In this work, I define the nature of emotional mechanisms in detail and use a theory of emotion to generate hypotheses regarding timing and targets of ethnic violence.

Focal Mechanisms

Given a motivation to resist, focal-point mechanisms provide for the coordination of action and the communication of the desire to accept risk. The power of focal-point mechanisms relies on the nature of cultural symbol sets: the same action may not convey the same message or provide for the same coordination against different occupiers or regimes. This point was supported by the case material examining the different historically based symbol sets operative between Lithuanians and Germans in comparison to those between Lithuanians and Russians-Soviets.

Most social scientists agree that focal-point mechanisms are universal and important; however, they debate the relative weight of culture versus elite manipulation in the operation of these mechanisms. In both the perestroika era and the first Soviet occupation of Lithuania, focal mechanisms operated without significant manipulation from elites. Czechs knew to show up at Wenceslas Square without any direction; East Germans went to Nikolai Church on Mondays without direct leadership; the meaning of the clash on All Souls' Day in 1940 Lithuania needed no further definition by elites. Political scientists often stress the elite manipulation of culture, but the cases here have provided ample evidence of the power of culture and history to generate actions in the absence of elite engineering. The previous chapter, with the discussion of cultural schema, further underlines the subtle, but sometimes critical, influence of culture on the nature of rebellion. Similar to resentment formation, focal mechanisms call out for interdisciplinary treatment. Political scientists concentrate on strategic action and anthropologists on culture, but the two should be brought together to understand how motivations are communicated under repressive conditions.

Status Reward Mechanisms

The conferral of honor for a given act of resistance and rebellion can help balance out the risks involved with that action. Status reward helps explain the rapidity of movement to +1 in the Lithuanian case as well as the dynamics of rebellion in Montenegro. In other cases, however, this mechanism does not appear to play a large role. When the chances of death and deportation increase, as in the Lithuanian postwar case or wartime Ukraine and Belorussia, status (in general) appears irrelevant. When the strength of community declines, as in the perestroika cases, status again plays a limited role. The findings suggest that this factor varies significantly across cases but is most important when communities are strong and costs are relatively low.

Norms

Norms inform the individual about what *should* be done. As defined here, norms may work to reduce (and sometimes increase) the level of risk that an individual accepts. A simple notion of reciprocity lies at the heart of the norms most relevant to rebellion: "Because my family and friends have acted, I should act as well." The second chapter outlines three norms common to family, work, and social organization. The movement from passive, unorganized resistance (+1) to armed, community-based rebellion depends in large part upon whether these norms are activated. In turn, the triggering of these norms depends on the structural features of the community itself. This reasoning ties into the sociological literature on centralization, heterogeneity, density, and size effects and leads to hypotheses linking these features to the likelihood of the development of local rebellion organization.

Perhaps the most crucial theoretical contribution here is the linkage of normative mechanisms to threshold mechanisms. How did ordinary people, often risk-averse farmers, end up in a hopeless battle against the Soviets in the postwar era? The answer is that they were drawn in through their normative relationships with friends and family. Norms change the way individuals relate to risk. Along with resentment formation, these normative mechanisms function to shape preferences. Emotions such as resentment change motivations to resist; norms, such as the community-based norms examined here, change levels of risk acceptance. For methodological reasons, many social-science approaches assume one stable preference ordering, but for the subject of rebellion against powerful regimes, this assumption is too simplistic. Rebellion develops as a *process,* and, within this process, mechanisms can be triggered that change motivations and attitudes. Clearly, debates over the stability of preferences will continue as a fundamental methodological question. This work has aimed to provide both theoretical and empirical material to further fuel this debate.

Threshold Mechanisms

"I will act if X percent of others act." This general logic of the threshold mechanism has taken two specific forms, differentiated by reference group:

societal and corporate groups form the reference for movement from 0 to +1, whereas the community forms the reference for movement from +1 to +2 positions. The cases demonstrate the essential role played by this mechanism. Threshold mechanisms operate at multiple levels of the rebellion process; they function, with some modification, across different eras. In almost every case, threshold mechanisms play a key role in explaining puzzling variation.

A sizable literature on thresholds exists. The work here contributes to this literature in at least three ways. First, it emphasizes that the social scientist can and should connect thresholds to social structures. In the 1940s cases, the mix of various community subsets provides an estimate of threshold distributions. In the perestroika era cases, the corporate nature of modern Communist society provides a base line for estimating thresholds. By linking thresholds to observable features of social structure, hypotheses predicting which types of communities and societies will reach high-resistance equilibria can be formed. As the case studies show, the amount of work necessary to link structure, especially community-level structure, to threshold distributions is extensive. But the payoffs are high.

Second, thresholds have not been treated as static. Emotions and norms can both affect thresholds at junctures within the rebellion process. This work has not only recognized that thresholds are not static but has identified specific mechanisms (A, B, C norms) that reduce or increase thresholds.

Third, as touched on earlier, this work studies the interaction of thresholds and norms within community structures. Why does one community develop an extensive rebellion organization while a neighboring community does not? Many urban communities do not develop rebellion organization, but what accounts for the ones that do? The study of community structure, norms of reciprocity, and local thresholds *work together* to provide answers. Different structures produce different distributions of thresholds and different chances of generating rebellion-enhancing norms. Given this reasoning, and relying on the literature on centralization, heterogeneity, density, and size effects, hypotheses linking community structure and likelihood of community-based rebellion organization were formed. While it is very difficult to test empirically these community-level dynamics, the fieldwork was sufficient to provide support for certain positions and to challenge others. For instance, the optimality of an intermediate density of ties in producing community rebellion organization was theoretically demonstrated and empirically illustrated. The importance of the structural location of low-threshold first-acting groups, as opposed to simply their existence, was supported by theory and case material. The combined use of these theoretical elements produces an understanding of several counterintuitive phenomena. For instance, to highlight one important insight, a social unit with high numbers of individuals motivated to rebel may never develop rebellion, whereas another social unit with fewer numbers of antiregime actors may indeed develop and maintain rebellion. The outcome depends more on specific structural factors, such as the position of first actors, than on the numbers of those motivated to rebel.

One particular structurally based hypothesis is perhaps most important: the mechanisms producing armed, locally based rebellion organization can only be found operating in *strong community* structures. In societies comprised of weak communities, certain mechanisms (resentment formation, focal points) may very well lead to unarmed resistance, mass rallies, and other forms of protest, but the very highest levels of risk are far more likely to be overcome with the set of mechanisms found in strong community.

Again, the nature of this analysis suggests the need for interdisciplinary cooperation. The reasoning of network scholars, the strategic insights of game theorists, and the extensive fieldwork and intuitions of anthropologists can all play a role in understanding the community-level dynamics of rebellion.

Resistance and Rebellion in One Small Nation

Much of the case material in this work has covered a fifty-year period of resistance and rebellion of one small nation. One can easily find figures that sum up the grisly drama that has taken place in Lithuania: hundreds of thousands deported, tens of thousands killed, 200,000 Jews murdered, and so on. One can list the significant resistance events: the rebellion of June 1941, the partisan warfare of the postwar period, the mass rallies and early declaration of independence during perestroika, the deadly protests at the television facilities in January 1991. This book has tried to provide some sense of the emotions, norms, and strategic thinking of ordinary people that go beyond the facts and figures of this bloody history. This goal drove the forty interviews so fundamental to the work.

For many of the interviewees, the recollection of this history was extremely painful. One day, I interviewed respondent S (the woman from whom I was renting a room while doing fieldwork in Lithuania). I went through the usual interview process, starting with her earliest recollections of the village where she grew up and proceeding through the changes of the 1940s. S had left her rural community in the mid-1940s to attend the university in Vilnius. Like many of the respondents in my project, S painted a positive, almost idyllic, picture of prewar life in her community: "There were very good times. Very beautiful relations between neighbors." S recalled beekeeping operations and relations among god-families with visible joy. I interceded to ask factual questions about the structure of the village or community. How many hectares did this neighbor have? Who owned a threshing machine? And so on. Eventually, her narrative led to recollections of tragic and violent events. Like many other Balts who had lived through this period, respondent S had witnessed considerable tragedy and atrocity during the Soviet occupations: a brother had been shot in the crossfire between Soviets and partisans, her father was tied to horses and dragged to death, her cousin had been imprisoned and tortured during the first Soviet occupation. S had personally witnessed the Soviets display dead partisans in the town square, a common deterrent tactic; she had twice seen scores of individuals and families destined for Siberia herded onto trucks. While horrific, her experiences were similar to those of most of the other interviewees. Also, like many other interviewees, S broke down and wept during the session.

On the first pages of this book, the reader encountered maps of rural villages. I placed them there in an effort to give some sense of the reality and intimacy of life in those communities. I still recall the interviews with the individuals who had lived, rebelled, and were captured in those communities. I vividly recall places that I saw during my fieldwork: the locations of the bunkers where rebels hid, the killing fields outside Merkine where the Nazis murdered the local Jewish population. I can easily recollect standing in the crowd on the night of January 13, 1991, and attending the massive funerals that followed.

There are excellent social science reasons for using Lithuania as a base line for the study of resistance and rebellion. The case provides multiple occupations, temporal and spatial variations, and ready comparison with neighboring states. The case has provided insight for the mathematical formulation of social norms and an analysis of network density and centralization. Hopefully, the work here can lead to a broader understanding of the dynamics of political protest. Beyond the development of more sophisticated social-science methodology, beyond a convincing explanation of variation, I sincerely hope that I have accurately told the story of how ordinary people lived through these events. That alone would make this book worthwhile.

Bibliography

Alexiev, Alex. 1982. *Soviet Nationalities in German Wartime Strategy, 1941–1945.* Rand Corporation, Rand Reports, R-2772-NA, August.

Arad, Yitzhak. 1979. *The Partisan: From the Valley of Death to Mount Zion.* New York: Holocaust Library.

Armstrong, John. 1964. *Soviet Partisans in World War II.* Madison: University of Wisconsin Press.

1968. "The Ethnic Scene in the Soviet Union: The View of Dictatorship." In Erich Goldhagen, ed., *Ethnic Minorities in the Soviet Union*, pp. 3–49. New York: Praeger.

1990. *Ukrainian Nationalism.* Englewood, N.J.: Ukrainian Academic Press.

Ash, Timoty Garton. 1993. *The Magic Lantern: The Revolution of '89 Witnessed in Warsaw, Budapest, and Prague.* New York: Vintage Books.

Aspray, Robert. 1965. *War in the Shadows.* Vol. 1. Garden City, N.Y.: Doubleday.

Audenas, Juozas. 1959. "The Cooperative Movement." *Lituanas* 5: 13–17.

Axelrod, Robert. 1984. *The Evolution of Cooperation.* New York: Basic Books.

Banac, Ivo. 1984. *The National Question in Yugoslavia: Origins, History, Politics.* Ithaca: Cornell University Press.

Banfield, Edward. 1970. *The Unheavenly City Revisited.* Boston: Little, Brown.

Bates, Robert, Avner Greif, Margaret Levi, Jean-Laurent Rosenthal, and Barry Weingast. 1998. *Analytic Narratives.* Princeton: Princeton University Press.

Benn, Stanley. 1979. "The Problematic Rationality of Political Participation." In Peter Laslett and James Fishkin, eds., *Philosophy, Politics, and Society (Fifth Series).* New Haven: Yale University Press.

Biggart, John. 1990. "The Collectivization of Agriculture in Soviet Lithuania." *East European Quarterly* 9: 53–75.

Boehm, Christopher. 1983. *Montenegrin Social Organization and Values: A Political Ethnography of a Refuge Area Tribal Adaptation.* New York: AMS Press.

Bonnell, Victoria. 1983. *Roots of Rebellion: Workers' Politics and Organizations in St. Petersburg and Moscow, 1900–1914.* Berkeley: University of California Press.

Booth, A., and N. Babchuk. 1969. "Personal Influence Networks and Voluntary Association Affiliation." *Sociological Inquiry* 39: 179–188.

Boshyk, Yury, ed. 1986. *Ukraine during World War II: History and Its Aftermath.* Edmonton: Canadian Institute of Ukrainian Studies.

Bowen, John, and Roger Petersen. 1999. *Critical Comparisons in Politics and Culture.* Cambridge: Cambridge University Press.

Brown, J. F. 1991. *Surge to Freedom: The End of Communist Rule in Eastern Europe.* Durham: Duke University Press.

Budreckis, Algirdas Martin. 1968. *The Lithuanian National Revolt of 1941.* South Boston, Mass.: Lithuanian Encyclopedia Press.

Bunce, Valerie, and Dennis Chong. 1990. "The Party's Over: Mass Protest and the End of Communist Rule in Eastern Europe." Paper presented at the annual meeting of the American Political Science Association, San Francisco.

Chavis, David, James Hogge, David McMillan, and Abraham Wandersman. 1986. "Sense of Community through Brunswik's Lens: A First Look." *Journal of Community Psychology* 14: 24–40.

Chong, Dennis. 1991. *Collective Action and the Civil Rights Movement.* Chicago: University of Chicago Press.

Clark, Robert. 1984. *The Basque Insurgents: ETA, 1952–1980.* Madison: University of Wisconsin Press.

Coleman, James. 1994. "The Realization of Effective Norms." In Randall Collins, ed., *Four Sociological Traditions,* pp. 171–189. Oxford: University of Oxford Press.

Dallin, Alexander. 1978. "The Baltic States between Nazi Germany and Soviet Russia." In V. Stanley Vardys and Romuald J. Misiunas, eds., *The Baltic States in Peace and War, 1917–1945,* pp. 97–109. University Park: Pennsylvania State University Press.

——— 1981. *German Rule in Russia, 1941–1945: A Study of Occupation Policies.* Boulder, Colo.: Westview Press.

Daumantas, Juozas. 1975. *Fighters for Freedom.* New York: Maryland Books.

Daunys, Stasys. 1962. "The Development of Resistance and the National Revolt against the Soviet Regime in Lithuania in 1940–41." *Lituanus* 8: 11–15.

Dawes, Robyn M., Jeanne McTavish, and Harriet Shaklee. 1977. "Behavior, Communication, and Assumptions about Other People's Behavior in a Commons Dilemma Situation." *Journal of Personality and Social Psychology* 35: 1–11.

Ditmer, Lowell. 1977. "Political Culture.and Political Symbolism: Toward a Theoretical Synthesis." *World Politics* 29: 552–583.

Djilas, Milovan. 1958. *Land without Justice.* New York: Harcourt, Brace, Jovanovich. ——— 1962. *Conversations with Stalin.* New York: Harcourt, Brace & World.

Dmytryshyn, V. 1956. "The Nazis and the SS Volunteer Division 'Galicia.'" *American Slavic and East European Review* 15: 1–10.

Dunn, Dennis J. 1978. "The Catholic Church and the Soviet Government in the Baltic States, 1940–41." In V. Stanley Vardys and Romuald Misiunas, eds., *The Baltic States in Peace and War, 1917–1945,* pp. 149–158. University Park: Pennsylvania State University Press.

Echikson, William. 1990. *Lighting the Night: Revolution in Eastern Europe.* New York: William Morrow.

Eidintas, Alfonsas, Vytautas Zalys, and Alfred Erich Senn, eds. 1998. *Lithuania in European Politics: The Years of the First Republic.* New York: St. Martin's Press.

Eisenstadt, Schmuel Noah, and Bernhard Giesen. 1995. "The Construction of Collective Identity." *European Journal of Sociology* 36: 72–102.

Elliott, Mark R. 1986. "Soviet Military Collaborators during World War II." In Yury Boshyk, ed., *Ukraine during World War II: History and Its Aftermath,* pp. 89–104. Edmonton: Canadian Institute of Ukrainian Studies.

Elster, Jon. 1986. Introduction. In Jon Elster, ed., *Rational Choice,* pp. 1–33. Oxford: Blackwell.

——— 1989. *Nuts and Bolts for the Social Sciences.* Cambridge: Cambridge University Press.

——— 1990. *The Cement of Society: A Study of Social Order.* Cambridge: Cambridge University Press.

——— 1990. "When Communism Dissolves." *London Review of Books,* January 25, pp. 3–6.

——— 1992. *Local Justice: How Institutions Allocate Scarce Goods and Necessary Burdens.* New York: Russell Sage Foundation.

——— 1999. *Alchemies of the Mind: Rationality and the Emotions.* Cambridge: Cambridge University Press.

Evans-Pritchard, E. E. 1940. *The Nuer: A Description of the Modes of Livelihood and Political Institutions of a Nilotic People.* Oxford: Clarendon Press.

Finkel, Steven E., E. N. Muller, and Karl-Dieter Opp. 1989. "Personal Influence, Collective Rationality, and Mass Political Action." *American Political Science Review* 83: 885–903.

Fireman, Bruce, and William Gamson. 1979. "Utilitarian Logic in the Resource Mobilization Perspective." In M. N. Zald and J. D. MacCarthy, eds., *Dynamics of Social Movements,* pp. 8–44. Cambridge, Mass.: Winthrop.

Frankel, Benjamin, and Brian D. Kux. 1990. "Recalling the Dark Past of Lithuanian Nationalism." *Los Angeles Times,* April 29, p. M2.

Frome, Frieda. 1988. *Some Dare to Dream: Frieda Frome's Escape from Lithuania.* Ames: Iowa State University Press.

Gambetta, Diego. 1998. "Concatenations of Mechanisms." In Peter Hedström and Richard Swedberg, eds., *Social Mechanisms: An Analytic Approach to Social Theory,* pp. 102–124. Cambridge: Cambridge University Press.

Gilbert, Martin. 1972. *Atlas of Russian History.* Great Britain: Dorset Press.

Gilliam, Sylvia, and Alexander Dallin. 1954. "Aspects of the German Occupation of the Soviet Union." In *Project on the Soviet Social System* (AF no. 33(038)-12909). Russian Research Center, Harvard University.

Girnius, Kestutis. 1988. "The Collectivization of Lithuanian Agriculture, 1944–1950." *Soviet Studies* 40: 460–478.

——— 1988. "Three Months of Change in Lithuania." *Radio Free Europe Research,* August 31, pp. 1–5.

——— 1988. "Lithuanian Dissent: Proud Past, Uncertain Future." *Radio Free Europe Research,* October 5, 1988, pp. 33–37.

——— 1989. "Catholicism and Nationalism in Lithuania." In Pedro Ramet, ed., *Religion and Nationalism in Soviet and East European Politics,* pp. 109–137. Durham: Duke University Press.

1991. "The Party and Popular Movements." In Jan Arveds Trapans, ed., *Toward Independence: The Baltic Popular Movements,* pp. 57–69. Boulder, Colo.: Westview Press.

Girnius, Saulius. 1988. "The Lithuanian Restructuring Movement." *Radio Free Europe Research,* August 4, pp. 19–24.

1988. "A New Party Secretary: Algirdas Brazauskas." *Radio Free Europe Research,* October 28, pp. 19–22.

1989. "Sajudis Candidates Sweep Elections." *Radio Free Europe Research,* April 21, pp. 19–22.

Gliauda, Jurgis. 1984. *The Agony.* Chicago: Lithuanian National Guard in Exile.

Glynn, Thomas J. 1981. "Psychological Sense of Community: Measurement and Application." *Human Relations* 34: 789–818.

Goldstone, Jack A. 1991. *Revolution and Rebellion in the Early Modern World.* Berkeley: University of California Press.

1994. "Is Revolution Individually Rational? Groups and Individuals in Revolutionary Collective Action." *Rationality and Society* 6: 139–166.

Gould, Roger. 1993. "Collective Action and Network Structure." *American Sociological Review* 58: 182–196.

Granauskas, Romualdas. 1992. *The Red Forest.* In Violeta Kelertas, ed., *Come into My Time: Lithuania in Prose Fiction, 1970–1990.* Urbana: University of Illinois Press.

Granovetter, Mark. 1978. "Threshold Models of Collective Behavior." *American Journal of Sociology* 83: 1420–1443.

Grinius, Liutas. 1985. "Soviet Consequences to Lithuanian Jews: A Comparison with the Lot of the Lithuanians." *Lituanas* 31: 28–44.

Gross, Jan T. 1988. *Revolution from Abroad: The Soviet Conquest of Poland's West Ukraine and Western Belorussia.* Princeton: Princeton University Press.

Gureckas, Algimantas P. 1962. "The National Resistance during the German Occupation of Lithuania." *Lituanas* 8: 23–28.

Gwertzman, Bernard, and Michael T. Kaufman, eds. 1990. *The Collapse of Communism.* New York: New York Times Press.

Hardin, Russell. 1982. *Collective Action.* Baltimore: Johns Hopkins University Press.

1995. *One for All: The Logic of Group Conflict.* Princeton: Princeton University Press.

Hechter, Michael. 1987. *Principles of Group Solidarity.* Berkeley: University of California Press.

Hiden, John, and Patrick Salmon. 1994. *The Baltic Nations and Europe: Estonia, Latvia, and Lithuania in the Twentieth Century.* London: Longman.

Hobsbawm, Eric J. 1990. *Nations and Nationalism since 1780: Programme, Myth, Reality.* Cambridge: Cambridge University Press.

Horowitz, Donald. 1985. *Ethnic Groups in Conflict.* Berkeley: University of California Press.

Hroch, Miroslav. 1985. *Social Preconditions of National Revival in Europe: A Comparative Analysis of the Social Composition of Patriotic Groups among the Smaller European Nations*. Cambridge: Cambridge University Press.

Hunczack, Taras. 1990. "The Ukrainian Losses during World War II." In Michael Berenbaum, ed., *A Mosaic of Victims: Non-Jews Persecuted and Murdered by the Nazis*, pp. 116–127. New York: New York University Press.

Idzelis, Augustine. 1990. *Rural Change in Soviet Lithuania, 1945–1980: Problems and Trends*. Chicago: Lithuanian Research and Studies Center.

Ivinskis, Zeonas. 1965. "Lithuania during the War: Resistance against the Soviet and Nazi Occupants." In V. Stanley Vardys, ed., *Lithuania under the Soviets: Portrait of a Nation, 1940–1965*. New York: Macmillan.

Johnson, Jim. 1991. "Symbol and Strategy: On the Cultural Analysis of Politics." Ph.D. dissertation, University of Chicago.

——— 1996. "How Not to Criticize Rational Choice Theory: Pathologies of Common Sense." *Philosophy of the Social Sciences* 26: 77–91.

Judt, Tony. 1992. "Metamorphosis: The Democratic Revolution in Czechoslovakia." In Ivo Banac, ed., *Eastern Europe in Revolution*, pp. 96–116. Ithaca: Cornell University Press.

Jurgela, C. R. 1948. *History of the Lithuanian Nation*. New York: Lithuanian Cultural Institute.

Kalyvas, Stathis. 1996. *The Rise of Christian Democracy in Europe*. Ithaca: Cornell University Press.

Karklins, Rasma, and Roger Petersen. 1993. "Decision Calculus of Protestors and Regimes: Eastern Europe, 1989." *Journal of Politics* 55: 588–614.

Kazeta, Daniel J. 1988. "Lithuanian Resistance to Foreign Occupation, 1940–1952." *Lituanas* 34: 5–32.

Kelertas, Violeta, ed. 1992. *Come into My Time: Lithuania in Prose Fiction, 1970–1990*. Urbana: University of Illinois Press.

Keward, H. R. 1983. *Resistance in Vichy France*. Oxford: Oxford University Press.

Knight, Jack. 1992. *Institutions and Social Conflict*. Cambridge: Cambridge University Press.

Kobasa, S. C., S. R. Maddi, and S. Kahn. 1982. "Hardiness and Health: A Prospective Study." *Journal of Personality and Social Psychology* 42: 168–177.

Krawchenko, Bohdan. 1986. "Soviet Ukraine under Nazi Occupation, 1941–1944." In Yuri Boshyk, ed., *Ukraine during World War II: History and Its Aftermath*, pp. 15–38. Edmonton: Canadian Institute of Ukrainian Studies.

Kuran, Timur. 1992. "Now Out of Never: The Element of Surprise in the East European Revolution of 1989." *World Politics* 44: 7–48.

——— 1995. *Private Truths, Public Lies: The Social Consequences of Preference Falsification*. Cambridge, Mass.: Harvard University Press.

Laar, Mart. 1992. *War in the Woods: Estonia's Struggle for Survival, 1944–1956*. Translated by Tina Ets. Washington, D.C.: Compass Press.

Laitin, David. 1991. "The National Uprisings in the Soviet Union." *World Politics* 44: 139–177.

——— 1995. "National Revivals and Violence." *European Journal of Sociology* 36: 3–43.

Laitin, David, Roger Petersen, and Jon Slocum. 1991. "Language and the State: Russia and the Soviet Union in Comparative Perspective." In Alexander J. Motyl, ed., *Thinking Theoretically about Soviet Nationalities,* pp. 129–168. New York: Columbia University Press.

Landsbergis, Algirdas. 1977. *Five Posts in a Marketplace.* 1958. In Alfreds Straumanis, ed., *Confrontations with Tyranny,* pp. 38–93. Prospect Heights, Ill.: Waveland Press.

Lasic-Vasojevic, Milija M. 1976. *Enemies on All Sides: The Fall Of Yugoslavia.* Washington, D.C.: North American International.

Levesque, Jacques. 1997. *The Enigma of 1989: The USSR and the Liberation of Eastern Europe.* Berkeley: University of California Press.

Levi, Margaret. 1998. "Conscription: The Price of Citizenship." In Robert Bates, Avner Grief, Margaret Levi, Jean-Laurent Rosenthal, and Barry Weingast, eds., *Analytic Narratives.* Princeton: Princeton University Press.

Levin, Dov. 1980. "Jews in the Soviet Establishment, 1940–41." *Soviet Jewish Affairs* 10: 21–37.

——— 1985. *Fighting Back: Lithuanian Jewry's Armed Resistance to the Nazis, 1941–1945.* New York: Holmes and Meier.

——— 1987. "Jews and the Socio-Economic Sovietization of Lithuania, 1940–41, Part I." *Soviet Jewish Affairs* 2: 17–30.

Liber, George. 1989. "Urban Growth and Ethnic Change in the Ukrainian SSR, 1923–1933." *Soviet Studies* 41: 574–591.

Lichbach, Mark. 1994. "Rethinking Rationality and Rebellion: Theories of Collective Action and Problems of Collective Dissent." *Rationality and Society* 6: 8–39.

Liedke, Raymond V. 1991. "Who Do You Know in the Group? Location of Organizations in Interpersonal Networks." *Social Forces* 70: 455–474.

Lieven, Anatol. 1993. *The Baltic Revolution: Estonia, Latvia, and Lithuania and the Path to Independence.* New Haven: Yale University Press.

Liulevicius, Vejas Gabriel. 2000. *War Land: Culture, National Identity, and German Occupation on the Eastern Front in World War I.* Cambridge: Cambridge University Press.

Lohmann, Susanne. 1992. "Rationality, Revolution, and Revolt: The Dynamics of Informational Cascades." Graduate School of Business Research Paper no. 1213. Stanford University, Stanford, Calif.

Maciuka, Benedict Vytenis. 1963. "The Baltic States under Soviet Russia: A Case Study in Sovietization." Ph.D. dissertation, University of Chicago.

Mackevicius, Mecislovas. 1986. "Lithuanian Resistance to German Mobilization Attempts, 1941–1944. *Lituanas* 32: 9–22.

Macy, Michael. 1992. "Learning to Cooperate: Stochastic and Tacit Collusion in Social Exchange." *American Journal of Sociology* 97: 808–843.

Maier, Charles S. 1997. *Dissolution: The Crisis of Communism and the End of East Germany.* Princeton: Princeton University Press.

Marwell, Gerald, Pamela E. Oliver, and Ralph Prahl. 1988. "Social Networks and

Collective Action: A Theory of the Critical Mass III." *American Journal of Sociology* 94: 502–534.

Mason, T. David. 1994. "The Ethnic Dimension of Civil Violence in the Post Cold War Era: Structural Configurations and Rational Choices." Paper presented at the annual meeting of the American Political Science Association.

McMillan, David, and David Chavis. 1986. "Sense of Community: A Definition and Theory." *Journal of Community Psychology* 14: 6–23.

Mendelsohn, Ezra. 1983. *The Jews of East Central Europe between the Wars*. Bloomington: Indiana University Press.

Mishell, William W. 1988. *Kaddish for Kovno: Life and Death in a Lithuanian Ghetto, 1941–1945*. Chicago: Chicago Review Press.

Misiunas, Romuald J., and Rein Taagerpera. 1983. *The Baltic States: Years of Dependence, 1940–1980*. Berkeley: University of California Press.

Monroe, Kristen. 1991. "John Donne's People: Explaining Differences between Rational Actors and Altruists through Cognitive Frameworks." *Journal of Politics* 53: 394–433.

Motyl, Alexander. 1974. "The Organized Ukrainian Resistance Movement and the 1946 Elections to the USSR Supreme Soviet." Unpublished manuscript.

——— 1978. "The Rural Origins of the Communist and Nationalist Movements in Wolyn Wojewodztwo, 1921–1939. *Slavic Review* 37: 412–420.

Muller, Edward, and Karl-Dieter Opp. 1986. "Rational Choice and Rebellious Collective Action." *American Political Science Review* 80: 472–487.

Mulligan, Timothy P. 1982. "The OSS and the Nazi Occupation of the Baltic States, 1941–1945: A Note on Documentation." *Journal of Baltic Studies* 13: 53–58.

——— ed. 1988. *The Politics of Illusion and Empire: German Occupation Policy in the Soviet Union, 1942–43*. New York: Praeger.

Naimark, Norman. 1992. "'Ich will hier raus': Emigration and the Collapse of the German Democratic Republic." In Ivo Banac, ed., *Eastern Europe in Revolution*, pp. 72–95. Ithaca: Cornell University Press.

Nielson, Niels. 1991. *Revolutions in Eastern Europe: The Religious Roots*. Maryknoll, N.Y.: Orbis Books.

Nisbet, Robert. 1962. *Community and Power*. London: Oxford University Press.

Oberschall, Anthony. 1973. *Social Conflict and Social Movements*. Englewood Cliffs, N.J.: Prentice-Hall.

——— 1994. "Rational Choice in Collective Protests." *Rationality and Society* 6: 79–100.

Oliver, Pamela E., and Gerald Marwell. 1988. "The Paradox of Group Size in Collective Action: A Theory of the Critical Mass II." *American Sociological Review* 53: 1–8.

Oliver, Pamela E., with Gerald Marwell and Ruy Teixeira. 1985. "A Theory of the Critical Mass I: Interdependence, Group Heterogeneity, and the Production of Collective Action." *American Journal of Sociology* 91: 522–556.

Olson, Mancur. 1971. *The Logic of Collective Action: Public Goods and the Theory of Groups*. Cambridge, Mass.: Harvard University Press.

1990. "The Logic of Collective Action in Soviet-Type Societies." *Journal of Soviet Nationalities* 1: 8–27.

Opp, Karl-Dieter. 1994. "Repression and Revolutionary Action: East Germany in 1989." *Rationality and Society* 6: 107–108.

Opp, Karl-Dieter, Peter Voss, and Christine Gem. 1995. *Origin of a Spontaneous Revolution: East Germany, 1989.* Ann Arbor: University of Michigan Press.

Ortner, Sherry B. 1990. "Patterns of History: Cultural Schemas in the Foundings of Sherpa Religious Institutions." In Emiko Ohnuki-Tierney, ed., *Culture through Time: Anthropological Approaches.* Stanford: Stanford University Press.

Pajaujis-Javis, Joseph. 1980. *Soviet Genocide in Lithuania.* New York: Maryland Books.

Pakstas, K. 1947. *Lithuania and World War II.* Chicago: Lithuanian Cultural Institute.

Petersen, Roger. 1989. "Rationality, Ethnicity, and Military Enlistment." *Social Science Information* 28: 563–598.

1999. "Structures and Mechanisms in Comparisons." In John Bowen and Roger Petersen, eds., *Critical Comparisons in Politics and Culture,* pp. 61–77. Cambridge: Cambridge University Press.

Forthcoming. *Fear, Hatred and Resentment: Delineating Paths to Ethnic Conflict in Eastern Europe.* Cambridge: Cambridge Universtiy Press.

Philipsen, Dirk. 1993. *We Were the People: Voices from East Germany's Revolutionary Autumn of 1989.* Durham: Duke University Press.

Piliavin, J. A., and W. H. Charng. 1990. "Altruism: A Review of Recent Theory and Research." *Annual Review of Sociology* 16: 27–65.

Popkin, Samuel L. 1979. *The Rational Peasant: The Political Economy of Rural Society in Vietnam.* Berkeley: University of California Press.

1988. "Political Entrepreneurs and Peasant Movements in Vietnam." In Michael Taylor, ed., *Rationality and Revolution,* pp. 9–62. Cambridge: Cambridge University Press.

Radio Free Europe Research Reports. Various issues.

Rastikis, Stasys. 1962. "The Relations of the Provisional Government of Lithuania with the German Authorities." *Lituanas* 8: 16–22.

Reitlinger, Gerald. 1960. *The House Built on Sand: The Conflicts of German Policy in Russia, 1939–1945.* Westport, Conn.: Greenwood Press.

Remeikis, Thomas. 1962. "The Armed Struggle against the Sovietization of Lithuania after 1944." *Lituanas* 8: 29–40.

1980. *Opposition to Soviet Rule in Lithuania.* Chicago: Institute of Lithuanian Studies Press.

Sabaliunas, Leonas. 1972. *Lithuania in Crisis: Nationalism to Communism, 1939–1940.* Bloomington: Indiana University Press.

Sahlins, Marshall. 1961. "The Segmentary Lineage: An Instrument of Predatory Expansion." *American Anthropologist* 63: 322–345.

Sapoka, Adolfas. 1962. *Vilnius in the Life of Lithuania.* Toronto: Lithuanian Association of the Vilnius Region.

Schelling, Thomas C. 1960. *The Strategy of Conflict.* Cambridge, Mass.: Harvard University Press.

——— 1966. *Arms and Influence.* New Haven: Yale University Press.

——— 1985. *Micromotives and Macrobehavior.* New York: Gordon and Breach.

——— 1998. "Social Mechanisms and Social Dynamics." In Peter Hedström and Richard Swedberg, eds., *Social Mechanisms: An Analytical Approach to Social Theory,* pp. 32–44. Cambridge: Cambridge University Press.

Scott, James. 1976. *The Moral Economy of the Peasant: Rebellion and Subsistence in Southeast Asia.* New Haven: Yale University Press.

Sen, Amartya K. 1967. "Isolation, Assurance and the Social Rate of Discount." *Quarterly Journal of Economics* 81: 112–124.

Senn, Alfred E. 1959. *The Emergence of Modern Lithuania.* New York: Columbia University Press.

——— 1980. "Tsarist Authorities and Lithuanian Book-Smuggling." *Journal of Baltic Studies* 11: 334–340.

——— 1990. *Lithuania Awakening.* Berkeley: University of California Press.

——— 1990. "Toward Lithuanian Independence: Algirdas Brazauskas and the CPL." *Problems of Communism* 39: 21–28.

——— 1991. "The Crisis in Lithuania, January 1991: A Visitor's Account." *Association for the Advancement of Baltic Studies Newsletter* 15: 1–12.

Silver, Morris. 1974. "Political Revolution and Repression: An Economic Approach." *Public Choice* 17: 63–71.

Simmel, Georg. 1955. *Conflict and the Web of Group Affiliations.* London: Free Press.

Simutis, Ancietas. 1942. *The Economic Reconstruction of Lithuania after 1918.* New York: Columbia University Press.

Skocpol, Theda. 1979. *States and Social Revolutions: A Comparative Analysis of France, Russia, and China.* Cambridge: Cambridge University Press.

Slavenas, Julius R. 1960. "Deportations." *Lituanas* 6: 47–52.

——— 1978. "General Hans Von Seeckt and the Baltic Question." In V. Stanley Vardys and Romuald Misiunas, eds., *The Baltic States in Peace and War, 1917–1945,* pp. 120–125. University Park: Pennsylvania State University Press.

Smith, Hedrick. 1991. *The New Russians.* New York: Random House.

Steenberg, Sven. 1970. *Vlasov.* New York: Alfred A. Knopf.

Stein, George H. 1966. *The Waffen SS: Hitler's Elite Guard at War, 1939–1945.* Ithaca: Cornell University Press.

Stern, Paul. 1995. "Why Do Individuals Sacrifice for Their Nations?" *Political Psychology* 16: 217–236.

Stokes, Gale. 1933. *The Walls Come Tumbling Down: The Collapse of Communism in Eastern Europe.* New York: Oxford University Press.

Streit, Christian. 1990. "The Fate of the Soviet Prisoners of War." In Michael Berenbaum, ed., *A Mosaic of Victims: Non-Jews Persecuted and Murdered by the Nazis,* pp. 142–149. New York: New York University Press.

Stukas, Jack. 1966. *Awakening Lithuania: A Study on the Rise of Modern Lithuanian Nationalism.* Madison, N.J.: Florham Park Press.

Subtelny, Orest. 1986. "The Soviet Occupation of Western Ukraine, 1939–1941: An Overview." In Yury Boshyk, ed., *Ukraine during World War II: History and Its Aftermath,* pp. 5–14. Edmonton: Canadian Institute of Ukrainian Studies.

——— 1988. *Ukraine: A History.* Toronto: University of Toronto Press.

Suziedelis, Saulius, ed. 1988. *Vengeance on the Run: Documents on Stalinist Atrocities during the First Week of the German-Soviet War, June 1941.* Chicago: Lithuanian Studies Center.

——— 2000. "Thoughts on Lithuania's Shadows of the Past: A Historical Essay on the Legacy of War." <www.artium.lt/4/journal.html>.

——— 2000. "Thoughts on Lithuania's Shadows of the Past: A Historical Essay on the Legacy of War, Part II." <www.artium.lt/4/journal.html>.

Taagepera, Rein. 1980. "Soviet Collectivization of Estonian Agriculture: The Deportation Phase." *Soviet Studies* 32: 379–397.

Tauras, K. V. 1962. *Guerilla Warfare on the Amber Coast.* New York: Voyages Press.

Taylor, Michael. 1982. *Community, Anarchy, Liberty.* Cambridge: Cambridge University Press.

Tietzel, Manfred, and Marion Weber. 1994. "The Economics of the Iron Curtain and Berlin Wall." *Rationality and Society* 6: 58–78.

Tilly, Charles. 1974. "Do Communities Act?" *Sociological Inquiry* 43: 209–240.

——— 1978. *From Mobilization to Revolution.* Reading, Mass.: Addison-Wesley.

Toennies, Ferdinand. 1887. *Gemeinschaft und Gesellschaft.* Leipzig: Fue's Verlag.

Tory, Avraham. 1990. *Surviving the Holocaust: The Kovno Ghetto Diary.* Cambridge, Mass.: Harvard University Press.

Tullock, Gordon. 1971. "The Paradox of Revolution." *Public Choice* 11: 89–99.

Tys-Krokhmaliuk, Yuriy. 1972. *UPA Warfare in the Ukraine: Statistical, Tactical, and Organizational Problems of Ukrainian Resistance in World War II.* New York: Society of Veterans of Ukrainian Insurgent Army.

U.S. Congress. 1952. *Hearings: Communist Aggression Investigation.* Fourth Interim Report of the Select Committee on Communist Aggression. 82nd Cong., 2nd sess.

Vardys, V. Stanley. 1963. "The Partisan Movement in Postwar Lithuania." *Slavic Review* 22: 499–522.

——— 1965. "Aggression Soviet Style, 1939–1940." In V. Stanley Vardys, ed., *Lithuania under the Soviets: Portrait of a Nation, 1940–1965,* pp. 47–58. New York: Macmillan.

——— 1989. "Lithuanian National Politics." *Problems of Communism* 38: 58–75.

——— 1990. "Sajudis: National Revolution in Lithuania." In Jan Arneds Trapans, ed., *Toward Independence: The Baltic Popular Movements,* pp. 11–23. Boulder, Colo.: Westview Press.

Vardys, V. Stanley, and Romuald J. Misiunas, eds. 1978. *The Baltic States in Peace and War, 1917–1945.* University Park: Pennsylvania State University Press.

Vardys, V. Stanley, and Judith Sedaitis. 1997. *Lithuania: The Rebel Nation.* Boulder, Colo.: Westview Press.

Vitvitsky, Bohdan. 1990. "Slavs and Jews: Consistent and Inconsistent Perspectives on the Holocaust." In Michael Berenbaum, ed., *A Mosaic of Victims: Non-Jews Persecuted and Murdered by the Nazis*, pp. 101–108. New York: New York University Press.

von Rauch, Georg. 1995. *The Baltic States: The Years of Independence, 1917–1940*. New York: St. Martins.

Weick, Karl E. 1984. "Small Wins: Redefining the Scale of Social Problems." *American Psychologist* 39: 40–49.

Weiss, Aharon. 1990. "The Holocaust and Ukrainian Victims." In Michael Berenbaum, ed., *A Mosaic of Victims: Non-Jews Persecuted and Murdered by the Nazis*, pp. 109–115. New York: New York University Press.

Wheaton, Bernard, and Zdenek Kavan. 1992. *The Velvet Revolution: Czechoslovakia, 1988–1991*. Boulder, Colo.: Westview Press.

Zaprudnik, Jan. 1993. *Belarus: At a Crossroads in History*. Boulder, Colo.: Westview Press.

Index

Albania, 28, 231, 269
All Souls' Day demonstration of 1940,
    98–100, 133, 160, 299
altruists, 281
anthropological approaches, 47, 57, 299
Ash, Timothy Garton, 250
assurance game, 33, 47, 244
    interlocking, Perestroika period, 244–249
    See also de-assurance
Ateitis, 99, 108, 109, 116, 122, 124, 136,
    146
    Ateitininkai connections to work groups,
    140
    ethos of sacrifice and activism, 137
    relationship with Christian Democratic
    Party, 138
Atlantic Charter, 201, 206, 207

Barbarossa, 171, 174
Belorussia, 28, 30, 218–231, 297
Benn, Stanley, 284, 285, 290
Brazauskas, Algirdas, 259–262, 264
Brezhnev Doctrine, 245

Catholic influences, 85, 100, 109, 130,
    238–239, 276
    Chronicle of the Catholic Church in
    Lithuania, 258
    communities of Catholic professionals,
    139
Ceausescu, 257, 272
centralization, 68–71, 75, 128, 134–135, 300
Christian Democratic Party, 102–103, 114,
    137, 157
clan societies, 54, 231–233
cognitive dissonance reduction, 11, 12
collective action problem, 282
collectivization of agriculture, 30, 171, 206,
    207, 238, 287
Communist Party, 103–104, 109, 173

community, 15–27
    community-based mechanisms, 181, 203
    community-based status mechanisms,
    165, 241–242
    effects of modernization on, 237
    strong, 19–25, 51–52
    strong versus weak, 52, 62
    structure, 25, 172 (see also centralization;
        density of ties; heterogeneity and
        homogeneity; size effects)
    weak, 25
    weakening of, 237
comparative method, 27, 28–31
culture, 39, 293, 299
    malleability of culture, 38
    schema, 292, 299 (see also symbols)
Czechoslovakia, 28, 31, 237, 245, 247,
    civic forum, 253
    events of 1989, 249–257, 269, 270
    comparison with GDR, 263, 268
    comparison with Lithuania, 259, 262, 271
    general strike called for November 27,
        251–253
    Jakes, Milos, 254, 256

Dallin, Alexander, 159, 220, 221, 225
Damusis, Adolfis, 109, 136, 138, 140, 142,
    147, 171
de-assurance, 253–257
density of ties, 61–65, 122–123, 134,
    300–301
    dilution effects, 65
deportations
    German, to Stutthof, 164, 171
    Soviet, June 1940, 81
    Soviet, June 1941, 149, 173
    Soviet, postwar period, 184, 206
dissidents, 240, 245, 249, 252, 258, 264, 279
Djilas, Milovan, 234
Durkheim, Emile, 237

elections
   fraudulent, in Lithuania, July 14, 1940, 97
   fraudulent, in East Germany, 265, 267
   Soviet, postwar, 181
   symbolic significance of, 285
   See also election boycotts
election boycotts
   in Galicia, 1921–1922, 212, 214–217
   of Soviet elections in Lithuania, 1940,
      100
   of Soviet elections in Lithuania, late
      1940s, 172
   of Soviet elections in Galicia, 1946, 217
Elster, Jon, 10, 12, 15, 47
emotions, 35, 298
Estonia
   Estonian Legion, 163
   nationalism, 282–283
   postwar Soviet rule, 205–209
   Soviet rule, 1940–1941, 129–130
ethnic hierarchy, 224–225. See also
   resentment
Evans-Pritchard, E. E., 231
expressive motivations, 284, 294

falsifiability, 15
fanatical behavior, 273–278
first players, 64, 272
First World War, 160, 162, 201, 297
focal mechanisms
   definition, 10–14
   focal actions, 36–39
   focal events, 86, 97, 98, 257
   focal-point mechanism(s), 36, 299, 203,
      213
   focal points and status, 96
   focal points during first Soviet occupation
      of Lithuania, 157, 160
   focal points during German occupation,
      160–162, 167 11, 203, 213
   focal points during 1989 Eastern Europe
      demonstrations, 240–244, 266, 270
   focal points during second Soviet
      occupation, 203
Frank, Hans, 213
freedom fighters, 156–157

Galicia, 28, 30, 209–217, 297
   attack on Polish estates in, 215
   Bereza Kartuzka, 215
German Democratic Republic, 28, 31, 237,
   245, 262–269
   Monday prayer services in Leipzig, 266,
      270

New Forum, 267, 268
German rule in Lithuania
   colonization policy, 158
   invasion of June 21, 118
   March 1943 boycott of the SS legion,
      166
   occupation of Klaipeda (Memel), 86
   provisional government of Lithuania, 154,
      164
   territorial force, 166, 167
Germany, 37, 167
Gilliam, Sylvia, 220, 225
Goldstone, Jack, 279
Gorbachev, Mikhail, 264, 267
Gould, Roger, 64, 65, 68, 69
Granauskas, Romualdas, 289
Grandis fraternity, 135–140, 145
   filisters, 142, 151
Greif, Avner, 14

Hapsburg rule, 210, 213
Hardin, Russell, 282
Havel, Vaclav, 249
heterogeneity and homogeneity, 72–75, 134
   economic homogeneity, 75
   effects of economic fragmentation, 128
   heterogeneity of modern society, 271
hierarchy, 35, 240. See also resentment
Himmler, Heinrich,163, 213
Hitler, Adolf, 86, 104
Hitler's regime, 154
homogeneity. See heterogeneity and
   homogeneity
Honecker, Erich, 257, 262, 263, 264, 269
Horowitz, Donald, 298
Hungary, 237, 249, 267, 269

ideology, 185, 201, 228
Irish Republican Army, 3
Istrebiteli, 171, 180, 185, 186
   assassinations of, 181
   recruitment of, 198

Jews, 106, 155, 159
   in Merkine, 173
   property of, confiscated or looted, 174
   role of, in the NKVD, 94
   under first Soviet occupation, 92–94,
      130–133

Kalanta, Romas, 289, 291
Kaminsky Brigade, 221
Kavan, Zdenek, 251, 254
Kazimierietis, 179, 180, 184

Klaipeda, 89, 91, 100, 104
  German takeover of, 107
  crisis, 95, 96
  incident, 103
Knight, Jack, 19
Koch, Erich, 213, 219, 228
Komsomol, 93, 173, 181, 186, 260
Krenz, Egon, 267
Kreve-Mickevicius, Vincas, 91, 92
Kruglov, General, 170
Kudirka, Vincas, 161
Kuran, Timur, 47, 63

Laar, Mart, 206
Landsbergis, Algirdas, 288
Landsbergis, Vytautas, 260, 275, 276, 279, 290
Latvia, 28, 29, 129, 205, 283, 297
  Aizsargi, 129
  Latvian legion, 163
  postwar Soviet rule, 205–209
  Soviet rule, 1940–1941, 129–130
Lenin, 95
Levi, Margaret, 14
Lieven, Anatol, 275, 277, 294
Lithuania, 263, 269, 270
  agricultural laws of March 1922, 105
  book smugglers, 84, 161
  democratic awakening, 266
  economic groups in prewar Lithuania, 104–106
  Ignalina, 259
  Kasciunai, 176, 177, 191
  Kaunas, 93, 98, 99, 106, 124
  Klepocai, 4, 175, 184, 188, 189, 190
  land reform, 105
  Merkine, 4, 7, 8, 52, 168, 173–193, 198
  Panevezys, 108, 114
  political groups in prewar Lithuania, 102–104
  Russification policy, 83, 85
  Samogitia, 193, 194, 198
  Samuniskiu, 190, 191
  social groups in prewar Lithuania, 106–109
  social-patriotic groups, 122, 204
  Svainikai, 109–123, 125, 234
  Taurage, 195
  Utena, 108
  War of Independence, 1918–1920, 82
Lithuanian Activist Front (LAF), 81, 117, 140, 142,
  appeal, 96
  Berlin LAF, 95, 101, 142
  under German occupation, 155, 163
Lithuanian Boy Scouts, Girl Scouts, 88
Lithuanian Communist Party, 260
Lithuanian Freedom League, 258–259, 261
Lithuanian Nationalist Union, 103
Lithuanian Salvation Committee, 274
Lithuanian Union Movement, 157, 163
Lithuania's Movement of Freedom Fighters, 172
Lutheran Church, 266

Mao, 33
martyrdom, 284–292
  small risk of, 274, 284, 294
  See also pseudomartyrdom mechanism
Marwell, Gerald, 62, 68, 69
Marx, 62
Mechanisms
  definitions, 10–15
  irrational, 76
  mechanism-based approach, 296
  personality-based, 280–282
  See also focal mechanisms; resentment; status; thresholds; tyrrany of sunk costs; wishful thinking
Molotov-Ribbentrop Nonaggression Pact, 257, 261, 270
monitoring and retaliation, 24, 183, 185
Monroe, Kristen, 281
Montenegro, 28, 30, 231–235, 297, 299
Motyl, Alexander, 214, 216, 217
Muller, Edward, 280

Narutis, Pilipas, 136, 140–141, 148, 151, 171
nationalism, 103, 104, 106, 185, 214
NKVD
  in 1940–1941 Lithuania, 80, 93, 115, 118, 144,
  in postwar Lithuania, 170–171, 176, 179, 180, 183
  in Volhynia and Galicia, 209
norms
  of conformity, 55
  of fairness, 22, 65
  family, 123
  normative effects of centralization, 135
  normative mechanisms, 300
  normative pressures, 203
  of honor, 54, 56, 122
  of reciprocity, 11, 14, 21, 53, 122, 208, 233, 238, 301
  relationship with community structure, 52–56

norms (*cont.*)
  relationship with risk, 56–61
  unconditional norms, 53
Norway, 37, 167

Oliver, Pamela, 62, 69
Olson, Mancur, 71, 135, 254
Opp, Karl-Dieter, 280
Organization of Ukrainian Nationalists, 214, 216
Ortner, Sherry, 292, 293
ostracism, 184, 188

Palach, Jan, 249
Philipsen, Dirk, 263
Plechavicius, Povilas, 164, 165, 166, 167
Poland, 83, 91, 209, 237, 239, 269
  General Govournement, 213
  Poles and Ukrainians, 211
  Polish-Lithuanian uprising of 1863, 83
  Polish interwar rule, 212
political entrepreneurs, 134, 135
political parties, 50, 75, 114
Popkin, Samuel, 22, 66, 134, 135
Populists, 102, 103, 114, 141, 163
Prapuolenis, Leonas, 145, 146, 147, 148, 150, 155
prediction, 243, 244, 245, 255, 256, 270
Project of the Soviet Social System, 220, 229
pseudomartyrdom mechanism, 290–292.
  See also martyrdom

rational choice, 12, 13, 14, 77, 79, 278
reciprocity, 300. *See also* norms
Red Army, 78, 92, 93
relative deprivation, 11
religion, 160, 208, 214
reputation, 135, 150
resentment, 33–35, 38, 40, 44, 297–298,
  in Galicia and Volhynia, 213, 224–225
  in Lithuania in first Soviet occupation, 92–94
  in Lithuania under German Occupation, 157–160, 163, 167
  in 1989 Eastern Europe, 240, 242, 270
revenge, 77
Rumania, 237, 269

safety in numbers, 33, 242, 243. *See also* assurance game
Sajudis, 258, 261
Salaspils concentration camp, 167
Schelling, Thomas, 10, 47

Schelling diagrams, 40, 165
Scouts, 98, 99, 107, 108, 126
segmentary societies, 231–235
self-rehabilitation, 256, 271
Simmel, Georg, 237
Senn, Alfred, 261
size effects, 71–72, 75, 134, 300
Skirpa, Colonel Kazys, 142
Smetona, Antanas, 102, 104, 106, 107, 114, 132, 137
Social Democrats, 102, 138, 141
Socialist Union of Youth, 251
Solidarity, 249
solidarity. *See* density; heterogeneity and homogeneity
Stalin, 95
Stalingrad, 162, 230
status, 184
  hierarchies, 34, 92
  reward mechanisms, 299
  rewards, 20, 40, 166, 167, 270, 283
  sanctions, 166
  status-based rewards, 44
strategic hamlet program, 3, 227
structural characteristics of community. *See* centralization; density of ties; first players; heterogeneity and homogeneity
Stutthof concentration camp, 164, 171
Supreme Committee for the Liberation of Lithuania, 163
Supreme Committee for the Reconstruction of Lithuania, 172
sustaining mechanisms, 13, 14, 27, 217
  in postwar Lithuania, 183–184, 185, 200–202, 203
symbols, 38, 39, 44, 299
  in Eastern European demonstrations, 240
  in Galicia and Volhynia, 210, 211, 215, 217
  in 1991 Lithuanian demonstrations, 285, 291, 292, 294

Taylor, Michael, 16, 17, 21, 238
threats, 24, 76, 193, 200, 243, 245
  of physical beating, 243
  of retaliation, 185
  See also sustaining mechanisms
thresholds, 11, 99, 242
  cascading nature of, 150
  distribution of, 47, 70
  mechanisms, 165, 270, 300–302
  safety calculations, threshold-based, 23–24
Tilly, Charles, 18
triggering mechanisms, 13, 14, 27

trust, 73
tyranny of sunk costs, 11, 12, 14, 76, 200

Ukraine, 28, 30, 218, 228, 297
  Lviv, 211
  Reichskommisariat, 213
  Insurgent Army, 214, 216
  National Council, 211
  SS division, 213
Union of Freedom Fighters, 163
Union of Sauliai, 48, 55, 87, 107, 108, 109,
  115, 116, 122, 126, 163, 171, 173, 184,
  195, 239
Union of Young Lithuania, 106
United Democratic Resistance Movement,
  172, 202, 287
University of Vytautas the Great in Kaunas,
  4, 97, 107, 137, 157
urbanization, 239

value of small victories, 14, 76, 200
Vanagas, 179, 180, 184, 186, 189, 192

Vatican, 102
Vietnam, 3, 134
Vilnius, 93, 236, 257
  January 1991 events, 274–278
  question, 102, 106
Voldemaras, Augustinas, 143, 154, 157
Volhynia, 28, 30, 209, 297

Waffen SS, 156, 163, 164
Weber, Max, 237
Weingast, Barry, 14
West Ukrainian National Republic, 211
Wheaton, Bernard, 251, 254
wishful thinking, 14, 78, 185, 200, 201, 202,
  206
World War I, 153, 159

Yakovlev, Alexander, 261
Young Lithuanian organization, 107, 108
youth and youth groups, 48, 279, 283
Yugoslavia, 3, 298